SOCRATES

Fictions of a Philosopher

.

Socrates

Fictions of a Philosopher

SARAH KOFMAN

Translated by
CATHERINE PORTER

Cornell University Press
Ithaca, New York

First published in France 1989
© Editions Galilée 1989 *Socrate(s)*
English translation © 1998 The Athlone Press

Publisher's Note
The publishers wish to record their thanks to the French Ministry of Culture
for a grant towards the cost of translation.

First published 1998 by Cornell University Press

Library of Congress Cataloging-in-Publication Data

Kofman, Sarah.
 [Socrate(s). English]
 Socrates : fictions of a philosopher / Sarah Kofman ; translated by
Catherine Porter.
     p.   cm.
 Includes bibliographical references and index.
 ISBN 0-8014-8138-4 (cloth : alk. paper)
 1. Socrates.   I. Title.
B317.K6413   1998
183′.2--dc21   98-9840

International Standard Book Number: 0-8014-8138-4

Printed in Great Britain

Contents

III. KIERKEGAARD'S "SOCRATES": SOCRATES UNDER AN IRONIC LENS

Introduction
Representations of Socrates

'Socrates, whose birth occurs in the fourth year of the 77th Olympiad (469 B.C.), was the son of Sophroniscus, a sculptor, and of Phænarete, a midwife . . . Socrates died at sixty-nine years of age, in Olympiad 95, 1 (399-400 B.C.), an Olympiad after the end of the Peloponnesian War, twenty-nine years after the death of Pericles, and forty-four years before the birth of Alexander.'

A book on Socrates purporting to present an 'actualized' or even a 'necessary' conception of Socrates – these are Kierkegaard's terms[1] – could not go beyond the brief biographical 'data' given above, borrowed from Hegel's *Lectures on the History of Philosophy*.[2] Hegel's information came from Diogenes Laertius,[3] who was reporting what he learned from archival documents preserved in the Metroön temple in Athens. Socrates left no other historical 'remains'.

But in citing Hegel I have already gone beyond history; I have transfigured Socrates' remains. I have entered the realm of interpretation, the realm of images or fictions of Socrates; I have embarked upon a Socratic novel, one possible novel among others. The account I have taken from Hegel is seemingly objective, straightforward and factual. Nevertheless, the presentation of Socrates' death in relation to the death of Pericles and the birth of Alexander – and exclusively in relation to those two dates – is by no means 'innocent'. It is already informed by a specific type of reading; it situates Socrates not only in a given historical period but in a precise dialectical position. By inscribing his death within a heroic series, within a typically Hegelian constellation of heroes ('as a statesman, it is Pericles who represents the pinnacle of supple individuality, and arrayed around him like stars are Sophocles, Thucydides, Socrates, and so on'[4]), this presentation strips Socrates of his empirical death in all its uniqueness. It 'sublates' his death.

With Socrates, we cannot escape from fiction. Not only because, by and large, there are no 'facts'. Generally speaking, any reading of any philosopher will be a symptomatic interpretation of the types of forces that lay claim to the work. The 'case' of Socrates has unique features; it is not even precisely comparable to the case of the 'pre-Socratics', whose fragmentary leavings have facilitated all sorts of reappropriations and misinterpretations

– for example, those of the metaphysicians who depicted Socrates as a master and used him as a yardstick for his predecessors, the 'pre-Socratics,' who were then depicted, reductively, as children stammering out an obscure and inarticulate truth, or as inadequately trained soldiers who had to be 'sublated' by more adult, more enlightened, better-trained successors.[5]

It has been all the easier, and all the more necessary, to make a philosophical novel out of Socrates because he himself, as we know, wrote nothing at all. At least that is what we believe, although the matter is perhaps not as simple as we think: is there not a letter attributed to Plato declaring that some if not all of the texts signed by him were written by Socrates?[6] The letter has been a source of jubilation for Jacques Derrida,[7] who was fascinated by the 'Oxford scene' of writing that he found brilliantly depicted by Matthew Paris in the frontispiece of a thirteenth-century fortune-telling book and reproduced on a postcard available at Oxford's Bodleian Library. The picture appears to represent Socrates as Plato describes him in the 'Second Epistle': the master, in the process of writing, is young, tall, and handsome, while Plato, a much smaller figure standing behind him, is reminiscent of Aristodemus, the good disciple, the good double Plato identifies in *The Symposium* as Aristodemus *the small*.

Plato's second letter (and also the seventh one, presumed to be more authentic[8]), the post card featuring Matthew Paris's literally 'reversing' image and – especially – Derrida's *The Post Card* introduce noteworthy complications into the somewhat simplistic assertion found even in the writings of one of its subtlest interpreters, Nietzsche, who refers to Socrates as 'the one who does not write'.[9] Indeed, except for Derrida, this is what all the interpreters say. They all believe that Socrates preceded Plato and that Plato wrote under Socrates's dictation.[10] The thirteenth-century postcard, subjected to 'delirious speculation',[11] to infinite analyses, 'overturns every-thing. . . . it allegorizes the catastrophic unknown *[insu]* of the order. Finally one begins no longer to understand what to come *[venir]*, to come before, to come after, to foresee *[prévenir]*, to come back *[revenir]* all mean . . ., to write one's will, to dictate, to speak, to take dictation, etc'.[12] Derrida, fascinated, multiplies the reading hypotheses. As he pauses to contemplate the 'mugs' of the two buddies (whom he brings into postcard communication with the 'mug' of Freud's grandson), his playful text unsettles the reader as it overturns one interpretation after another in a series of fictitious letters, an unstoppable inventive proliferation with no end in sight: no 'pseudo-truth' offered by an allegedly competent specialist can bring it to a halt, for there is no 'truth' in painting. In its strange mutism, painting, which can neither question nor respond, as Plato had already pointed out, gives rise to an infinite discourse that does not claim to have the last word on the riddle of the most famous couple in the history of philosophy: Who is ahead, who behind? Who dictates, who writes? Who is captain, who is at the helm? Who impregnates whom? – which member of this odd couple is the man and which the woman? All these questions, among others, posit overly clearcut and simplistic alternatives; they have to remain unanswered, have to be asked only as a way of poking fun at all metaphysical oppositions and all rigid dogmatic discourse.

Socrates thus (perhaps) did not write, they all insist, paralyzed with fascination. And this absence of writing, perhaps the most bizarre of all of Socrates' bizarre and more or less pathological characteristics, according to Hegel and Nietzsche (his monstrous ugliness, his ecstatic immobility, his demonic voice), impels the interpreters, for their part, to write. If we can believe Plato's *Theaetetus,* Socrates declared that he was sterile, unable to conceive. He knew only one thing: that he knew nothing, that as his mother Phaenarete was a midwife for bodies, he was merely a midwife for minds (such was his divine mission).

The same Socrates has given rise to an immense literature reflecting a vast diversity of views on his life and his death.[13] For some, Socrates lived and died as a sage (Nietzsche offers this reading, among others[14]) who was the victim of an unjust condemnation, like Christ (a figure with whom he is routinely compared[15]). For others (Hegel), Socrates is neither a sage nor a saint but a tragic hero: his condemnation was both just and unjust. It is equally legitimate to represent the character on stage in a tragic scenario[16] and to make fun of him in a comedy, as Aristophanes did in *The Clouds*.[17] For still others, following Xenophon's flat, vulgar interpretation, which nevertheless in its way 'inspires' the Nietzsche of *Twilight of the Idols,* Socrates died simply because he had had enough of life, which he experienced as a disease. (For Nietzsche, Socrates' 'last word' – 'O Crito, I owe Asclepius a rooster' – was one too many; Nietzsche found the statement devastating, 'ridiculous and terrible', symptomatic of the disguised pessimism of a man who seemed to have led the joyous life of a soldier[18]). Under these conditions, there was nothing heroic about consenting to be condemned; as Xenophon says, it is a way to spare oneself the ills that old age holds in store for us all: *the economy of sacrifice.* Finally, in yet another hypothesis, Kierkegaard's, Socrates the ironist died out of irony – for nothing.

Now, there is no way to choose one of these interpretations over the others, no way to establish an 'actualized' and 'necessary' conception by going beyond the fictional reappropriations and returning, if not to the non-existent texts of Socrates himself, then at least to sources that transmit his thought accurately and clearly. On the one hand, even supposing that Socrates' 'living words' had been transcribed without betrayal (we shall see how Plato, in the *Symposium,* dramatizes the fiction of a so-called faithful tradition), like all language this speech is *écriture,* writing in the Derridean sense, a system of differences that always allows for a gap between what was said and what was thought. On the other hand, and all the interpreters agree on this point (Hegel deplores it whereas Kierkegaard delights in it and exploits it even more than Nietzsche does; the latter, curiously enough, seems to have been somewhat insensitive to it at times), Socrates' speech, because it is essentially ironic, is dissimulated, duplicitous, ambiguous at the very least; it lends itself to all kinds of misunderstandings, the height of irony being to take a nonserious discourse seriously and vice versa. More than any other, Socrates' speech is therefore *écriture* (perhaps that is why Socrates did not feel the need to write), and it could not have revealed his thought in a simple and immediate way – supposing that an ironist can have 'a' thought; Kierkegaard's interpretation consisted entirely in showing that the emptiness of thought is the correlative of irony and of the maieutic method, that Socrates teaches nothing, that his confession of ignorance must be taken 'seriously'.

The Socratic novel thus begins in Socrates' own lifetime: each of the 'disciples' heard Socrates' 'lesson' in his own way, from his own perspective (Nietzsche unmasks Plato's fictions in particular; he is less sensitive than Kierkegaard is to Xenophon's). As Kierkegaard put it, each one saw him through his own *stereoscope*: Xenophon, with the mentality of a shopkeeper, was able to create only the fiction of a down-to-earth Socrates, a flat, realistic, insignificant figure, so harmless and boring that one could legitimately ask why the Athenian nobility condemned him to death, unless it was precisely because of the unbearable boredom he exuded. Plato, on the other hand, tended to idealize Socrates, to make him an ally by transfiguring him – especially after his death. So did the Athenians, who condemned him and then, overcome with remorse and regret, elevated him post mortem to the status of a veritable totemic figure, made him a statue. It is Hegel, not Freud, who relates this anecdote, and for him there is nothing anecdotal about it. Plato, bowing to a non-dialectical necessity, especially after Socrates' death, congealed Socrates into a master figure, a founding father of philosophy. Plato's image seems to have won out over the one Xenophon fabricated, since Socrates is held up even today as a model by a good many philosophers who seem to have forgotten Hegel's lesson: if Socrates is a grandiose figure in the history of philosophy, he is still none the less a simple figure belonging to a necessary phase in dialectics, one that is necessarily surpassable and that has been surpassed.

For someone who, like Kierkegaard, seeks to conceive of a real and necessary Socrates, above and beyond all the fictions, what is the best source? And in Plato's dialogues in particular, how can one choose among the various images of Socrates? How can anyone sort out what belongs to Socrates and what to Plato? How can anyone manage to pry apart that inseparable couple and capture a 'pure and authentic' Socrates, a Socrates who has not been contaminated by his disciple, who has not been transfigured by someone who, under the influence of a somewhat excessive and suspect filial piety, attributes *all* his own thought to the other, someone who never speaks in his own name, someone who practices, more than anyone else does, the mimetic discourse that is condemned in Books II, III, and X of *The Republic*? On the pretext of veneration, and in order to settle an unpayable debt, by making Socrates his spokesman and having him play multiple roles is Plato not taking revenge on someone who had 'corrupted' him, had accepted him as a disciple only on condition that he burn his poems and make poetry a simple *ancilla*, a handmaiden of philosophy? Nietzsche offers this hypothesis among others.[19] In making this gesture, does Plato not make it forever impossible to differentiate between what properly belongs to each party – assuming that there is actually something 'proper' to Socrates and something 'proper' to Plato? In any event, if historians of philosophy from Diogenes Laertius on have agreed to distinguish the dialogues they call Socratic from the ones they call Platonic, they are hardly in agreement as to which belong to whom.

Among the interpreters, Kierkegaard spends the most time trying to sort things out; he does so in order to conceive of a 'quite real' Socrates (a Socrates seen in fact through Kierkegaard's own stereoscope), an ironic Socrates who has nothing of his own to affirm, properly speaking, except nothingness. As for Hegel, he appeals to one source after another (Plato, Xenophon, Aristophanes) according to the demands of 'his' cause, that of absolute Mind; whereas Nietzsche, guided by his unparalleled genealogical flair, strives as if motivated by jealousy to bring about the couple's divorce by ferreting out elements in the aristocratic Plato's dialogues that still reek of the plebeian. Each relying on 'sources' that are themselves fictitious, each equipped with his own method, the interpreters attempt to dispel the fascinating enigma that Socrates represents. Hegel, by situating him in a specific position within dialectics and universal history, tries to suppress his atopia. Kierkegaard, through an indirect and subtle polemics that is nevertheless derived from a certain Hegelianism, tries to displace Socrates from the position Hegel assigned him, and perhaps from all positions. As for Nietzsche, from *Philosophy in the Tragic Age of the Greeks* to *Twilight of the Idols*, from one text to another and sometimes within a single text, he forges several more or less contradictory representations of Socrates in an attempt to resolve the extraordinary enigma presented by that figure; he finds himself in a no less extraordinary muddle[20] every time he returns to the problem. And he returns to it repeatedly: he is torn between highly contradictory feelings toward Socrates, haunted by the ancient philosopher as if by an authentic double,[21] wholly fascinated by this individual who, despite the vast literature on the subject, has been and remains an obsessive puzzle, as if nothing at all had yet been said about him or his overwhelming influence on the art, ethics, and philosophy of his day, an influence that, 'like an infinitely lengthening shadow in the evening sun, casts itself far over posterity'.[22]

However divergent the interpretations may be, they all agree on the importance of the figure of Socrates. Long after the philosopher's death, the exasperating enigma he posed continues ironically to throw all his interpreters into aporia; this is one of the long-distance effects of the magic spells, the sorcerers' charms[23] that characterized the 'mocking and enamored monster and pied piper of Athens, who made the most overweening youths tremble and sob'.[24] Hegel positions Socrates as the great turning point in the history of the development of Mind; for him, Socrates with his tragic destiny is a remarkable figure, crucial for the history of philosophy, the most interesting in all Antiquity; Hegel goes so far as to rank him among the major personalities in world history. For Nietzsche, Socrates is the axis and the pivot of the world, and if in the early texts he is depicted more as a wise man than a hero, he is still linked with the great figures of Greek tragedy, Oedipus and Prometheus, who, under their Apollonian appearances, hint at Dionysian monstrosity. In Nietzsche's later texts, it is true that Socrates' monstrosity tends to be unmasked as a symptom of a pathology of decadence, and this monstrosity even leads to doubts about Socrates' Hellenity – doubts that begin to find expression in *The Gay Science*.[25] In that pivotal text, Socrates seems to have deeply disappointed Nietzsche by turning out to be too talkative; he had known how to hold his tongue during his lifetime, but his tongue was loosened when he was on the verge of death by poisoning. What made Socrates' 'last word' possible? How could a Greek have implied, vengefully and ungenerously, that life is a disease? Is Socrates not finally more Jew than Greek? From this point on, Nietzsche's problem is not that he does not know *where* Socrates is, what place he occupies in dialectics and in history, or who Socrates *'really'* is, but rather that he does not know how such a person, someone who wished – in suspect fashion to say the least – for death, could have lived. Through what magic spells – the height of irony – could he have been perceived as a saviour? How could that great erotician, such an ugly man,[26] have been so seductive?

For he seduced them all, in spite of and perhaps by means of his repellent ugliness, in spite of and perhaps because of his professions of ignorance. Plato stresses this point in the *Symposium*: the more Socrates proclaims his ignorance, the more knowledge and mastery the Athenians attribute to him, and the more he reduces them to the position of lovers, slaves forever chained to his side. And if seduction is essentially feminine (if we are to believe Xenophon, Socrates himself makes this assertion[27]), what does this tell us (here is another enigma) about the sex of this great master of seduction? This sculptor's son who spent his time – Hegel and Kierkegaard do not forgive him for it – denigrating all fathers, thus corrupting youth on the pretext of turning the young toward the only true father, the Good? What does this tell us about the sexual position of Socrates who, philosophizing before Nietzsche with blunt hammer-strokes, refused to take up sculpture, the art (the most superficial of the arts, according to Nietzsche) for which his father had destined him, so as instead to sculpt himself, to generate himself like 'a perfect classical work of art which has brought itself to this height of perfection'?[28] What can we make of the man who, killing off the fathers with the dagger-strokes of dialectical irony, rejected his own father's trade (while making free with his inheritance) so as to do philosophy, while identifying with a midwife, his mother Phaenarete? What can we make of Kierkegaard's sexual position, or Nietzsche's, given that, despite their differences, each identifies with Socrates as with a double?

The best-known readings of Socrates – which we are about to examine in more detail – have all attempted to answer these questions, to bring Socrates under control by forging, each in its own way, one or several Socrates(es) in their own image(s). Despite their best efforts at appropriation, they all more or less acknowledge that Socrates eludes all the conventional categories; he resists all mastery, and this is where his own mastery lies. Plato's *Symposium* suggests that Socrates can be reduced neither to the portrait sketched by his good twin Aristodemus nor to the satyric images born of the drunkenness of the bad twin Alcibiades; the *Symposium* hints that he most closely resembles – but here is yet another fiction – the demonic Eros, a mythic figure of the intermediary who is neither knowing nor ignorant, neither tragic nor comic, neither grotesque nor sublime, neither feminine nor masculine: Eros is atopic, outside of all common places.

If Hegel attempts to immobilize this atopia by enclosing it within a specific dialectical space, the position he confers on Socrates is an untenable one. Socrates is the *threshold* of philosophy, a two-faced Janus: he represents the *beginning* of philosophy, the moment when 'the subjectivity of thought was brought to consciousness in a more definite and more thorough manner'[29] but when, because philosophy was still in its infancy, conscious subjectivity was *still* marred by unconsciousness, by exteriority, and thus presented itself in a necessarily pathological form. 'It is in this way that, in Socrates, in a non-conscious form, what involves knowledge, resolution and determination properly speaking, meets what stems from a conscious and reflective attitude'[30] (ibid., p. 317). After portraying Socrates as a monolithic figure, as Hegel did,[31] depicting him as the pure prototype of theoretical man and related through that purity to the 'pre-Socratic' types, in his later texts Nietzsche imagines Socrates, to his own great disappointment, as a *mixed breed*, more Jew than Greek, an authentic living paradox. Kierkegaard, finally, imagining Socrates as an ironist, a figure of nothing, of nothingness, removes him from all stable positions. In Socrates and in the irony he emblematizes, Kierkegaard makes manifest a space of resistance to dialectics: Socrates is irreducible to all definitions and specifications: he is and is not.

Is it not the atopia of that *Janus bifrons* that fascinates and enchants us in Socrates, that makes him relevant to us even today? An atopia that is not dialecticizable, not masterable, despite Hegel's claims to have dialecticized and mastered it? And what matters to us in all these interpretations is not the possibility that we might cut through their diversity to find a single interpretation, the 'true' one, that would finally give us a 'real Socrates', bound over hand and foot; what is important to us is that these interpretations make manifest the impossibility of any reading that is not, no matter what approach it takes, a reappropriating fiction.

I. PLATO'S SOCRATES(ES)

A. Socrates and His Twins
(The Socrates[es] of Plato's *Symposium*)

1. 'BUT WHERE IS THE MAN?'[1]

Among all of Plato's Socratic dialogues, why should the *Symposium* warrant special attention? Is it because this dialogue may have handed down a more faithful portrait than any other? Might it be possible, in this dialogue in particular, to distinguish between the master's part and the disciple's? A whole tradition seems in fact to agree that this is the case. Alongside the *Phaedo* and the *Apology*, key dialogues for readers interested in the philosopher's final moments (we shall return to these in connection with Kierkegaard), this tradition views the *Symposium* as a crucial 'document' for anyone interested in Socrates' life. Alcibiades' portrait of him in particular – a portrait produced under the influence of alcohol – seems to have been taken at face value. Does not Alcibiades himself demand such a reading? *In vino veritas.*

The situation, however, is actually much more complicated than this. Countering the traditional view, I shall argue that Alcibiades' portrait is no more faithful than the usually neglected one offered by Aristodemus at the beginning of the dialogue. To take Alcibiades' portrait literally is to ignore the entire staging of the *Symposium,* to neglect Plato's own textual indications that the dialogue is more deeply rooted in fiction than in reality. Unlike practitioners of the traditional approach, I single out this text precisely because to me it seems to reveal, more than any other, the way Plato 'fictionalized' Socrates. Where Kierkegaard – who sees the *Symposium* as a product of dual authorship – attempts to spot traces of what truly belongs to Socrates, I attempt instead to find traces showing the hand of Plato, the distinguished director and stage manager.

Let me begin with a Jewish-American joke as related by Freud:
Two self-made men have had their portraits painted. Very proud of the likenesses, they put the paintings on display side by side, at an evening party, along with other marvels. Instead of admiring the portraits, however, one art critic exclaims: 'But where's the Saviour?'[2]

It may seem odd to begin with this story when we are dealing with Socrates, someone whose destiny, if we take Hegel's word for it, is properly tragic, someone who is comparable in Nietzsche's eyes to the great figures of tragedy. But Socrates cannot be confined to a single category. If he is a tragic hero, he is no less a comic figure, even for Hegel, who shows that the sublime and the grotesque are two sides of the same coin, and that the appearance of Aristophanes and his comedy in Athens was as necessary as the appearance of Socrates and his tragic destiny. Nietzsche begins by comparing Socrates to the venerable masters of Greek philosophy and ends up turning this figure – who never ceases to haunt and trouble him – into a veritable monster, a hybrid creature, more Jew than Greek, a caricature buffoon who looks more like a satyr than a figure of tragedy. In any event, Xenophon, whose Socrates is fond of laughter, dancing, and word-play, seems to assure us that the person who attended a performance of *The Clouds* so that the Athenian audience could judge for itself how well Aristophanes had captured his likeness would have savored Freud's anecdote, since by asking the disconcerting question 'Where's the Saviour?' the story brings to light the true nature of the two self-made men, a pair of scoundrels who can be likened to the thieves hung on either side of Christ.

For Socrates, whose name indicates his status as master-Saviour, could have identified with that other Saviour. Did he not save Alcibiades at the battle of Potidaea, and Xenophon, 'another of his favourites', during a different campaign?[3] The entire philosophical tradition (apart from Kierkegaard, although he too sees Socrates as a 'doctor', a necessary remedy against the Sophists) has set him up as a saviour figure. For Hegel, Socrates stands in opposition to his Athenian contemporaries: their minds, remaining in a state of internal division and conflict, continue to believe in the old gods and in external oracles, whereas Socrates appeals to the voice of his demon, to an inner oracle (for this he was justifiably sentenced to death), as the only source of value, virtue, and knowledge, the sole principle of healing and redemption.

For Nietzsche (the Nietzsche who wrote *The Twilight of the Idols*), the grotesque buffoon Socrates, despite his ugliness – which for a Greek was paradoxical – and his plebeian crudeness, managed to 'seduce' the most well-bred Athenians because they saw him as a saviour, a healer: they found a necessary 'life raft' in the remedy he proposed for their unhealthy instincts (unhealthy in the sense that they developed anarchically, excessively and disproportionately, each one for itself in bulimic pursuit of its own goals, because they had become unable to subordinate themselves to a single point of view). Socrates fascinated them because he represented in his own person – as a figure whose frightful, monstrous ugliness symbolized the anarchic power of impulses – an antidote to the malady. Against the tyranny of competing instincts he offered a stronger counter-tyrant: reason in a hypertrophical form, reason carried to absurd extremes. And the Athenians had no choice; in their life-threatening distress, this was their last resort: 'One must . . . counter the dark appetites with a permanent daylight –

the daylight of reason. One must be clever, clear, bright at any price; any concession to the instincts, to the unconscious, leads *downward*.[4]

From this standpoint, Socrates holds the fascination of a Saviour, a Saviour from decadence, one who is himself decadent, unhealthy, and degenerate. The remedy he offers – rationality at all costs – is a symptom of decadence, worse than the sickness itself, 'by no means a return to "virtue", to "health", to "happiness".'[5] That is why the Athenians were right to condemn him. By agreeing to drink the hemlock, by willing his own death, Socrates acknowledged ironically that he was a charlatan, that death alone is a true healer: he himself had been only a patient whose duty it was, at the moment of death, to sacrifice a cock to Asclepius.

By bringing 'light' to the Athenians, did Socrates give them the gift of life, or death? Was he a good doctor or a bad one, in the end? The philosophical tradition has established him as a saviour figure, like a fetish to be simultaneously attacked – since it legitimizes his condemnation – and venerated – since the same tradition holds him to be 'divine'. This tradition seems to be both unable and unwilling to choose between the two approaches.

Can we hang the saviour figure, in its undecidability, like a third painting in the empty space between the two others painted respectively by Xenophon and Plato, the first overly realistic and the second overly idealistic? Can we see a third painting that would show up the other two as counterfeit and unmask their creators as scoundrels? Be this as it may, this third portrait, like the one in Freud's story, exists nowhere except in the minds of its inventors: Socrates-as-Saviour is yet another fiction. Just as the philosopher's soul flies about freely, leaving only his corpse behind in the city, according to the *Theaetetus,* so only simulacra of Socrates remain. He is never present in person: only the interest on the debt owed this founding saviour and 'father' has been paid. And to speak of him as 'father' is already to fall under the sway of the Platonic phantasmagoria.

2. GOOD AND BAD TWINS

Thus it would be naive to suppose that somewhere there is one 'authentic' portrait of Socrates that we can use as a yardstick for evaluating all others. Plato's *Symposium,* which seems to offer a faithful rendering of statements actually made by Socrates, may in fact be the most 'mimetic' of all the Platonic dialogues. Many passages in the text indicate that we are dealing with a fiction here, even if it is a fictionalized version of actual discourse.

Two portraits of Socrates frame the *Symposium,* one painted by Aristodemus, the good thief, the best of the *deme,* the other by Alcibiades, the bad thief. Between the two, the figure of Diotima-Socrates-Plato hangs a third mythical portrait, that of the demon Eros, son of Poverty (Penia) and Resource (Poros),[6] an atopic figure of the intermediary. This third portrait, even if it too is fictitious, uses the blank space left between the others to sketch in Socrates' erotic and demonic identity (Socrates resists both a logic of identity and a speculative logic); it discredits the other two portraits and discredits in advance all the readings offered by his philosophical posterity that seek to make sense of Socrates, that attempt to reconcile his paradoxical atopicity and his 'contradictions' in a dialectical synthesis.

The two 'thieves' who offer us portraits of Socrates in the *Symposium*, each in his own way, may be viewed on more than one account as Socrates' *doubles,* as his good and bad twins.

Each is *attached* to Socrates like a *shadow,* following him step by step. Their love remains attached to a single body, or at least to a single soul; they are unable to rise to the higher dialectical level of generalization, let alone to the level of exclusive love for the essence of the beautiful. They remain 'fixated' on Socrates. When Alcibiades tries to get away from him, he finds Socrates reappearing 'uncannily' at every turn. When Aristodemus arrives alone at Agathon's house, everyone is astonished to see him without Socrates: 'But how is it that you do not bring us Socrates? . . . Very good of you to come, . . . but where is the man?' (174e). Moreover, Aristodemus is as surprised as everyone else, since Socrates had been walking alongside him – the 'two go along together', he said – right before Socrates went off on his own, sending his shadow ahead as a forerunner to Agathon's house, a shadow as disconcerted and disquieted at having lost its sun as a German Romantic hero is distressed, conversely, to lose his shadow or reflection. However, Socrates for his part feels no distress, since detaching himself from shadows is what he is trying to do at that very moment in order to 'recollect' his soul, to remember it, whereas he runs the risk of forgetting it if he goes on to Agathon's banquet. When he detaches Aristodemus and sends him on ahead, the act symbolizes the spiritual detachment that Socrates is trying to achieve, the goal of which is to incite the twin to pull away, to cut the umbilical cord, for the greater good of both disciple and master. That same master, for fear of being imprisoned by his attachments, chooses to refuse the crown he had been offered for saving Alcibiades; no doubt he recalls the equivalence between crowns and bondage that Aeschylus had established in his *Prometheus*.[7] (And Alcibiades clearly has not forgotten the equivalence either: taking a braided wreath he had earlier offered Agathon, he places it on Socrates' 'magnificent head'.)

It is because they are indeed Socrates's doubles that Aristodemus and Alcibiades both show up at the banquet *uninvited.* In this they resemble Penia (Poverty), a double for the human soul who slips in like a phantom at the gods' banquet of nectar and ambrosia on Aphrodite's birthday: there, owing to her own cunning and Poros's (Resource's) drunkenness she gives birth to Eros (Love), who offers men a means (*mechanê*) to acquire a substitute for immortality, since Zeus has definitively excluded them from the feasts of the gods.[8] In Greek, the word *skia*, meaning 'shadow', 'phantom', 'simulacrum', may also mean 'to come uninvited to a banquet'. It is always the most powerful individual who neglects or refuses to invite a weaker one; the latter then takes revenge by coming to haunt the feast like an evil twin. (In a different tradition, Dostoevski's *The Double* similarly links the problematics of doubles to the absence of an invitation to a feast. Golyadkin turns up as a 'double' for the first time when his benefactor, his substitute 'father', refuses him entry to his home on the occasion of a party.[9]) Aristodemus goes to Agathon's house at Socrates' invitation, backed by Socrates' ironic reference to a proverb according to which respectable people may turn up of their own accord at parties given by their own kind ('What if they go of their own accord, / The good men to our Goodman's board?' [174b]). This proverb is then immediately contradicted by a reference to Homer, who reports that Menelaus, a warrior lacking in courage, showed up uninvited at a meal given by Agamemnon. Aristodemus, nicknamed 'the little one', also gives the lie to the proverb, for he hastens to compare himself to Menelaus in all humility.

But when he sent his shadow on ahead, Socrates may have been thinking of yet another proverb: 'People often need someone smaller than themselves'. Philip the buffoon, the parasite who also attends the banquet uninvited (as we know from Xenophon), must have been acquainted with that saying; if he arrives 'prepared, in all varieties – to dine on some other person's [food]' (*Symposium*, I, 11), and if he finds it more amusing to come without an invitation than with one, it is because this clownish parasite knows that he is more necessary to the people involved than is the feast itself, because he contributes laughter, a supplement that gives the feast its full flavor. Similarly, without the indigent Penia, Eros would never have been born: in her extreme aporia, Penia weaves the plot that gets her pregnant by Poros, that overflowing repository of resources ensnared in the bonds of sleep.[10] Without little Aristodemus, without Aristodemus as his shadow and 'good' twin, Socrates, the Socrates of the *Symposium*, the master and model whom Aristodemus follows step by step, would never have been born or immortalized. Everything begins and ends with a double. Aristodemus precedes Socrates to Agathon's feast and will follow him out 'in the usual manner' (223d). His presence and his absences, the fact that he falls asleep and the fact that he forgets things, account for the unique features of the banquet narrative, its tenor and its duration.

After Alcibiades' eulogy, the ongoing dialogue between Socrates, Agathon, and Aristophanes about the relation between comedy and tragedy cannot be reported, for Aristodemus has fallen asleep: in a contingent way, his sleeping signifies the end of the *Symposium*. Furthermore, because he is Socrates' shadow, he guarantees the accuracy of the narrative: a simple man, in love with Socrates, he *follows* Socrates everywhere, in all senses of the term. Aristodemus identifies with his model, imitates him in his dress, goes barefoot as Socrates does. His identification is presumed to lend the narrative as much authenticity as if it had been related by Socrates himself; moreover, according to Apollodorus, Socrates would have confirmed the validity of his double's testimony, for the double's version, presumed purely repetitive, is deemed preferable to that of Philip's son Phoenix. As for Apollodorus, who transmits Aristodemus's narrative, his account purports to be above suspicion as well: he too is one of Socrates' admirers, a recent convert to Socratic philosophy. Head over heels in love, he *drinks in* the loved one's words: whether he has heard Socrates' discourse directly or *indirectly*, its effect on him, as on everyone else, is overwhelming. Alcibiades highlights the influence Socrates exercises from a distance; it makes him more powerfully seductive than Pericles, the greatest of the orators, or the best flute player, for Socratic discourse, even distanced from its source, like the most remote link in the magnetic chain of the *Ion*, loses none of its effectiveness or charm. Apollodorus, who like Aristodemus follows close upon Socrates' heels, can thus serve as a warning. Assiduous in keeping Socrates company, putting all the zeal of a new convert into learning what the master has said or done each day (172d), Apollodorus seems more capable than anyone else of reporting Aristodemus's narrative faithfully.

However, what qualifies Aristodemus and Apollodorus as faithful narrators disqualifies them as philosophers, for they are more in love with Socrates, whom they idolize, than they are with *Sophia;* their ability to remember outstrips their gift for recollection. Thinking they are imitating Socrates, each one goes too far. Aristodemus always shows up barefoot, whereas Socrates is willing to put on slippers for a banquet. Apollodorus's conversion, his 'reversal of values', is hardly 'philosophical': it consists in an exaggerated repudiation of everything he valued previously. He devalues without reservation everything that can be perceived by the senses; this is something Socrates does not do. Aristodemus scorns all men for their ignorance; he excepts only Socrates, whom he views as knowledgeable and happy. But Aristodemus has forgotten that Socrates scorns no one, that if he knows anything at all it is that he knows nothing; like the 'son' of Poros and Penia, Socrates rejects all simple oppositions and is no more ignorant than he is wise. Glaucon, chatting with Apollodurus, sees this plainly. He teases Apollodorus about his extravagant temperament, which verges on melancholy: by overestimating the object of his affections (of which he sees only the poretic aspect), by pouring out all his 'narcissistic libido' onto his idol, Apollodorus is actually merely indulging in self-deprecation, and making himself miserable. After 'shedding' his ego in favor of Socrates, after rejecting all his old friends, he is no more than a shadow of his old self, and of Socrates. He is fit only to play his assigned role, faithfully repeating the speech that Aristodemus had already recounted to Phoenix.

As a narrative of a narrative of a narrative, since Plato is after all the one who writes it down, the *Symposium* is a paragon of indirect discourse, a form that is thoroughly discredited in the *Republic* and that stands in stark contrast to Socrates' own pronouncements at the beginning of the *Symposium*. Socrates in effect condemns Agathon (and thus also Aristodemus and Apollodorus), for they imagine that to philosophize is to pour knowledge from a full vessel into an empty one by simple contact. This approach is an intoxicating one for the disciple, who is simply required to remember, to repeat with the greatest fidelity (which amounts to infidelity), the inebriating words of the master, instead of giving himself over to recollection or 'conning', to what Diotima calls a 'fresh' memory' (208a).

Does the disciples' fervor at least ensure that, in the mimetic genre of dialogue, untruthful par excellence, such a narrative is the least untruthful one possible? Plato, who would like to convince the reader that such is the case, nevertheless emphasizes that there is no identification without distancing, no repetition without difference, no memory without deformation, selection, and approximation: 'Now the entire speech in each case was beyond Aristodemus's recollection, and so too the whole of what he told me is beyond mine: but those parts which, on account also of the speakers, I deemed most memorable, I will tell you successively as they were delivered' (178a). Far from being an asset, the disciple's fervor may simply compound the inevitable deficiencies of memory with lapses caused by his fanaticism, which threatens to rob his narrative of its objectivity. Instead of sketching a faithful portrait of the master, the disciple merely elaborates an imagined figure of Socrates, a master figure presented as an exemplary model for all to follow; in the same way, according to the suggestion in the Phaedrus myth, every human soul must follow the chariot of the god with which it seeks to be identified.

The portrait of Socrates drawn by the good twin is thus as suspect as the portrait fantasized by the bad one. We have access to the latter, moreover, only through the narrative of good twins who report 'somewhat as follows' (173e), if we are to believe Plato himself. And it is ultimately Plato alone who creates, *poetically*, these two fictional portraits of Socrates – a fitting revenge against the master who had succeeded in 'corrupting' him, who had required him to burn his poems before he could become a disciple.

Might not the 'recollection' scene at the beginning of the *Symposium* be read, in this case, as a dismissive gesture in which Socrates not only attempts to exorcise what is perceptible to the senses before going on to Agathon's banquet, but also, as if in anticipation, places the reader ironically on guard against all the simulacra of his person that will be forged, in the *Symposium*, by the stage manager, his 'best disciple', Plato?

3. ATOPIA

The foregoing is one possible reading of the celebrated Socratic 'immobility' that has perhaps elicited more astonishment than any of his other characteristics and has perhaps contributed the most to making Socrates a demoniacal figure even more than a demonic, atopic one. According to this view he is an odd, disconcerting creature who is never where he is believed to be; his behaviour is always unexpected; he occupies a position outside genres and categories; he is an eminently paradoxical, outsized, monstrous, excessive and exceptional figure who is therefore exempt from competition and rivalry. Socrates' unexpected and unusual choice of footwear for Agathon's party astonishes Aristodemus, who is used to seeing him barefoot (and who seems mistakenly to associate him here with Penia, or ascetics). The master's bizarre behaviour is disconcerting for his disciple, who seems unaware that Socrates is master of his own body as well as of opposing possibilities; he has not pledged himself either to sobriety or to self-mortification, and he is not committed to limiting his pleasures, for he has an astonishing capacity to retain his full strength, consciousness and lucidity in the midst of bodily excesses.[11] Alcibiades recalls his tolerance for wine, for example: Socrates is able to drink more than anyone else without getting drunk, for the balanced measure of goodness that governs his behaviour is not of the quantitative order. This exceptional mastery explains how he can walk barefoot on ice in winter and allow himself to wear sandals on occasion: while his object is not simply to obey conventions and customs (he does not hesitate to show up right in the middle of a meal), he does not set out to scandalize. His choice of dress is ironic: he takes pains with his appearance because he is going to a handsome young man's house, because as a true 'hunter of young men,' he makes a 'feminine'[12] effort to seduce his host, the better to attract his soul.

Dressing up also means putting on the other's costume, mimetically, in order to win him over more easily; and it is a way for Socrates to prepare to play the unaccustomed role he has been assigned, that of delivering a eulogy which, in keeping with the rhetorical genre, ought to be more concerned with beauty than with truth. Praise for Eros has been put on the agenda by Phaedrus, who initiates the contest; it has been prescribed by the prescription-man, the doctor Eryximachus, and placed under the auspices of the god Dionysus. Now because philosophy and its dialectical order have not been invited to the contest or to the banquet, Socrates is obliged to undergo a sort of ritual to exorcise 'bad influences' before he sets foot in

Agathon's theater: he suddenly stops moving, stops noticing anything that is happening outside his own soul, as if he were succumbing to the violent effects of a sudden illness. Hegel, among others, introduces this analogy,[13] comparing Socrates' abrupt immobilization to a state of catalepsy, ecstasy, or even magnetic somnambulism (we shall return to this analogy, which is dependent on the overall Hegelian reading of Socrates that reinscribes him within speculative dialectics).

Alcibiades recalls that Socrates is never free from his chronic illness, not even in wartime; indeed, in wartime an even longer period of recollection is required. In one such instance Socrates remains motionless not just for a few hours, as he does in Agathon's vestibule, but all night long. He remains standing, erect, like a rigid phallus, offering himself up as a spectacle to the amazed and fascinated warriors who bring their mattresses and rugs outdoors the better to lie in wait, to look on surreptitiously (220c). Socrates himself hears nothing; he remains deaf to all harsh assaults on the senses, assaults emblematized by Agathon's violence, for Agathon will not hear of letting Socrates spend the night outdoors: he sends slaves for him, despite Aristodemus's warnings. Aristodemus advises Agathon to leave Socrates in peace, knowing full well that, whatever happens, he will not move for any reason, for his attention is fully engaged in strengthening his resistance to sense perceptions, in mesmerizing himself, in turning his body into a corpse so that his soul can free itself. Agathon's violence turns out to be as ineffectual as that of the Athenian state when it confines Socrates to prison: it does not keep him from thinking, does not prevent his soul from evading its bodily envelope. The only prison Socrates fears is pleasure, which binds the soul to the body and which alone can constitute an obstacle to recollection.[14] Socrates' instinctual forces must be monstrous, Nietzsche says,[15] for him to need such highly plastic exercises to be able to remember his own soul and to obey the Apollonian imperative, the essentially inhibitory voice of his demon! Stupefaction, cadaverization, petrification, paralysis, catalepsy, catatonia: these are all in effect analogies for describing the difficult immobilization brought about by the period of reflection during which the soul, ceasing to wander, dies to the body and its madness.

But, paradoxically, it is precisely when the soul is closest to itself that Socrates' behaviour is most astonishing, fascinating, and strangely disturbing. Like an uncanny double, he seems to appear and disappear at will, immobilizing himself, mesmerizing himself and others through some magic trick, like a sorcerer with more power to charm than the finest flute player or the most eloquent orator. He is more powerful than Gorgias and his rhetoric, more powerful than Agathon, who hurls his Gorgon-like speeches at his listeners to frighten them and to hide the vacuity of his own thought. Socrates' seductive sorcery, on the contrary, makes him appear to be immobilizing himself in order to seek some divine wonder within, as if he possessed some tremendous secret, some knowledge he would prefer to conceal from everyone: the presumed knowledge of a presumed master, which, despite Socrates' profession of ignorance, the others persist in attempting to extract from him through a variety of strategies. Agathon thinks he can incorporate the master's science magically, through mere contact and influence, as if all Socrates had to do were to sit down beside him and wait for knowledge to be poured into him, as if from a full cup into an empty one. But Socrates rejects that image, as in the *Meno* he rejects the image of the torpedo fish, He shows that contact with him does not convey learning: on the contrary, it strips the interlocutor of whatever learning he had thought he possessed up to that point.[16] Socrates cannot pour out anything at all, for, being a man, he is himself sterile; unlike the gods, who possess true knowledge, he possesses 'merely the knowledge of dreams,' a simulacrum of knowledge. His disciples' desire, which is oneiric in nature and inspired by Socrates' seductiveness (his only source of mastery) transforms that simulacrum of knowledge into divine knowledge, a hidden adornment or *agalma* that he might bequeath them through 'magnetic transfer'.

But Socrates contrasts the magical influence of poets capable of subjugating crowds – more than thirty thousand Greeks were subjugated by Agathon – with the clarity of the Good, the condition that makes knowledge as recollection possible. To the Sun-Good, the only god, Socrates addresses his morning prayer after he has remained standing all night so as to recollect not some idea, like a dove – that is Alcibiades' version – but his soul's infinite power to think. At the risk of being taken for a madman, a magician, a master:

> Immersed in some problem at dawn, he stood in the same spot considering (σκοπῶν) it; and when he found it a tough one, he would not give it up but stood there trying (Ζητῶν). The time drew on to midday, and the men began to notice him, and said to one another in wonder (θαυμάζοντες): 'Socrates has been standing there (ἑστήκει) in a study (φροντιζών τι) ever since dawn!' The end of it was that in the evening some of the Ionians after they had supped – this time it was summer – brought out their mattresses and rugs and took their sleep in the cool; thus they waited to see if he would go on standing all night too. He stood till dawn came and the sun rose; then walked away, after offering a prayer to the Sun. (*Symposium*, 220c-d).

Fascinated by the power that Socrates, like Eros, exercises over them (all the protagonists of the *Symposium* wonder more about the *power* of love and its effects than about its essence), the Greeks congeal the philosopher for all eternity as a shamanic figure,[17] the figure of a master *in spite of himself*.

Interpreting his profession of ignorance as a pure pose, his disavowal of mastery as a strategy of mastery, they attempt to take possession of a phallus as fantasmatic as that of the woman (the mother) whose clothes, the best fetishes of all, create the impression that she conceals an enigma, a veiled secret. Socrates, who identifies with his mother Phaenarete, with the sterility of her midwife's role, is metamorphosed fetishistically not so much into a paternal figure as into an omnipotent phallic mother from whom no one can steal the phallus, and for good reason.

Alcibiades learns this lesson the hard way. Although he places Socrates above everyone else, Alcibiades in his presumptuousness wants to make an exchange *between equals;* he seeks to swap his own beauty for the other's knowledge. Socrates does not go along with this fool's bargain; for, even if he were to possess the coveted object of exchange (this is Alcibiades' first illusion, for Socrates, full of resources, like Eros, nevertheless never holds onto anything; he dwells no more in euporia than in aporia), there can be no equivalence, no common measure (here is Alcibiades' second illusion) between the two objects of exchange, any more than there can be equivalence between the idea and its simulacrum. From these attempts at seduction, Alcibiades gains only by learning (if we may translate Plato into Lacanian language) that the law of desire is castration.[18] The hunter gets caught in his own trap; when the seducer's efforts are frustrated, the one he desires as a lover becomes the eternal loved one, a plebeian in relation to whom he himself, a well-bred nobleman, suffers a humiliation not unlike that of being enslaved to a master.

This may account for the necessary ambivalence – to say the least – of Alcibiades' feelings as revealed in his portrait of Socrates.

4. ALCIBIADES' SATYRIC DRAMA

As in all stories about doubles, the evil twin Alcibiades (like the idea of the beautiful) makes a sudden (ἐξαιφνῆς) appearance, announced by a commotion outdoors that introduces static into the discussion; earlier, Aristophanes' hiccups had disrupted the orderly progression of eulogies in a similar way. With Alcibiades' unexpected entrance, the outside intrudes violently upon the inside, with a disproportionate intoxication of the senses, in the form of the returning flute players. These voices external to the logos had been dismissed at the start of the *Symposium* (although in various forms they had in fact already surreptitiously snuck back into all the eulogies except the one pronounced by Socrates). Alcibiades comes in propped up by the musicians: their support is comical but crucial to someone who lacks the assistance of the paternal *logos* that has been abandoned in favor of the Athenian *demos* and projected onto the outside in the form of a persecuting double from which he tries vainly to escape. Alcibiades is hunted down and trapped by this double, waylaid by him always precisely where he least expects it – for example, at Agathon's banquet, where he is lurking in the dark, near the man with whom Alcibiades himself is in love and upon whom he is about to confer a garland when he catches sight of Socrates. 'Save us, what a surprise! Socrates here! So it was to lie in wait for me again that you were sitting there – your old trick of turning up on a sudden where least I expected you!' (213b) Alcibiades is surprised, jealous of the double and rival who is seeking to take his place next to Agathon, attempting to separate him from Agathon along with all the other handsome youths Socrates would like to keep for himself – or so Alcibiades believes. For his part, Socrates interprets Alcibiades' 'eulogy' as an attempt to enlighten Agathon about the risks involved in becoming Socrates' lover, so Alcibiades can keep Agathon for himself as a friend and have Socrates as his own exclusive lover. Alcibiades suspects Socrates of the same maneuver: Socrates seems to be trying to make him jealous, pretending to forget him in favor of Agathon (he does the same thing elsewhere in favor of Protagoras[19]) in order to make Alcibiades his lover and slave, fraudulently and crudely compelling Alcibiades to love him instead of being loved by him. Socrates always pretends to play the role of lover in order to be the loved one and in order to subject the other to his own desire. For the Greeks, this is an intolerable situation (as the eulogies of Phaedrus and Pausanias also attest[20]); subjection to another's desire is the true aporetic trap, a dead end from which, after his failed attempt to seize the unseizable, Alcibiades cannot escape:

'In what I thought was my sole means of catching him he had eluded me. So I was at a loss (ἠπόρουν), and wandered about in the most abject thraldom to this man that ever was known' (219e).

The position of lover-in-subjection is intolerable, for it convinces the lover of his own inferiority and even of his infirmity; he dreads the ridicule, shame and dishonor this position confers. Just as the other guests at the banquet had produced 'beautiful and magnificent descriptions' of Love's qualities, Alcibiades puts Socrates' performances on display, performances that show him as an incomparable being, unrivaled, superior to everyone else in all respects. This is excessive praise, a counterpart to the excessiveness of Alcibiades' own desire, which identifies Socrates' virtue with the extraordinary power (he always succeeds in doing and in having others do things that no one else can accomplish) that humiliates them all (220c), and especially Alcibiades himself: '[Socrates] has set his heart on having the better of me in every way' (222e). His 'amorous' failure affects him because he runs the risk of damaging his glorious reputation as an invincible seducer and thus damaging the high opinion he has of himself (in this respect he is the opposite of Apollodorus), of his own good looks and his wealth, both spurned by Socrates: 'for I was enormously proud of my youthful charms' (217a). '[Socrates] despises [beauty] more than any of you can believe; nor does wealth attract him, nor any sort of honor that is the envied prize of the crowd. All of these possessions he counts as nothing worth' (216d). Alcibiades felt 'affronted' (219e). In seeking to seduce Socrates, Alcibiades is not betraying a desire to 'see' or to have his 'tail' but rather his phallus,[21] precisely the thing that confers on him all his power, his *Agalma*, the marvel that Socrates is thought – because he has disavowed it – to possess, his knowledge, which Alcibiades would like to incorporate as his own in order to reverse the situation of mastery. And to that end, Alcibiades is ready to strike any bargain; he is prepared to sell his own good looks – which he believes are invincible – to the devil.[22]

But what Alcibiades finds even less tolerable than the loss of his social *timè* (honor) is the permanent sense of shame aroused in him by Socrates and Socrates alone: 'And there is one experience I have in presence of this man alone, such as nobody would expect in me, – to be made to feel ashamed by anyone; he alone can make me feel it' (216b). 'I was ashamed' (217d). Alcibiades' sense of shame is intolerable to his fragile narcissism because it brings to light his divided inner state. If Alcibiades flees Socrates as vigorously as he desires him, if he stops up his ears as if he were trying to avoid the Sirens, it is because Socrates forces him to pay attention to himself[23] rather than to the affairs of Athens; it is because Socrates would like to 'reconcile' him with the part of himself projected onto the outside that continues to haunt him in the form of Socrates, like an invincible, omnipotent phantom. Socrates is a double who pursues Alcibiades because he is more tenacious, more in love with Alcibiades than Alcibiades is 'himself', and stronger than 'he': this is the secret of Socrates' invincible superiority. For it is impossible to detach yourself from someone who is permanently attached to your soul (unlike all those who, loving only your body, will abandon it as soon as the prime of life has passed).

So long as Alcibiades seeks to improve himself, he is sure to meet Socrates, and he is not fooled by his own threat to do away with Socrates: he knows perfectly well that in death Socrates would haunt him more than ever. He understands that, as in all twin stories, killing the double would be tantamount to pronouncing his own death sentence, would kill the best part of himself, the part that still resists the Athenian *demos*. With the death of Socrates, Alcibiades would lose the eye that can look into his own soul, the mirror that alone allows him to recognize his true kinship, the divinity of his soul:[24] in other words, he would lose the 'ideal self' with which Socrates seeks in vain to reconcile him. 'No reconcilement for you and me', says Alcibiades (213d); if he flees Socrates, it is because the latter unsettles his sense of identity, the narcissistic unity which he has sought to protect by projecting outside of himself the part of himself that separates him from himself. Even though he cannot get along without the ideal other who defends him against annihilation, he cannot help feeling overcome, ridiculed, betrayed by the one whom he does not succeed either in seducing or abandoning.

Of Socrates, the divine part of his own soul who is the only invited guest at the banquet of immortality as he is at Agathon's feast, Alcibiades can thus only sketch in an ambivalent portrait, one whose ambivalence is betrayed by a cleavage into a series of opposing terms (inside and outside, appearance and reality, knowledge and ignorance, and so on) that bear negative or positive connotations as the case may be. Despite these reversing images, Alcibiades' portrait of Socrates still depends upon a logic of identity, and thus it differs from the portrait of Eros, which eludes such logic. And yet the philosophic tradition, seduced by Alcibiades' eulogy, seems to have taken his affirmations at face value and to have credited his portrait as accurate – probably because it corresponds, at best, to a tenacious, hysterical fantasy that holds Socrates to be a master seducer.

Alcibiades claims to be praising Socrates truthfully, even though a eulogy by definition focuses on beauty rather than truth. Like Socrates, whom he parodies, and unlike the other guests, Alcibiades thus offers a derisive echo of his double's words. But how could a eulogy, especially one delivered in a state of drunkenness, be truthful? To be sure, for Plato, wine is not a bad thing in itself, since it has the nature – and the ambiguity – of a *pharmakon*; consumed in moderation, it is capable of softening souls and making them susceptible, as children are, to the truths embedded in fables.[25] However, Alcibiades seems to have gone beyond the bounds of temperance, since he is drunk, and sufficiently outside his normal state to claim to be telling the truth in a eulogy. In fact, the wine he has drunk simply puts Alcibiades into a state of mind that allows him to ignore social conventions and thus to speak without shame or embarrassment about his attempts at seduction and their failure, so as to tell the 'truth' – not the truth about Socrates, but the truth of desire – and, anticipating Lacan, to formulate the law of desire: to love is to want to be loved; there is no human desire without castration, without desire for the Other's desire. The wine emboldens Alcibiades to describe love in its full violence (and in so doing he refutes the effeminate discourse in which Agathon depicted Eros, in his own image, as a tender and delicate god). It is in this sense alone that Alcibiades is right to say '*in vino veritas*'.[26]

Alcibiades' claim to be telling the truth might still be justified by the argument that drunken discourse, veering off in all directions, is more appropriate to the Socratic atopia than straightforward, reasonable, rational discourse. Is this not the lesson that Alcibiades is seeking to put across, as he multiplies images in his attempt to capture Socrates? In the Platonic optic in which images are ontologically discredited, Alcibiades' claim is paradoxical at the very least. His recourse to images seems in fact to stem from some psychological necessity rather than from an epistemological requirement: his images allow him to 'compare' the incomparable, to abolish Socrates' exceptional singularity, to reduce the extraordinary to a common standard that allows him to enter into a relation of mimetic rivalry and try to strike a bargain based on a supposed equivalence with the rival, and perhaps, finally, to take the rival's place. And yet the images proffered all tend to show that Socrates *cannot be equaled,* that he cannot be compared to ordinary mortals, that a god alone may be his rival. But Alcibiades does not compare him to a god: this singular being whose very abnormality denies him a place in the human world (the Athenian democracy, unable to tolerate exceptional beings, condemns him to death – which is one form of ostracism) instead resembles one of those hybrid creatures who are closer to animality than to divinity. This comparison does not signify that Alcibiades has grasped Socrates' demonic nature; rather, it reflects his desire to heap ridicule on this peerless being who is admirable in all respects, like a father or an elder brother; it reflects his desire to punish Socrates for his infidelity by making him look ridiculous, creating an image worthy of Aristophanes (who had already profaned Love in recounting his own myth). Viewed in this light, Alcibiades' eulogy begins to resemble a counter-trial in which he accuses Socrates of not having sufficiently corrupted young people and of having been incorruptible himself, of having resisted Alcibiades' own beauty, his wealth, his cunning and his violence. Before the tribunal of the Athenians present at the banquet, in his inebriated state,[27] he does not hesitate to denounce Socrates, to exhibit for all to see what that atopic being conceals; he does not hesitate to crack open the outer shell before their eyes so as to uncover behind the grotesque exterior a sublime inner aspect against which Alcibiades seeks to defend himself by laughter and buffoonery, turning Socrates not into a tragic hero, as Hegel will, but into a character suited to a satyric drama.

The first image Alcibiades proposes is that of a silenus, an image that echoes and responds to Socrates' own image for the Athenian people in *Alcibiades* (131b): 'For my chiefest fear is of your being blighted by becoming a lover of the people, since many a good Athenian has come to that ere now. For fair of face is "the people of great-hearted Erechtheus", but you should get a view of it stripped: so take the precaution that I recommend. . . . You must wait till you have learnt, in order that you may be armed with an antidote' (132a-b). Conversely, the image of the silenus as applied to Socrates uncovers, beneath his monstrous ugliness and repulsive exterior, a secret beauty, a divine marvel. Alcibiades does not seem to have invented this comparison. In Xenophon's *Banquet,* the same comparison is attributed to Critobulus, who declares that Socrates is the ugliest of all the silenuses that appear in satyric dramas. And it is Socrates himself who unmasks the beauty behind his ugliness, for this pseudo-ugliness is 'functional' and actually to his advantage: thus his eyes see not only straight ahead but also to the side, for they are positioned on the sides of his head like those of the crayfish – which by this criterion would be the most beautiful animal there is. Socrates' flat nose is the most beautiful of all, for it allows his nostrils to receive scents from all sides. And his mouth, which according to Critobulus is more hideous than a donkey's, can also be viewed as purposeful, and thus as beautiful, for if it were to bite, it would make off with the largest portions; as for his thick lips, they present no obstacle to the tenderness of his kisses. In any event, if Socrates resembles silenuses, these after all are children of goddesses, the Naiads, and this fact is irrefutable proof of their beauty and his.

Socrates' ugliness – fascinating and enigmatic for the Greeks, for whom *Agathos* is always also *Kalos* – is also what triggers Alcibiades' comparison with the flat-nosed, thick-lipped, bull-eyed silenus that Socrates could have seen as a statuette in his father's workshop; identifying himself with this representation, Socrates seeks to reject the identification and to avenge himself, as it were, by an act of auto-generation, an exceptional exercise in plastic art, turning himself into a statue in order to recollect his own soul, the wonder concealed under his silenus-like exterior.[28] The most important aspect of the silenus image – and Alcibiades' ambivalence leads him to go farther than Critobulus does on this point – is in fact less the ugliness itself than the contrast between external ugliness and inner beauty, between a rough-hewn lubricious exterior whose Dionysian character is attested by the statuette's customary Pan-pipes, and the marvelous hidden Apollonian inner reality, the divine Agalma. Socrates' beauty no longer lies in his ugliness, as it does for Xenophon (for Alcibiades such ambivalence is intolerable); rather, it is dissociated from that ugliness, located behind it, as an effect of cleavage: it is an extraordinary pure beauty contrasted with pure ugliness, with a pure deceptive appearance, a beauty construed as an additional ruse devised by Socrates the better to entrap and fascinate, the equivalent in a way to the torpedo fish with which Meno compares it.

The torpedo fish 'appears as a flabby body, quite without vigour but, Oppian tells us, "its flanks conceal a cunning trick, a *dólos,* its strength in weakness". Its *dólos* consists of the sudden electric shock which its harmless appearance masks and which takes its adversary by surprise, leaving it at the torpedo fish's mercy'[29] paralyzing and overcoming its prey.[30] By means of this living trap, a veritable apotrope that prevents access to his 'insides', Socrates conceals the source of his power and superiority, his knowledge, so as to keep it for himself, proclaiming aloud, too loudly to be credible, that his ignorance is general and that he knows nothing: a pure ruse, according to Alcibiades, comparable to the roughness of his seemingly foolish discourse. Anyone who can see through his defenses and perceive Socrates himself, anyone who can unmask the beauty beneath the ugliness, the knowledge beneath his self-proclaimed ignorance and the seriousness beneath his irony, anyone who does not fear to crack open this silenus cannot fail to be amazed and overwhelmed by the prodigious internal richness of the 'phallic mother' spewing forth figurines, who subdues you once and for all:

> He is utterly stupid and ignorant, as he affects (σχῆμα). Is this not like a Silenus? Exactly. It is an outward casing (ἔξωθεν) he wears, similarly to the sculptured Silenus. But if you opened his inside (ἔνδοθεν), you cannot imagine how full he is, good companions, of sobriety . . . [He] spends his life in chaffing and making game of his fellow-men. Whether anyone else has caught him in a serious moment and opened him, and seen the images inside, I know not; but I saw them one day, and thought them so divine and golden, so perfectly fair and wondrous, that I simply had to do as Socrates bade me. (216d-217a).

> His talk most of all resembles the Silenuses that are made to open. If you chose to listen to Socrates' discourses you would feel them at first to be quite ridiculous; on the outside they are clothed with such absurd words and phrases – all, of course, the hide of a mocking satyr. His talk is of pack-asses, smiths, cobblers, and tanners, and he seems always to be using the same terms for the same things; so that anyone inexpert and thoughtless might laugh his speeches to scorn. But when these are opened, and you obtain a fresh view of them by getting inside, first of all you will discover that they are the only speeches which have any sense in them; and secondly, that none are so divine, so rich in images of virtue, so largely – nay, so completely – proper for the study of such as would attain both grace and worth. (221e-222a).

By cracking the mother's womb open again without embarrassment before the tribunal of banquet guests, by exhibiting the divinity concealed beneath its ugliness (that of its genital organs?), the fecundity beneath its self-proclaimed sterility, just as Aristophanes, in a pastiche of Empedocles, had revealed the powers of Eros, Alcibiades reveals Socrates' *dynamis* (power), which he unmasks the better to denounce him: for, compared now not to a silenus-figure but to the mythological Silenus himself,[31] Socrates only gives up his secrets when he is required, compelled, to do so.

Alcibiades does not hesitate to tell how he himself tried to seduce Socrates on several occasions in order to drag his *dynamis* out of him, but he was not as lucky as King Midas, for Socrates managed to resist all his ploys, stood up to all the trials he imposed: the trial of solitude (for, as someone for whom *aidos* (self-mastery) is the only value, Socrates ought to be more susceptible, more 'takable' in private than in public, since it is less shameful for a Greek to laugh or cry at home than in the theater; see *The Republic*, X), the trial of nudity in the gymnasium, the trial of treacherous violence and even rape.

Socrates gave up nothing, revealed nothing at all, and by that very token he succeeded in subjugating Alcibiades for all time. Unmasking him before the Athenians is thus not a way of betraying his secret, to which Alcibiades has no more access than anyone else; it is rather a way of warning the Athenians against the perverse duplicity that endows Socrates with mastery over all: 'I assure you, not one of you knows him; well, I shall reveal him, now that I have begun' (216d).

Just as behind a woman's veil there is always another veil, according to Nietzsche, if you take off a silenus's mask you will find another mask, that of the satyr *Marsyas*. Whereas the first image implies the whole system of oppositions upon which metaphysics will come to depend, the second, above and beyond the cleavages it operates, attempts to reconcile those oppositions.

The image of Marsyas is a mythical representation of a dual being, no longer an equivocal, ambiguous man *or* god but man *and* animal in ambivalent fashion; in the coherence of its form this image creates the illusion of a possible reunion of opposites, a reconciliation, over and beyond the anguish of fragmentation, of Alcibiades with himself, of the animal portion with the divine or human portion, projected onto the outside. This image, which is reassuring for Alcibiades, seems to work against Socrates. Just as the other protagonists of the *Symposium* were convinced, wrongly, that Eros was an admirable god, the silenus image could lead to the conclusion that Socrates' divinity is 'real'. The image of the satyr turns him into a buffoon, a lubricious figure, a familiar character in satyric dramas. Satyrs were represented with goat or horse features from the waist down; their upper body was that of a man. They had long, wide tails and perpetually erect male members of superhuman proportions; they belonged to Dionysus's following. While this view of Socrates deems him comparable to satyrs in every respect, he bears a special resemblance to the satyr Marsyas, the inventor of the double-piped flute. According to another tradition, Marsyas merely appropriated the flute that Athena had invented, and was castrated by Apollo as punishment. Challenged to produce music on his lyre comparable to Marsyas's flute music, Apollo invites Marsyas to play his instrument backwards, the way he himself plays his lyre. Defeated by Apollo, Marsyas is flayed by him.

Socrates, for his part, is not castrated (contrary to Lacan's contention); he is invincible, more powerful than Marsyas. It is his disproportionate, excessive, monstrous power that allows him to be compared not so much to Apollo, whom he invokes (this gesture would be a manifestation of the dissimulation and irony practiced by Socrates and unmasked by Alcibiades here), but more to Dionysus and his band of flute-girls. For Alcibiades, only Socrates' duplicity accounts for his dismissal of the flute-girls at the beginning of the *Symposium* (the flute being a polyphonic instrument par excellence; Plato banishes it from the ideal education he describes in *The Republic* in favor of the lyre, because the flute leaves all those who hear it 'beside themselves'). And if the comparison between Socrates and a female flute-player[32] may seem surprising and even insolent, it is only because Socrates misleads us by working his magic without exhibiting a flute or any other phallic instrument: he works his charms more surely with the help of mere words than the best flute player, the greatest orator;[33] an orator may impose himself by his presence, but he does not really possess you. Socrates succeeds even when he is absent. He operates at a distance; far from being degraded, his words as reported by even the most mediocre speaker (little Aristodemus?) retain their seductive effects, their magico-magnetic power. His words may be said to be all the more powerful in his absence (and even when he is present he is always already absent, dead).

The enthusiasm Socrates provokes is analogous, but superior, to the enthusiasm produced by the corybants in their transports; his words have an unsoothable sting, more powerful than a serpent's.[34] Everyone bears witness to the power of Socrates' words, for their impact is universal: men, women, adolescents, all succumb to possession and subjugation: 'For when I hear him I am worse than any wild fanatic; I find my heart leaping and my tears gushing forth at the sound of his speech, and I see great numbers of other people having the same experience' (215e). Socrates is a true man of the theater; it is he, not Agathon, who deserved to be crowned by the thirty thousand assembled Greeks. Alcibiades carries out this hierarchical displacement by symbolically transferring a garland with which he has crowned Agathon to Socrates' head. Since the essence of beauty and the transports to which it gives rise are more powerful than perceptible beauty and its effects, Socrates himself surpasses Agathon decisively in seductiveness. His is a formidable seductiveness, for, through the disturbance it generates, it leads to a general overturning of values, to a conversion of the *thumos* (spirit), which is henceforth indignant over its subjection to the perceptible. If you think you have escaped this dangerous Marsyas, this siren, by plugging your ears, think again; you will depend on him more than ever. For if Socrates' voice can charm to such an extent, it is because it belongs neither to an exceptional individual nor to an elder brother or father nor to a silenus, satyr, serpent, or siren – these mythological monsters remain overly reassuring – but to the logos itself. It is Alcibiades' own voice, the one from which he turned away to subject himself to the other, flattering voice of the Athenian *demos*, one that covers him with honor *and* with shame because it distances him from concern with himself and his true kinship. Because Alciabiades fails to hear his own voice in that of Socrates – the voice of the philosophical Eros, which ought to direct him toward exclusive commerce with his own soul – he remains necessarily fixed at a lower degree of the dialectics of love, attached and subjected to the person of Socrates alone.

The end of the eulogy abandons the apparently deprecatory mythological images. Just as the other protagonists had showered fulsome praise on the god of love by enumerating his virtues and his good deeds, Alcibiades exhibits those of 'his' god whom he can call, after the reassuring mythological detour, an extraordinary *man*, one who resists all comparisons as he stands up to all trials, including fatigue, cold, and sleep; he is superior to all by virtue of his temperance, his courage, his indifference to honors, his mastery – even in the most perilous situations, he always knows what to do at the crucial moment; this man from whom Alcibiades seeks to save himself has saved his, Alciabiades', life at his own risk. The greatest of all orators, musicians, strategists, and so on, he has no peer among men of the past or the present; he is worthy of unreserved admiration. At the end of the eulogy, as if his drunkenness has subsided and he has remembered that the rhetorical genre he is using requires not truth but an accumulation of the virtues of the object being praised, Alcibiades abandons all ambivalence and 'deifies' Socrates, as someone to whom no image – no human, all too human image – and no mythological figure could do justice. As Socrates' own rough discourse is an envelope concealing profound wisdom, so the crude images of silenuses and satyrs are cloaks that cover over the portrait of Socrates the perfect, peerless man; they are comical only for the masses, for imbeciles and ignoramuses. Anyone who is capable of seeing through the satyric hide of Alcibiades' discourse, capable of discerning his admiration and his love, will no longer wish to mock Socrates or condemn him to death. Only one complaint against Socrates will remain: he claims to be everyone's lover the better to make himself the loved one and master of all. But in the final analysis this accusation is perhaps a ruse on Alcibiades' part, an attempt to frighten Agathon into breaking off with Socrates and thus to have Socrates all to himself.

As a simple either/or alternative, the initial question raised – 'Is Alcibiades' eulogy aimed at buffoonery or truth?' – is moot, for it does not take into account either Alcibiades' ambivalence or his irony (or Plato's), nor does it take into account the end of the *Symposium,* with its suggestion that the capacity for contraries belongs to Plato, that he may be at once a comic and a tragic author, and thus also the author of this two-faced satyric drama that Alcibiades has just performed and that Plato has staged. For in the succession of eulogies pronounced by the various protagonists – each one in conformity with his own Muse – it is Plato who has succeeded in demonstrating unsurpassable mastery in the most diverse genres;[35] Plato is the sole stage manager of the *Symposium.* It is he who, concealed under the features of Aristodemus, Apollodorus, and Alcibiades, has created the fictional figure of Socrates as a figure of mastery. If he has hidden himself behind his privileged spokesperson, if he has transferred his own thoughts to that figure, it is because he knows perfectly well that there is no mastery without disavowal of mastery. By making it impossible for all time to sort out what belongs to him and what belongs to his master, Plato takes away with one hand what he gives with the other, and makes the debt unpayable.

In any event, Plato produces a veritable omnipotent *deus ex machina*, relying on the fiction of a sudden commotion, a new hubbub from outside that signals the double's disappearance just as a similar disturbance had signaled his arrival, to conclude the *Symposium* and *arrest* the portrayal of Socrates.

B. Plato's Chimerical Socrates, as Seen by Nietzsche

There is something in the morality of Plato that does not really belong to Plato but is merely encountered in his philosophy – one might say, in spite of Plato: namely, the Socratism for which he was really too noble. 'Nobody wants to do harm to himself, therefore all that is bad is done involuntarily. For the bad do harm to themselves: this they would not do if they knew that the bad is bad. Hence the bad are bad only because of an error; if one removes the error, one necessarily makes them – good'.

This type of inference smells of the *rabble* that sees nothing in bad actions but the unpleasant consequences and really judges, 'it is *stupid* to do what is bad', while 'good' is taken without further ado to be identical with 'useful and agreeable'. In the case of every moral utiliarianism one may immediately infer the same origin and follow one's nose: one will rarely go astray.

Plato did everything he could in order to read something refined and noble into the proposition of his teacher – above all, himself. He was the most audacious of all interpreters and took the whole Socrates only the way one picks a popular tune and folk song from the streets in order to vary it into the infinite and impossible – namely, into all of his own masks and multiplicities. In a jest, Homeric at that: what is the Platonic Socrates after all if not *prosthe Platōn opithen te Platōn Messē te Chimaira*.[36]

In Nietzsche's reading of Greek philosophy, the enigmatic figure of Socrates occupies an unstable position. At some points, Socrates is linked with his predecessors, the great venerable masters of philosophy, owing to his purity (Socrates is the last exemplary sage who triumphs over the passions), in which case it is Plato, the first of the great hybrids, who institutes a break. At other points, Socrates is depicted as a veritable monster of theory who introduces schisms and oppositions (labeled 'metaphysical') in every domain and introduces a simultaneous rift in history; this Socrates represents a critical turning point. According to the second view, Plato's noble and highborn soul, 'the most beautiful growth of antiquity',[37] is led astray under the unhealthy influence of Socrates the uncultivated plebeian. Armed with matchless medical skill and genealogical flair, Nietzsche works like a police dog, sniffing out suspicious traces of Socratism in Plato's dialogues, traces not suspected even by their author – in order to restore to the disciple his initial nobility and purity, in order to separate Plato in spite of himself from his master, from that demonic (demoniacal?) corruptor, from the criminal poisoner who decidedly deserved to drink hemlock.[38]

One of the traces is particularly symptomatic, for it 'reeks' undeniably of commonality and lack of distinction: it includes everything in the noble Plato's ethics that hints excessively at utilitarianism in the noble Plato's morality,[39] a utilitarian ethics that betrays its popular, Socratic origins through its assimilation of the good to the useful or the agreeable. Take the well-known adage, 'No one is wilfully evil', which could sum up what is called Plato's 'moral intellectualism': when it is dissected and subjected to genealogical insight, it appears as the conclusion of an implicit argument whose popular presuppositions Nietzsche brings to light. It results from a veritable calculation of interests that proclaims its own true genealogical affiliations, for anyone who knows how to listen and sniff it out:

> *First premise:* no one wants to hurt himself.
> *Second premise:* a bad person who does evil hurts himself.
> *Conclusion:* a bad person does evil only through ignorance (of the second premise). Thus he is not really bad, except by mistake.
> *Negative counter-proof:* take away his mistake and the bad person will necessarily become good.

In this 'syllogism', a particularly subtle and sensitive genealogical insight, one that for its part rarely makes mistakes (would popular wisdom thus judge it particularly 'good'?), can sniff out some postulates that smell particularly foul.

The first premise, in fact, seems self-evident only to someone for whom pain is intolerable, to someone who is not strong enough to love and desire pain, and who does not know that pain and pleasure are inseparable twins.[40] The second premise does not recognize that the one who does 'evil', the bad person, harms himself less than the 'good person' does, since the former, by doing 'evil', discharges his will to power on the outside, enjoying his power directly, whereas the latter, compelled to turn his will to power against himself, enjoys it only in oblique fashion, so that he does not recognize the pleasure in the 'pain' he feels, and he can bear the pain only by giving it a meaning, by disguising it under the tawdry cloaks of religion and divinity.[41]

Both premises of the argument are thus symptomatic of a weak will to power. The weakness of that will is betrayed by an inability to bear suffering that causes it to identify what is *evil* with what is *harmful*, that is, to evaluate the act from the point of view of the affected third party, from the point of view of its consequences and not its origin. Such an evaluation is characteristic of the plebeian perspective and its democratic prejudice, which constitutes an obstacle to any research into the question of origins. This perspective runs counter to that of the nobility, which begins by evaluating the 'good' act, not in relation to someone who has been the recipient of an act of goodness, but in relation to the agent of the act, who considers himself 'good' and judges his actions good simply because in carrying them out he enjoys the feeling of his own power.[42]

As for the conclusion of the argument, it leads to what Nietzsche elsewhere calls an overwhelming affirmation:[43] the affirmation of a moral optimism that believes, wrongly, that evil resides in ignorance and virtue in knowledge, that it is therefore sufficient to teach the good for everyone to become 'good'. Such an affirmation postulates the *universality of good will;* but it implies total 'ignorance' as to the true nature of will, its true nature being the will to power, the will to life that is not singular but multiple and '*essentially* appropriation, injury, overpowering of what is alien and weaker; suppression, hardness, imposition of one's own forms, incorporation and at least, at its mildest, exploitation'.[44] Will, understood in this way, is thus not at all 'moral' in the popular sense of the term; as an aggressive force, seeking to extend and enlarge itself, aiming at preponderance, it cannot be subjected or subordinated to knowledge of the good. The 'devastation' that is produced by moral optimism amounts to an illegitimate hierarchical reversal carried out between 'will' and knowledge. Moral optimism takes the means for the end; it wrongly believes that 'rationality', *ratio,* a calculation of interests, can allow one to choose and evaluate a course of action, whereas in fact instinct alone evaluates, chooses, decides, 'deserves more authority than rationality, which wants us to evaluate and act in accordance with reasons, with a "why" – in other words, in accordance with expedience and utility'.[45] To believe that reason can dictate behaviour and that it therefore suffices to teach virtue in order to make everyone virtuous is to 'neglect' the entire irrational dimension of moral judgments.

The plebeian presuppositions sniffed out in the 'Platonic' formula lead to the revelation that this formula in fact belongs to Socratic 'foolishness',[46] that Socrates is its father as he is the father of all utilitarianism, whose popular origin is easy to detect provided that one relies not on reason but on one's nose. By turning to his subtle sense of smell, and also to Xenophon, who had the nose of a shopkeeper, Nietzsche indeed manages to trace a utilitarian Socrates in Plato's dialogues, a Socrates who is more or less hidden behind his 'best disciple', Plato: the disciple masks his master's plebeian origins by embellishing them in noble style. By projecting his own aristocratism into Socrates' doctrine, by introducing his own interpretations into that doctrine, by introducing himself into it erotically so as to make disciple and master an inseparable, symbiotic couple, Plato in effect made it impossible to distinguish between what properly belongs to each one of them, except for a reader armed with the genealogical criterion of distinction, that is, precisely the *distinction* or lack thereof of the propositions: the degree to which the propositions are *distinguished*.

If this criterion makes it possible to ferret out traces of plebeianism in Plato's dialogues, symptoms of an unhealthy contamination by Socrates, it also makes it possible, conversely, to appreciate to what extent the figure of the master has been contaminated by that of the disciple, has been transfigured by that hybrid being, covered over by the latter's multiple masks and faces. You would thus seek in vain, in Plato's texts, the original text of 'Socrates'. You would find there only Plato's more or less chimerical interpretations.[47] 'Socrates' is only a more or less anonymous popular theme on which Plato, like an authentic musician, embroiders his noble variations ad infinitum and to the point of impossibility, since there is no common typological measure between the original theme and its variations – which have entirely different origins. Whereas Cicero[48] creates a fictional Socrates who brings philosophy down from heaven to earth, into homes and streets (he spends his time on the agora interrogating the humble and the powerful alike, all blended together in their shared lack of knowledge), Plato, with unparalleled audacity, brings Socrates up from the street where he picked him up in some filthy dive and elevates him to the Platonic heaven of ideas – where he transforms him, actually, into a Chimera.

The Chimera, according to Homer, was 'in the fore part a lion, in the hinder a serpent, and in the midst a goat'.[49] Socrates, as 'imagined' by the poet Plato, becomes 'in the fore part Plato, in the hinder Plato, and in the midst a chimera': an entirely fictitious being created in the hybrid image of his author, who must have taken a wicked pleasure in thus avenging himself on the master who required him to give up poetry and music as the price he had to pay for becoming a disciple.

By offering a pastiche of Homer, not without irony, Nietzsche in turn takes revenge on Plato, who may have had a good eye and a good ear but probably not a very good nose, since he did not manage to keep his distance from the plebeian Socrates and did not avoid being poisoned by him. Nietzsche in the end thus brings Homer back from the exile to which Plato, to please his master, had condemned him. Nietzsche unmasks the hypocrisy of the disciple who had actually never stopped identifying with, never lost his fondness for, Homer, since under the mask of the philosopher, disciple of Socrates, he never stopped constructing Homeric fictions and chimeras, and those alone.

Nietzsche's genealogical reading, which emphasizes the reciprocal relations of love and contamination between master and disciple, remains nostalgic – and this is what I should like to emphasize – for something that would properly 'belong' to Plato or 'belong' to Socrates, something that it *would like* to be able to distinguish subtly. In this it remains contaminated by the Plato of Books II and III of the *Republic*. It is itself a fiction in the image of its author (he would acknowledge this), in the image of Nietzsche's own multiple facets, 'Plato' and 'Socrates' at once. Nietzsche in fact carries his own double within himself, in the form of a dual system of evaluation, and that is what makes him more apt than anyone to sniff out signs of rise and fall, nobility and baseness – 'I have a subtler sense of smell for the signs of ascent and decline than any other human being before me'[50] – which are what, as he sees it, beyond corruption and mixture, forever separate Plato from Socrates. And 'Nietzsche' from 'Nietzsche'.

II. HEGEL'S TWO-FACED SOCRATES

Introduction
Putting Socrates in his Place

The Hegelian Socrates figure has had more impact on philosophers than any other since Plato's, whether they have adopted his fictionalized version or have tried to conceive of an entirely different Socrates, sidestepping speculative dialectics without opposing Hegel's view. Kierkegaard's Socrates was conceived in the margins and gaps of the Hegelian system, on the basis of what Hegel did not say or seemed to say only in passing, in casual remarks. Nietzsche, for his part, attempted by displacing the questions to dislodge Socrates from the place dialectics had assigned him. For Nietzsche the terms of the problem were no longer dialectical and topical ('Where is Socrates? What position does he occupy in the history of philosophy and in the historical development of Mind?'), but typological and genealogical ('Who is Socrates? Is he alive or dead? Greek or Jew?'). Answers to these questions would allow us to assign Socrates a definitive place in the history of philosophy. From Nietzsche's standpoint, Hegel 'reversed' the order of questions. By privileging the 'topical' question, what was Hegel getting at? What did he 'want'? By pinning down the disconcerting atopicity of the individual, by depicting Socrates as a figure of Mind, a stage in Mind's development that would inevitably have to be surpassed, was not Hegel's intent more than anything else to put Socrates to death a second time? Did he not aim to make Socrates more than a tragic hero, not just a necessary victim of the conflict between two equally legitimate forms of law, but a victim of the Hegelian system as well?

According to Hegel, Socrates' originality lay in the fact that he himself called for and announced his second death. He prophesied, as it were, what would follow in his wake, although his contemporaries could not understand his discourse or his position. Moreover (and in this he was unlike the prophets), he himself did not have a clear grasp of what he was announcing; he could do no more than allude to it because he had only an abstract, indefinite, indeterminate relation with what he was declaring, namely, the universality of the Idea. This puts Socrates in an ambivalent position as the *beginning* or *threshold* of philosophy. He may serve as a yardstick for his predecessors, the pre-Socratics, but he is still not a fully accomplished philosopher himself. He is not yet entirely serious or entirely speculative; he is less so, paradoxically, than was his predecessor Heraclites, whom Hegel saw as the ancestor of speculative logic.[1] As Kierkegaard sums it up, Socrates had the idea of dialectics but not yet the dialectics of the Idea. His dialectics was more negative than positive; ruinous to his contemporaries' opinions, it brought in the new Idea only allusively and abstractly. According to Kierkegaard, the supplement of novelty that Socrates contributed made him irreducible to his historical period and incapable of being fully explained by that period. It put him ahead of his time, and established him as someone who paved the way for the future. This supplement remained an unconscious one for the very person whose appearance in history nevertheless coincided with the emergence of self-consciousness, subjectivity, interiority. But it is precisely because consciousness was appearing for the first time that it could not grasp itself with full awareness; that is why it remained tarnished with pathological exteriority, with negativity.

Kierkegaard identified this negativity with Socratic irony. Hegel, however, did not place much stock in that irony; on the contrary, as Kierkegaard noted reproachfully,[2] he minimized it, because he essentially equated irony with Romantic irony – Fichte's, Friedrich Schlegel's, or Sölger's. Hegel's relation to those authors was one of rivalry, as attested by the very pointed way he always evoked the Socratic irony that his contemporaries identified with the infinite and infinitely negative freedom of subjectivity – for irony has no place as such within Hegel's system at this stage of the development of Mind. And this rubbed Hegel the wrong way: it annoyed him, and it kept him from grasping the importance of Socrates' irony. In order to come to terms with Socrates, Hegel was compelled to credit him with at least a minimal amount of seriousness and positivity, if only in the mode of allusion. (Hegel viewed positivity as operative chiefly in the moral realm, in the privileged relation that Socrates, the founder of moral philosophy, maintained with the idea of the good.) Unlike Kierkegaard's Socrates, who is conceived in 'reaction' to the still overly positive Hegelian figure and who is identified with irony and its infinite negativity, Hegel's Socrates occupies a Janus-like position at the threshold of philosophy. It is a *two-faced* Socrates, oscillating ambivalently between negativity and positivity (this accounts for the diversity of the Socratic schools, which, in contradictory ways, may all claim to be 'his').

Hegel's reading thus privileges one aspect of Socrates or another as his argument requires. Sometimes he refers to a source that presents a more or less positive Socrates (Xenophon), at other times he draws upon a different source that forges a negative Socrates instead (Aristophanes), and on still other occasions he appeals to Plato, without ever quite managing to choose between them or to thematize the question of sources and their compatibility as such (whereas he does this explicitly when he is dealing with the pre-Socratics[3]). Thus – and this occurs only in the section immediately after the one devoted to Socrates – he writes regarding the Socratics: 'If we inquire whether [Xenophon] or Plato depicts Socrates to us most faithfully in his personality and teaching, there is no question that in regard to the personality and method, the externals of his teaching, we may certainly receive from Plato a satisfactory, and perhaps a more complete representation of what Socrates was. But in regard to the content of his teaching and the point reached by him in the development of his thought, we have in the main to look to Xenophon' (p. 414). When Hegel is getting his information from Plato, he does not seem to distinguish, either, between Socrates' contributions and Plato's, even if (in a slip pointed out by Kierkegaard), at a certain point in his reading, he uses expressions that he seems to take for granted: 'Socratic dialogues', 'Platonic dialogues'.

For Kierkegaard, whose aim is to abort all the fictional Socrates figures (Xenophon's overly prosaic Socrates, Plato's overly poetic one), it is essential to separate Socrates from Plato; Nietzsche's genealogical and typological project likewise requires a divorce between the two. We may wonder, then, why Hegel is so little concerned with discovering what 'properly' belongs to Socrates and what to Plato. In other respects he does not conflate them, after all; he even assigns them somewhat different positions in the history of the development of Mind. In fact, the dialectical project itself requires indifference to ideas as private property.[4] From 'Socrates', 'Plato' necessarily retained, preserved, sublated *(aufgehebt)* and developed only what was essential, only what in any event could not be lost: the profound or speculative aspects of Socratic thought, aspects which, as such, belong neither to Socrates nor to Plato but to Mind. It is because the 'eclectic' Plato understood that ideas belong to no one that he did not hesitate to 'spend much money' (p. 166) to procure the writings of the ancient philosophers for himself, did not hesitate simply to 'develop' their doctrines even at the risk of being charged with plagiarism;[5] this is also why he hid behind multiple spokespersons and never spoke in his own name:

'Because in his writings he never himself appeared as a teacher, but always represented other people in his dialogues as the philosophers, a distinction has never been made between what really belonged to them in history and what was added by him through the further development which he effected in their thoughts' (p. 167).

A dialectical conception of the history of philosophy may thus view as negligible 'remainders' what is 'proper' to Socrates and what is 'proper' to Plato, as it necessarily leaves unexamined the master- disciple relations of love and reciprocal contamination, for such relations are external to the development of ideas (p. 168). The development of ideas proceeds according to its own objective logic, a logic that is 'cold, pure and divinely unconcerned': these are the terms in which Nietzsche denounced what he saw as a prejudice typical of philosophers, play-actors who pretend not to know that 'ideas' are unacknowledged confessions, that they are born of their authors just as surely as a tree is born of the soil from which it grows, and that it is therefore pointless and dishonest to seek to do without the empirical individuality of philosophers, to dispense with the system of instincts and impulses of which their systems and ideas are merely symptoms.[6]

Contrary to Nietzsche, then, and to the horror of Kierkegaard (who transposes the dialectics of the Idea to the personal level and views stages in the development of Mind as phases in the development of personal life – where irony again finds its rightful place), Hegel reserves very little room for philosophers in his history of philosophy; he has little to say about their lives and their empirical individuality.

In the case of Socrates, this causes him certain problems, since, as he acknowledges, Socrates' philosophy and his way of philosophizing are inseparable from his way of life. His philosophy 'is in a piece with his life' (p. 396). Where Socrates is concerned, Hegel is compelled (not without regret!), as he declares at the end of his text, to be 'more detailed' (p. 448); in other words, he cannot entirely neglect the philosopher's 'life' or his 'death' in their empirical uniqueness, since it is that very uniqueness – Socrates' refusal to take his place within a statist totality and to let himself be imprisoned by it – which alone justifies, for example, his death sentence. Hegel thus cannot shrug off Socrates' individuality, but he gives meaning to its slightest, apparently least significant empirical features in a supremely audacious interpretive gesture: if it is impossible to eliminate Socrates the individual, this is because the Socratic 'moment' is that of the still contingent subjectivity that the figure of Socrates embodies, a figure henceforth reduced to a 'great figure', 'a most important figure *[Figur]* in the history of Philosophy – perhaps the most interesting in the philosophy of antiquity . . . a world-famed personage' (p. 384) whose appearance and disappearance stem from a systemic and dialectical necessity.

The appearance *hic et nunc* in 469 B. C., in the fourth year of the 77th Olympiad, of Socrates, son of Sophroniscus, a sculptor, and Phaenarete, a midwife ('details' of which Hegel makes nothing, even though he insists that Socrates is 'one of those great plastic natures . . ., resembling a perfect classical work of art which has brought itself to this height of perfection' [p. 393] and, later, without comment, that 'the art of midwifery . . . came to him from his mother' [p. 402]), this contingent appearance coincides, then, with the 'moment' of the emergence of consciousness in Greece: as if this singular moment in the universal history of Mind had required the appearance of Socrates in all his contingency, specifically that of his birth and his death (which is always already announced as soon as he is reduced to an inevitably passing 'moment' that is destined to be surpassed).

'Consciousness had reached this point in Greece, when in Athens the great form [*die große Gestalt*] of Socrates, in whom the subjectivity of thought was brought to consciousness in a more definite and more thorough manner, now appeared' (p. 384; this is the opening passage of the section devoted to Socrates).

'Consciousness had reached *this point* in Greece': in other words, first of all, the moment when Socrates was born, *hic et nunc,* in Greece, coincides with *the Greek moment* of the development of Mind, that is, with the first stage in this development; more precisely, 'Socrates' moment' belongs to the first period of that first stage that extends from Thales to Aristotle (the second period of that first stage being the Greek moment in the Roman world and the third that of neo-Platonic philosophy). The first period of the first stage starts from a wholly abstract, natural or perceptible thought, and elevates itself to the conceptualized idea. This period presents the beginning of the philosophizing thought that Plato develops and elaborates; he pulls the work of all his predecessors together without bringing the task to its conclusion (for 'there is only the idea in general'). Completion of the task falls to Aristotle, who develops an entire science, a system.

The first period of the first stage is in turn broken down into three divisions, and Socrates has his place in the second of these.

1. The first [division] extends from Thales to Anaxagoras, from abstract thought which is in immediate determinateness to the thought of the self-determining Thought. ...
2. The second division comprises the Sophists, Socrates, and the followers of Socrates. Here the self- determining thought is conceived of as present and concrete in me; that constitutes the principle of subjectivity if not also of infinite subjectivity, for thought still shows itself here only partly as abstract principle and partly as contingent subjectivity.
3. The third division, which deals with Plato and Aristotle, is found in Greek science where objective thought, the Idea, forms itself into a whole. The concrete, in itself determining Thought, is, with Plato, the still abstract Idea, but in the form of universality; while with Aristotle that Idea was conceived of as the self-determining, or in the determination of its efficacity or activity. (P. 165)

On this dialectical line, within its divisions and dizzying tripartite subdivisions, Socrates' place is thus predetermined, necessitated, as it were – it occupies the second division of the first period of the first stage of the history of the development of Mind: 'Socrates', Hegel says, 'did not grow like a mushroom out of the earth' (p. 384).[7] His place, which is that of (still) contingent subjectivity, is not at all contingent in itself: according to Hegel, Socrates 'stands in continuity with his time' (ibid.), that is, with his 'spiritual' epoch. This does not prevent him from being in a certain state of rupture with respect to his epoch, in the empirical sense, in a state of discontinuity that alone can account for his death sentence. Being in continuity with his time means that Socrates simply develops and goes deeper into what had already begun in the first division of the first period. 'In Socrates, the subjectivity of thought is brought to consciousness in a more definite and more thorough manner' (ibid.). And yet, in this simple continuous development of Mind, the appearance of the great figure of Socrates constitutes a decisive and definitive irruption, marks a *date*, since 'a mental turning-point exhibited itself in him in the form of philosophic thought' (ibid.). To be sure, he does not 'grow like a mushroom out of the earth', and yet he is an *inaugural* figure, 'perhaps the most interesting in the philosophy of antiquity' (ibid.). He marks a turning point which is his mark: while he remains in continuity with the pre-Socratics, especially Anaxagoras, he surpasses them all, and yet he is still not Plato, or, *a fortiori*, Aristotle. His function – like that of the demon Eros – is that of a *metaxu*, an intermediary: he belongs to the second division of the first period, but he oscillates between the first and the third divisions, between 'already beyond' and 'not yet'. His position is that of threshold of philosophy; however uncomfortable this position may be, it is none the less a place of such specificity that it allows the Socratic moment to be distinguished from the Platonic moment (even if Hegel is not concerned with determining what belongs properly to Socrates and what to Plato, for 'Socrates' and 'Plato' are merely names, figures of Mind, not 'proper' names): only a dialectical flair, and not a genealogical one, ensures the separation of these two moments, distinguishes the 'master' figure from the 'disciple' by stripping them both of precisely the sort of scholastic relation that disrupts the unity and linearity of development and introduces an imperfect linkage, one that is external to dialectics.[8]

In this intermediate position that cuts him off from Plato, Socrates turns out to be associated, on the contrary, with the other Socratics[9] and put on virtually the same level as his traditional 'enemies,' the Sophistsfrom whom he is now separated by only one subdivision of the second division of the first period of the first stage. (Aristophanes thus seems to have had more dialectical flair than Plato: in *The Clouds*, he seems to want – rightly – to depict Socrates as a Sophist, at least if we are to believe Hegel. Kierkegaard, who reads *The Clouds* more attentively, more 'literally' than Hegel, distinguishes the position of the chorus – which alone takes Socrates to be a Sophist – from that of Aristophanes 'himself'.[10]

Socrates' specific dialectical position is thus one of still contingent subjectivity; with the necessity inherent to a system, it requires that empirical details neglected elsewhere be taken into account. Hegel says it time and again: Socrates' life and his death are inseparable from his philosophy. 'We must examine more closely this noteworthy phenomenon, and begin with the history of Socrates' life. This is, however, closely intertwined with his interest in Philosophy, and the events of his life are bound up with his principles' (p. 389).

'His philosophy, which asserts that real existence is in consciousness as a universal, is still not a properly speculative philosophy, but remained individual; yet the aim of his philosophy was that it should have a universal significance. Hence we have to speak of his own individual being . . .' (p. 392).

The moment proper to Socrates – which causes him to oscillate between the empirical and the ideal (as Kierkegaard, a reader of Hegel, will put it) – thus explains Hegel's two-fold approach to Socrates. He pays exceptional attention to the philosopher's 'life', to empirical details (his character, comprising all 'the virtues adorning the life of the private citizen' [p. 392], his external aspect, which 'indicated naturally low and hateful qualities' [p. 393], and his death); and, since this life is all of a piece with his philosophy, he attempts to inscribe it as a whole – with no remainder – in dialectics, in the universal history of Mind, of which Socrates, the figure of Socrates, would represent the great turning point.

The final lines of the section on Socrates in *Lectures on the History of Philosophy* reveal this dual treatment with particular clarity, while betraying Hegel's ambivalence toward the ambivalent figure of Socrates. Thus he writes:

> We are done with Socrates. I have been more detailed here because all the features of the case have been so completely in harmony, and he constitutes a great historical turning point. Socrates died at sixty-nine years of age, in Olympiad 95 (399-400 B. C.), an Olympiad after the end of the Peloponnesian war, twenty-nine years after the death of Pericles, and forty-four years before the birth of Alexander. He saw Athens in its greatness and the beginning of its fall; he experienced the height of its bloom and the beginning of its misfortunes. (P. 448)

The tone here is reminiscent of a funeral oration. Hegel seems to be invoking coldly and with perfect objectivity the place and date of the hero's birth and death. But behind the impassibility and the objectivity of the numbers[11] lined up like so many protective incantations, there is a hint of a certain anxiety about death on Hegel's part, and an attempt to master it.

To be sure, he seems relieved to be 'done' (*fertig*) with this Socrates over whom he has lingered so long, as if he had had trouble letting go of the great figure, as if he were having a hard time saying goodbye to someone he admires. By declaring that he is 'done' with him, he is recalling above all that, however admirable, remarkable, indeed capital the figure of Socrates may have been, it has met its end, it has been surpassed, decapitalized if not decapitated, and his own lingering over the details finally serves simply to postpone the necessary moment of cutting the figure down.

The need to put an end to Socrates does not arise from the conclusion of Aristotle's well-known Aristotelian syllogism: 'All men are mortal; Socrates is a man; therefore Socrates is mortal'. By demonstrating in the paragraphs that immediately precede the concluding passage that the death sentence the Athenians imposed on Socrates was just and legitimate (legal?), Hegel is in effect stripping Socrates of 'his own' empirical and singular death, of the solitude of that death. He turns the event into the death of a tragic hero whose destiny is indistinguishable on the one hand from that of Athens (for the historical development of Athens is at a decisive crossroads; it is entering a decadent phase, experiencing the onset of its 'ruin' and 'misfortune'), and indistinguishable on the other hand from the destiny of Mind, whose 'great historic turning point' (p. 448) he embodies (and here the turn in question is a positive one).

It is precisely because Socrates' death was that of a hero and not that of some randomly-selected empirical human individual that Hegel situates it within a star-studded series. He does not relate it, as Diogenes Laertius does, to the death of Euripides (a tragic poet whom Socrates may have more or less inspired[12]), but rather, in a much more surprising fashion, to the death of two great men, the exemplary statesman Pericles and the great conqueror Alexander. And this is no accident on Hegel's part. For although the individuality of Pericles was, like that of Socrates, of the highest plasticity, Pericles was not condemned to death, because he was able to stop laughing in time: once he began to devote himself to affairs of State, as Hegel notes, 'he laughed no more' (p. 394). This remark, unexpected to say the least, has to be understood as indicating that, unlike Socrates, Pericles was able to renounce his own individuality from one day to the next; he succeeded in submitting himself 'to the judgment of the people as sovereign' (p. 441).

As for Alexander, Hegel cites him in *Reason in History* alongside Caesar and Napoleon as exemplifying those great men in whom the 'cunning of reason' exploits the passions in pursuit of its own ends. As Hegel notes, 'when we contemplate the struggle of the Greeks against the Persians, or the momentous reign of Alexander, we are fully aware of where our interests lie: we wish to see the Greeks liberated from the barbarians'.[13] What interests Hegel is not the individual Alexander, with his passions, his tastes, and his obsessional mania for conquest through which a psychologizing, moralizing and belittling history (history as seen from the standpoint of domestic servants, for whom heroes do not exist) assumes it can explain his actions by giving them a subjective form that is not the Good. For 'let us imagine for a moment how we would feel if Alexander had failed in his enterprise. We would certainly have no sense of loss if we were interested only in human passions, for we would still not have been denied the spectacle of passions in action. But this would not have satisfied us'.[14] The interest Hegel brings to this history is 'material' and 'objective', that is, his dialectical flair detects in the goal toward which great men's passions are directed not happiness, which belongs to private life, but the same goal as that of the Idea, the Universal. To be sure, Alexander died young (and Caesar was assassinated, and Napoleon was deported). But this is not to be deplored, for he died after reaching the end of his road. And that is every hero's destiny: 'When their end is attained, they fall aside like empty husks' (ibid., p 85).

By bringing the figure of Socrates into the picture between the figures of Pericles and Alexander, those two great men who were able, each in his own way, to sacrifice their individuality to the service of the State and Mind, Hegel reintegrates Socrates the individual, as it were, into the beautiful statist totality; it is as if by legitimizing Socrates, by depicting his death as heroic, Hegel were inscribing his individual death within the history of the development of Mind. And, in the same move, he strips that death of its singularity and its solitude: like Alexander's, Socrates' death belongs henceforth to the dialectical economy and its necessary sacrifices.

> The particular has its own interests in world history: it is of a finite nature, and as such, it must perish. Particular interests contend with one another, and some are destroyed in the process. But it is from this very conflict and destruction of particular things that the universal emerges, and it remains unscathed itself. For it is not the universal Idea which enters into opposition, conflict, and danger; it keeps itself in the background, untouched and unharmed, and sends forth the particular interests of passion to fight and wear themselves out in its stead. It is what we may call the *cunning of freedom* that it sets the passions to work in its service, so that the agents by which it gives itself existence must pay the penalty and suffer the loss.[15]

Although Socrates' particular interest, unlike Alexander's, apparently did not lead him to satisfy his passions but rather to struggle against them, Socrates did die, and thereby lost possession of his own death – he lost its solitude, and he gained a glorious 'sublation' in the process. As both Diogenes Laertius and Hegel note,[16] the Athenians repented and honored him with a bronze statue almost immediately after his death:[17] because Socrates dies a hero, he does not really die. By justifying Socrates' death sentence, Hegel ensures the 'sublation' of his death, guarantees his redemption. The gesture is ambivalent, to say the least; it allows Hegel to be done with Socrates without finishing him off, allows him to take leave of that grandiose figure without lapsing into melancholy. We still have to discover whether, in this economy, Socrates really comes out ahead: whether saving him, thanks to dialectics, does not really amount to losing him, and whether he would not be better protected, on the contrary, if he were exempted from any reappropriative and redemptive 'sublation'.

To look into these questions, we shall have to pinpoint the aspects of Socrates' life and death that might escape dialectics. We shall be obliged to read between the lines of Hegel's text, in order to interrogate not only what he says but what he does not say: his negligences, his lapses, and indeed his contradictions, the 'details' that make it possible, if not to 'think', at least to 'conceive' (like Kierkegaard) or to 'fictionalize' (like Nietzsche) a Socrates quite different from Hegel's.

1. Life and Philosophy Intertwined

Let us look, then, 'in detail' at the chapter Hegel devotes to Socrates in his *Lectures on the History of Philosophy*, far and away the longest chapter in the book (64 pages in the Haldane translation, pp. 384-448). Although Hegel declares that Socrates' life and death are all of a piece with his philosophy, that the history of his life 'is closely intertwined with his interest in Philosophy' (p. 389), the order in which he presents his information reveals that the alleged 'intermingling' of life and philosophy works entirely to the benefit of philosophy. Indeed, Hegel begins by reducing Socrates, or at least an apparition of Socrates,to a figure of Mind whose specific 'moment' is spelled out and analyzed (pp. 384-89). Only after determining that moment and at the same time – already – the general meaning of the Socratic principle and doctrine, does Hegel declare that it is necessary 'to examine more closely this noteworthy phenomenon' and '*first of all*' (p. 389, emphasis added) the story of his life, which concerns the particular individual on the one hand, his philosophy on the other. But this initial declaration, which appears to distinguish between the person and the thought, turns out to be a purely rhetorical move, since Hegel specifies immediately afterward that Socrates' philosophical activity is closely bound up with his life, that the events of his life are inextricably linked with his principles (p. 389), that his destiny and his philosophy must be dealt with only insofar as they constitute a unity (p. 389). And since Socrates' destiny is 'truly tragic' (p. 446), the story of his life begins by evoking his properly tragic death (p. 388; Hegel will have more to say about the death toward the end of his text, pp. 425-48); the story begins by 'killing off' its hero even before it mentions his birth (p. 389). It begins with the end, because only the end gives the beginning of the life its full meaning; only the end truly transforms the life into a destiny, a heroic and philosophical destiny.

Hegel's presentation of Socrates 'life' (pp. 389-97) reviews his birth, his education, and the three military campaigns in which he participated. The details of these campaigns are evoked only because none of them is trivial or purely anecdotal: either they manifest Socrates' moral character (his exemplary courage) or else they embody in empirical daily life the philosophical moment proper to Socrates (for example, the ecstatic immobility whose significance Hegel discusses at length, 'forgetting' Socrates' life in favor of his philosophy). And if Hegel also recalls Socrates' various civic roles (pp. 391-92), he does so in order to emphasize that in carrying out those functions Socrates always manifested his opposition to the State and – this is the only way Hegel could announce and justify in advance his ultimate condemnation – to emphasize that affairs of state were not his principal activity, that his true life's work was the exercise of moral philosophy. Hegel thus begins to present the philosophy – whose principle finds itself perfectly embodied in Socrates' individual way of acting, his virtues and his character – even as he is summarizing the events of the philosopher's life (pp. 393-96), even before he comes to the *philosophy* heading, which appears in italics in some editions as if to signal an entirely different 'subject'. In reality, Socrates' life and his philosophy turn out to be intimately intertwined throughout Hegel's text because they are of a piece (p. 396). The connection has its basis not in Socrates' life as expressed by his philosophy, but in the philosophy itself, because the latter is not developed into a system and because Socrates' way of philosophizing through dialogue is inseparable from everyday life (p. 396).

A presentation of the Socratic *method* follows (p. 397) as the first point, subdivided, as one might expect, into three moments: (a) Socrates' irony (pp. 398-402); (b) his midwifery (pp. 402-404); (c) his results, which are both negative (this is their most important aspect) and positive (pp. 404-406). After describing Socrates' way of proceeding, which was of a piece with his philosophy, Hegel attributes the fact that he has not yet said very much about the Socratic principle to a deficiency in the principle itself, for the principle is 'concrete within itself' but 'not yet manifested in its development', so that 'nothing that is affirmative can, beyond this, be adduced' (p. 407). However, he proposes to return at greater length to the Socratic principle when he examines it once again in three points (pp. 407-25). (a) The formal definition appears first. The principle in question is the principle of subjective liberty, which consists in causing consciousness to return to itself (pp. 407-414). 'Everything that has value to men' – the true and the good' – is contained in man himself and has to be developed from himself' (p. 410): the universal belongs to thought. (b) The universal itself has a positive side and a negative side (pp. 414-21; this second point in turn has three subdivisions). Finally, taking a closer look at what the true in consciousness might be, Hegel comes to the third point: (c) *The principle by which the universal is attained* occurred to Socrates himself by way of his well- known *demon* or *genius* (pp. 421-25).

Hegel's investigation leads him to a third stage in the presentation of Socrates' *philosophy* – after presenting the Socratic method and the principle behind it, Hegel deals with Socrates' *condemnation to death* (pp. 425-48). The first-time reader of Hegel, who is doubtless used to seeing the death sentence as an event in the life of Socrates rather than as an essential element of his philosophy, will inevitably find this third category surprising.

Yet if Hegel refers to Socrates' death both before and after discussing his 'life', if he attaches Socrates' death to his philosophy as its third stage, he does so because what is in question is not just the empirical death of an individual, but rather a dialectically legitimated condemnation that transforms Socrates' actual death into a destiny that follows necessarily from the principle of his philosophy. 'With this Genius of Socrates as one of the chief points of his indictment, we now enter upon the subject of his fate, which ends with his condemnation. We may find this fate out of harmony with his professed business of instructing his fellow-citizens in what is good, but taken in connection with what Socrates and his people were, we shall recognize the necessity of it' (pp. 425-26). The condemnation is itself subdivided into three phases: (a) the accusation (pp. 431-40); (b) the death sentence; c) Socrates' redemption. These three moments constitute the three aspects of Socrates' properly tragic destiny.

Thus, throughout his entire reading of Socrates, Hegel intermingles Socrates' philosophy and his 'life', because the life is intimately dependent on a determining philosophical principle. This principle is what makes Socrates a great man, a 'hero who possessed for himself the absolute right of the mind, certain of itself and of the inwardly deciding consciousness, and thus expressed the higher principle of mind with consciousness' (p. 444). The principle gives the life its highly 'plastic' character and makes Socrates 'consistent through and through', 'a perfect classical work of art' (p. 393); despite his unattractive appearance (ibid.), and his empirical death, he is in fact eternally alive and beautiful. And in the last analysis it is owing to his beauty alone that Hegel can be 'more detailed' on the subject 'because all the features of the case have been so completely in harmony' (p. 448).

2. The Socratic Moment (pp. 384-89)

The crucial task, then, is to define the Socratic principle that governs the thinker's life and/or his philosophy. To this end, the figure of Socrates has to be situated within the history of philosophy, has to be assigned a place in the history of the development of Mind. As we know, Socrates belongs to the second division of the first period of the first stage. And, within this second division, he still occupies an intermediate or intermediary place between the Sophists, to whom Hegel devotes the previous chapter, and the Socratics, to whom he devotes the subsequent chapter. Socrates has his place within a developmental cycle; he 'did not grow like a mushroom out of the earth', he 'stands in continuity with his time', and for this reason he merely develops and explores more deeply something that has already manifested itself among his predecessors: the subjectivity of thought. But at the same time his figure is more remarkable, more interesting than that of his predecessors; Socrates is a major figure; his personality stands out among all others in world history (even though Socrates too is destined to pass on). 'A mental turning-point exhibited itself in him in the form of philosophic thought' (p. 384).

In what way, then, does Socrates take up where his predecessors left off, and why is he more interesting and more remarkable than they are, despite the continuities? Why is he more interesting, for example, than the thinkers who embody the first division of the first period (the ones who move from abstract thought that is in a state of immediate determinacy to thought of a thought that is self-determining): the ancient Ionians, the Atomists, and Anaxagoras? What makes him more remarkable, too, than the figures who precede him in the second division, the Sophists, Protagoras in particular?

The Ionians, the Atomists and Anaxagoras have one essential characteristic in common: they are all already *thinkers* (Hegel convokes them on the basis of their thought; he reinscribes them all within the dialectic of the development of Mind but retains from their thought only what 'deserves' to be saved). Of these, only Anaxagoras is 'taken up again', 'sublated' by Socrates, whom he prefigures, for he thinks thought as such for the first time. Translated into Hegelian language, Anaxagoras's thought is already the 'all-powerful Notion', 'the negative power over all that is definite and existent', the movement of the 'all-resolving consciousness' (p. 385): it is already the Hegelian unrest of the Notion. From Anaxagoras, in short, what Socrates retains is a doctrine that prefigures Hegel: 'Thought, the understanding is the ruling and self-determining universal. . . . Self-conscious thought . . . [is] real existence' (ibid.). But the Sophists, Protagoras in particular, had also already adopted the same doctrine. So where does Socrates' superiority lie? What places him at a higher stage of dialectics? The answer is that Socrates goes beyond the unrest and movement of the Notion; he also specifies the 'rest', the 'firmness' inherent in that unrest.[18] The Sophists are Hegel's real 'bête noire.' The Sophists see this firmness as residing in the self, a singular negative entity that is not a universal reflected in itself. Their dialectics leads to the disappearance of the objective and leaves the nature of the subjective ambiguous; it does not allow us to determine whether the subjective is opposed to the objective and is thus singular, contingent, arbitrary, or whether the subjective is itself objective and universal. In this ambiguity, Socrates comes down on the side of the Universal. What is firm and at rest is apprehended in thought. What is purely and simply preserved, substance, being (*Sein*) in itself and for itself, is defined as the end, the true, the good.

To this first characterization of the Universal Socrates adds a second. The good as such is 'free from existent reality, free from individual sensuous consciousness of feeling and desire, free finally from the theoretically speculative thought about nature' (ibid.). The good inherent in thought must necessarily be recognized by consciousness. What comes to light with Socrates, what awakens in the clarity of consciousness, is precisely the presence to self of consciousness in its subjectivity and its infinite liberty. The process of awakening will continue to develop; in the modern era, it takes on the redoubtable form of a requirement of infinite, unrestricted freedom. With Socrates, we have simply the beginning of this requirement (and this is why his 'irony' must never be mistaken for that of the German Romantics, for the latter is disproportionate, not subject to mastery by dialectics). But the beginning is of 'infinite importance':[19] it inaugurates the movement of reappropriation of Mind by itself, the reduction of truth, of what is objective, to consciousness, to the thinking of the subject; in short, it inaugurates the movement of spiritualization that alone makes a man, properly speaking, a human being. To be sure, the Sophists too refer the objective to the subjective; they attribute their personal decisions to the power of consciousness and reflection, and they proclaim that man finds his own measure, direction and goals within himself. (The Sophists and Socrates alike grant primacy to consciousness and to the presence of consciousness to self; thus we can see why in any event the war that Socrates [or Plato – Hegel does not distinguish between them in this regard] is waging against the Sophists is not aimed at preserving the interests of Greek morality and religion, the ancient mores; these Socrates too can only strive to destroy). But Socrates – and here is the second distinctive feature of his 'moment', here is what distinguishes him from the Sophists – defines the return of consciousness to itself as an exit from individual subjectivity, a proscription of contingency, fantasy, arbitrariness and particularity, in favor of objectivity understood as universality in-and-for-itself.

In opposition to authentically naive morality and religion, which, like Sophocles' Antigone, rely on custom and on existing laws, Socrates posits truth as having to be mediatized, produced, posited by thought: 'Truth is now posited as a product mediated through thought' (p. 386). But the position of thought and its production – and this is what distinguishes Socrates from the Sophists – are simultaneously those of something whose character is not to be posited:

> The objective produced through thought, is at the same time in and for itself. . . . Hence because, on the one hand, to Socrates and Plato [here it is very much in Hegel's interest to link them in a common position, for it is only because he does not distinguish Socrates from Plato at this point, even though Plato is situated in a different division of the development of Mind, that he can give Socrates a certain positivity and thus a fixed and assured position within the system, a position distinct from that of the Sophists] the moment of subjective freedom is the directing of consciousness into itself, on the other, this return is also determined as a coming out from particular subjectivity. It is hereby implied that contingency of events is abolished, and man has this outside within him, as the spiritual universal. This is the true, the unity of subjective and objective in modern terminology. (P. 387)

'In modern terminology' [*in heuerer Terminologie*], Hegel adds, as if by this formulation he were only beginning to reduce or elevate Socrates, to translate the Socratic moment into the Hegelian moment, a translation that is nevertheless legitimate in his eyes because between these two moments there is not heterogeneity but dialectical continuity, and because the second is the end result of the development of the first, and its truth.

Because Socrates – unlike Plato, here (and Aristotle) – first gave the good a particular and practical signification, there is (as we might have expected) a *third specification* of the Socratic moment: Socrates is the one who introduced *moral philosophy* [*Moralphilosophie*] – which he invented – into a philosophy that had been previously oriented toward nature. Hegel depicts Socrates as the inventor of morality [*Moralität*] and not of ethics (which includes both *Sittlichkeit* and *Moralität*), in order to emphasize what distinguishes his reading from those of the ancient historians of philosophy, Diogenes Laertius in particular. Hegel does not much care for Diogenes' widely-cited reading[20] because it lacks a philosophical and critical spirit; Diogenes tells shoddy, superficial anecdotes, and is more interested in the philosophers themselves than in philosophemes (*Lectures*, pp. 167-68). Hegel seeks to distance himself from Cicero, too, who is at least as unreliable as Diogenes, and just as lacking in the philosophical spirit. Cicero reads the Ancients by way of ratiocination, not speculation (pp. 388-89); he attributes no content to philosophy, which ought to be accommodating, he believes; and he adopts the ways of thinking of his time (p. 167). His interpretations are thus excessively banal and commonplace. If one were to rely, then, on these two not-very-reliable sources – and as always when he evokes them, Hegel's irony becomes biting here even though in general he does not have much use for irony – Socrates would rank far below Plato and Aristotle, who take the good not in a particular sense but in a more elevated, universal sense. If we were to listen to Diogenes and Cicero and were to be moved by Socrates' 'innocent' death, we would make him out to be the patron saint of moralizing babble and popular philosophy, that is, of non-philosophy. What is original and sublime about Socrates would be the fact that he brought philosophy from the heavens down to earth, introduced it into homes and the marketplace! That he produced a philosophy for housewives (*Hausmittel*), suitable for kitchen use, 'only a domestic or fireside philosophy which conforms to all the ordinary ideas of men [*Menschen*]' (p. 389)! His singular – heroic! – audacity would reside in the fact that he discussed the truths of everyday life, without venturing forth into the depths of the heavens – into the depths of consciousness! – and this would be the extent of his innovation!!

If we abandon this insipid reading, however, and look into the matter more closely, we note that Socrates' doctrine is neither an ethics (in the sense of *Sittlichkeit*) nor a form of moralizing babble for the ladies; it is rather – because, on the contrary, Socrates was the first to dare to turn toward the depths of consciousness – a moral philosophy worthy of the name. For the defining characteristic of morality is discernment, the subjective intention and aim of the good through which the freedom of the subject posits the determinations of what is moral and legitimate, surpassing the immediate determinations of natural morality (*Sittlichkeit*). Moral men before Socrates knew the good and did good, but without reflection and without being aware of their own excellence. Naively. With the mediation of thought and reflection, ethics, natural morality (*Sittlichkeit*) becomes abstract morality (*Moralität*). We owe this distinction to Kantian philosophy in particular, but if Socrates' moral philosophy cannot be reduced to Cicero's caricature of it, it is because it is a prelude to Kant's. To Kant's, that is to say, and not quite to Hegel's. 'It was not incumbent on him to reflect upon all the speculations of past Philosophy, in order to be able to come down in practical philosophy to inward thought' (p. 389). He would not have had the time, as it were, to reach the later stage, that of the submission of inward thought to the beautiful statist totality. Here is where the moment proper to Socrates reaches its limit, and here is what legitimates his death sentence. It is thus not astonishing that the story of Socrates' life – which Hegel confronts after he has identified the general meaning of the Socratic principle that determined the life – begins with an evocation of Socrates' death and his tragic destiny.

3. Socrates' Tragic Death (p. 388)

Socrates' death is not the sort of pitiful, romantic death that arouses the interest of people – women in particular[21] – who are inclined to be moved by the suffering of a just and innocent man. Socrates' death is tragic not in the superficial, popular sense but in the proper sense of the term: it is highly tragic, truly tragic. And what is truly tragic does not stem from pathos, has nothing to do with feelings of sadness at some innocent victim's misfortune. The truly tragic is rational, and Socrates is not simply a victim. A misfortune is rational and authentically worthy when it is produced not by the forces of nature or tyranny, but by a clash between two competing and equally legitimate moral forces. Socrates' destiny corresponds to this definition. On the one hand, his action – his will – is infinitely free, legitimate and moral, and thus he is guilty of causing his own misfortune. On the other hand, the force that condemns his action is equally legitimate and moral. Moral legitimacy derives from different rights in each case; hence the conflict. The force that condemns Socrates depends on the right of the State, a divine right stemming from the naive customs, morality, and religion of the populace – the will to live a free, moral and noble life under the laws of the land – which Hegel calls objective freedom and natural morality (*Sittlichkeit*). The right to which the victim, Socrates, lays claim is no less divine; it is the right to consciousness, knowledge, and subjective freedom, the right to reason in all its spontaneity. The rational tragic thus grows out of the encounter between two necessary and legitimate principles. 'The one power is the divine right, the natural morality whose laws are identical with the will which dwells therein as in its own essence, freely and nobly; we may call it abstractly objective freedom. The other principle, on the contrary, is the right, as really divine, of consciousness or of subjective freedom; this is the fruit of the tree of the knowledge of good and evil, *i.e.*, of self-creative reason; and it is the universal principle of Philosophy for all successive times' (pp. 446-47).

That conflict between two rights is the reason Socrates' destiny is not purely personal, is not a romantic, individual destiny. His destiny is tragic in that it represents and enacts the tragedy of Athens, the tragedy of Greece. Socrates' life, his death and his philosophy embody two principles that surpass him; their conflict and collision determine not only his personal destiny but also that of Greece, and of Mind.

Just as Christ died for the sins of the world and took those sins upon himself, Socrates may be said to have paid in advance for all generations to come. He paid the price for bringing to light for all time the universal principle of philosophy: subjective freedom, the right to consciousness and knowledge. But this right was not fully recognized in Socrates' own historical and dialectical moment; the philosopher, who appeared prematurely, in a sense, was thus a necessary and legitimate 'victim' of destiny. And so he died the death of a hero, a tragic hero.

On this point, we should recall what Hegel had to say about the death of tragic heroes in *Aesthetics,* in the section devoted to *the principle of tragedy, comedy,* and *drama,* in the chapter on *the genres of dramatic poetry;* we can also refer to a long note in *Philosophy of Right.* In these passages, Hegel is discussing Romantic irony, the extreme end point of subjectivity affirming itself as a supreme affirmation, inaugurated within certain limits by Socrates. In this context, not coincidentally, he returns to the question of the tragic fall. Contrary to Sölger, Hegel sees the fall not simply as the defeat of the best but as the triumph of the true. In these two texts, returning to the topos of tragic pity, one of the essential wellsprings of tragedy according to Aristotle, Hegel shows that the pity aroused by that great art is not the same as the pity inspired by the death of a rogue, a scoundrel or a criminal: 'provincial females are always ready with compassion of this [latter] sort'.[22] For scoundrels may arouse the interest of the police, but they are unworthy of the true art of tragedy.[23] Socrates' death, like that of a tragic hero, does not provoke a humiliating pity but a true, manly pity, which

> is sympathy . . . with the sufferer's moral justification, with the affirmative aspect, the substantive thing that must be present in him. . . . For it is only something of intrinsic worth which strikes the heart of a man of noble feelings and shakes it to its depths. . . . A truly tragic suffering . . . is only inflicted on the individual agents as a consequence of their own deed which is both legitimate and, owing to the resulting collision, blameworthy, and for which their whole self is answerable.[24]

So although he is neither a knave nor a villain, Socrates deserves to die. His death is deserving of the highest form of pity, masculine pity, because he dies for the benefit of a justice higher than his own, that of the State or of absolute Mind. Only a remarkable 'great figure' like that of Socrates can and must die heroically, tragically. And if the death of a highly moral figure interests and moves us – 'us', not the womenfolk but 'men' worthy of the name – it is because it ultimately elevates us and reconciles us with ourselves. For by bringing to the surface the rights and wrongs of the two conflicting forces, the tragic situation brings to light the true moral idea of its partiality – purified, triumphant, and thus reconciled in us.

Accordingly, it is not the highest in us which perishes; we are elevated not by the destruction of the best but by the triumph of the true. This it is which constitutes the true, purely ethical, interest of ancient tragedy . . . But the ethical Idea is actual and present in the world of social institutions without the misfortune of tragic clashes and the destruction of individuals overcome by this misfortune. And this Idea's (the highest's) revelation of itself in its actuality as anything but a nullity is what the external embodiment of ethical life, the state, purposes and effects, and what the ethical self-consciousness possesses, intuits, and knows in the state and what the thinking mind comprehends there.[25]

Above mere fear and tragic sympathy there therefore stands that sense of reconciliation which the tragedy affords by the glimpse of eternal justice. In its absolute sway this justice overrides the relative justification of one-sided aims and passions because it cannot suffer the conflict and contradiction of naturally harmonious ethical powers to be victorious and permanent in truth and actuality.[26]

If *Philosophy of Right* and *Aesthetics* emphasize that tragic conflict is necessarily followed by the moment of *reconciliation*, the chapter on Socrates in the *Lectures on the History of Philosophy* initially has nothing to say about that moment. For the whole object of the chapter is precisely to expose the conflict between the two opposing principles 'which we see coming into opposition in Socrates' life and philosophy' (p. 447). 'The sense of reconciliation' is present only at the end of the text when Hegel, once again and at greater length, returns to Socrates' death sentence. The third, properly tragic aspect of his destiny is indeed that of redemption, 'the last act in this drama' in which 'the Athenians recognized through their repentance the individual greatness of the man; . . . they also recognized that this principle in Socrates . . . has . . . been introduced even into their own spirit, and that they themselves are in the dilemma of having in Socrates only condemned their own principle' (p. 445). In punishing Socrates, the Athenian people has thus punished its own 'moment', has condemned its own spirit to disappear from the world, but in so doing it has caused a higher principle to arise 'out of its ashes', and thus with its help 'the world-spirit [has] raised itself into a higher consciousness' (p. 447).

To accept this beautiful, tragic story and allow it to reconcile us with ourselves and with fate, we clearly have to accept the entire Hegelian system and its dialectics, the structure of opposition and the reference to a historical necessity with respect to which two rights are in conflict at a given moment. Kierkegaard, as we shall see, offers an entirely different reading of Socrates' death. For him it is not a tragic death. On the one hand, Socrates himself does not recognize the legitimacy and divinity of state power or its law. And, on the other hand, he is not guilty; by choosing death, he does not produce his own misfortune. Death is not a misfortune, as he sees it: our very ignorance reduces death to nothing at all. Choosing death is an ironic gesture through which Socrates dupes the State, since he chooses a punishment that cannot hurt: death, about which nothing is known.

Only a reading that stresses the fundamental importance of Socrates' irony can counter, without countering, a tragic interpretation of Socrates' death. Hegel himself was well aware of this. In the *Philosophy of Right,* in a footnote to a chapter called 'Morality', it is with reference to Socrates' irony (which is more or less conflated with Plato's for the sake of the argument) that he attacks Romantic irony and its absolute negativity, 'the culminating form of this subjectivity which conceives itself as the final court of appeal.[27] Romantic irony is an extreme form that must be distinguished from Socratic irony if Socrates is to be saved and made worthy of a heroic and tragic death. Hegel in fact reduces Socrates' irony to the following: 'Plato used [the name 'irony'] to describe a way of speaking which Socrates employed in conversation when defending the Idea of truth and justice against the conceit of the Sophists and the uneducated. What he treated ironically, however, was only their type of mind, not the Idea itself. Irony is only a manner of talking against *people*'.[28]

Socratic irony, thus restricted, is indeed compatible with a tragic death and destiny. The same cannot be said of Romantic irony: in its extreme negativity, this latter form holds that the death of the tragic hero condemns the objective moral Idea to death at the same time; it undermines what is noblest within us. It allows for no reconciliation. By which we are given to understand that, unlike Romantic irony, Socratic irony as Hegel sees it can be inscribed within his system, although perhaps within a very small space. For it points in the direction of morality and justice; it does not endanger the Idea itself, or reason, or the reason of State, whose ultimate triumph it finally ensures. For if Socrates accredits his conflict with the State and the State's legitimacy (even if his aim is to contest that legitimacy), if he recognizes that he himself is at once innocent and guilty, he definitively saves the objective ethical Idea, which turns out to be exempt 'from the misfortune of tragic clashes and the destruction of individuals overcome by this misfortune'.[29] Socrates' tragic destiny, marked through and through by the collision between two contrary principles, justifies Hegel's point of view – as he sees it – over that of Sölger and the other German Romantics. For if there are two opposing principles there has to be a third moment, a final reconciliation; everything will not collapse into the void of infinite negativity – into irony.

To save reason and the reason of State, to save Socrates and his own system, Hegel is thus forced to minimize Socratic irony and to stress that the philosopher's life and his philosophy, closely intertwined, are essentially marked by the collision of the two opposing principles. So after recalling his tragic death, the emblem of that collision, after killing off Socrates 'rationally' and without pathos the better to save him (or after elevating him the better to do away with him), Hegel proceeds to the presentation of his life, an account placed wholly under the sign of the heroic death by which Socrates is always already tragically threatened.

4. Socrates' Life (pp. 389-96)

Borrowing quite selectively from Diogenes Laertius and Xenophon, Hegel says very little about Socrates' early life, and does not make much of what he does mention. He recalls that Socrates' father was a sculptor and that, pushed by his father, Socrates himself was skilled in the paternal art. But sculpture – the most superficial art of all, according to Nietzsche – did not satisfy him; he gave it up in favor of philosophy and scientific research, except insofar as he needed to practice it in order to earn a living. Hegel points out parenthetically, without comment, that, as death approached, Socrates' father took pains to bequeath him a small fortune.[30] But we can only suppose that the fortune must have been small indeed, since, even coupled with what the sculptor's trade brought in, it did not suffice to pay for his education: Crito – already Crito – is said to have been the source of financial support, allowing Socrates to polish his instruction at the hands of masters in all the arts. The same Socrates whom Nietzsche calls an 'uncultured plebeian' was – Hegel insists on this both at the beginning and at the end of his account of the philosopher's life – 'a man of culture, who was instructed in everything then requisite thereto' (p. 390): philosophy (he read the works of the ancient philosophers, listened to Anaxagoras and Archelaus, the Sophists, Prodicus, the master of eloquence), music, poetry, and so on.

Unlike Nietzsche but like Kierkegaard (for whom Socratic ignorance needed to be essential rather than empirical in nature), Hegel emphasizes, echoing his sources in the interest of his own argument, that Socrates was an extremely well-educated man in all areas. It seemed of little concern to the ancients, but of great concern to Hegel, that in order to achieve such a cultivated status one needed money! Socrates therefore cannot be blamed for having procured funds; this is in no way a sign of greed.[31] The proof is that, contrary to the customary practice of his day, he did not take payment for his philosophy lessons – through his own free choice, out of indifference to money. Does this mean that Socrates, that paragon of virtue, must be taken as an example to follow even in modern times? No: today it is perfectly normal and customary to be paid for giving courses and lessons. If you were to refuse money, you would be considered eccentric, or crazy; you might be criticized and even provoke a scandal: since the time of the Roman emperors, teaching has become the State's business. The State pays teachers; thus to refuse money is to oppose the State. And Socrates did not oppose the State on this point at least, for teaching 'was not yet a State affair' (p. 394). At that time, it was thus virtuous and glorious to refrain from asking for payment; it was proof of one's strength of conscience and of one's total absence of greed.[32] Unless – in a hypothesis suggested by Kierkegaard, obviously not by Hegel – Socrates refrains from asking for money because, unlike the Sophists, he is not a master, teaches nothing, and knows perfectly well that he does not deserve to be paid.

Out of a need for money 'for a necessary subsistence' (p. 389), then, Socrates continued to practice the trade bequeathed to him, along with a small fortune, by his father, even as he was putting his curiosity and his love at the service of philosophy, which for its part brought him nothing. A little further on (p. 402), with reference to the art of midwifery that characterizes the second element or moment of his method, Hegel notes without further comment that Socrates got his philosophy from his mother (but, as we learn from *Philosophy of Mind*,[33] the mother is always her child's inspiring genius). Socrates' mother had already made an initial, modest appearance in the text, after the father's, with only her name (*Phaenarete*) and profession (midwife) noted, as they might appear in a civil register. Hegel does not specify whether his father's death is what triggered Socrates' turn toward philosophy and his mother, even as he continued to exploit his father's fortune, or whether the 'murder of the father', the son's distancing of himself from his father in favor of his mother, who was as seductive as philosophy, was what caused his father's death. Hegel says nothing more about Socrates' mother, nor does he even mention the name of the shrewish Xanthippe,[34] of whom the ancient sources and, later, Nietzsche[35] make a great deal. Nor does he point out Socrates' bigamy. As Plato does in the *Phaedo*, Hegel evacuates the women and children; he dismisses the housewives with their pathos, their lamentations and their cackling, which might offer resistance to the dialectics of his system.

As for the 'Oedipal' scenario that one might easily imagine or construct between the lines of his text, Hegel has essentially nothing at all to say. Not that he does not suspect a certain affinity between Socrates and Oedipus, but he gives the relationship a totally different slant from the one Freud and Nietzsche give it. Socrates does not 'resemble' Oedipus; rather, the figure of Oedipus responds or corresponds to that of Socrates. Nietzsche will reproach Hegel for failing to grasp the excessive, Dionysian qualities of the Oedipean wisdom, and indeed, in his *Aesthetics,* Hegel makes Oedipus the quintessential figure of light and clarity of consciousness, one who can solve every riddle and defeat any monster. 'Oedipus found the simple answer: a man, and he tumbled the Sphinx from the rock. The explanation of the symbol lies in the absolute meaning, in the spirit, just as the famous Greek inscription calls to man: Know thyself. The light of consciousness is the clarity which makes its concrete content shine clearly through the shape belonging and appropriate to itself, and in its [objective] existence reveals itself alone'.[36] In *Oedipus Rex* and *Oedipus at Colonna,* for Hegel

> what is at issue . . . is the right of the wide awake consciousness, the justification of what the man has self-consciously willed and knowingly done, as contrasted with what he was fated by the gods to do and actually did unconsciously and without having willed it. Oedipus has killed his father; he has married his mother and begotten children in this incestuous alliance; and yet he has been involved in these most evil crimes without either knowing or willing them. The right of our deeper consciousness today would consist in recognizing that since he had neither intended nor known these crimes himself, they were not to be regarded as his own deeds. But the Greek, with his plasticity of consciousness, takes responsibility for what he has done as an individual and does not cut his purely subjective self-consciousness apart from what is objectively the case.[37]

In his *Lectures on the History of Philosophy,* Hegel never alludes to Oedipus. However, as he does for Oedipus in *Aesthetics,* in the *Lectures* he pronounces Socrates a great plastic nature, 'a perfect classical work of art which has brought itself to this height of perfection' (p. 393). Socrates shaped himself in autonomous fashion, became what he wanted to become, embodied a unique principle that took shape in his being-there as a whole. In other words, it was not his sculptor father who carved his statue; he sculpted himself. Following the maternal model, he gave birth to himself all by himself. But for Hegel this self-midwifery has nothing to do with 'psychoanalysis'; it is only an empirical figure for the advent of self-awareness, wholly inscribable within the dialectics of Mind and the history of its development. Thus Hegel's remark that Socrates gave up his father's trade early in life is neither 'anecdotal' nor insignificant. By 'disobeying' his father, Socrates obeys the principle that is his own, the very principle that will later set him in opposition to all fathers and to the State, the principle that will get him accused of corrupting youth and have him condemned to death. It is not the destiny of his instincts but his heroic destiny that always already, teleologically, commands the 'murder of the father' and the identification with the mother. That is why you are wrong to seek to put Socrates on the couch – it is entirely normal and legitimate for the child, after obeying his father, to leave the family and become autonomous. That is the goal of education properly understood.[38] The child, because he is not a slave, is 'raised' only to raise himself up to self-awareness – and thus to 'kill' his father; we are all Oedipus, because we should all be Socrates.

Hegel thus replaces the Oedipal scenario with the great scene of Mind's self-gestation, the advent of self-awareness, the best anthropological model for which is the infant's gestation in the maternal womb.

B. Socrates' later life

a) His campaigns; the saviour figure

Hegel shows us Socrates on the battlefield – not coincidentally – immediately after he has presented the philosopher's early life, at a point when his approach still seems to be strictly chronological: after the depiction of Socrates' birth and education we have a portrait of Socrates as citizen, carrying out his duties as defender of the fatherland. The scene of Socrates' 'ecstatic immobility' – a scene of self-reappropriation of consciousness – takes place (and here Hegel is faithful to Plato's *Symposium*, to which he refers) during one of the three military campaigns in which the philosopher participated during the Peloponnesian war. More precisely, it is situated between two scenes in which Socrates appears twice in the guise of saviour, first of Alcibiades and then of Xenophon, 'another of his favourites' (p. 391). This remarkable situation highlights the fact that the advent of self-awareness, the emergence of the light of consciousness, is the advent of a saving, redemptive power. If Socrates is a saviour, it is first and foremost because he embodies the awakening of self-awareness; it is that awareness alone, the strength of his consciousness, that explains how he had the courage to save two men at great risk to himself in completely disinterested fashion (for he kept the *'corona civica'*, the prize awarded for the highest bravery, only to give it to Alcibiades[39]).

Just as Oedipus saved the Thebans from the monster, the Sphinx, just as Diotima, according to Plato, spared Athens from an outbreak of the plague for ten years, so Socrates saves not only Alcibiades and Xenophon but also all the Athenians alive at the time of the Peloponnesian war, a war that 'led to the dissolution of Greek life' (p. 390). He did so by making them a gift of what they initially perceived as a corrupting principle, the principle of reflective consciousness, of interiority – a gift that cost him his life. According to Hegel (and in his own way Nietzsche says the same thing), Socrates fascinated the Greeks at the beginning of the period of decadence because they needed a saviour, a healer; as an antidote to their extravagant and anarchic passions, he offered the remedy that he had applied to himself: reason. He fascinated them, but they condemned him to death, because in their eyes he struck them initially as an odd, unhealthy creature rather than as a healer or saviour. And in Hegel's eyes too (as will also be the case for

Nietzsche, although in a different sense), Socrates is indeed diseased, and necessarily so: in this historical and dialectical epoch of the development of Mind, he could not avoid illness. The disease that manifests itself in sudden and repeated attacks is called catalepsy.[40]

b) Catalepsy

Because Socrates' specific moment is that of a commencement, the beginning of the internalization of consciousness, consciousness had to be presented to him in a physical form, in an anthropological mode. The work that goes on in the depths of his mind, because it is taking place for the first time and has not yet become habitual (although, as Hegel reminds us, Socrates found himself in a cataleptic state several times), is work through which Socrates *dies to the perceptible,* as Plato puts it, work that leaves him dead *as a perceiving consciousness,* in Hegelian terms, work that involves a 'physical setting free of the inward abstract self from the concrete bodily existence of the individual' (p. 391). This work is manifested in an external phenomenon, the state of ecstatic immobility. Here Hegel picks up Alcibiades' description of that state in the *Symposium,*[41] but he adds that what is in question is a cataleptic state, a disease of the mind. Hegel's diagnosis presupposes that normalcy, Mind's health, is purely a matter of self-positioning, self-production. It is in view of that ultimate state of health, and thus necessarily 'after the fact', that the initial moment is described as pathological – and necessarily so.[42] The dialectical necessity of this initial moment robs Socrates of the individual singularity of the disease that is no more 'his' than his death. This disease of Mind was inevitable, and it will just as inevitably be surpassed; there is no need to resort to any sort of psychoanalysis of the individual who, because he was the first to internalize consciousness, suffered empirically from its attacks. Thought has merely to take on the *habit* of thinking – repeating its moments of reappropriating ecstasy, its moments of recollection – in order to find health at the end of its road of dialectical development. The passage through catalepsy – which may be analogous to, or even akin to, somnambulism and hypnotism – is thus a necessary one.

Hegel's *Philosophy of Mind* makes it possible to elucidate this analogy. Here, he describes affective life as a disease related to hypnotic somnambulism. It is a disease, because the individual's behaviour is unmediated with respect to his own concrete content. 'The individual in such a morbid state stands in direct contact with the concrete contents of his own self, whilst he keeps his self-possessed consciousness of self and of the causal order of things apart as a distinct state of mind' (§406, p. 30). (Hegel inveighs vociferously against those who, despite many reliable witnesses, and because they are *a priori* slaves of the categories of understanding, view unchallengeable accounts of 'the remarkable condition produced by animal magnetism [hypnotism]' (ibid.) as illusions and deceptions. Surprising, for in these diseased states (hypnotic sleep, catalepsy and other morbid conditions like those that appear in young women at puberty, at the approach of death, and so on), the essential characteristic, that of affective life itself, is that of being in

> a *state of passivity*, like that of the child in the womb. The patient in this condition is accordingly made, and continues to be, subject to *the power of another person*, the magnetiser; so that when the two are thus in psychical *rapport*, the selfless individual, not really a 'person,' has for his subjective consciousness the consciousness of the other. This latter self-possessed individual is thus the effective subjective soul of the former, and the genius[43] which may even supply him with a train of ideas. That the somnambulist perceives in himself tastes and smells which are present in the person with whom he stands *en rapport*, and that he is aware of the other inner ideas and present perceptions of the latter as if they were his own, shows the substantial identity which the soul (which even in its concreteness is also truly immaterial) is capable of holding with another. When the substance of both is thus made one, there is only one subjectivity of consciousness: the patient has a sort of individuality, but it is empty, not on the spot, not actual: and this nominal self accordingly derives its whole stock of ideas from the sensations and ideas of the other, in whom it sees, smells, tastes, reads, and hears. It is further to be noted on this point that the somnambulist is thus brought into *rapport* with two genii and a twofold set of ideas, his own and that of the magnetiser. But it is impossible to say precisely which sensations and which visions he, in this nominal perception, receives, beholds and brings to knowledge from his own inward self, and which from the suggestions of the person with whom he stands in relation. This uncertainty may be the source of many deceptions . . . The purely sensitive life . . ., even when it retains that mere nominal consciousness, as in the morbid state alluded to, is just this form of immediacy, without any distinctions between subjective and objective, between intelligent personality and objective world, and without the aforementioned finite ties between them. Hence to understand this intimate conjunction, which, though all-embracing, is without any definite points of attachment, is impossible, so long as we assume independent personalities, independent one of another and of the objective world which is their content – so long as we assume the absolute spatial and material externality of one part of being to another.[44]

The analogy with sleepwalking and hypnotic states makes it possible to say that catalepsy implies a state of passivity, heteronomy and alienation akin to that of the child within the body of the mother,[45] who is the child's real 'inspiring' genius. Thus it is a magical relation of dependency and sharing, a relation without relationship and a sharing without division, a relation of substantial identity lacking all absoluteness in which there is no distinction between other and same, subjective and objective, internal and external.

This, then, is the state in which Socrates finds himself several times: the ecstatic state (consubstantial with the natural state) during which consciousness awakens, emerges from its initial torpor and numbness[46], separates itself from the soul, that is, from affective life, and presents itself as consciousness. Separating physically from the concrete corporeal being with which it had been unified, it separates from its own internal self like a child born of its mother; it dies as sensible consciousness and becomes pure interiority. The identity of consciousness with itself, pure unity of self in itself that differentiates man from nature and from animals, thus begins necessarily with a pathological schism from the self, in a state of unhealthy dependence upon an *aliud* and a state of symbiotic union with that *aliud*: for consciousness to be cured is for it to cut the umbilical cord, to become autonomous, to cease to be 'inspired' by the maternal genius. Because Socrates is only in the very first stage of his separation, he remains dependent upon exteriority; he retains pathological traces of passivity, sharing, and heteronomy (the identification of his philosophical method with the maternal model of childbirth might be envisaged as an empirical symptom of these traces, but Hegel does not make the point).

If Socrates repeatedly finds himself falling into ecstatic states, it is because Mind can only emerge from its unhealthy condition by force of habit. Only exercise makes it possible to move beyond violent separation from the corporeity in which consciousness had been buried toward a painless schism leading to a normal state in which consciousness is no longer dependent on the 'body', no longer affected and inspired by the body, but in which, on the contrary, the body is entirely at the service of consciousness. Philosophy is training for death, that is, for schism, separation from that with which one had first been unified. One becomes thought, pure interiority freed from all bodily attachments, by repeatedly making the effort to pull oneself away from corporeity in order to think. Contrary here again to Kant,[47] for whom any habit is basically a 'bad habit' because it mechanizes the mind and thus counters its freedom, for Hegel habit alone frees Mind and allows the soul's spiritualization. Far from 'bestializing' man, it elevates him, brings forth Mind into its normal state.

> The main point about Habit is that by its means man gets emancipated from the feelings, even in being affected by them. . . . In habit regarded as *aptitude,* or skill, not merely has the abstract psychical life to be kept intact *per se,* but it has to be imposed as a subjective aim, to be made

a power in the bodily part, which is rendered subject and thoroughly pervious to it. Conceived as having the inward purpose of the subjective soul thus imposed upon it, the body is treated as an immediate externality and a barrier. Thus comes out the more decided rupture between the soul as simple self-concentration, and its earlier naturalness and immediacy; it has lost its original and immediate identity with the bodily nature, and as external has first to be reduced to that position. . . . In this way an aptitude shows the corporeity rendered completely pervious, made into an instrument, so that when the conception (e.g. a series of musical notes) is in me, then without resistance and with ease the body gives them correct utterance.

The form of habit applies to all kinds and grades of mental action. The most external of them, i.e. the spatial direction of an individual, viz. his upright posture, has been by will made a habit – a position taken without adjustment and without consciousness – which continues to be an affair of his persistent will; for the man stands only because and in so far as he wills to stand, and only so long as he wills it without consciousness. Similarly our eyesight is the concrete habit which, without an express adjustment, combines in a single act the several modifications of sensation, consciousness, intuition, intelligence, &c., which make it up. Thinking, too, however free and active in its own pure element it becomes, no less requires habit and familiarity (this impromptuity or form of immediacy), by which it is the property of my single self where I can freely and in all directions range. It is through this habit that I come to realise my *existence* as a thinking being. Even here, in this spontaneity of self-centred thought, there is a partnership of soul and body (hence, want of habit and too-long-continued thinking cause headache);[48] habit diminishes this feeling, by making the natural function an immediacy of the soul. Habit on an ampler scale, and carried out in the strictly intellectual range, is recollection and memory . . .

Habit is often spoken of disparagingly and called lifeless, casual and particular. And it is true that the form of habit, like any other, is open to anything we chance to put into it; and it is habit of living which brings on death, or, if quite abstract, is death itself: and yet habit is indispensable, for the *existence* of all intellectual life in the individual, enabling the subject to be a concrete immediacy, an 'ideality' of soul – enabling the matter of consciousness, religious, moral, &c., to be his as *this* self, *this* soul, and no other, and be neither a mere latent possibility, nor a transient emotion or idea, nor an abstract inwardness, cut off from action and reality, but part and parcel of his being.[49]

The soul, . . . setting in opposition its being to its (conscious) self, absorbing it, and making it its own, has lost the meaning of mere soul, or the 'immediacy' of mind. The actual soul with its sensation and its concrete self-feeling turned into habit, has implicitly realised the 'ideality' of its qualities; in this externality it has recollected and inwardised itself, and is infinite self-relation. This free universality thus made explicit shows the soul awaking to the higher stage of the ego, or abstract universality in so far as it is *for* the abstract universality. In this way it gains the position of thinker and subject – specially a subject of the judgment in which the ego excludes from itself the sum total of its merely natural features as an object, a world external to it, – but with such respect to that object that in it it is immediately reflected into itself. Thus soul rises to become *Consciousness*.[50]

Because the internalization of consciousness is not yet a habit in Socrates, because the possibility of recollection that it opens up is still at the stage of a pure imperative, it manifests itself in him initially in a physical form and in an anthropological guise: in the form of ecstatic immobility. Socrates' upright posture, the habit of which he seems already to have acquired, mimics the erection of consciousness, the habit of which he is only in the process of acquiring. Like a true *Colossus*, he offers the spectacle of a double erection to the fascinated Greeks during his military campaigns: the spectacle of the spiritualization and the interiorization of man, his only and unique occupation and preoccupation.

c) *The citizen and his virtues*

His preoccupation with the inner life does not prevent Socrates from carrying out his civic duties, even though the business of the State is never of fundamental importance to him. We must understand that he has no real interest in politics, that he never aspires to any position of leadership (otherwise, how can his final condemnation to death be explained?). He acts consistently and exclusively in a spirit of justice; obeying only his internal principle, he does not fear to set himself in opposition to the democratic people if need be. His real occupation is not politics but the exercise of moral philosophy, which is of a piece with his behaviour as an individual, insofar as his own conduct is instituted as a universal model.

Socrates' individual character and his virtues simply embody his moral principle. Indeed, his virtues do not have the form of custom or of some natural entity. They arise from his will; they are engendered by his will owing to an autonomous determination. They are thus authentic virtues that constitute his characteristic features, his *habitus*, his second nature. This second nature is in complete disharmony with his external appearance, which for its part betrays 'naturally low and hateful qualities' (*Lectures*, 393). The lack of correlation between the inner and the outer man (which makes Socrates enigmatic for the Greeks, as Nietzsche notes) is what confirms Socrates' moral personality and his perfect mastery. Drawing upon

Xenophon[51] without citing him, Hegel reports that Socrates recognized that he had a 'bad' nature, but added that he had been able to control it. Socrates' virtue lies precisely here, in the capacity of his internal principle to dominate his nature; this unique principle takes shape within him and transforms his entire being. 'Socrates formed himself, through his art and through the power of self-conscious will, into this particular character, and acquired this capacity for the business of his life. Through his principle he attained that far-reaching influence which has lasted to the present day . . ., for since his time the genius of inward conviction has been the basis which must be fundamental' (p. 394).

By virtue of his mastery over his primary nature, Socrates is not only a moral being but an accomplished work of art, a work of classical art, all of a piece (a solid block, Nietzsche will say) in which each feature is determined by an idea, a will: because Socrates has become what he wanted to be, he is alive and consummately beautiful, for 'the highest beauty is just the most perfect carrying out of all sides of the individuality in accordance with the one inward principle' (p. 393; *jeder Zug durch diese Idee bestimmt ist*). By virtue of his plastic nature, he belongs to the series of great men of his day (Sophocles, Thucydides, and so on), to the stars who gravitate around Pericles, the highest plastic individuality. All these men were in fact self- generated, and each remained faithful to the statue of himself that he had created (fidelity to the internal model is more important, according to Xenophon's Socrates, than a statue's resemblance to its external model'[52]; each remained faithful to his internal principle and to his goal. Thus Pericles, once he became a statesman, 'laughed no more', Hegel says, 'and never again attended a feast' (p. 394); we are to understand that, at the expense of his personal happiness, he subordinated his individuality to the seriousness of the statist totality.

We still need to understand why Hegel describes the work of art that Socrates represents as classical. At first glance, indeed, the figure of Socrates, marked by a schism between inside and outside (as Alcibiades notes in Plato's *Symposium*), would seem to fit better within the category of symbolic art (if we refer to the classifications Hegel offers in his *Aesthetics*). For Kierkegaard, the lack of consonance between Socrates' inner beauty and his external ugliness attests – by embodying it, as it were – to the irony through which the philosopher shattered the Greek belief in harmony between body and soul. For Nietzsche, physical ugliness is the symptom of a nature constituted by violent, extravagant, anarchic instincts, so that Socrates is likened to criminals and decadents. Hegel, for his part – and in this respect, in his own way, his own position is not far from Nietzsche's – recognizes that to a certain extent the outer body reflects the inner soul (here again Hegel's position is opposed to Kant's[53]). This is even, according to Hegel's *Aesthetics,* one of the points that differentiates the human body, which is expressive through and through, from the body of an animal, whose outer form betrays no inner being.

With animals, and this is the main cause of their inferiority from the standpoint of beauty,

> what is visible to us in the organism is not the soul; what is turned outwards and appears everywhere is not the inner life, but forms drawn from a lower stage than that of life proper. The animal is living only *within* its covering, i.e. this 'insideness' is not itself real in the form of an inner consciousness and therefore this life is not visible over all the animal. Because the inside remains *just* an inside, the outside too appears *only* as an outside and not completely penetrated in every part by the soul.
>
> The *human* body, on the contrary, stands in this respect at a higher stage, since in it there is everywhere and always represented the fact that man is an ensouled and feeling unit.[54]

Hegel's Philosophy of Mind, §411, establishes a relation of sign to signified between inside and outside:

> In this identity of interior and exterior, the latter subject to the former, the soul is *actual:* in its corporeity it has its free shape, in which it *feels itself* and *makes itself felt*, and which as the Soul's work of art has *human* pathognomic and physiognomic expression. Under the head of human expression are included, e.g., the upright figure in general, and the formation of the limbs, especially the hand, as the absolute instrument, of the mouth – laughter, weeping, &c., and the note of mentality diffused over the whole, which at once announces the body a[s] the externality of a higher nature.[55]

However – and on this point Hegel agrees with Kant and Kierkegaard – physiognomy cannot be raised to the rank of science. This is 'one of the vainest fancies, still vainer than a *signatura rerum,* which supposed the shape of a plant to afford indication of its medicinal virtue'.[56] For shape, by virtue of its externality, is immediate and natural, and thus to the mind it can be nothing but an indeterminate and completely imperfect *sign*; it cannot represent the mind as it is for itself, as something *universal.* To the mind, the shape of the human body is only the primary phenomenon; from the outset, *language* is its most perfect expression. If, unlike an animal body, the human body manifests its being-alive externally, there are limits to expressivity, and lacunae: a certain number of organs work together to serve the animal functions, whereas others serve to externalize psychic life, feelings and passions. The soul, the inner life, is not manifested in *all* the reality of the human form. Moreover, to the mind, physiognomic and pathognomic determinacy represents something *contingent.* There is an accidental element in expressivity that explains the differences in aspect of the human organism according to race, family, occupation or trade, temperament and character; these are all particularities that lack the character of Mind.

> Poverty, worries, anger, coldness and indifference, the frenesy of passions, the stubborn pursuit of unilateral aims, variability and spiritual dissociation, dependence with respect to external nature, and in a general way all the finitude of human existence are specified to give rise, depending on chance, to particular physiognomies each of which ends up taking on a durable expression. Thus there are ravaged physiognomies that bear traces of destructive storms of passion, while others reveal nothing but an internal platitude and sterility, and still others are so particular as to have lost the general type of forms. There is no limit to the accidental quality of faces. That is why children are, by and large, the most beautiful beings: in children, all the particularities are still slumbering as in a closed seed, no limited passion stirs their breast, and none of the multiple human interests has yet succeeded in imprinting on their changing features the mark of their sad necessity. But to this innocence, and even though its childhood vivacity seems to contain all possibilities, are lacking the deepest features of the mind whose activity must only occur within itself, following essential directions and in view of essential goals.
>
> This defectiveness of immediate existence, whether physical or spiritual, is essentially to be regarded as *finitude,* more precisely as a finitude which does not correspond with its inner essence, and through this lack of correspondence just proclaims its finitude. For the Concept, and, more concretely still, the Idea, is inherently *infinite* and *free.* Although animal life, as life, is Idea, it does not itself display the infinity and freedom which only appear when the Concept so completely pervades its appropriate reality that therein it has only itself, with nothing but itself emerging there. In that event alone is the Concept genuinely free and infinite individuality. [57]

It is because Mind and its infinite liberty find no expression in the finitude of existence and its dependence with respect to the outer forms that Mind seeks to satisfy its need for liberty at a higher level. 'It is from the deficiencies of immediate reality that the necessity of the beauty of art is derived'. [58] Art must make the external aspect conform to the concept. Thanks to art, truth acquires an external expression through which one sees an existence that is affirming its freedom and autonomy, its self-definition from within, and not in relation to otherness.

'Art . . . has to convert every shape in all points of its visible surface into an eye, which is the seat of the soul and brings the spirit into appearance. . . . Art makes every one of its productions into a thousand-eyed Argus, whereby the inner soul and spirit is seen at every point' in all their internal freedom and infinity.[59]

Socrates' ugliness is a sign that the philosopher no longer has the innocence of a child. His face is ravaged by the passions that he expresses in their contingent particularity. To be sure, Socrates is the paragon of all virtues ('wisdom, discretion, temperance, moderation, justice, courage, inflexibility, firm sense of rectitude in relation to tyrants and people' [*Lectures*, p. 394]); but, as Plato's *Symposium* shows (and Hegel refers to Plato's text in this connection), being virtuous implies neither reduced pleasure nor ascetic sobriety nor intentional mortification. Socrates experienced all the passions. His virtue lies in the force of consciousness that manages to keep itself intact throughout any bodily excess. This is what constitutes Socrates' beauty,[60] for it is expressive of the infinite liberty of his mind and of Mind. Through the mastery he has been able to achieve over the violent passions to which his ugliness bears witness, he shows that he has become what he wanted to be and has remained faithful to his intent; he is a true work of classical art, reflecting the infinite liberty of Mind. His passions, his primary nature, are a perceptible material that he has managed to reappropriate and reshape, sculpting a second nature for himself that is the sign of his freedom. By virtue of his spiritual self-generation, Socrates indeed belongs to the stage of Greek consciousness, to the stage of beauty, belongs to the autochthonous people that became what it is on its own, on the basis not of nothing but of a foreign material that it managed to reappropriate for itself, while transforming, elaborating and metamorphosizing it to the point of making it essentially its own and of becoming able to perceive its real beginning in itself. The foreign rudiment is a rudiment only in relation to this work of elaboration, and it served only as a necessary shock, a driving thrust behind the process of development of Greek Mind and culture.

The Greeks' work of culture is a work of art, on the one hand, because 'the form which they have given to the foreign principle is this characteristic breath of spirituality, the spirit of freedom and of beauty which can in the one aspect be regarded as form, but which in another and higher sense is simply substance' (p. 150). They created the spiritual element of their culture through an appropriation that shunted its foreign origin into oblivion, in such a way that they appear to themselves as transparent to themselves. They are indeed works of art; they created themselves, fashioned a native land from their own existence. However, they also honored this self-creation in artistic representations properly speaking. Themselves works of art, they represented themselves in works of art. With joy and gratitude (Nietzsche says much the same thing in his own way), they represented their own existence as a native land, not in order to be that land, to have it or to use it, but as a simple sign of gratefulness for their rebirth, for they were conscious of having as their distinguishing characteristic the fact that they had been born of a spiritual renaissance. Thus they represented their existence as separate from themselves in the form of an object that engenders itself for itself and as such has fallen to them as their lot. They knew that they were the foundation and origin of foundations and origins. Thus they represented for themselves the origin of everything, the way it was produced among them. Beneath the external aspect, they saw these origins arise historically among themselves as their own works and their own merits. They represented the mind of beings within themselves in their civil, juridical, moral and political existence; here is the seed of reflective freedom that allows *philosophy to be born* among them as well.[61]

Like the Greek people, Socrates, a plastic nature, is a beginning. His real birth is his spiritual rebirth. However, he is not yet abstract modern subjectivity, because the natural sense-based mode still exists in him, even if it is entirely subordinated to spirituality, which has the highest status. For Mind does not yet have full command of itself, cannot use itself as an intermediary to (re)present itself and base its world on that self-representation. If Socratic self-generation implies the 'murder of the father', it cannot yet do without the perceptible material, the maternal model. That is why his milieu is one of beauty; that is why the figure of Socrates belongs among the great Greeks of his era, all of whom transformed themselves, each of whom was a star reflecting the freedom of Mind – the comparison is fully justified if we refer to Hegel's *Aesthetics*.[62] In that text, when Hegel describes art as an Argus with a thousand eyes, he is in fact recalling (and reversing the meaning of) the distich in which Plato addresses an invocation to Aster: 'When thou lookest on the stars, my star, oh! would I were the heavens and could see thee with a thousand eyes'. (p. 153).[63]

If, despite the lack of correspondence between his 'outside' and his 'inside', Socrates is indeed a classical work of art, it is because there is a perfect correspondence between his second nature – nature made his own by an overall operation of mastery – and the mind. The material of art that reflects the mind is a material transformed. Socrates is beautiful and alive because he has become what he has been through elaboration of his first nature according to a unique inner principle.

Hegel and Nietzsche agree that Socrates' ugliness is the sign of a violent instinctual nature governed by reason. But whereas for Nietzsche the pseudo-triumph of reason is the symptom of the degeneration and failure of instinct and an indication that the uncultivated plebeian Socrates belongs to a decadent type, for Hegel the fact that Socrates was able to master his passions reveals an unshakable strength of consciousness, a self-mastery that is of a piece with his attitude toward others. Far from being the attitude of a coarse, uncultivated being, Socrates' self-mastery exemplifies a consummate urbanity that couples universality of discourse with a free and vital relation to individuals and to the situation in which that relation takes place: 'The intercourse is that of a most highly cultured man who, in his relation to others, never places anything personal in all his wit, and sets aside anything that is unpleasant' (p. 396). Plato and even Xenophon provide evidence of this.

The end of the 'presentation of Socrates' *life*' leads into the presentation of his '*philosophy*' – a philosophy entirely based on the urbane relations characteristic of Socratic dialogue. Socrates' 'life' – as a beautiful work of art – was forged by his philosophical principle and his philosophy constitutes part of his way of life. Life and philosophy, intimately intermingled, have been disentangled by Hegel only for didactic reasons. Thus when the presentation of Socrates' philosophy begins, under a new heading, it has already been under way for some time. Socrates' philosophy has always already haunted his life just as his life, like a ghost, will not cease to haunt his philosophy, and this is so because the philosophy is not developed into a system, because Socrates' way of philosophizing as a retreat from political affairs – from functional reality – is in intimate connection with daily life.

5. The Philosophy (pp. 396-440)

The life and the philosophy may form an indissoluble whole, and Hegel may linger more, with Socrates, than he does with any other philosopher over the 'details' of the life; nevertheless, he gives more space to the philosophy: forty-four pages (in the English translation) as opposed to seven devoted to Socrates' life. There are systemic reasons for this disproportion. The connection between Socrates' life and his philosophy is not to be explained, in Nietzsche's fashion, by the life, but by the nature of the Socratic philosophy itself, which, as such, contains an intrinsic link to life: the daily life of a free citizen of Athens of his day, a citizen with ample leisure – for he had slaves at his service – to stroll around outdoors, in broad daylight, chatting with one and all. The notion that, owing to his wife's shrewish humor, Socrates may have been more impelled than others to spend time outside his own home (that is Nietzsche's ironic hypothesis, as we have seen) does not concern Hegel at all; for him philosophy, public business transacted out of doors, does not stem from private quarrels but from contemporary Athenian life and customs. Socrates' life was thus spent outdoors in conversations about questions posed orally; that was his characteristic occupation and his philosophy. That philosophy was not a set of teachings after the manner of the Sophists, nor was it a way of moralizing in the modern style of pathetic religious predication aimed at indoctrination. Socrates' style – in harmony with that of the period and with Attic urbanity – was dialogue, that is to say, a rational, reciprocal, free relation from which all harshness was eliminated, the very model of a refined and sociable culture. At least if one believes Xenophon's dialogues and Plato's – 'where there is, in this regard, particular skill displayed', Hegel adds (p. 403), suggesting by the slight difference he establishes between the two sources that perhaps all the refinement the noble Plato could muster was needed to transfigure the coarseness of the uncultivated plebeian into his own image. But it is not Hegel, it is Nietzsche, as we know, who draws this consequence. Hegel's primary concern is to show the urbanity of Socrates himself, inasmuch as that urbanity is the sign of the internal principle, of the strength of consciousness that governs him, and of his self-mastery.

A. *The method* (pp. 397-406)

Socrates' life is of a piece with his manner of philosophizing, that is, with his method, which is by nature dialectical. Dialogue is not a formal artifice, as it is in the modern period; it is justified by the very principle of Socratic philosophy and by its content, which is of an ethical order: the search for good as the absolute. Referring to Xenophon's *Memorabilia* and to Aristotle's *Metaphysics*[64] Hegel succeeds in giving the Socratic method a positive content and aim from the outset. He emphasizes his opposition to the 'modern' reading of Socrates (the 'Romantics' reading, and also Kierkegaard's), which depicts Socrates as the initiator of the infinite negativity and freedom of consciousness. In his presentation of the Socratic method, Hegel is thus seeking to minimize its negative aspect, which is reduced to a simple phase. He can succeed only by privileging certain sources (Xenophon and Aristotle) at the expense of another (Aristophanes) and by generally neglecting to distinguish Socrates' contributions from Plato's. In short, his project requires him to reinscribe the Socratic dialogue within the speculative dialogue. He recalls that Socrates engaged citizens of all sorts, classes, and ages in 'conversation'; any pretext at all might serve to get them to reflect on their responsibilities. (This reminder has the particular advantage of allowing Hegel to stress that Socrates got involved in the domestic interests of citizens, that he interposed himself between fathers and sons, and thus to justify in advance the first of the charges used to condemn Socrates, his corruption of youth.)

Hegel thus translates the Socratic method into speculative language: the method consists, he says, in leading one's interlocutors on 'from a definite case to think of the universal, and of truths and beauties which had absolute value' (p. 398). He can bring off this operation of translation only because he has already read Socrates by way of Aristotle (whom he views as the richest and most reliable source for anyone seeking to know Greek philosophy[65]). Thanks to this relevant and reappropriating double translation, Hegel can describe the two characteristic features[66] of the Socratic method. The first is a positive feature: the method starts with a concrete case to work toward a universal, and it brings to light the concept that is in itself in every consciousness; this is the method's maieutic phase. The second characteristic feature is negative: the method dissolves universals, solidified and immediate opinions; it consists in an ironic phase that results in a third phase, the troubling of consciousness (this negative phase is the only one that Kierkegaard will retain; he accuses Hegel of confusing Socrates with Plato, because he failed to distinguish between two different dialectics, two ways of interrogating).

a) Irony

The most detailed discussion of the method begins, not coincidentally, with the negative phase, that of irony. Even if, within the presentation of the third phase, that of the aporetic result to which the method leads, Hegel indicates that the purely negative side is the essential one, to make irony a single, initial phase is instantly to reduce its dissolving impact. If it is true that philosophy must necessarily begin with disquiet and universal doubt, this is still only a beginning. Socrates' goal is to encourage reflection, to arouse skepticism: 'Everything must be doubted, all presuppositions given up, to reach the truth as created through the Notion' (p. 406). The negative phase is always followed by an affirmative element. Socrates shakes the faith of his interlocutors, to be sure, but he does so in order to make them seek what lies within themselves, and to 'awaken' – this is all that matters to him – 'the thinker' within man, that is, to bring consciousness out of its native torpor and numbness by prodding each individual to assert his own internal principle. Negativity is thus not an end in itself; it is wholly oriented toward the affirmative and positive element: Socrates' goal is to get other people to come up with their own principles (pp. 398-99). Far from seeking to destroy morality by positioning himself above it through the distancing power of irony, Hegel aims to lead his interlocutors to the true good, to the universal idea.

Socrates' irony, like Plato's, does not grow out of purely negative, mocking and hypocritical behaviour that denies all reality to the Idea and treats it as nothing but a big joke. No, his irony has a very limited and specific meaning: it is a way of conversing, an attitude of affable serenity. As Hegel also emphasizes in *Philosophy of Right* (§140), Socrates treats individual consciousness ironically but not the Idea itself. Irony 'is a particular mode of carrying on intercourse between one person and another, and it is thus only a subjective form of dialectic' (*Lectures*, p. 398). Irony is simply Socrates' way of testing his interlocutors – who are most often young people – by provoking them to speak. The philosopher's pseudo-naivete and his attitude of feigned ignorance leads his interlocutors to contradict themselves; his method is to show them only that they believe in contradictory principles, each equally well-grounded. To this end, Socrates does not affirm the contrary of the interlocutor's thesis, but, in a profound and speculative fashion, anticipating Hegel, he shows how the contrary of the thesis is implied in the initial thesis itself: he acknowledges the latter as valid and lets the process of internal destruction, 'the universal irony of the world', unfold on its own (*Lectures*, p. 400). The result of his method is that he teaches his interlocutors – and this is all he teaches – that they know nothing at all.

Socrates was said to have been falsely naive and to have feigned ignorance; however, this does not mean that he 'really' possessed a body of knowledge and aimed to teach it. Socrates knew perfectly well that he knew nothing, and that his goal was not the possession and imparting of knowledge. One must thus conclude that it was others who took his admission of ignorance as a sham, and a strategy. However, Hegel does not say this in so many words; in contradictory fashion – Kierkegaard notes this contradiction among others – he seems to acknowledge simultaneously that Socrates' ignorance was a strategic pretense, a necessary correlative of his irony, and that his ignorance was real, since it belonged only to the second division of the first phase of the first stage of the development of Mind: Socrates is not yet either Plato or Aristotle; that is, he has not yet managed to have a philosophy or to elaborate a science. And yet – and this is what Hegel seeks to imply – Socrates' ironic method must not be equated with the Sophists' approach, which it aims to confound, and which is itself purely negative. Socrates' irony is always used 'in defending the Idea of truth and justice against the conceit of the Sophists and the uneducated'.[67] That is why if Socrates' irony seems lacking in truthfulness on the one hand, it is not lacking in greatness on the other: it is a serious irony, for it is profound and speculative. Far from being idle chatter, it allows Socrates and his interlocutors to move beyond oppositions and reach an understanding, to bring to light what they hold in common. It allows Mind to progress: 'The irony of Socrates has this great quality of showing how to make abstract ideas concrete and affect their development, for on that alone depends the bringing of the Notion into consciousness' (*Lectures*, p. 400). Socrates succeeds in making totally abstract representations explicit: 'Herein lies the truth of Socratic irony. . . . It is a matter of the development of that which is only representation and which as such is something abstract'.[68]

In support of the progress that the Socratic method made it possible to achieve, Hegel, in a way that is to say the least unexpected, takes the example *a contrario* of the pointless contemporary arguments over faith and reason, sterile debates that cannot lead to mutual comprehension because the interlocutors, unlike Socrates, do not examine their own presuppositions.

This example, borrowed from the modern period, reveals with perfect clarity the thought Hegel has 'in the back of his mind': if he is so determined to restrict the negative import of Socratic irony and to stress its specificity (which he can do, however, only by identifying Socrates with Plato in this respect[69]), it is because he wants to save the figure of Socrates, the tragic hero, from the reappropriation that has been made of him by those very moderns who argue in such a vain and sterile fashion: that is, the German Romantics, who want to make Socrates the founding father of an irony that is totally negative, destructive and immoral, an irony established as a universal principle. Hegel wants to make a radical distinction between this contemporary, 'diabolical', non-dialectizable irony, and Socrates' *tragic* irony, an irony that can be reinscribed, by means of a thoroughgoing operation of reappropriating translation, within speculative dialectics, in a place that is highly circumscribed, limited, and reduced to a simple opposition between subjective reflection and existing morality, that is, to the opposition between two equally positive and legitimate principles.

So Hegel does not hesitate to devote two pages to Romantic irony, which, according to Kierkegaard, he deems 'abominable': he vents his greatest indignation against Friedrich Schlegel in particular, because the latter sought to make irony the highest and most godlike attitude of the mind. A product of Fichtean philosophy, Romantic irony is the way in which 'subjective consciousness' can maintain 'its independence from everything' (p. 400) – from law, morality, and the good – by situating itself as master of all determinations and, following the Sophists but not Socrates (as Ast claimed), by making itself the arbitrary measure of all things. For Romantic irony, nothing is serious any longer, or rather the serious is only taken seriously so as to be destroyed and reduced to a play of pure appearances: everything that is lofty and divine is susceptible to becoming a pointless and trivial joke. In this view, the *ultima ratio* of all things is subjective consciousness and its intuition of the vanity of all things. To validate irony, to affirm that it constitutes the '"inmost and deepest life"' (p. 401), is in fact to validate the depth of the void.

Romantic irony is reserved for the modern world, but Aristophanes managed to represent it in advance, instead of staging Socratic irony (so Kierkegaard claims); still, this does not mean that Hegel condemns *The Clouds*. He eventually turns to Aristophanes' text as one of the best sources for understanding the 'comic' aspect of Socrates, an aspect that counterbalances his tragic and heroic aspect but that (contrary to what Kierkegaard says) does not reside in his irony. For *Aesthetics*[70] makes it clear that the comic is not to be confused with irony. Because irony destroys all that is noble, great and perfect, even in its objective productions, ironic art finds itself reduced to the representation of absolute subjectivity. Whereas irony takes seriously neither justice nor morality nor virtue nor the sublime nor the best, the comic 'must be restricted to showing that what destroys itself is something inherently null, a false and contradictory phenomenon, a whim, e.g., an oddity, a particular caprice in comparison with a mighty passion, or even a *supposedly* tenable principle and firm maxim'.[71]

The difference between the ironic and the comic thus bears essentially upon the content of what is destroyed. The comic safeguards true values; irony leaves nothing behind but a void.

Hegel criticizes the Romantics for drawing Socrates and Plato into the depth of the void (their void) and for trying, therefore – as Kierkegaard would do later – to separate him from (his) speculative profundity. By seeking to make Socrates their 'initiator', they wrongly conflate two epochs of Mind, a subjectivity whose negativity is limited and a subjectivity whose negativity is infinite – an irony compatible with Greek, Homeric serenity and an irony that causes everything to shift from one extreme to another, that moves from the best to the worst without retaining any value, any affirmative or objective element. But in order to be able to oppose the infinite negativity of Romantic consciousness and its attempt to reappropriate Socratic irony, Hegel is forced to leave Socrates coupled with Plato, and even to associate Homer with them; neglecting Aristophanes, whose *Clouds* he will reinterpret later on quite differently, he is forced to distinguish the more positive Socratic moment from the Sophistic moment, reversing the relation that the Romantics (and later Kierkegaard) establish between the two moments when they affirm, in order to justify taking Socrates as their own precursor, that in his ironic negativity he rose up against the Sophists' pretention to knowledge.

The exasperated tone (once again, Kierkegaard did not fail to point it out) with which Hegel speaks of contemporary irony throughout his works shows how threatening that irony is to his entire system of dialectics, his whole system of security. Thus at every turn he has to protect the alleged alliance between Socrates and Plato from the enemy whom he attacks with unparalleled vitriol.

Only Sölger (and Tieck, but to a lesser degree) really escape Hegel's exasperation, and Sölger's rehabilitation reveals what is at stake in the whole affair. Though Sölger in fact returns to the term 'irony' as proposed by Friedrich Schlegel (whom Hegel thoroughly detests because Schlegel raises irony to the highest degree), he nevertheless gave the term a favorable meaning – that is, one more favorable to Hegel's system. A reading of *Philosophy of Right*, §140 (the last section devoted to subjective morality), leaves no room for doubt about this. After distinguishing Socratic and Platonic irony from Romantic irony once again, in a lengthy, revealing note Hegel attempts to 'save' Sölger, who has maintained in the word 'irony' 'that part of Schlegel's view which was dialectic in the strict sense, i.e., dialectic as the pulsating drive of speculative inquiry'.[72] The greatest merit of Sölger's last work would be that he undertook a complete critique of A. G. Schlegel's lectures on dramatic art and literature and that he returned to a Platonic sense of irony.

In the second chapter of the introduction to *Aesthetics,* devoted to Romantic irony, Hegel repeats the same redeeming gesture with respect to Sölger – not in a note, here, but in some brief concluding remarks, a sort of appendix symptomatic of what is really at stake.

In this text, as in *Lectures on the Philosophy of History* and *Philosophy of Right,* Hegel begins by linking Romantic irony to Fichte's philosophy, in which the Ego is the absolute principle of all knowledge and value (and thus also of their dissolution), a sovereign and absolute master that can arbitrarily overturn its own choices and decisions at any moment. The artist who adopts this point of view, according to which no content is absolute nor does any content exist by itself, no longer takes the formalism of the Ego seriously. Detached from everything, the creator views himself as a divine genius who, from the pinnacle of his irony, holds in contempt those who remain attached to the trifles that are, for him, morality and law, and derives pleasure only from himself before ending up as an empty and vain subjectivity aspiring paradoxically and nostalgically to the absolute, or enjoying the morbid state of the beautiful soul dying of tedium.[73] The result is that ironic art, because it destroys all that is noble, great and perfect, eliminates the substantial; it is necessarily an inferior art. Its productions, because they take the non-artistic principle of irony as the basis for artistic creation, are vulgar, absurd and characterless; they resemble the ironic subject, who is endowed with a petty and contemptible character and who, through his negations, proves only his weakness and moral inferiority, his inability to posit a definite and worthwhile goal. And even though Hegel does not quote Socrates in the text in question, he seems to be describing the 'bad' ironic subject by antithesis with the plastic individual capable, for his part, of assigning himself a single goal and remaining faithful to it. The latter is depicted as an authentic character worthy of appearing on a tragic or comic stage; in any case such a character cannot be produced by ironic art, which is destined to fail in any case. For – and here Hegel is delighted to get his revenge – the public does not like ironic art, and 'it is a good thing that these worthless yearning natures do not please; it is a comfort that this insincerity and hypocrisy are not to people's liking, and that on the contrary people want full and genuine interests as well as characters which remain true to their important intrinsic worth'.[74]

Romantic irony is thus condemned overtly in the name of morality, but the real import of the condemnation is revealed by the rehabilitation *in extremis* of two artists who nevertheless 'adopted irony as the supreme principle of art', Tieck and Sölger.[75]

Tieck, although he continually glorifies irony, is in fact perfectly capable of appreciating the true value of great works of art. Hegel is grateful to him, for example, for not emphasizing the irony of *Romeo and Juliet*,[76] thereby proving the trustworthiness of his aesthetic judgments – and his profound lack of affinity for ironic art. But it is Sölger in particular who deserves to be 'saved', and Hegel volunteers for the task: in fact, 'in his life, philosophy, and art [he] deserves to be distinguished from the previously mentioned apostles of irony'.[77] Sölger experienced a true speculative need that allowed him to reach the dialectical stage of the Idea as absolute and infinite negativity. However, he did not see that negativity was not all there was to the speculative idea, that it was only a single phase of that idea. Kierkegaard will depict Sölger as 'the metaphysical knight of the negative'[78]: owing to irony, Sölger saw the true meaning of negativity, the nothingness of all things. But in Hegel's eyes, that was what kept him from fully comprehending the tragic; it kept him from separating the objective moral idea from the unhappy accident of the collision of two opposing 'moral' principles, kept him from understanding that that idea is real and present in the objective moral world.[79]

Despite his limitations, however, and unlike the other Romantics, Sölger is not to blame for having grasped only the negative aspect of the idea. For, Hegel declares, it is only his premature death (Kierkegaard will suggest that he was perhaps a victim of Hegel's positive system) that prevented him from going beyond negativity to achieve full elaboration of the philosophical idea. The proof (but here Hegel is really begging the question) is to be found in his real life, which manifests a firmness, a seriousness, a distinction of character that makes it impossible to assign him without reservation to the ranks of the ironic artists (who could not possibly be serious). A supplementary proof: as for Tieck, Sölger's profound understanding of authentic works of art could have nothing ironic about it, 'properly speaking'.

In other words, the seriousness of his conduct is what ultimately determines whether an artist belongs to one 'genre' or another; one can produce good literature and appreciate it as such only if one is endowed with good positive feelings that permit one to be inscribable within speculative dialectics, to become its hero or its victim – just like Socrates, or almost.

For behind Sölger's 'recuperation', over the merits of which Hegel lingers with pleasure (even though 'here' is not the place to speak of it, he says), one can in fact discern in profile that of Socrates. The seriousness of his life and his strength of character authorize Hegel to distinguish him, too, from the apostles of irony – to make of him only a *tragic ironist*. But unlike Sölger, Socrates did not die prematurely; he had time to comprehend the tragic, which, as an authentic hero, he embodied; he had time to recognize the positivity of the Idea, to make it his goal to lead people to the true good, the universal Idea. And he lived long enough to die for the Idea; but not before the moment set by his destiny.

b) The art of giving birth

That is why, after the negative phase of irony, the Socratic method includes a second, positive phase: the delivery of minds.

In his presentation of the well-known maieutics, or art of midwifery, Hegel seems to retain just one thing from the *Theaetetus*: that Socrates learned his art from his mother Phaenarete. He adds no commentary, makes nothing of the fact that Plato develops the comparison, term for term, in great detail. Hegel lets the 'details' slip by in silence, for it is important to him to accentuate the positive aspect of the Socratic method, and the details might well show that maieutics has at least as many negative aspects as positive ones: indeed, Socrates engages in at least as many abortions as in deliveries of thoughts worth keeping. Far from helping minds give birth to the positive truth with which they are deemed to be pregnant, maieutics implies an 'exhibition scene' in which the newborn, shown off to all and sundry, is subjected to a test of legitimacy. Is it a fruit of life and truth that deserves to live, or a vain and untruthful appearance that must be eradicated? It is the cruel virgin Artemis, twin sister of Apollo, the god of philosophers, who presides over childbirth, and she does not hesitate to put newborns to death as circumstances dictate. Hegel overlooks these 'details' cited by Plato: the better to reinscribe maieutics within his dialectics, he exposes this aspect of Socrates' method by relying more on Aristotle than on the *Theaetetus*. As it happens, Aristotle borrowed from maieutics only what he could reappropriate for his system, and Hegel translates Aristotle's borrowings into speculative language for his own purposes.

By virtue of this double operation, the result of which is to eliminate all negative aspect of maieutics, Hegel can declare that maieutics consists in developing the universal principle on the basis of concrete cases and in bringing to light the concept that is in itself within every consciousness. The goal of Socrates' interrogative method is to bring to light the universality of the concrete within non- reflective consciousness itself. There is thus in this method 'more than can be given in questions and replies' (p. 402). There is a targeted positive supplement that directs the entire interrogation and constitutes its specificity. This supplement alone makes for a true interrogation: contrary to what would happen in a real conversational exchange, the response given, in fact, is not contingent; it does not derive from personal arbitrariness on the part of the respondent, who may, depending on the circumstances, give an answer that is beside the point, situate the question in a different light, or bring to bear a different point of view, his own. These are all legitimate options in a live conversational exchange governed by the psychological laws of mimetic rivalry, by claims that one is right or that one has won, an exchange in which the interlocutor, if he is caught short, does not hesitate to break off the conversation, or he may go against prevailing custom and change the subject through joking or criticism. The arbitrary contingency of the response is encountered in life or in modern dialogues, not in Socratic exchanges, at least as they are transcribed in Plato's dialogues, or Xenophon's, which are 'altogether under the author's control' (ibid.; *Ganz in der Hand des Verfassers*).

In the description of the 'bad respondent', readers may have imagined they recognized one of Socrates' individual interlocutors, such as Polus, Gorgias, or Meno. These individuals are often called unsatisfactory interlocutors, because they do not conform to the rules of dialectical exchange: they are none the less present in the dialogues, more especially in those traditionally called 'Socratic'. These latter are in general livelier and more aporetic than Plato's later dialogues, which are more properly called 'Platonic' and which some view as 'false dialogues'. Let us not be misled: Hegel does not find any bad respondents in the 'Socratic dialogues' as transcribed by Plato. All of Socrates' interlocutors are satisfied to answer the questions asked. The questions are asked in a way that makes it easy to reply (for Hegel, this is praise), and the response is necessarily offered from the same point of view as that of the questioner; there is no room for deviation, no possibility of changing the subject. The respondents are seen as pliable youths – produced by art and responding with art – because in their responses they conform to a single idea. If the Socratic dialogue is truly a dialogue – a dialogue in truth – it is because, directed as it is toward a goal and purified of all empirical 'living' elements, it makes it possible to reestablish on a better footing the linearity of speculative dialectical development – the development of the idea that is not concerned, in its necessary cold objectivity, either with the interlocutors' psychology or with their contingent and arbitrary passions.

The 'external' and 'formal' aspect of the Socratic-Platonic dialogue, its 'mimetic' character, is thus suppressed by Hegel in favor of 'content' alone. As Hegel sees it, the true aim of maieutics would be to gain access to this content by deducing the universal from the particular, from immediate naive experience. However, the Socratic method is not deductive or conceptual, properly speaking; instead, it is inductive, since – and here again Hegel refers to Aristotle and betrays him – it extracts the universal principle as universal, such as it is in natural consciousness without being thought; it makes the interlocutor conscious of the universal principle by separating it from the contingent concrete, a process that we *also* see quite frequently in Plato's dialogues (Plato displays particular skill in this respect), Hegel adds. This time he seems to be distinguishing Plato from Socrates, but without specifying 'which' Socrates he is talking about or according to what criteria he can determine that Socrates is not simply a mouthpiece for Plato.

What Socrates would have inaugurated and Plato exemplified by maieutics thus defined would be nothing other than the process of the formation of self-awareness, the development of reason, that is, of consciousness of universals. Such awareness characterizes a healthy, cultivated adult consciousness; once formed, after it has emerged from childhood with its singular concrete representations, adult consciousness circulates in complete freedom among abstractions, thoughts, universals. It moves without the slightest fatigue; what this cultivated adult consciousness finds tiring, rather, is the Socratic process – for, in order to be accessible to all, this process is prodigal with wordy examples and does not hesitate to resort to, and settle for, concrete representations. Socrates makes 'us' regress to the state of childhood; he bores 'us', we who are now cultivated enough to express our boredom

(*Tädiosität, taediositas*) even in Latin (or almost); because 'we' have been trained in abstraction, from childhood on, because 'we' are now accustomed to the universal principle, 'we' tire quickly of chatter that is now useless and painful: 'we' no longer need a hodgepodge of examples to arrive at abstraction and to establish it in its universality, as was the case in the Socratic phase of childhood when Mind was not yet accustomed to universals, when thinking tired people out or made them ill. Fortified by his adulthood and his health, looking back from the lofty vantage point of his entire culture, Hegel casts a disdainful glance on the past of Mind, on its sickly childhood, now fortunately left behind, which threatens, if 'we' take too much pleasure in returning to it, to provoke 'our' boredom, even 'our' disgust (another possible meaning of *taediositas*). To stave off nausea, Hegel thus wipes out all the examples and paradigms that proliferate in the 'Socratic-Platonic' dialogues. He eradicates all empirical elements, everything that derives from a live conversational exchange and that *dates* them; he keeps only what is essential, only what is worthy of being 'sublated' by a 'modern' reader, only what Aristotle, modern before his time, had already 'retained' from Socrates: the development of the universal principle on the basis of a well-known representation, the consciousness of the interlocutors themselves.

Because for Socrates' interlocutors the universal principle had not yet become second nature, finding it via its separation from the concrete could not fail to provoke astonishment (Plato knew this quite well: in the *Theaetetus* he locates the origin of philosophy in this admiring sentiment). But 'we' who are accustomed, perhaps overly accustomed, to the abstract and the universal, 'we' are no longer astonished at that marvel. In order to reactivate, as it were, this now outdated astonishment, Hegel gives an example of what, even today, retains the power of appearing prodigious to 'us': the unity of being and nonbeing in the simple representation of becoming. This unity was perceived for the first time by Heraclitus, a bold thinker who dared to make the profound claim that being and non-being are the same. Hegel's translation of this statement allows him to make Heraclitus, a 'pre- Socratic', the ancestor of his own grand logic. 'We say [is this "we" the same as "we" adults, healthy and cultivated, or is it only a royal "we", as they say? But for Hegel, who identifies himself with modern consciousness that has reached the end point of its development, these two possibilities seem to be one and the same], in place of using the expression of Heraclitus, that the Absolute is the unity of being and non-being' (p. 282).

What still strikes 'us', we who are not quite Hegel, as prodigious is the identity of terms between which there is such a tremendous [*ungeheuerer*] difference: 'If we reflect, for example, on the universally known idea of Becoming, we find that what becomes is not and yet it is; it is the identity of Being and non-being, and it may surprise us that in this simple conception so great a distinction should exist' (p. 404). This identity still has such power to surprise 'us' that we may find Hegel obscure, as Socrates and Plato found Heraclitus obscure, precisely because of the speculative depth he was able to express (pp. 280-82).[80] For while 'we' may be accustomed to the mathematical abstraction that stems from understanding, 'we' are not yet entirely accustomed to speculative thought, which is always difficult and obscure for understanding that cannot grasp it.

c) The aporetic result

The example Hegel provides allows us in any event to grasp the initial astonishment that must have been provoked by the discovery of the universal principle. The *third phase* of the Socratic method consists in the result of this discovery and its development. In presenting the second phase, Hegel has underlined the affirmative element in order to make the negative element, irony, stand out more clearly as a simple phase, the first; when he presents the third phase he oscillates between a negative Socrates and a positive one. He begins by insisting on the negative result, which he deems crucial for the beginning of philosophy. By developing points of view opposed to those immediately available to consciousness, Socrates makes his interlocutors aware that what they take to be true is not yet truth; stripping away their confidence in their own opinions, he leaves them in a troubled and aporetic state. Hegel's sources here are the *Lysis*, the *Republic*, and especially the *Meno*: the celebrated passage in which Meno compares Socrates to a paralyzing torpedo fish is cited at length in support of the negative aspect of the outcome. Unconcerned about contradicting himself, Hegel notes in passing that Meno (who in this respect is an 'unsatisfactory interlocutor' according to the terms of the foregoing analysis) does not answer the question directly, for he does not know what the universal character of all the virtues may be, or that Socrates is setting him back on the 'right' road.

    For while the negative aspect is the essential one (and Socrates differs from the Sophists in this respect), the philosopher does not intend to leave his interlocutors in a state of immobilizing aporia: that is why in Plato's text Socrates rejects Meno's torpedo fish image. Although Hegel is apparently more faithful than ever to Plato, following his text quite closely here, he leaves out this 'detail'. For Socrates explains his rejection of the image as follows: if he were seeking to paralyze the others, he ought to paralyze himself as well, since he is as ignorant as his interlocutors. Now, according to Hegel, Socrates cannot be in an authentic aporia himself, one provoked by the absence of knowledge: he is rather in a state of astonishment triggered by the discovery of the universal principle, and he aims to bring his interlocutors to the point where they share his astonishment. The disruption he fosters has a positive goal (on this Hegel and Plato agree): it is designed to lead to reflection, to provoke a more serious effort to acquire knowledge. That is to say, says Hegel in his own language which is no longer Plato's, it aims to re-engender, via the concept, the interlocutor's abandoned presuppositions – which are thus not truly abandoned, but 'sublated' at a higher dialectical level.

By folding Plato's dialectics into speculative dialectics in this way, by translating Plato into his own language, Hegel can finally emphasize the *positive* aspect of Socrates' results. Through the Socratic method, an affirmative element is developed in consciousness, namely, the good in so far as the good is produced by the knowledge that draws it from consciousness, that is, the universal in-and-for-itself that is determined by thought. This free thought produces the universal, the true, and to the extent that it is the goal, the good. This targeting of truth and goodness is what differentiates Socrates from the Sophists. The latter take man as the measure of all things, but they still define man as particular and not universal. With Socrates, as read by Plato and translated by Hegel, man is the measure of things inasmuch as he is thought; and that is the true and the good. (Hegel has nothing at all to say about the *Good* of Book VI of the *Republic,* a non-hypothetic principle that transcends man's thought, which it 'produces' – possibly because this time he is distinguishing between Socrates and Plato?) The Sophists are nevertheless not to blame for their attitude, which also corresponds to a degree of development or culture of Mind scarcely inferior to that of Socrates. And Socrates in turn does not warrant praise because he recognized the good as a goal in itself: that discovery corresponded to his 'moment', his epoch. Every discovery is made in its own time; individuals are to be neither praised nor blamed, since they merely represent moments in a development that surpasses them and that implies that they will be surpassed in turn. By inscribing the Sophists and Socrates within this development, Hegel shows that, from his own vantage point at the end of the process, he knows perfectly well that man is not the measure of all things, either in the Sophistic sense or in the Socratic sense; the measure of all things is absolute Mind.

B. *THE SOCRATIC PRINCIPLE, OR SOCRATES' DISCOVERY* (pp. 396-425)

After presenting the three phases in the Socratic method, which are coextensive with his own philosophy, Hegel attributes the fact that he has not yet said very much about the Socratic principle to its inherent deficiency. That principle (the good is universal, it is produced by thought) is intrinsically concrete, but it has not yet been given concrete expression. It is less abstract than Anaxagoras', but Socrates' principle still remains abstract. That is why 'nothing that is affirmative can beyond this, be adduced' (p. 407).

Hegel nevertheless proposes to 'develop' the Socratic principle, and this development constitutes the second part of the presentation of his philosophy, which he makes, of course, in three points.

a) The reversal
The first distinguishing characteristic of this principle is the still purely formal one of subjective freedom. Socrates teaches that consciousness must turn inward to draw from within itself the true, the universal and the absolute. Manifestations previously situated in the realm of being – the law, the true, the good – Socrates now moves back (*zurückkehren*) into consciousness. But this 'reversal', this return from outside to inside, is not a revolutionary and contingent invention of a brilliant individual named Socrates: 'his' discovery must not be imputed to him individually as if it were to his personal credit. 'Socrates' did not spring up like a mushroom; 'his' principle had to appear just when it did, for it corresponds to a determined stage in the history of Mind. The 'Socratic' reversal is a manifestation of the reversal (*Umkehr*) that the world's Mind was initiating at that moment in Athens and that it would later bring to fruition elsewhere. Socrates is only in the vanguard of the necessary change that consists in passing from natural morality to abstract morality; he is the consciousness of this change which, as such, is independent of his own singular, contingent, empirical individuality. And it is because Hegel's vantage point is the higher one of universal consciousness, the world history of Mind and its unfolding, that he can know that Socrates is at the head of the reversal and that that head, like every head, has to be and will be chopped off. Only this higher viewpoint, the vantage point of accomplishment, makes it possible to evaluate the beginning as such, and to situate Socrates in his proper place within the totality of a people and within the world history of which he represents only a specific stage, that of the beginning of reflection and consciousness.

The 'epoch' inaugurated by Socrates begins at the moment when essence considered as being is abandoned. Among a people at the height of its flowering, this abandonment seemingly threatens to corrupt the natural morality according to which the good has the form of the immediate absolute, of the universal present – the form of actually existing law that has not yet been mediated by consciousness. With Socrates, the good takes the form of the conviction of a singular consciousness, an abstract moral consciousness which by its critical interrogations disrupts the universal validity and the presumed divinity of statist law and proceeds to disturb the repose of natural moral consciousness. If the latter believes it can regain its repose by condemning Socrates, it is mistaken, for the movement of disruption and 'corruption' begun by Socrates is inscribed within an irreversible, universal movement, that of the return of consciousness into itself (*Rückkehr-in-sich*), which the Athenians collectively were also in the process of bringing about, a movement of the greatest freedom with respect to everything that possesses being and validity: this was the 'highest point reached by the mind of Greece' (p. 408). At this level – that of a living consciousness of Greek mores that retains the same content as those mores, even as it circulates freely among them – there is something like a joyful equilibrium between what is and the consciousness that freely enjoys its content. Consciousness has not yet become abstract; it is not yet opposed to its content as if that content were a being; it is merely on the verge of abandoning its content, of losing its equilibrium in order to assert itself in its autonomy and its solitude. At this point, having reached the stage of abstract morality, consciousness will seek to legitimize everything that has appeared to it to be immediately valid; it will seek to conceive of itself in this immediacy. This point marks the separation (*Trennung*) between the singular and the universal, the isolation of the individual, who will no longer be concerned with anything but his personal salvation at the expense of that of the State, which for him has lost the force of law.

This concern for the self (*Sorge für sich*), which already foreshadows the idolatry of modern subjective consciousness, ironic consciousness, comes into view at the time of the Peloponnesian war. It is a fundamental factor in the decomposition of Greek life owing to the decisive importance that all Greeks attribute to their own participation in that life. The concern for self is criminal (*Verbrechen*); it interrupts the continuity of the universal principle and destabilizes the mores of the public. For if this disruption is not actually caused by the valorization of individual consciousness (with each individual taking responsibility for his own morality), it is nevertheless contemporaneous with the appearance of abstract morality and is closely related to it: for Hegel, all evil and misfortune always reside in separation. In other words, Socrates, who participated in the three Peloponnesian wars (as Hegel reminds us insistently), could not have made his appearance on the stage of history and philosophy without this general breakdown of mores, but, conversely, mores would not have become unstable if, in that era, the new perspective of abstract morality inaugurated by Socrates had not opened up and produced the feeling that 'everyone has to look after his own morality' (p. 409). Socrates' specific philosophy – to teach everyone to turn back to his own consciousness in search of the universal mind, the good and the true that have disappeared as realities – can thus be understood only in the overall context to which it belongs, a context that alone renders his singular destiny intelligible and necessary and that transforms his life, which is reinscribed and internalized within the history of Athens and the history of the development of Mind, into a destiny.

And because the discovery of 'Socrates' is part of a larger context that surpasses it, the best way – indeed, the only way – to comprehend 'his' principle is to turn to his successor and disciple Plato: the famous Platonic reminiscence according to which 'what man seems to receive he only remembers' (p. 411) is in fact, in Hegel's view, only an amplified variation on a Socratic theme. As interpreted by Hegel, it signifies that man can learn *nothing*. Virtue is not the only thing he cannot learn; virtue is merely an example of man's overall inability to receive anything at all from the outside, passively, the way wax receives the imprint of a form.[81] He only appears to learn what is in fact contained in the very nature of Mind, the eternal and truly universal in-itself-and-for-itself. If man believes that everything comes from without, it is because Mind is initially alienated, does not recognize itself in the external realm. Nothing derives from that realm, however; everything simply begins there. The external realm merely gives impetus to the development of Mind.

Owing to Plato's mediation (and this is why Hegel needed to turn to him) the Socratic principle – an external shock that might also be deemed necessary to the development of the mind of his disciple – is more easily translatable into Hegelian language. As reappropriated by Hegel, this principle, according to which nothing would have validity for man if Mind did not bear witness to it, did not make it its own, is transformed into the principle of Mind's subjectivity and freedom, into the Hegelian principle of reappropriation. Moreover, Hegel continues to put this principle to work for his own benefit by translating it yet again, this time into Biblical language. '"Flesh of my flesh, and bone of my bone", that which is held by me as truth and right is spirit of my spirit [*Geist von meinem Geiste*]' (p. 410). This translation, which emphasizes the continuity between Platonism and Judeo-Christianism, which are both animated by the same principle of spiritual reappropriation (Nietzsche, in his own way, will turn Christianity into Platonism for the use of the people), reveals in particular that Hegel feels that he is on his home ground with Socrates, as he was already, earlier, with Heraclitus[82], and he revels in the situation. By and large, Hegel feels quite at home among the Greeks, in the big family dwelling of Mind, and this is because the Greeks felt at home in transforming, elaborating, overturning the rudiments of their culture that had come to them from outside, from abroad, using these rudiments as raw material that provided the impetus for their spiritual development. They proceeded to transform that material until it was entirely their own, thus making it analogous to the Greeks themselves.

Hegel reappropriates the earlier culture for himself. Taking all that is 'foreign' to him, he gives it the value of law and truth, transforming it into mind of his mind, flesh of his flesh. Only such a metamorphosis can free him to experience pleasure and to feel perfectly at home elsewhere, outside, abroad, particularly in Greece. For 'philosophy is being at home with self, just like the homeliness of the Greek; it is man's being at home in his mind, at home with himself' (p. 152).[83] That is why Hegel, suffering from 'homesickness' from the beginning of his history of philosophy, turns nostalgically toward Greece, the birthplace and homeland of philosophical science and art, the source of everything that offers satisfaction to spiritual life, a place where 'we' can find our own origins and homeland, because the Greeks, owing to this movement of spiritual reappropriation, really did have, for their part, a homeland.

It is more particularly in the Greeks' philosophy that 'we' find ourselves again in our own country, not because we are in their land but because we are truly in our own, because philosophy is to be truly at home, in one's Mind, in one's birthplace, and Mind is free of all particularity. That is why Greek philosophy, a specific stage in the development of Mind, the very first stage, that of beauty, also represents philosophy as a whole as Mind's being at home with itself. Because even though Mind is not from the outset fully at home or with itself, and even though there exists a gap, a lack of correspondence between Mind proper and its various manifestations, there is a history and a history of philosophy whose driving force is this nostalgic movement of reappropriation, of return to oneself. But this history of Mind (its Odyssey) is a false history, because Mind's exit from itself, its voyage outside itself, oriented and driven by nostalgia for its own country, brings it back even before it has truly left; Mind is always already at home. (In this Mind can be compared with the heroes of the cultural novels of a Novalis or a Hoffmann.[84] These protagonists leave their birthplace, travel throughout the world, have narrow escapes and acquire wisdom and reason through their detour outside the self. Molded by the experience of life, they always come back home, restored to themselves at last. Thus the history of Mind, its dialectical development, sublates the negative – that is, anything that separates consciousness from itself, divides itself from itself – in order to allow it to find itself again, definitively, in its homeland, in complete proximity and identity of self to self.)

From this contemplative movement, oriented by the values of ownership, propriety, proximity of self to self, and homeland, Socrates and his outside-to-inside reversal marks the emergence of self- awareness. By making man the measure of all things, a formula that Socrates understands in a totally different way from Protagoras (for Socrates, man is not a set of particular interests, passions and desires but a thinking being, 'a spirit which acts in a universal manner' [p. 410]), Socrates in fact invites men to turn inward, toward what properly belongs to them, toward what is really and truly theirs. For there is property and property. The passions also belong, indeed, to our inside, to our own inward selves, but they are proper to us only in a natural (*aber nur auf natürliche Weise unser eigenes*), particular and contingent way – and thus they are not proper. The true 'inward' (*wahrhaftes Innere*), the authentic property toward which Socrates directs men, is the universal 'inward' of thought; it awakens them not to consciousness of their own particular interests, as the Sophists do, but to universal moral consciousness, where what is subjective is objective as well.

Socrates inaugurates this movement of return toward the self in the moral realm, for moral philosophy is his overriding concern, as Hegel notes on more than one occasion (pp. 388, 392). Socrates' basic line of questioning concerns the essence of the good, which he relates to people's actions and needs in particular. Under the terms of the reflective, abstract morality that begins with Socrates, individuals may no longer simply do the appropriate thing unconsciously the way they could under natural morality. They need to know what is appropriate and to act accordingly with full consciousness; they must make choices. They must know what good is, must know that the human subject is good, that goodness is its character, its virtue, its *habitus*. Goodness is defined in relation to subjectivity which, given individuals endowed with decision-making capacity, is linked to the inner universal principle. But while this turning inward is necessary, it is nevertheless doubly dangerous. On the one hand, by emphasizing choice, by making consciousness the agency of decision-making, it leads to modern crime, to the absolute self-sufficiency of ironic consciousness, the pride of mastery, the presumptuous and arbitrary folly of human will, which, in the excellence it attributes to its own choices and to itself, believes that it is equal to God. On the other hand, because Socrates is situated at the very beginning of the reversal, his idea of the good still remains indeterminate; its defining feature is simply formal, abstract subjectivity in general. Socrates anticipates and announces Kant rather than Hegel; in other words, he foreshadows the countless false representations and oppositions of modern culture, which draws a line between good, virtue, and practical reason (everything that makes up the abstract moral realm) on the one hand, and evil, sensibility, penchants and passions (which are equally abstract) on the other.

Contesting this double abstraction and going beyond Kant, Hegel appeals to Aristotle. Once again, Hegel depicts Aristotle as having seen things more clearly, as having genuinely anticipated him, Hegel, by demonstrating in his *Nicomachean Ethics* (VI, 13) that the a-logical, feeling side of the soul, *pathos*, cannot be eliminated from virtue any more than rational discernment, or custom, *ethos*, can. In other words (in Hegelian language), virtue cannot do without the heart (*wollendes Gemüt*), the effective subjective reality without which the good lacks the opportunity to come into being, to be realized. To define virtue as discernment alone is to cut it off from substantiality or matter, from the natural spirit of a people; it is to forget reality as custom (*ethos*) and as *pathos*. Yet *ethos* and *pathos* are indispensable to the realization of the universal principle, which operates through the activity of the consciousness of individual beings, thus through individual passions, and these, while they do not constitute the true 'proper nature' of man, are nonetheless necessary for effective action.

Aristotle was right, then, to reproach Socrates for depicting virtue, even though it implies discernment, as a science. For virtue is not *logos,* although it is accompanied by *logos.* Translated into Hegelian language, we may say that the universal principle indeed begins with thought; the universal element of the goal indeed belongs to thought, but virtue cannot be reduced to thought, for it also implies the heart, individuality in action, the natural mind.

Since Socrates grasped only the first ingredient of virtue, the universal principle of thought, Hegel undertakes to examine this principle more closely in the second part of his discussion of the Socratic principle.

b) The ambivalence of the universal principle
The Socratic universal is a *Janus bifrons.* It has two faces, one positive and one negative: that is what Hegel *declares* at the outset. But what he *does* tends to bring the negative face into relief, because Socrates is still not yet Plato, the Plato of *The Republic.* For in the last analysis, if Socrates was condemned to death, the fault must lie in the dominant side of his principle, its negative face.

The *positive side* consists in Socrates' elevation of the moral consciousness of his time to the level of perception or discernment: a gesture possible only because Socrates – and here is where his greatness lies – became conscious of the unsettled state of natural morality as it had been delineated. Socrates represents – in a good translation – the power of the concept that suppresses and dissolves the being, the immediate validity of mores and moral laws. The power of this concept is thus entirely permeated by the negative element, even where discernment recognizes real law positively as law. Through discernment, real law, in so far as it has objective lineaments, is deprived of its supposed truth and universality. Only the universal in itself, absolute good, is true, and truly positive; but since in its formal purity the latter turns out to be devoid of any reality, since it remains empty and indeterminate, the positive universal results solely in fact from the *negation* of the particular whose reflection has brought the limitation to light. Through its rigorous formal character, the 'positive' Socratic universal is at least as dangerous as if it were purely negative, since it emphasizes only what is lacking in the particular, which from that point on lacks all solidity. In any case, it would be more dangerous, according to Hegel, than the inconsistency of immediate consciousness, which considers the particular as limited as the absolute, for immediate consciousness finds its own unconscious correctives in natural morality, in the whole of common life. To be sure, these spontaneous correctives do not always work very well and in that case can give rise to excesses, collisions (like the ones, for example, that led to Socrates' death sentence?) – unfortunate but rare, unusual, exceptional collisions that confirm the rule.

Socrates paid the ultimate price, one might say, for having brought to light a dangerous principle, more dangerous than the principle of which he was one of the rare non-innocent victims: for if the particular is deficient, the universal as abstract in itself is not what has validity either.

Hegel has just indirectly justified the condemnation of Socrates. At this point in the text, as if he is feeling guilty, he takes a step backward and appeals to Xenophon's *Memorabilia,* suggesting that in this instance Xenophon is a more accurate and reliable source than Plato[85]. Xenophon's text provides the best illustration, Hegel indicates, of the danger represented by abstract formalism, for Xenophon had a good grasp of the two-faced nature of the Socratic universal, the indissoluble link it assured between positive and negative. Thus immediately after he has underscored the negative aspect of Socrates, Hegel turns to Xenophon, a source that Kierkegaard will later discredit on the grounds that it merely reflects the petty bourgeois realist or 'positive' mind of its author. But might not Hegel's move actually be, on the contrary, a way of attempting – on the pretext of offering an illustrative example – to cover over the negative face with the positive one? What the example shows, in fact, is that Socrates was less guilty than one might have thought, for he did not limit himself to the purely abstract universal (in other words, he prefigures, but is not identical with, Kant, Hegel's own *bête noire,* who would for his part have richly deserved to drink the hemlock). He showed young people that the universal principle constitutes the good and the true in the objective sphere to which in the last analysis he always returned. By turning to Xenophon, who is not overly concerned with Platonic or Hegelian dialectical subtleties, Hegel thus does something quite different from illustrating the argument he has just made. As if struck by remorse for reducing the double-faced Socratic universal to a one-sided negativity, but also for the sake of his argument, he restores (or adds) the positive face; this is the only way he can avoid portraying Socrates as a pure 'ironist' in the modern sense of the term, or in Kierkegaard's fashion.

According to Hegel, Xenophon shows that Socrates, without torturing his young interlocutors or confusing their minds with subtleties, taught them the good in the clearest and most obvious way, the way least open to doubt, the most 'realistic' and concrete way there is. In *Memorabilia,* IV, 4, Socrates urges Hippias to obey the laws, despite the fact that the people themselves acknowledge that laws are not absolute, for they are often changed. 'Now this is the one side in which Socrates looks away from the contradiction and makes laws and justice, as they are accepted by each individual, to be the affirmative content. But if we here ask what these laws are, they are, we find, just those which have a value at some one time, as they happen to be present in the State and in the idea; at another time they abrogate themselves as determined, and are not held to be absolute' (p. 416). In this way Socrates restored an affirmative content to the abstract universal, a content that is even more positive than immediate concrete consciousness, since the latter unconsciously secretes its own correctives, whereas Socrates asserts the absolute value of law as such. He urges people to obey the law whether it is just or unjust in its specific applications; the necessary obverse of his formalism would be absolute 'realism' and 'positivism'.

In any case, the positive face cannot be dissociated from the negative face, with which it forms a system. The negative face is illustrated by another passage in Xenophon's *Memorabilia* (IV, 2). Here, in order to incite Euthydemus to use discernment, Socrates unsettles the certainty of his interlocutor's opinions on the subject of the just and the unjust, by showing that the various behaviours (lies, deception, destruction of property and freedom – and each of these examples will take on a life of its own) can be placed in either category, thus bringing to light the mutual contradiction of the contents. But Socrates, who is neither a Sophist nor an 'ironist', does not stop with this negative aspect. His goal is not to overturn everything. If he challenges the laws, it is the better to establish the universality of obedience to them, a formalism of obedience: for laws as such do not lie, do not deceive, even if true discernment can identify their limits, their finite scope. Because Socratic discernment has an indeterminate content, it leads not to the contingent suppression of laws but rather to formalist obedience. To train young people to be discerning is thus not to corrupt them, not to make them grasp the limits of the validity of real laws and keep them fixated on this negative aspect. From Xenophon's perspective, the time spent conversing with Socrates, far from teaching young people to challenge the force of the laws, instead helps them strengthen their own character. The accusation of corruption may have been leveled against Socrates simply because many of his followers turned away: 'many no longer approached him'.[86]

But if there was widespread infidelity to Socrates, it was because to a certain extent he made infidelity possible, and even necessary. After all, by arousing consciousness of the conditional character of the content of the laws, he contributed to challenging the solidity that they derive from their universality. Because the positive element that Socrates puts in the place of what is solid is only an indeterminate universal whose definition remains to be filled in, the *first result* to which the formation of consciousness leads is indeed the disruption of custom and law. In other words, the first result is a negative one, just as, at the gnoseological level, the first result of the Socratic method was aporia, a disturbance of consciousness. In each case, the negative aspect wins out in the first instance.

If Xenophon fails to highlight the negative moment, it is because he himself is a faithful disciple whose work is intended to justify Socrates, to cleanse him of all suspicion. But the moment is amply developed by Aristophanes, to whom the reader is now referred.

For, after attempting to 'save' Socrates from unilateral negativity, thanks to and in collaboration with Xenophon, Hegel swings back, pendulum-fashion, to Socrates' negative aspect; he turns this time to the source that best succeeded in apprehending Socratic philosophy through its negative side alone, namely, Aristophanes. The playwright's attitude anticipates that of the Athenian people, who 'likewise certainly recognized his negative methods in condemning him' (p. 426). In keeping with the stages of the dialectic process, then, Hegel validates one source at the expense of another, oscillates between one and the other as he oscillates between a positive Socrates and a negative Socrates, putting forward now one face, now the other of this *Janus bifrons*.

However, before he turns to Aristophanes, Hegel feels compelled to justify – in the mode of denegation – his appeal to a source that has been discredited by certain German historians such as Ast. As a comic author, Aristophanes has been accused of contributing with malice to the unjust condemnation of an honest man. This is a two-pronged charge, both gnoseological and moral; Hegel refutes it by turning it against the accusers and accusing them in turn, by virtue of their excessive seriousness, of being so lacking in seriousness that they neglected as profound and serious a source as Aristophanes' comedy – a source, in other words, that is in perfect harmony with the dialectical movement of history, with my (Hegel's) fictionalized Socrates, with my conception of philosophy, morality, politics, and also – even if I, Hegel, do not proclaim this aloud – with my phallocratism.

First of all, there was nothing unusual about portraying a great man on stage during his lifetime. In addition to Socrates, Aristophanes depicts Aeschylus, Euripides, Athenian generals, Athenians in general, the Athenian people personified. He does not even hesitate to portray the gods on stage, and none of his contemporaries – at least not Socrates, if we are to believe Diogenes Laertius[87] – seems to have taken offense at such a profanation, at a degree of license that would be unthinkable today. No one can find this astonishing but certain historians who, lacking a sense of history and endowed with a German, all too German,[88] seriousness, are incapable of appreciating the freedom of the Greek mind.

Furthermore (here is the second premise of the 'melting-pot reasoning' in which Hegel indulges in order to exonerate himself), Socrates is perhaps not as honest, as innocent, as he seems, even if, as I (Hegel) have shown, he is neither a rogue nor an assassin. Had he been perfectly innocent or wholly corrupt, he would not have been worthy of representation either on a tragic or a comic stage. For, to borrow an expression used by Nietzsche,[89] who agrees with Hegel on this point, in condemning Aristophanes, modern Germans simply that they have completely misunderstood the essence of the comic, Aristophanes' comedy, and *The Clouds* in particular. That play may have helped condemn Socrates, but not without good reasons, not *without reason*. Contrary to what modern Germans may think, Aristophanes is neither a buffoon nor a practical joker nor a superficial jokester who makes Socrates look ridiculous with the casual, frivolous aim of simply making the Athenian public laugh.

The Germans, in their supposed seriousness, mistakenly believe that there is a simple answer to the question 'Why do people laugh?' This viewpoint is narrow and simplistic, for not all laughter is the same: 'In general, nowhere can more contradiction be found than in the things that people laugh at'.[90] What is truly comic must be distinguished from what is purely and simply ridiculous; what elicits laughter must be distinguished from any action devoid of substance by virtue of its simple emptiness. Of course human vices and absurdities or the most banal instances of ineptitude can make people laugh. Laughter may stem from a sense of superiority, from mockery, scorn, or despair, but there is nothing truly comic in any of these forms. The truly comic has more profound requirements: it simply demolishes what is 'inherently null, a false and contradictory phenomenon'.[91] By its very nature, comic action depends on contrasts, on a contradiction between something that is true in itself and an individual realization of that truth. For example, a comic situation arises when individuals who have conceived grandiose goals and great ambitions turn out to be particularly ill-adapted instruments for accomplishing their own aims. A contradiction between the goal and the individual, the action and the character, thus destroys any possibility of achievement: this is the case with Aristophanes' *Women in Parliament,* in which the women, capricious, unstable, and passionate by nature (in his speculative profundity, Aristophanes certainly hit his mark!), turn out to be totally inappropriate instruments for accomplishing the lofty, sublime (virile!) goal they had laughably set for themselves: creating a new constitution for the State.

Comedy depends by nature on a contradiction. Akin in this respect to tragedy, comedy therefore requires (even more than tragedy does) a conclusion in the course of which neither of the two opposing entities, neither the substantial nor the subjective, is destroyed. On this point Hegel opposes Kant once again. For the latter, the comic genre cannot belong to the fine arts, for 'the object of [beautiful art] must always show proper worth in itself, and hence requires a certain seriousness in the presentation, as taste does in the act of judging'.[92] It stems solely from the art of pleasing, and has nothing to do, *a fortiori*, with morality or reason. For Hegel, comedy, the obverse of tragedy (with which it maintains a relation of close solidarity), is worthy of being counted among the authentic arts, the arts of *reason*. On the one hand, in fact, it presents the triumph of the rational, which always wins out over foolishness, over all the unreasonable aspects of reality; on the other hand (and this is something that 'rigid understanding' can never comprehend), it also safeguards its opposite, subjectivity. Nor can the truly comic exist if the subject has to feel unhappy or lost once his project has failed, no matter what petty and insignificant goals he may pursue with apparent seriousness and complicated devices: the comic is present only if, confronted with the collapse of all finitude, subjectivity preserves its freedom and remains sure of itself, behaves in sovereign fashion with respect to the appearances of the real, maintains its full serenity and good humor. There is no comic, one might say, without humor in the Freudian sense of the term, without a Superego strong enough to console the Ego no matter what vicissitudes it encounters, strong enough to spare the Ego any suffering by shoring up its narcissism, which remains intact.

'The comical as such implies an infinite light-heartedness and confidence felt by someone raised altogether above his own inner contradiction and not bitter or miserable in it at all: this is the bliss and ease of a man who, being sure of himself, can bear the frustration of his aims and achievements. A narrow and pedantic mind is least of all capable of this when for others his behaviour is laughable in the extreme'.[93]

It is clear, then, that a 'comic' source, with a comic thus reinscribed in speculative dialectics, can be taken seriously by Hegel. With very Germanic seriousness, his utterly flat and sterile dialectical flair that has little use for gratuitous jokes, banter, mockery, or the purely ridiculous, succeeds in detecting the profundity and fruitful seriousness of Aristophanes' comedy.

Aristophanes is right to mock, for his mockery and his jokes, unlike those of modern Romantic irony, do not attack what is respectable and eminent for the purpose of profanation. His mockery is rational and substantial; it conforms to true comedy, which shows how men and things, in their ostentation, are undone from within. It is based – and this is what makes it profound – on the contradictions that are immanent in things themselves. It is based, in other words, on genuine irony, on the contradiction that the thing mocked already incorporates. 'Aristophanes, for example, did not make fun of what was truly moral in the life of the Athenians, or of their genuine philosophy, true religious faith, and serious art. On the contrary, . . . what he exhibits is sophistry, the deplorable and lamentable character of tragedy, flighty gossip, litigiousness, etc., and the aberrations of the democracy . . .'[94] In short, Aristophanes highlights the self-destructive foolishness of anything that runs counter to the true reality of the State, religion or art. If he does not make people laugh in a sacrilegious manner, at the expense of the gods, the 'great' men or the Athenian people whom he puts on stage, it is because underneath his hearty laughter lies the profound seriousness of his patriotism, which is identical to the seriousness of dialectics – or to its irony (which is the same thing; and the pinnacle of irony is precisely to have oneself taken seriously – or vice versa).

In any event, it behooves us to take Aristophanes 'seriously', according to Hegel: his appearance among the Athenian people has the same necessity as that of the other historical figures, the sublime Pericles, the frivolous Alcibiades, the divine Sophocles or the moral Socrates, all admirable or laughable figures, heroes of tragedy or comedy (for both genres are equally essential and necessary to the Athenians).

Aristophanes, who specialized in making people laugh, and Pericles, who decided he would never laugh again once he became head of state, both belonged to that circle of stars. For dialectical seriousness ignores differences between genres; all genres (tragic, comic, frivolous, sublime, divine, moral, and so on) are equally necessary and equally destined to disappear, and they are made equal by the profound irony of the dialectics that lines up opposites back to back and in the final analysis carries everything – except absolute Mind – away in derision. So you may as well go ahead and laugh, so long as your laughter is not insane (senseless), miserable or false, clownish or farcical, so long as you know why you are laughing[95]; in short, so long as your laugh is a 'good' one, is rational, can be internalized within the system, can be supervised by philosophy and enlisted by politics. While Hegel recognizes the heterogeneity of laughter and even the heterogeneity internal to any instance of laughter, by privileging one single form of laughter as good and true he in fact degrades and scorns all the others, all those that might threaten to disturb his system. The laughter of the profound and enlightened patriot Aristophanes is worth more than anyone else's, and it is equivalent to the absence of laughter in the sublime Pericles. For, anticipating its triumph in reality, Aristophanes makes Reason triumph on stage, along with the reason of State. Nevertheless, he is not a politician and not a tragic author; if he remains an author of comedies, it is because, while his plays preserve reason, their conclusions at the same time safeguard the subjectivity that takes pleasure in itself even in failure, because he shows the sure, happy enjoyment of a people that abandons itself to itself. 'We enjoy in Aristophanes this side of the free Athenian spirit, this perfect enjoyment of itself in loss, this untroubled certainty of itself in all miscarriage of the result in real life, and this is the height of humor' (p. 428). Aristophanes offers a supreme form of comedy which, although it excludes insane laughter, is perhaps not, through the blindness to the contradicting of reality that it implies on the part of subjectivity, foreign to the profound laughter and enjoyment characteristic of the insane[96]; comedy could thus offer the spectator this latter form of laughter and enjoyment as well, for the duration of the spectacle.

Thus Hegel can use Aristophanes – *The Clouds* in particular – to shore up his position. In his summary of the play,[97] Hegel mentions only the elements that serve to illustrate and confirm his thesis; he fails to take into account – and Kierkegaard will reproach him for his neglect – the staging, the difference between the chorus (the Clouds properly speaking) and the characters, in short all the elements that he views as literary and thus as negligible.[98] Aristophanes' play attests judiciously to the negative aspect of the Socratic universe: provided that, after summarizing, interpreting and analyzing the text, the reader proceeds to exclude every element that does not stem from the highest form of comedy and that is not truly inscribable within dialectics (for example, the fact that Aristophanes makes fun of Socrates for his preoccupation with such basic research as the distance a flea can jump – a detail that does not correspond to any historical reality). Although the play's representation of Socrates is false, it nevertheless proves the accuracy with which Aristophanes managed to grasp Socratic philosophy.

In a more general way, Aristophanes' play seems to 'embarrass' Hegel, who declares that it does not correspond to the highest form of comedy, the naive comedy that is characteristic of the author and that he has just described. *The Clouds* is a play with a thesis; it is destined in advance, as it were, but perhaps not only in advance, to illustrate the Hegelian thesis. It stages contradiction with a specific intention: to show how Socrates' moral strivings lead to the opposite of his aims. It seeks to show, too, how Socrates' disciples, including Strepsiades, make useful discoveries, or so they believe, and then watch them backfire: specifically, they acquire a higher discernment that allows them to recognize the inanity of laws taken as truths by naive consciousness. By learning dialectics from Socrates, Strepsiades learns to use argumentative thrusts to overturn specific aspects of the law, for example, those governing the payment of debts. When his creditors arrive, he pays them with good reasons he has learned at Socrates' school. But he who laughs last laughs best. Strepsiades sends his son to study with Socrates; the son behaves unbecomingly towards his father, demonstrating by equally good reasons why he has every right to beat the old man up – a conclusion that his father fails to find amusing. Henceforth Strepsiades curses dialectics, returns to his old habits, and ends up setting fire to the master's Thinkery.

By pushing Socrates' dialectics to its extreme consequences, Aristophanes does it no harm; he merely shows that he has a profound understanding of its negative side, even though he has described it, 'after his own way' (p. 430; *nach seiner Weise freilich*), as Hegel indicates in a small addition that points toward the scrap heap of dialectics, the 'literary' aspect – a negligible vestige that Hegel points out in passing and then ignores, for to make something of it might topple his entire system. This vestige nevertheless marks the entire distance between Aristophanes' play and the Hegelian 'thesis', a distance that for his own reasons Hegel prefers not to measure.

The story of Strepsiades thus 'illustrates' the following phenomenon: when the individual subject, moral consciousness, is endowed with decision-making capacity, in conformity with the Socratic principle, and when the decision is bad (and that is the danger), it will necessarily have unfortunate consequences. Because the freedom acquired by Socratic dialectics is an empty freedom, is *whatever* presents itself to consciousness, the manner in which that freedom is conceptualized as universal, its fulfillment, is, in Aristophanes, interest deprived of consciousness; the mind that is only the negative consciousness of the content of the laws is filled with the bad mind of Strepsiades and his son. The formal universal principle, indifferent to all definite content, thus disrupts the uncultivated mind, leads to the suppression of the truth of the laws (the need to pay one's debts, or to respect one's father) to the benefit of the freedom of consciousness that dominates all content. Consciousness has become free but empty, and, along with its contents, it has lost the representation of truth.

Thus *The Clouds* did not provide Hegel simply with clouds, that is, something he had always already known: Aristophanes' profundity, while it resides for Hegel in the anticipation and confirmation of his own thesis, nevertheless has by that very token been reduced, one may say, to the depth of a void. For, in the final analysis, the detour by way of this comedy has only been a recourse, and a return to the always-already known; it has served only to illustrate a stage in a speculative thesis of the highest seriousness. Hegel's move outside himself has been, as always, a false exit; it has merely allowed him to return home, in the greatest proximity of self to self, and to enjoy, if not to laugh at, that state, before leading him to the third point of the development of the Socratic principle.

c) *The actualizing principle of the universal: demon or genius*
The Clouds show that the first step toward becoming a spiritual conscious-ness has an aspect that is negative, therefore dangerous. The absence of a positive truth can be understood in one of two ways: either as lack of the real moment of activity for the freedom manifested (Aristotle had already offered this reading), or as absence of content.

But Socrates has begun to take the second step. To a certain extent, he has filled the universal with content through a return to obedience to laws. One might say that Strepsiades made such a return at the end of *The Clouds;* in that case, Strepsiades would represent Reason, except that for Socrates, unlike the ridiculous old man, the return to obedience is accompanied by discernment of the truth of individual laws. Hegel cannot actually fill the intolerable void of the Socratic principle with which, if we are to believe Kierkegaard, *The Clouds* would leave us – a void where everything dissolves in clouds or goes up in smoke – except by moving beyond Aristophanes and returning implicitly, in his customary oscillating manner, to Xenophon the 'realist'.

The result, for Socrates, is a contradiction to which Hegel closes his eyes. On the one hand, Socrates' concepts manifest the pure universal principle as the essence in which all determinacy is dissolved; on the other hand, because the universal *must* (*soll*) have a content (but is it Hegel or Socrates who imposes this necessity, or obligation?), Socrates restores its original content. Socrates at once destroys and reinstates that content; he places truth – and here is the positive gain – at the level of the discernment that spiritualizes the old content and gives it a universal, purely formal foundation.

For the Socratic universal is not yet – here is its limit – the essence, the absolutely real universal principle that can contain opposites. Recognition of the universal in its specificity is possible only within a fully coherent system of effective reality. Custom – which is the unique universal mind, the mind of the people – brings a spontaneous correction to the inconsistency that would otherwise obtain if one were to enunciate a given specific content while crediting it with absolute validity. In the case of Socrates, custom is replaced, in its corrective function, by the individual mind, by individuality, by consciousness, the decision-making agency that then disrupts the particulars of law. Whether the individual mind in question is good (Socrates) or bad (Strepsiades and his son), it is now the subject that is the determining factor. What was up to that point unconscious determination becomes conscious decision; the deciding mind is transferred into subjective human consciousness. This is what is beginning to come to light with Socrates.

That is why it is necessary – the dialectical moment requires it – to return to Socrates' own *personality,* in order to ask in this new light how subjectivity appears in Socrates 'himself'. Such a line of questioning is crucial to our understanding of his destiny and his death sentence.

The transfer of decision-making to subjectivity was not without danger, both for Athens and for Socrates, since from that point on decision-making would be conditioned by the contingency of the individual character of the decision-maker. Now, while Socrates, as we have seen, was a good 'character', or a good mind, a noble, plastic individuality, and while he was surrounded mainly by noble individuals whose own characters were strengthened (as Xenophon tells us) through contact with him, the fact remains that some of his contacts turned out badly. Critias and Alcibiades – the 'frivolous' Alcibiades, who was nevertheless an essential element among the Athenians (although they did not know this) – were considered traitors, corrupting influences, tyrants, by their contemporaries. Although both were endowed with brilliant natures (*genialistichsten Naturell*), they were nonetheless badly inspired by their genius, to say the least. Their most serious flaw was perhaps that each believed in his own genius; he trusted his own inspiration, his individual mind, the absolute validity of his own perception. Now, Socrates bears some responsibility for such a belief, since it is with him that individual subjectivity took the form of *genius* or *demon*: through contact with him, as if by magnetic communication and direct assimilation, fascinated by the great hypnotist, their 'evil demon', Critias and Alcibiades thought that they too were possessed. They believed that they had a genius, a good genius in whose inspiration they thought they could trust enough to make decisions running counter to the ones that Socrates' demon had inspired in him. They became unfaithful to Socrates while remaining fully faithful to the principle that he had hypnotically instilled in them. By his own genius, he had inculcated them with his own discovery, just as the mother, the inspiring genius of the child she carries in her womb and with whom she forms a single substantial identity, shares with him her 'own' contents.

As we have seen, Hegel proposes the analogy with the child in the mother's womb in *Philosophy of Mind* to describe the hypnotic relation and others similar to it, a magical relation of dependency and sharing, a relation without relation in which the other is not distinct from the same, nor the subjective from the objective, nor the inside from the outside. Now, if we are to understand the nature of the Socratic 'genius' appropriately, without mistaking it, as some do, for a sort of guardian angel, the anthropological analogy must be retained. The analogy also allows us to distinguish the Socratic 'genius' from moral consciousness, which is at once a representation of the universal individuality of the self-confident mind and also universal truth. Socrates' demon simply represents the other side of the coin, the mind in its individuality; it is the mark of the mind's divided state, its native finitude, its passivity, its deficiency. In a representation by Socrates' genius, the deficiency proper to the universal principle is compensated for in a singular, deficient manner, so that it looks like an eccentricity; it appears to be peculiar to the atopical character known as Socrates, one of his fantasies or superstitions, a product of his unhealthy imagination. As with the ecstatic catalepsy that struck Socrates repeatedly, as we know, and that is of a piece with his system, Hegel strives to remove the peculiarity and thus to strip Socrates of what the philosopher thought was most properly his own, 'his' genius. Hegel does this by depicting Socrates' singular pathological state as a necessary disease of Mind, an affliction that was required at this precise dialectical moment in the Mind's development, the moment of its very first conversion. Socrates' way of seeing was necessary at that particular moment, with one caveat: because Socrates – this is the price of genius – did not yet have Hegel's perfect health, he was unaware of that necessity; he believed – owing to his genius once again, but mistakenly – that his genius was a peculiar characteristic of a single individual. It did not appear to him as it really was, in its necessity;

its true nature can be grasped only 'after the fact', in the final moment of Mind's development.

If the Socratic stage is the stage of subjective, conscious, internal decision-making, the decision-making in question nevertheless takes on an external, non-conscious form, that of knowledge allied with an absence of consciousness. This is precisely what a demon or a genius represents. The representation is bizarre because it emanates from an unconscious consciousness or subjectivity, from something that is oneself without being oneself, something that decides in one's place, alienates one maternally, and renders one's will heteronomous, since it is this genius which impels one to act without being an external force. As peculiar as this representation may be, it is nevertheless not entirely unique. It occurs in other forms and at other 'moments', in more or less pathological states, in phenomena such as seeing the past or the future at the moment of death, in states of catalepsy, hypnotic somnambulism or hypnosis – which are all states of dissociation of consciousness in which the subject is in the power of a different subject that fills him with its own 'contents'.

Despite the absolute and summary denegations that these 'enigmatic' phenomena provoke, Hegel strives to reduce their obscurity and to defend their plausibility, as he does in *Philosophy of Mind* against the slaves of categories of understanding who view such 'panic' states as illusory or deceptive. Dissociative states arouse feelings of panic for more than one reason. On the one hand, it is difficult to admit the existence of knowledge of anything but the present, that which is currently present to consciousness; on the other hand, it is difficult to accept the principle that a given individual consciousness – or rather unconsciousness – might be privileged or chosen, might be the only one to have 'revelations', and that these revelations might concern purely individual problems.

If Hegel strives to show the possibility and the reality of the forms of knowledge that can accompany an absence of consciousness, it is because the Socratic genius is related to these forms, and because the history of consciousness depends upon their necessary morbidity. The Socratic genius for its part also turns consciousness away from its real interest, the universal principle, in favor of individual interests, which as such are derisory and insignificant. This is easier to grasp once we recognize that Socrates' genius is nothing other than his personal oracle; it functions as an internal replacement for the earlier decision-making agency, the external oracle. Hegel can bring about such an identification, which is crucial for his understanding of Socrates' condemnation to death, because he refers only to Xenophon (*Memorabilia*, Book I), and Xenophon is the only source that presents the demon as a positive force. Kierkegaard and Nietzsche draw instead on Plato, who describes the demon as an instinctual but inhibiting force; they depict the genius as a negative force that is in keeping, in Kierkegaard's case, with the image of an ironic, strictly negative Socrates, and, in Nietzsche's case, with that of a decadent Socrates inspired by a will to nothingness, of which the vital paradox of a negative instinct is one of the most glaring symptoms.

Now, according to Xenophon as 'translated' by Hegel, the external oracle played the role of spontaneous corrective to the universality of laws. The Greek people turned to oracles in cases where concrete decisions were required. Because the subject did not yet know that his interiority was sufficiently independent and free to make decisions and take responsibility for them (such a consciousness of infinite freedom and subjective responsibility belongs exclusively to the modern age), he necessarily allowed himself to be determined by something external, 'the oracle'. The Greeks consulted oracles in particular in connection with issues related to the contingent future and stemming from the uncertainties of that future; they believed that they were thus reserving the most important matters – individual interests, unique situations – for the gods. They deemed it extremely important to find out whether they were going to be happy with a new spouse; whether the power of some relative, a source of delight today, might not be used against them tomorrow; whether there would be a good harvest; whether a given business venture would succeed or fail. These are all questions that we healthy moderns know to be derisory and insignificant in relation to the only true interests, those of the universal principle relating for example to legal institutions, the State, agriculture, or marriage. By bringing about this hierarchical inversion of interests, the Greeks signalled, for 'us', their more or less morbid state of childhood; they allow 'us' to take pleasure, we who owe them so much, in 'our' modern, adult superiority.

Now in situations where the Greeks left decision-making to an external oracle, Socrates confers this responsibility to the interiority that he represents to himself as a personal demon or genius, an internal 'oracle' different from human will. Because man was not yet accustomed to turning back toward the pure interiority of the mind, Socrates initially represented this interiority by means of an external form. The demon (as Plato had seen – but Hegel does not cite Plato, for he gives the Platonic *metaxu* an entirely different meaning) is an intermediary figure: he occupies a middle position between the pure exteriority of the oracle and the pure interiority of the mind.

Socrates' transformation of world history, through which the subject took the place of external oracles and took on decision-making power, was obliged to pass initially through a morbid form of genius, an original disease of the mind still divided from itself; the subject thus had to experience an inversion of centers of interest. This was the price Socrates had to pay for grasping the other side of the universality of Mind, its singularity and its finitude or deficiency.

C. *Socrates' tragic destiny* (pp. 425-48)

Socrates also paid the price through his condemnation to death, since the substitution of his internal oracle for the external ones led to the accusation that he had *introduced new gods into the city-state*. That was one of the two charges against him; the second, a corollary, is that he had corrupted the youth of Athens. Hegel's whole aim is to show that the celebrated condemnation is perhaps not as shocking as 'one' might have thought. Countering the pleasing and edifying tableau offered by the apologists Xenophon and Plato, and opposing the claims of most German historians (Tennemann, for example, whose indignant clamor revealed only the dull, narrow mind that unwittingly confines itself to a single viewpoint, that of the right to abstract moral freedom), Hegel shows that Socrates' death is not purely and simply that of an innocent victim who succumbs to the unwarranted attacks of a crowd that has been aroused by theatrical statements (statements that were not always entirely baseless, moreover, as we have seen). Socrates' condemnation was just and rational, necessary and legal; it was carried out for good reason by the Athenian people as a whole in all its majesty. By allowing truth to be decided by internal consciousness (in the still-deficient form of a genius or internal oracle), Socrates had come into conflict with the mind of the people, with real morality, with what for the Athenians was just, true, solid and established (this is what characterizes his specific dialectical moment); for this reason, the Athenians were obliged to accuse him. They could not have done otherwise: in complete necessity and legitimacy, they took a stand not so much against an individual as against a principle that had become a force of corruption in their eyes. Properly speaking, Socrates' condemnation results not from the content of the charges against him but from Socrates' behaviour in the course of the trial, behaviour that could lead to the suspicion (and readers more subtle or less sympathetic than Hegel, Kierkegaard and Nietzsche, have entertained this suspicion) that Socrates himself was seeking to die.

a) *The first face of his destiny*

So far as the *charges* are concerned, and the way Socrates thought he could defend himself against them, Hegel, without any apologetic intent whatsoever, turns to Plato's and Xenophon's *Apologies*. Once again, he privileges Socrates' 'favorite': only Xenophon, in spite of himself, permits Hegel to justify the charges and to show that Socrates' fate is a necessary consequence of the conflict opposing the new oracle to the old.

In response to the *first charge*, according to Xenophon, Socrates shows that he has not done or said anything impious, that he has always carried out his religious duties at the public altars. He does not deny the existence of the gods, for, unlike the Sophists, or Anaxagoras, he has never undertaken speculative research on nature. As for his 'demon', the inner oracle that offers him personal revelations in such a singular fashion, there is nothing about it that should shock popular belief, which does not take much offense at the even more bizarre devices chosen by its own oracles to make equally personal revelations.

Hegel finds it quite natural that Socrates' apology on this point should 'displease' his judges, as Xenophon reports. Their displeasure can be explained by consious or unconscious psychological laws, universal laws that are valid not only for the still child-like Greeks but also for us moderns, who are healthy adults. In other words, we are not to believe that we can arrange things by attributing Socrates' condemnation to a contingent motive, the bad humor of the judges of his day; the death sentence is not attributable to such circumstantial conditions. No, even contemporary judges would accuse Socrates and would be displeased by his defense. Indeed, in similar cases, judges today behave no differently: they remain incredulous regarding everything having to do with revelations, especially when these purport to concern individual destinies, and they condemn those who seek to exercise the trade of divination (which the Greeks did not yet do). And I, Hegel, remind you, even though I do not think they are right on this point, that the moderns remain skeptical about the phenomenon of hypnosis, for the same reasons.

In any event, the personal and contingent character of the Socratic 'oracle' invites skepticism on two counts. On the one hand, it eludes the grasp of scientific understanding, it does not contribute to the advance of knowledge. On the other hand (and this is the more important reason), it seems to presuppose the divine election of a particular individual, so it arouses envy and jealousy and, consequently, denegation. The democratic spirit of the Greeks in particular ostracized anyone who could be viewed as superior (and this is why that 'idiot', Tennemann, who is ignorant of the most elementary psychology, is quite wrong to be astonished that Socrates was condemned under a democratic regime, not during the reign of the Thirty Tyrants); any incomprehensible personal privilege was deemed unacceptable. The Greeks could not accept the idea that divinity should attach itself to the trivial concerns of individuals: for if we suppose that divinity is capable of prescience – although absolute consciousness knows only the present – it must be capable at a minimum of knowing that the universal principle, the life of entire States, is more important than the particular, which is insignificant, and, for Mind, slated to disappear.

Like an external oracle, Socrates' internal oracle made only individual revelations to him, much less important ones than those made by his thought. The Greeks' incredulity with respect to his demon – a finite and subjective aspect of Mind – was thus comprehensible and lacked seriousness. History was destined to retain, to sublate, only the worthwhile element of the Socratic principle: its universal aspect. In condemning Socrates' demon along with the philosopher himself, the Greeks were thus proceeding along the lines of the world history of Mind. By condemning the demon, they were condemning something that was still tied to their old mind in favor of the only thing that was really new in the Socratic principle, something that was beginning to come to light for everyone (as their later repentance proves): the universal aspect of Mind, which is in fact the only thing in which it is appropriate to believe.

Hegel's demonstration remains awkward nevertheless. On the one hand, in place of the simplistic psychology described by Xenophon (envy or jealousy is the essential motive), he attributes to the judges – the better to justify their displeasure – an overly modern psychology and an awareness of the real hierarchy of interests (the universal wins out over the particular). Moreover, he still refuses to credit the Greeks in general with the same awareness: the Greeks do not hesitate to attribute the most personal revelations to their gods. On the other hand, in the very next paragraph, he declares that the Greeks' representation of oracles incorporated Socrates' way of seeing things, the viewpoint of his demon. For the philosopher, this entity was not yet the voice of a moral consciousness; it had the form of a being distinct from consciousness. The oracle had indeed been transposed from outside to inside, but not yet in the same manner as for 'us' moderns; the transposition was not quite complete. The demon appeared to be a personal trait, an individual peculiarity; it did not have universal individuality. If what the judges could not tolerate was the personal character of the oracle, because they knew that what is truly divine belongs to everyone, we would have to acknowledge that Hegel was not alone (Hegel who, on the strength of his superiority as a modern, always thinks he knows more about the subject than anyone else): Socrates' judges were further advanced in historical terms than the rest of the Greeks, further advanced even than Socrates, who still believed in a personal representation of divinity, in individual oracles. Hegel cannot exit from this aporia except by affirming, finally, that the Greeks did acknowledge personal revelations, but only when they emanated from official non-subjective oracles (trees, Pythia, and so on), not from ordinary private citizens; in the latter case, because they are so extraordinary, they have to be judged false.

Because Hegel fails, despite his best efforts, in his attempt at reappropriation – fails in his attempt to transfer the Athenian tribunal into a modern court of law – he can only conclude, banally and with a certain appearance of self-contradiction, that Socrates' demon – which he nevertheless declares to be in harmony with the Greek view of things (for the Greeks, 'the category of the contingency of consciousness was an existent, a knowledge of it as an oracle' [p. 434; *'Die Griechen hatten eben diese Seite in der Vorstellung'*]) – was rejected because it was a medium of a different kind (*eine andere*

Weise) from the one that prevailed in Greek religion. Yet Hegel dissolves and 'sublates' the contradiction by moving surreptitiously from the demon's personal aspect, which he has emphasized up to this point by referring to Xenophon, to its universal aspect (the other side of the two-faced intermediary). To make this move, Hegel invokes Plato's *Apology*. By shifting sides and sources, he can now assert that there is an irreducible difference between the modes of revelation of external and internal oracles: in declaring Socrates the wisest of men, the Pythian Apollo of Delphi, that knowing god, also pronounced him wiser than his own oracle, Pythia. By exhorting Socrates to know himself, the oracle was not commanding him to turn toward his own personal demon, but toward his own mind, in order to recognize it in its universality; the external oracle was thus inviting Socrates to 'kill' him, Apollo, as a source of truth, and no longer to seek the truth anywhere but within himself.

The revolution Socrates brings about thus does not consist in replacing external oracles with an internal one that would remain homogeneous with them in terms of goals; the search for the revelation of some individual good is a trivial matter. (This is Xenophon's version. Now, Xenophon is a source of truth from which it is appropriate – at least provisionally – to turn away, as from the Delphic oracle, even though in his chapter on the Socratics Hegel declares categorically that, so far as factual knowledge about Socrates and the degree of elaboration of his thought are concerned, 'we have in the main to look to Xenophon' [p. 414]. We are to rely on him, then, provided that we translate him by occasionally using the Platonic dictionary that elevates Xenophon to the level of truth). The real Socratic conversion does not consist in turning away from an external oracle in favor of an internal one, but in overturning the hierarchy of interests, in bringing about the triumph (and it is a triumph that presupposes the death of all oracles) of the universal consciousness of everyone's thought over individual self-consciousness and its certainty. This universal consciousness, rather than the internal oracle, is the new god that Socrates has introduced into the city-state.

Owing to the shift from the subjective to the universal aspect of the 'demon', owing to the sophism or the 'dialectics' (?) of his demonstration, Hegel can conclude that the first charge brought against Socrates by the Athenians was entirely well-founded, and can proceed to the second: *the corruption of young people.*

If we are to believe Xenophon once again, Socrates defended himself against this second charge by invoking the Delphic oracle's well-known declarations on wisdom (declarations that were credible in the eyes of the Greeks and were interpreted by Xenophon as moral wisdom in the ordinary sense), and the exemplary character of his life. The testimony of Melitus and Anytus runs counter to this second justification: they accuse Socrates of inciting young people to obey him rather than their parents, thus of turning them away from their parents and drawing them to himself; in short, Socrates is accused of *seducing* them. On this specific point, according to Hegel translating Xenophon, Socrates was able to respond only indirectly, displacing the question from the moral level to the technical level, stifling the essential point by virtue of the paradigm adopted. By skillfully encouraging the people to return to its own practice of electing the most qualified and competent persons in all areas, he thought he could get them to acknowledge without difficulty that, *a fortiori*, 'he was preferred to parents by the sons in their aspirations after the highest human good' (p. 436), which is an education suited to making them noble men.

Socrates responded to this second charge the way the child does in a modern *Witz* that Hegel might have cited in support of his interpretation, if the comic aspect of the witticism had appeared sufficiently serious to him. A father reminds his child that parents must always be respected and obeyed because they always know more than their children; the child answers by asking why, in that case, James Watt invented the steam engine instead of his father, who by his own account must be more competent and knowledgeable. Socrates sidesteps the question, as in a *Witz*, (this is one of the techniques described in Freud's inventory of jokes, and Xenophon reports in his *Banquet* that Socrates enjoyed word play; Xenophon emphasizes a whole ludic side to Socrates that Hegel neglected – just as he minimized the importance of Socrates' irony – but that Kierkegaard and Nietzsche exploited), as if he were trying to make fun of his judges or else to bring them around to his side by means of laughter in a game where he is risking his life.

In so doing, Socrates pretends to be unaware of the essential reproach (essential for Hegel in any case): his moral interference in the parent-child relationship. According to Hegel, if not according to Socrates' judges (and on this point, for once, Kierkegaard's position is closer to Hegel's than to Nietzsche's), the parent-child relationship must be considered as absolutely inviolate; it must not be interfered with or interrupted by the unnecessary intervention of a third party, especially if that party is a private individual who comes along in a contingent and inappropriate fashion and cuts the umbilical cord. The parent-child relationship is an absolute: it defines children in the family as its members rather than as independent persons in themselves. In such a relationship, the children are still bound to the parents as if by way of the umbilical cord (to say 'as if' is not to indicate a mere analogy, but the very nature of the bond that connects them with one another, a 'visceral' bond through which children constitute with their parents, like the fetus in the mother's womb, a substantial identity of the hypnotic type). The absolute character of the parent-child bond is the real, primary and immediate moral relationship, a relationship constituted entirely of love, trust, and obedience, which Hegel also describes as such in his *Philosophy of Right*.[99]

The tight bond, the family feeling ('children must have the feeling of unity with their parents' [p. 437]), must be respected by education, at least in one of its phases; it must be maintained and cultivated in its purity; it must not be shattered by any outside interference that would turn children away from their parents in a disgusting manner, by seducing them. Undertaking to loosen or destroy this bond that must (*muß*) always be respected, and *a fortiori* if the bond is turned into hatred, contempt, or ill will, is even, Hegel adds, 'the worst thing [das Schlimmeste] which can happen to children in regard to their morality [*auf Sitte*] and their mind [*Gemüt*]. . . . Whoever does this, does injury to morality in its truest form' (ibid.). One might say that, by turning filial love into hatred, the bad teacher, the seducer, sours the mother's milk of natural morality (*Muttermilch der Sittlichkeit*) that nourishes mankind. Hegel uses the metaphor of mother's milk to describe the originary unity and confidence that reign at the heart of (*au sein de*) the family;[100] here again, it is more than a simple metaphor. In *Philosophy of Right*[101] Hegel demonstrates that objective natural morality is first introduced in the form of immediate impressions and without opposition within (*au sein de*) the natural family unit. The family nourishes its members in order to form them (this is the positive side of familial education) by instilling its 'milk' in them, that is, the content, thoughts and actions that it breathes into them or inspires in them by means of 'genius', hypnosis or maternal care – all of which amount to the same thing, as we have seen. Thus the premature loss of one's parents may sour the mother's milk or deprive the infant of it by sudden weaning;[102] it cuts the umbilical cord that attaches the infant to the family too soon; it is a 'great misfortune' (*großes Unglück*) – that is, it may be the object of a tragic action – since the loss of one's parents opens the way to seduction by principles entirely different from, and even in conflict with, the parental ones.

Such a collision of principles is the very driving force of tragedy, as we have seen. Does this mean that for Hegel there is some point at which the loss of parents ceases to be a misfortune? Or at least ceases to be a great, tragic misfortune? Is it a great misfortune only because it happens 'too early'? But in what sense? In a dialectical sense, quite clearly: indeed, since in order to become consciousness the soul has to separate itself from the corporeity with which it initially formed a substantial unity, despite and because of the strength and necessity of the immediate substantial bond, children (sons or daughters: gender difference is not relevant here) have to pull out of the natural unity of the family (*der Sohn wie die Tochter muß sich aus seiner natürlichen Einheit mit der Familie reißen*) and become autonomous. For, as Hegel declares in *Philosophy of Right*, children are not slaves, they are free beings. This is why family education also includes a negative aim: 'raising children out of the instinctive, physical, level on which they are originally, to self-subsistence and freedom of personality and so to the level on which they have power to leave the natural unity of the family'.[103] Although the term for 'leave' used by Hegel (*reißen*) seems to imply that daughters and sons must do violence to themselves in order to pull away from the family unit, this is not the case at all: Hegel adds that separation takes place without fear or force, since it emanates from the heart of the family itself, from the education it provides, from the dialectical necessity of its negative moment.

The negative aim of education within the family contributes to the family's own decomposition, to its necessary self-destruction: because it is natural and internal, familial education, which functions without hostility and without contempt for the family mind and its unity, functions without violence and without constraint. If, to pull away from the family, one must do violence to oneself, the violence in question is of a gentle sort; it does not inflict irreparable harm[104] as an overly harsh weaning would, either through the premature loss of parents or through the revolting effect of an ill-intentioned external education. In these latter cases, the heartache produced is not easy to overcome: one might even add, although Hegel does not do so, that a forced premature weaning produces pathological phenomena that are as enigmatic as those of which they are the obverse, those that Hegel used as anthropological models in order to describe the unity and substantial identity of the soul with corporeity, the primary substantial unity within the family. That identity is not at all pathological at an early stage of development; on the contrary, if it is broken off too soon, it cannot fail to generate real illnesses as well as tragedies. Everything depends, then, on *timing*: if the umbilical cord is cut too soon, the child experiences great misfortune or lapses into irreparable melancholy. If it is cut too late, less severe misfortunes ensue – the child simply risks being stifled within the family that has loved him so much; he risks becoming its slave, its possession, unless – because of this overly prolonged absorption of the familial 'mother's milk', without any distancing or breaks, the child becomes schizophrenic. The latter scenario, however, is not the stuff of tragedy.

Still, if the essential primordial unity is so strong, how can there ever be a 'good moment' for the break? Is it not always already too late? Is the child not always already locked into psychosis, incapable of becoming autonomous and free one day? It seems that there may be an opportune moment for weaning only if the second phase of family education, the one with a negative aim, forms part and parcel of the first, the one with a positive aim – if division is always already present at the heart of the family's substantial unity or identity, if absorption of the mother's milk is not continuous, if it is always already cut off by weaning. In other words, authentic family education must keep the child within the family only the better to detach him from it, and must detach him from it the better to keep him. This is to say that the second 'phase', which is not really a phase at all in the temporal sense, only serves as 'sublation' for the first, and so it conserves the first: separation from the heart of the family must come about without ill will, must ensure the retention of the full initial respect accorded the family, even dismembered, by its detached members, who are thus no longer members. One has to 'kill' one's father, though not during the Oedipal stage or as a consequence of that stage; and one must also preserve all one's good will toward him. In order to kill the father, one must do gentle violence to oneself and act against him without violence. Even when it comes apart and disappears, the family bond must always be respected. Such is the logic of sublation, *Aufhebung*[105] which, because it may appear contradictory to understanding, requires recourse to metaphors that are more speculative than the concepts themselves.[106]

So how can Socrates be faulted for intervening between parents and children, between Anytus and his father, for example, given that the family bond was to be dissolved in any event? Given that in the case in point a state of discord had prevailed over that bond from its inception? Socrates is guilty – to his misfortune, in this case – not really of coming on the scene too soon, but of encouraging and thus reinforcing the state of contradiction, discord and discontent that characterized the young man's attitude toward his father; Socrates was at fault for stabilizing the rupture.[107] He was not really accused of doing away with the family, but introducing its death from the outside, violently, instead of letting it die a death of its own, a proper, bloodless, dialectical death that guarantees the 'sublation' of those it kills, the 'sublation' of fathers by their children, who immortalize their fathers at the same time they are putting them to death. A 'proper' death inflicted on the family, at the heart of the family, by the family, is a death 'sublated', a death denied. If the premature loss of parents is a great misfortune, the loss is at least as great for the parents themselves as for their children. If that loss leads the children to neglect the parents' principles, to stop respecting them, thus to deny them immortality (but the contrary is often the case, a fact that Hegel overlooks), one might say that, by teaching young people to turn away from their biological parents in favor of their true kin, their only legitimate father, the *Logos*, Socrates subordinates (as he does in Plato's *Symposium*) the immortality conferred by natural procreation to the immortality procured by spiritual procreation; for him, this implies the empirical death of the father, a death 'unsublatable' through dialectics.

Because he destroyed the family economy of death, Socrates thus deserved death himself, and not just a dialectical death; he deserved to appear not only before the tribunal of History and Mind, but before the tribunal of Athens. The State is not a physical but a spiritual realm whose existence depends on men's mental dispositions. If the State senses that it is being attacked by principles that do not maintain the cohesiveness of the whole, it is obliged to intervene, and it was right to condemn Socrates. If Socrates was advocating disobedience to parents and was destroying the family from without, he was not doing so for the benefit of a higher moral unity, that of the State; or at least, for his own purposes, Hegel is attempting to eradicate (and even in the literal sense[108]) everything that might lead readers to imagine that Socratic education might have had the formation of good citizens as its goal. Even when he points out that Socrates did fulfill his civic duties, he takes pains to add that his primary preoccupation lay elsewhere.

So the Athenian State had two good reasons to accuse Socrates. For both offenses with which he was charged were destructive of the Athenian Mind. In the first place, by overturning public religion, which in those days was intimately linked with public life in general, he threatened the entire State. The Socratic demon, a divinity different from the officially recognized gods (but we have seen the sophism that Hegel is compelled to adopt in order to maintain the difference), exposed the State to subjective arbitrariness: the introduction of a new god whose principle was self-consciousness and who provoked disobedience was necessarily a crime in the public eye. The Athenians' judgment was consistent and obligatory, even if 'ours' would have been more nuanced.

In the second place, the accusation that Socrates brought 'trouble' into filial relations was not without truth either, for the moral bond between parents and children was even more solid than it is for 'us', who have the subjective freedom inaugurated precisely by the Socratic principle that underlies all the 'crimes' of Romantic consciousness. For the Athenians, piety toward the gods and one's parents was absolutely essential. Socrates thus injured Athenian life on two fundamental points, tearing apart both the bosom of the family and that of the State; he introduced pain from which both have had trouble recovering, perhaps because it was not 'sublatable' without residue.

b) The second face of his destiny

The double charge against Socrates was thus necessary; it was inscribed in his destiny, of which it constitutes the first of two faces. The *death sentence*, contrary to what Tenneman says, was not an inevitable consequence of the two-fold accusation. It represents the other facet of his trial and the *second face of his destiny*; it results from Socrates' attitude, from his refusal to assess his penalty himself, his refusal to establish its modality (a fine, banishment or death) as the procedures demanded; for, according to Xenophon, submitting to that customary practice would have amounted to acknowledging that he had been in the wrong. In Hegel's eyes, far from being the sign of an admirable and exemplary moral grandeur, Socrates' refusal is a crime that properly warrants death: indeed, it confirms the opposition between natural morality and abstract moral consciousness. The latter is conscious of its right and its autonomy; it clings to them in its *splendid isolation* and its guilty pride, recognizing as just not the judicial sentence of the tribunal, but what it has itself, as the only legitimate tribunal, decreed to be just. Socrates' refusal was inconsistent with his own principle of formal obedience to the laws, for that principle obliged him to remain in prison. He refused in order to avoid humiliation; he acted out of pride, a dangerous corollary of the newly-acquired consciousness of subjective freedom – 'this miserable freedom of thinking and believing what men will' (p. 443)! Although he recognized the sovereignty of the people *in general,* in this *particular* case he refused to submit to the people's judgment and majesty, manifesting by his gesture the hypocrisy of the abstract morality that sets forth universal laws in order to exempt some particular individual from obeying them, on the strength of the superiority of his individual judgment over that of an entire people.

Now (and Hegel could have cited Aristotle in support of his own argument here), if the people can be mistaken, the individual can be even more mistaken, for the people constitute the universal principle. Socrates is guilty of acquitting himself on his own before the tribunal of his own moral consciousness, whereas no people, *a fortiori* no free people, is obliged to recognize the validity of such a tribunal, but rather must recognize the validity of its own, which for it is the only authentic moral consciousness. The first principle of any State is that there is no reason superior to the reason of State, to what the State recognizes as law: 'The conscience of the court alone possesses any value as being the universal legalized conscience, which does not require to recognize the particular conscience of the accused' (p. 443). Socrates' crime is that he feared, wrongly, that he would dishonor himself, as a free individual, by bowing to the power of the people, the noblest of the universal powers. In the *Phaedo,* where the account of the philosopher's last moments 'forms an elevating picture' (p. 443), Plato shows that Socrates went to his death in the noblest and most serene manner possible (the most virile – *männlich* – manner, Hegel adds parenthetically, doubtless remembering that Socrates had sent away the women whose wailings and lamentations might have disturbed his last conversations about immortality – conversations that he burnished, moreover, only for the people's benefit, since he himself, much more noble and manly in this respect than Achilles, did not fear death).

Nevertheless, despite all his manliness, Socrates misunderstood true nobility. True nobility appears to be independent of sexual difference, since Antigone,[109] 'the heavenly Antigone, that noblest of figures that ever appeared on earth' (p. 441), did not fear to humiliate herself by acknowledging her guilt, when the laws had decided to punish her; by accepting the state's judgment, she subordinated subjective consciousness of her fault to punishment, to objective natural morality. Pericles, who was not simply an unparalleled mythical figure but a contemporary of Socrates, was fed at the same breast as the philosopher by the same milk of Athens' natural morality, which he had assimilated better than Socrates; as a good, grateful son, he too was able to submit to the people's judgment as he would to a sovereign. Even if it did not bring him to the point of laughter (that day or any other), he was not afraid to humiliate himself by looking for citizens to support Aspasia and Anaxagoras and pleading with the people on their behalf.

Socrates, on the contrary, harmed the Athenian people, its mind and its moral life – perhaps because he was weaned (or weaned himself) too early. (After all, did he not ask more or less ironically, that, as sole punishment, he be provided with free food at the town hall – a request that Hegel fails to mention?) The premature loss of the maternal breast was irreparable both for Socrates and for the Athenians. Punished for injuring the maternal breast, he fully deserved to die.

By refusing to choose his punishment, did he not in effect choose death? Did he not acquiesce in this way in the popular judgment? And if that is the case, did he then deserve to die? Hegel does not raise these questions; he sees the Socratic gesture as strictly motivated by pride, the *hubris* of subjective consciousness, with its exaggerated claim to divinity. Regarding Socrates' refusal and its consequences, Kierkegaard and Nietzsche offer entirely different versions, based on texts Hegel does not mention. For Kierkegaard, precisely because Socrates was not guilty, he had to make the ironic choice of death, for death is the only punishment that is not really a punishment, since death is nothing at all. For Nietzsche, the choice of death fits in perfectly with Socrates' last words, when he entrusts Crito with the duty of sacrificing a cock to Asclepius, thereby signifying that life is an illness and that he himself is a dubious living being since he prefers death to life; the choice is symptomatic of his participation in the ascetic ideal and in decadence.

It is noteworthy that Hegel, who up to this point has privileged Xenophon over Plato, prefers to evoke at the end, and in connection with Socrates' end, the 'serene and noble' picture offered in the *Phaedo* rather than the prosaic and pragmatic one (on which Nietzsche, on the contrary, relies), offered in Xenophon's *Apology*. According to Xenophon, Socrates allowed himself to be condemned to death in order to escape the illnesses of old age, to escape an existence overshadowed by disease that would be far worse than death. For if Socrates is not endowed with the nobility of Antigone or Pericles, in Hegel's eyes, neither is he a pitiful old man or a scoundrel – if he were, he would be unworthy of appearing on a tragic stage. He is in fact a heroic figure (and Hegel had no doubt about this from the start): if he opposes natural moral law and refuses to bow to the people, he does so in the name of another law that is just as absolute, the law of a mind that is sure of itself, the law of a decision-making consciousness.

The conflict between these two forms of legitimate right was inevitable, and the reaction to the collision, Socrates' death sentence, was equally inevitable. But, as in any tragedy, even though the individual may be annihilated – this is the difference between tragedy and comedy – the universal principle, because it is absolute and just, is preserved. It even gains something by way of the punishment inflicted: it appears in all its purity, for it is stripped of the inadequate shape it still had in Socrates' case, that of a personal demon, the property of an *individual,* an unjust privilege spurring the individual to an excess of braggadocio that leads him to crime and its rightful expiation. The punishment of Socrates, by putting the individual to death, allows the principle to be elevated to its true stature, that is, to appear in the universal mode – not, henceforth, as the figure of a person, but as the figure of the Mind of the world, a truth that can be understood, as always, only after the fact. That is why Socrates' world is not guilty of his death. Only the future world, which looks down on Socrates and his world from the height of its definitive historical superiority, can understand them by mastering and reappropriating them.

Here we are given to understand that the true master is Hegel. Looking down from his full height – but not out of culpable pride, of course not; he does not mistake himself for a god! – he distributes merits and demerits to each party; he assigns each to its proper place in the world history of Mind. He makes a place – an elevated position of honor – for something that without him might have been tossed onto the trash heap of history, devoid as it is of any necessity or intelligibility. By representing Socrates' death as tragic and necessary, Hegel strips him of his essential solitude and contingency, of what he has that is most truly his own, what he would have kept if he had lived and died as a private philosopher, at peace among his disciples. By situating his life and his death on the public stage, on the contrary, Hegel has him 'win' immortality – 'win' in spite of himself, since for his final conversations on the subject seem to have been along the lines of 'popular philosophy', and since he willed his own death.

But Hegel has no use for Socrates' individual will. By saving and immortalizing the philosopher he aims only to do honor to 'his' principle, precisely because it is not really his; it is an absolutely essential principle in the development of self-consciousness, a principle destined to spawn a new and superior effective reality. It is because this principle cannot be reduced to a doctrine or to an individual opinion that it deserves to be honored and preserved, that it warrants its place in the history of Athens and that of Mind, and that it had a role to play in that same history: it had to stand up against another principle, that of the Greek mind. By tragically condemning Socrates to death, the Athenians did him the honor of recognizing that 'his' principle was truly a principle, a real and universal principle, not just in relation to his individuality alone but also in relation to effective reality. Even though he rose up against 'their own' principle, the principle 'of Socrates' was also 'their own', and, even though they judged and condemned Socrates, as they had to, they themselves were already imbued with his principle.

c) The last act of the drama
Do not believe, Hegel says in effect, that once again, despite the language I use and the logic I deploy, which are indeed 'mine' (for I could translate what happened by saying that in killing Socrates, the Athenians were killing themselves, that they were ensuring Socrates' 'sublation' and thus were preserving him, that Socrates is not really dead, since the essential thing, his principle, was preserved in them), I myself, Hegel, am the only one who knows this and understands it. The Athenians themselves already recognized it, as we see from what follows: the *last act of the drama* or rather of the tragedy of fate (which alone provides the truth of the matter), the third act, the act of reconciliation and the triumph of reason that begins with the Athenians' act of *repentance*.

After Socrates' death, the Athenians in fact punished his accusers. Diogenes Laertius[110] even reports that they erected a statue to Socrates and that such reversals were common occurrences; Hegel is silent on these points, which might invite a 'psychologizing' interpretation of their repentance (deification of the father after his murder). The Athenians' repentance stems not from a 'psychoanalytic' but from a 'dialectical' necessity: that is, 'their' repentance does not really have anything to do with 'Socrates'. Although by the gesture of repentance they acknowledge the philosopher's individual greatness, to be sure, they particularly want to signify (we are supposed to believe Hegel rather than Diogenes or Freud on this point) that the principle through which Socrates introduced new gods into the city-state and advocated disobedience to parents was already a principle in their own minds. They recognized that they were in a state of internal division; they acknowledged that in condemning Socrates they had condemned their own state. According to this view, Socrates played the role of *pharmakon*, or scapegoat; he paid the price, was condemned to drink their *pharmakon*, because he embodied a necessary movement of division, a prelude to a no less necessary movement of *Aufhebung*, of elevation and sublation. That is why the Athenians' repentance does not mean that things could and should have had a different outcome: only the subjective viewpoint of consciousness could express such a nonsensical desire, after the fact. It proves only that the Athenian people was not a vile tyrannical figure that undertook a relentless offensive against an innocent victim, Socrates, but that the Athenian people and Socrates are both innocent, both guilty, and that expiation was required of both. And there was nothing to give offense to either, for to declare them guilty in spite of themselves is to assert their spirituality, their freedom, and their tragic greatness.

In the conflict between the Athenians and Socrates, one law confronted another, one met destruction in the other: 'both suffer loss and yet both are mutually justified' (*Lectures*, p. 446). The Athenian people, having reached the stage in which consciousness separates itself from universal Mind, knew intuitively, in punishing Socrates, that they were *right* and so was he. The Athenians recognized that they had 'in Socrates only condemned their own principle' (p. 445). Because the Greek Mind has now become a consciousness that returns to itself, the Athenians now view Socrates as having committed no crime; their gratitude abrogates his condemnation and confirms their own dissolution as a people; they have just played a game where everyone loses. The only real winner is absolute Mind: indeed, a higher principle arises from the ashes of the two condemned, dead phoenixes, the Greek mind and Socrates. After demanding this double victim, which its economy required as an expiatory sacrifice, the Mind of the world – which for its part emerged completely unscathed – is elevated to higher consciousness.

Socrates is thus, for Hegel, the hero who *consciously* recognized and expressed the higher principle of Mind. In this end stage, in his need to depict Socrates and the Greek people as equals in their guilt and greatness, Hegel seems to have forgotten that Socrates' consciousness is nevertheless not yet entirely conscious, since it represents the new, universal principle to itself in the form of a personal demon, and since this individual representation, as he has shown, was one of the grounds for his accusation, if not his condemnation, by the Greeks. Like absolute Mind in its own development, in order to depict Socrates as a truly tragic hero and assign him a corresponding place in world history Hegel is compelled, at this particular *stage* in his own undertaking, to gloss over the personal aspect of the Socratic principle, an aspect that was decisive for Socrates' condemnation but that was wiped out with and by that condemnation. Through 'Socrates', which is no longer a proper name but the figure that arises from the ashes of the phoenix to give it its truth, a new world saw the light of day, the world of subjective reflection, a world in contradiction with the one that had existed previously. That is why, like all heroes, Socrates was judged violent and subversive, even if his principle was already beginning to emerge *also* within the Greek mind.

On the individual level, Socrates' violence earned him his death sentence; but like another great man, Christ, whose individuality was shattered by conflict but whose divine good news, once brought to light, was preserved like all that is great,[111] was raised up from his ashes or 'resuscitated' from his tomb. (The comparison between Socrates and Christ has become traditional; it allows Hegel once again to feel at home with Socrates in 'his own' country, in a truly Christian, perhaps overly Christian land; he reserves the right to understand that in the last analysis this 'new god introduced by Socrates into Athens' was already – in a different form – Christ, or else, conversely, that Christ's divinity, his truth, is the same as Socrates' universal divinity and truth.) Like Christ, then, Socrates was condemned, but 'his' principle penetrated and undermined the existing principle nonetheless. That principle, the principle of discernment, lay behind the figures of Alcibiades and Critias, his favorites, who in their ingratitude only served to bring him into disfavor; these followers, whom he had nourished with his maternal milk by entrancing them hypnotically (in his penetrating power Socrates had more affinity with 'Jews' than with Christ,[112] though Hegel does not stress this point), had left him (*abgetrennt*) too early, inspired by their evil genius, without a word of thanks (as he himself had done with his parents and the Athenian people). They had therefore turned out badly: the Socratic principle that has been misdirected away from its target by the tyrant Critias and the feckless, frivolous Alcibiades (*dieses Genie des Leichsinns*) is what consummates the ruin of Athens.

Despite their differences, Socrates, Alcibiades and Critias are part of a single constellation; they are identical in that they are all instruments of the cunning of Reason – and in seeking to achieve its own ends, in seeking to bring about the triumph of one principle over another at the desired moment, Reason does not hesitate as to the choice of means. For Nietzsche, Socrates will be the symptom of the death of tragedy; for Hegel, on the contrary, he was necessary for the birth of tragedy, or at least necessary for the birth of its destiny. Critias and Alcibiades were equally necessary for its outcome, and all three were necessary for the final triumph of Reason or Mind. Owing to the Hegelian ruse that works as an authentic *Deus ex machina,* all three, although Greek, might corroborate the Jewish adage according to which original sin comes through knowledge, since the Socratic principle of self-knowledge is what corrupted his two disciples and led Athens to its ruin. But only Socrates could anticipate Christ and his redemption of sins, because he had perceived the universal aspect of his principle and had perceived that it also contained the remedy: it thus allowed the history of Mind to be raised to a higher level and to be completed in the end, after a long detour, by a return home.

Because the principle of the interiority of consciousness had not yet arrived at its final stage, was not yet united with the constitution of the people, it appeared and became a principle of corruption for that people: the Athenians found themselves in a state of internal division and became so weak that they lapsed into dependence on Lacedaemon and later on Macedonia. Because of this principle, philosophers withdrew from public affairs (this had already begun, moreover, with Heraclitus). They ceased to be in harmony with the universal goal of the natural moral formation of the people; they became separated from the people to the point of hostility, to the benefit of the formation of an inner world and the triumph of private interests and goals. On this point, a certain Nietzsche, in his own language, says the same thing: metaphysics begins with Socrates. In other words, with Socrates are inaugurated all the schisms and divisions that philosophy – which had previously been an integral part of the civilization for which its various systems represented potential correctives – transforms into a set of sects preoccupied solely with individual salvation. Philosophy cuts itself off from civilization and thus loses all necessity; from this point on it has the aspect of a random comet. It is no longer the consciousness but the bad conscience of its time.

Hegel wraps up his discussion of Socrates ('we are done with Socrates' [p. 448; *wir sind so mit Sokrates fertig*]) in connection with the ruin of Athens and the corruption of philosophy, which Socrates *also* provoked. With Socrates, even though Hegel has been 'more detailed' (*ausführlicher*) on the subject, he had in fact been finished with him at the outset, since he had noted and adapted only what he thought worth keeping, nothing of what was properly speaking 'him', Socrates, but the 'universal': Hegel encompassed 'his' principle which, as such, could only surpass him, in the totalizing movement of the history of Mind. Socrates represents only the great turning point in that history, alongside other figures that are just as necessary as his: that of Pericles, who is still faithful to the mind of the Athenian people, which Socrates destroyed; that of Alexander, whose figure is summoned up by that of Socrates, since in the final analysis it is the dissolving character of the Socratic principle that accounts for the ultimate subordination of Athens to Macedonia.

In the brief funeral oration offered by Hegel, in which he robs Socrates of his own death, he frames the figure of Socrates, not coincidentally, between that of Pericles, representing the magnificence and supreme flowering of Athens, and that of Alexander, representing Athens' ruin and decadence. Socrates, an intermediary demon, a *Janus bifrons,* necessarily faces in both directions at once; looking both backward and forward, he is an agent, through his principle, of the death of the one and the birth of the other.

Hegel opens the conclusion of his text onto the future, of which as a consciousness he cannot of course have advance knowledge, but which he can know because the future of Athens is now past, and because inasmuch as the past has taken shape there is knowledge of it, 'for the past is the preservation of the present as reality' (p. 434); he thus finally turns his gaze away from this great historical turning point, the cause of so many triumphs and misfortunes, after having (not without ambivalence) assassinated and saved Socrates, after having condemned and absolved that *Janus bifrons.*

It remains to be seen whether, to conceptualize Socrates and his death, 'we' can turn around or get around Hegelian dialectics. Whether there is a way – one that perhaps no longer stems from thought in the Hegelian sense and can no longer be sublated by it – for us to 'represent' him other than as a figure of Mind, even as the ambivalent one of a *Janus bifrons*. Whether we can also 'represent' his death for ourselves in some way other than as the death, always already assured of redemption, of a tragic hero. Both Kierkegaard and Nietzsche tried to do this; both sought to position Socrates outside of dialectics. The question that remains is whether they succeeded, and whether they succeeded equally well.

III. KIERKEGAARD'S 'SOCRATES': SOCRATES UNDER AN IRONIC LENS

Introduction
Socrates Displaced

1. *Expositions*

Kierkegaard's 'conception' of Socrates is an attempt to abort Hegel's figure of the philosopher. Not in order to put a different figure in its place – the 'figure', properly understood, is only a fictitious concept – but in order to bring to light a conception of the individual that is possible, 'actualized', and even necessary: a new Socrates who gives birth to himself. The title of Kierkegaard's thesis – *The Concept of Irony with Continual Reference to Socrates*[1] – is subversive in itself, because it declares straight away that the author's project, the opposite of Hegel's, is to judge a concept by the yardstick of an individual. The thesis is in fact a long argument with Hegel. Kierkegaard deals explicitly with the Hegelian conception of Socrates only in an Appendix to Part One, but he knew that one can reserve what is most important, *as women sometimes do,* for a post-script.[2]

Part One, 'The Position of Socrates Viewed as Irony', is much longer than Part Two, 'The Concept of Irony' (230 pages versus 90 in the English translation). The disproportion puts subjectivity back in its proper place, triumphant, while the concept of irony is relegated to a secondary position. Under the apparently more Hegelian title of Part Two, Kierkegaard's primary focus is on Romantic irony according to Fichte, Friedrich Schlegel, Tieck, and Sölger. Operating subversively once again, Kierkegaard does not relate Socratic irony, as Hegel did, to the much-maligned irony of the Romantics. In his eyes, the Romantic yardstick does Socratic irony a disservice. Although Hegel distinguished between the two forms of irony, in his treatment the Romantic version ends up discrediting the Socratic form. Kierkegaard, on the contrary, consistently relates modern irony to Socrates, whose irony may be irreducible to the modern form but is closely allied with it.

Kierkegaard does not value modern irony any more highly than Hegel did, even though he condemns the peremptory, disdainful, superior tone Hegel adopted in inveighing against the practitioners of the irony he found so irritating. Hegel's tone, Kierkegaard says, is that of a schoolmaster who treats the practitioners of modern irony as impenitent and hardened sinners. Because he dealt with them arrogantly while allowing himself to become absorbed in the problems they raised, Hegel did not pay enough attention to Socratic irony, which he had sought to distinguish, to rescue, from the modern form; he failed to see that Socratic irony was for its part also entirely negative, and that the Romantic version deserved to be judged by the Socratic yardstick, not the other way around. For in Kierkegaard's view, Socrates is the first ironist and represents the truth of all irony.

This, then, is the 'conception' that Kierkegaard seeks to justify in Part One. In three devastating chapters, he echoes Hegel's categories the better to displace them, in a parody of the ternary, military rhythm of dialectics: '*Ein, zwei, drei*'. Emulating Artemis, the goddess who presided over births, Kierkegaard lets loose his arrows against other 'fictive' conceptions of Socrates in order to abort them in favor of the only possible, actualized and necessary one: his own. In the opening chapter, which is directed primarily against Xenophon, Kierkegaard borrows from Plato and especially from Aristophanes to present the *possibility* of an entirely negative Socrates, whose *actuality* is confirmed, in the second chapter, by 'real' documents concerning Socrates' demon and his death sentence; in the third chapter, Kierkegaard demonstrates the *necessity* of his own conception.

Part One of *The Concept of Irony* is a harsh, devastating text in which Kierkegaard identifies himself with the Socrates/Artemis figure in Plato's *Theaetetus*. In the appendix to Part One, Kierkegaard exposes Hegel's concept of irony (in the Greek sense of the term 'expose'), on the horizon of which his entire text is located; his aim is to cause that concept, too, to abort. Kierkegaard *exposes* Hegel's concept; he does not *oppose* it. By taking up the vocabulary of maieutics, midwifery, for his own purposes, Kierkegaard locates himself outside speculative dialectics and its system of oppositions; he opts for a more purely Socratic dialectics, which he thereby removes from Hegel's reappropriating 'sublation'. By making the Socratic 'conception' work against the Hegelian 'concept', Kierkegaard can challenge speculative dialectics without appearing to do so, without playing its game.

2. Gaps

In a more general way, Kierkegaard sets out to subvert the Hegelian system with subtle moves, such as the disproportion between the two parts of the dissertation, and the reversal of terms in his titles – not only the overall title of the thesis, but also the title of Part One, 'The Position of Socrates Viewed as Irony', in which the emphasis is placed on a finite subjectivity reduced to a *point of view*, reduced to a perspective that is at once *negative* – it has nothing in view but nothingness – and *singular*, characterized by an unsurpassable empirical individuality whose irreducible phenomenal reality must now be established. As we have seen, Hegel sought to circumscribe that singularity by depicting Socrates' subjective consciousness and individuality as a simple stage, an unsurpassable moment. To speak of Socrates' position or point of view is thus to give him back in so many words what Hegel had taken away by presenting 'Socrates'' principle neither as opinion nor as doctrine but as nothing less than a universal principle. Kierkegaard's titles implicitly restore Socrates' ownership – his ownership of nothing – and in so doing they remove him from dialectics; they resist dialectics without opposing it. Was it not Hegel himself who said that 'Socrates has no philosophy'?

Through the elaborate and subtle play of his writing, then (and at his thesis defense, the jury, in its own way, manifested a certain awareness of the game[3]), Kierkegaard positions himself almost imperceptibly at a slight remove, distances himself from dialectics, detaches himself ironically. For example, he multiplies metaphors in a way that is unprecedented, especially for a university thesis, but he *also* retains the entire old speculative arsenal, the Hegelian concepts of 'moment', 'subjectivity', 'negative' and 'positive'. Indeed, he maintains the whole Hegelian system of oppositions to such an extent that he later confesses to having been 'a Hegelian fool' when he wrote that early work[4] (not unlike the Nietzsche of *Ecce Homo,* who condemns *The Birth of Tragedy*). In fact, this ongoing double-edged gesture already allows Kierkegaard's 'folly' to efface the Hegelianism that it destabilizes without appearing to touch it at all.

By holding onto the old words, Kierkegaard seems to be taking up where Hegel left off, making himself an ally, at the very moment when he is actually pulling away from Hegel, ironically displacing him by beating him at his own game, having fun with him and undoing him with consummate seriousness – his own – or with consummate irony; for the height of irony is to work surreptitiously, *incognito,* so as to be taken quite seriously.

Kierkegaard's ironic writing, which allows him to escape the Hegelian reappropriation without seeming to do anything of the sort, mimics Socratic irony. As in an embedded reflection of the model, his writing declares that Socratic irony alone can preserve the individual from domination by the system, and that the terrain of irony is where the battle lines are drawn. Thus he strives to show, operating against Hegel and in close proximity to him, that Socrates' irony is not merely a stage in a method – not its negative moment, the moment of void to be surpassed and fulfilled by a presumably positive maieutic moment – but that Socratic irony is part and parcel of Socrates himself. For Socrates is a consummate ironist or midwife, and these amount to the same thing, since, like a good midwife, Socrates is completely sterile. He himself has nothing to affirm: like Charon at the helm of Death's ferryboat, Socrates takes others to their destination but never completes the journey himself.

3. *Theses*

Such is the thesis (to the extent that it lends itself to summary) of the Thesis written in Danish on the concept of irony that 'Søren Aabye Kierkegaard, B. Th. [candidate in theology], will endeavor to defend in a public colloquium [on] September 29 [at] 10 o'clock in order to obtain in the appointed manner the degree of Master of Arts [of the University of Copenhagen 1861]'.[5] The seriousness of the thesis[6] is attested at the outset by its division into fifteen 'theses' (pp. 5-6; these were printed in the original copies of the dissertation that were not intended for sale). Written in Latin, in a supremely serious academic style, and presented at the beginning as if to guarantee the seriousness of what is to come, these fifteen theses in fact destroy the 'thesis'. For one thing, their multiplicity and the apparent disorder of their presentation tend to arouse suspicion among academics. (A thesis, by definition, must have only *one* thesis, one that can be clearly summarized and mastered, just as there must be only *one* concept of irony.) In addition, each of the theses contains some element that is intriguing, even scandalous, perhaps as a way of getting the attention of the jury to whose verdict the candidate's 'offspring' is exposed – but also perhaps as a way of bringing about the 'abortion' of that offspring, as thesis, and of shielding it from the judgment of the academic institution at the very moment when it seems to be bowing to that judgment.

The *first thesis,* which responds to Ferdinand Christian Baur's comparison between Socrates and Christ (a comparison Kierkegaard discusses in his opening chapter), announces paradoxically and ironically that the *similarity* between the two lies in their *dissimilarity.* The *second* and *third theses* dismiss Xenophon and Plato simultaneously and – from the academic standpoint – scandalously, as sources equally devoid of truth; the former because he *gives Socrates too little credit,* confining him to the level of empirical usefulness; the latter because he *gives him too much credit.* Kierkegaard thus establishes the ironic equality of 'too little' and 'too much', each source having allowed Hegel to pull Socrates, erroneously, toward positivity. The *fourth thesis* incongruously identifies 'the form of interrogation employed by Plato' with the Hegelian negative.

The *fifth thesis* puts jury members before an alternative that is awkward, to say the least. Either they must accept the scandalous hypothesis that Plato's *Apology* – a canonical text whose authenticity has never been challenged and which attests to Socrates' innocence – is false, or else they must interpret that text as ironic from start to finish, a hypothesis that is not without audacity. For if it is true that nothing can settle the question of a text's seriousness or irony as such (and while Kierkegaard is aware of this impossibility, his jury may not be), all the virtuosity the candidate can muster is needed to prove, supporting texts in hand, that Socrates' death was neither an unhappy accident nor the result of a tragic confrontation, but that it arose from an ironic necessity. For the ironist, death is a necessarily desired state of nothingness; ignorance on the subject of death makes death the only possible punishment that is not a punishment for the ironist, since, for someone who does not know whether it is a good thing or bad, death is nothing at all.

Socrates' admission of ignorance must be taken seriously and lightly at the same time: he knew something, since he was aware of his own ignorance, but that knowledge has no positive content, thus he knew nothing. The ironist is incapable of formulating affirmations. He can only play endlessly, lightly, with the 'nothing' that he takes seriously, to the extent that he takes nothing seriously. Socrates' ignorance thus short-circuits any significant communication with death. By condemning him to death, by its own certainty that it has punished him, the State gives a foothold to irony, which in the last analysis is the only thing that condemns him. Death is to the ironist what the negative result is to his questioning: self-destruction, autophagia. Socrates' death, as the *sixth thesis* indicates, results from his irony itself, from his own *vampirism* that turns against him, as with the sorcerer in the folktale who ends up devouring his own stomach.

Whether or not Socrates explicitly desired this outcome, by virtue of its self-destructive aspect irony ends up undoing the ironist himself with all his vain vanity; he is caught up in the vanity of all things. Irony thus announces the form of religious piety that seeks the death of finite subjectivity in favor of an infinite divine subjectivity. That is why the *fifteenth* and final thesis indicates, paradoxically, that no human life worthy of the name can do without irony, any more than philosophy at its inception can do without doubt. This second necessity will be easier for the jury to accept; it may allow the jury, carried along by its momentum, to 'swallow' the first, more resistant one as well. But to say that these two existential and gnoseological necessities are inaugural is to indicate at the same time that they have to be surpassed. Not, however, in Hegel's manner, as stages in a dialectics, for that would imply only that neither one is an end, that they are both merely means, access routes. Thus Kierkegaard's last chapter will make irony a necessary stage of existence, but a simple stage, a route – the route of detachment. Skirting everything finite and remaining in very close proximity to religious humor, this route leads to the ethical stage.

The *seventh thesis* proclaims that Aristophanes' depiction of Socrates is by and large truthful. Here is a paradox for the many readers who are inclined to 'throw the book at Aristophanes', though not for the potential Hegelians on the jury who may believe that on this point at least their candidate agrees with Hegel. But they could erase the differences between the two only if they were to overlook the fact that the thesis speaks only about the truth of Aristophanes' *portrait* of Socrates; it deals only with the extent to which the picture presented in *The Clouds* resembles the original. As we have seen, the resemblance or lack of it is of little concern to Hegel, indifferent as he is – this is one of the things for which Kierkegaard reproaches him – to the phenomenal reality of Socrates as an individual. The word 'depiction', introduced in the *seventh thesis* – in just as subversive a way as it is by Nietzsche when he declares that he is attempting not to tell the 'truth' about the 'presocratic' philosophers, but to 'depict' them, to paint their *portraits* a hundred times over on the walls – distances Kierkegaard once again from Hegel and his 'truth', without appearing to do so. So far as Socrates was concerned, in any event (as Hegel saw it), Aristophanes could only have illustrated the negative aspect of his principle, and could not have revealed, as he did for Kierkegaard, the absolute vanity of the character whose speculative profundity was reduced for him, Hegel, to the profundity of the void.

As if to reassure the jury, the *eighth thesis*, taken on its own terms, seems to manifest for once a straightforward complicity with Hegel by using Hegel's own language to condemn irony: 'irony as infinite and absolute negativity is the lightest and weakest indication of subjectivity'. But on the one hand, for Hegel, irony thus defined is actually the result of the extreme 'development' of subjectivity, a sign of its triumph rather than of its weakness; on the other hand, 'after the fact', in its confrontation with the theses that follow, in which the alliance with Hegel disappears, the *eighth thesis* seems to be more distracting than reassuring. The *ninth* and *tenth theses* in fact present Socrates as the founder of irony – irony as described in the *eighth thesis*. The *twelfth thesis* asserts that Hegel paid less attention to the ancient than to the modern form of irony; thus he failed to see that Socrates was the first ironist, that his irony was totally negative and destructive of all reality. In his violence, Socrates drove his contemporaries away from substantiality, but, like his namesake in *The Clouds* who stripped Strepsiades of his cloak, he gave them nothing in return; he left them as naked as victims of a shipwreck. Socrates' vision – his eyesight – was deficient (and, if we are to believe Aristotle, whose hierarchy of the senses Kierkegaard seems to respect here even as he disrupts it, touch, a subservient organ that operates in contact with matter, is less speculative than sight, which works at a distance and whose organs are situated high up in the face): he could see the truth only from a distance, without being able to grasp or possess it (though this would seem to belong more to touch than to sight). Owing to the disturbance of all his senses, he leaves his contemporaries in a state of extreme aporia: it is as if they had been abruptly awakened from the dogmatic sleep of substantiality by the bite of a horsefly, and left in confusion as to where – in what positive direction – to turn.

Theses eleven through fourteen present for examination certain character-istics of recent manifestations of irony that have been inappropriately foregrounded by Hegel. Kierkegaard reattaches them to ethics and gives them a psychological foundation: as he sees it, these manifestations are based on a bitterness that grows out of mimetic rivalry, jealousy, or the desire to appropriate the pleasure of someone who has seized the object of one's own desire. He offers the case of Sölger, the only Romantic 'saved' by Hegel. Sölger's acosmic position is explained – ironically – by his jealousy of Hegel, whose negative he could not even have imagined; once his rival credited him with the capacity to do such a thing, Sölger could never get the better of him, not even through thought.

The last thesis, the *fifteenth,* represents irony as the beginning of all human life worthy of the name, but it does not specify what form of irony is at issue. Being a man of good will, and hoping to elicit good will on the part of the jury members at the point where they are about to confront the dissertation properly speaking, candidate Kierkegaard perhaps believes that he is helping the jury – whom he has just disoriented, to say the least – to land on its feet again, by appearing to maintain the unity and homogeneity of the concept that he has just split apart and displaced from the speculative realm to the existential, psychological and moral realms.

Notwithstanding the fact, then, that the fifteen 'theses' were written in Latin, with the utmost seriousness, they still helped undermine the seriousness of the *Thesis* and the university as an institution, at the outset; moreover, appearances to the contrary, they enabled Kierkegaard to make sport of his jury and its verdict.

In his dissertation, because he is still addressing a thesis jury, and because it is the only way to resist Hegel without opposing him, Kierkegaard, like a true *Janus,* continues to play on at least two boards and to advance on two fronts at once.

4. *The critical front*

On a 'first front', drawing upon his arsenal of speculative concepts, Kierkegaard embarks on a dense and serious academic critique of Hegel's writings. Summoning up citations and references in support of his arguments, he denounces Hegel's inconsistencies, contradictions, and slippages (sometimes unfairly, for his own operations are carried out with inflexible understanding more than with speculative reason). For example, he points out that Hegel asserts in one passage that there is no need to distinguish between Plato and Socrates, while in another passage he appeals, as if making a slip of the tongue, to the traditional distinctions between the so-called Socratic dialogues and the so-called Platonic ones. (It is true that Hegel confuses the Socratic dialectics with the Platonic version. He fails to note Socrates' particular approach, which moves from the concrete to the abstract rather than the other way around; he fails to distinguish between two types of questions, those that call for an answer and those that seek only to confound. At one point, he declares that Socrates is teaching himself a lesson and thus that his not-knowing has to be taken ironically, and at another point he asserts that the not-knowing has to be taken seriously and that Socrates aims only to confound.)

More generally speaking, Kierkegaard reproaches Hegel for inadequately thematizing the question of sources (he himself, being more 'serious' than Hegel, devotes the whole first – and longest – part of his thesis to the project of aborting those sources). He reproaches Hegel, too, for failing to distinguish between different types of dialogues in Plato's texts: for example, Hegel cites the *Lysis* without justifying his choice of that dialogue rather than some other. Kierkegaard faults Hegel for not being *concerned* with certain questions: for believing that the essential question had to do with Socrates' life as an individual – unlike Schleiermacher, who saw Socrates as a philosopher. (Even as he paid homage to Socrates, Hegel marked his conviction clearly by beginning and ending his study of Socrates with discussions of the philosopher's life.) Kierkegaard criticizes Hegel for failing to question the phenomenal reality of the individual: this was a fundamental question in his own eyes. Last but not least, he condemns Hegel for missing the concept of irony: for saying so little about irony, and for making what little he did say – in a tone that was to say the least polemical – quite inconsistent. Hegel did not really disapprove of Socrates' irony, because he failed to grasp its full importance; he represented it as a weak concept and reduced it to a simple 'moment', a stage in dialectics, without seeing its infinite and absolute negativity.

As for irony in its Romantic form, according to Hegel, it has no justification; it was not useful in the period of world history when it appeared, for it was not at the service of the Mind of the world. Romantic irony was not a phase that had to be negated and supplanted by a new one, given the historical circumstances; Romantic irony denies all historical reality in order to leave room for a reality generated by its own works. Unlike Socrates' irony, Romantic irony does not manifest a subjectivity already present in the world, but a subjectivity to the second power, a subjectivity that has the limitless power to negate and deny ideas as well as phenomena. Destructive of reality as a whole, Romantic irony does not recognize the value of each historical moment as a moment: sometimes it attributes absolute value to reality, sometimes no value at all. It seeks merely to produce reality itself, poetically; it has no precise goals, for it is, properly speaking, good for nothing. That is why Romantic irony is unjustifiable in Hegel's eyes (and Kierkegaard recognizes that Hegel is right on this point); he will not rest until he has broken it down and wiped it out. But owing to his exasperation with this form of irony to which he had – out of envy or jealousy? – become allergic (Friedrich Schlegel in particular served as a scapegoat), by launching a vigorous attack on the post-Fichtean irony that caused him the greatest concern and left him in a state of aporia – to the detriment of the Socratic irony that he analyzed succinctly – Hegel did a disservice to the concept of irony, despite all his seriousness. He had lost sight of its truth.

In his second point, as every good dissertation-writer does, Kierkegaard acknowledges that Hegel nevertheless made 'many excellent particular comments' (p. 225). Provided that one knows how to find them, for (the height of irony!) contrary to what Hegel believes, everything that is 'good' and true turns out to lie, dispersed and incoherent, outside his system. If one pays attention, then, to the small details that Hegel appears to deem negligeable, if one notes what he seems to be saying only in passing remarks, if one picks up the tone in which he makes such remarks, one discovers that to a certain extent Hegel can corroborate the candidate's initial view of Socrates, for if one knows how to read between the lines, one observes that Hegel, too, has stressed Socrates' negative aspect, in spite of himself. For example, and despite his contradictory statements on the subject (in reality, as we have seen, if one adopts the Hegelian perspective, these apparent contradictions are contradictory only for understanding that does not grasp them as opposing 'moments' within a speculative dialectics), Hegel did indeed see that Socratic teaching is negative, that it aims to unsettle and not to strengthen, that its negativity is not immanent to any positivity but is itself its own object. This viewpoint is particularly easy to detect in the section he devotes to Aristophanes, with whom he does not disagree. (Aristophanes is a privileged source for Kierkegaard, for the playwright correctly presents an absolutely negative Socrates who has nothing to say or to give.) But as we have seen, Hegel actually invokes the playwright simply in order to illustrate the negative side of the Socratic principle, which is merely the counterpart of its positive side, the one illustrated by Xenophon.

Hegel also perceived that Socrates' philosophy was not speculative, that Socrates was essentially *the founder of moral philosophy*. This view might seem incompatible with that of the ironist, but in reality such is not the case at all, for, according to Hegel, Socrates' moral position consisted in teaching people to universalize subjectivity, that is, in making people conscious of subjectivity's infinite and infinitely negative freedom. All the specific features of Socrates' moral philosophy as Hegel sees them can be 'recuperated' to the benefit of the Kierkegaardian thesis, that of Socrates' absolute negativity. What this moral philosophy has to offer is the notion that the individual must no longer act out of respect for laws but must act consciously, knowledgeably. This is an essentially negative proposition, as much with respect to the established order as with respect to the deeper positivity that, because it is speculative, presupposes a negative condition.

If Hegel did endow Socrates with a certain positivity, the principle of subjective freedom that makes consciousness return to itself, he went on to declare at once that Socrates' abstract attitude with regard to the good stripped his positivity of any affirmative character. Although Socrates seemed to take a giant step forward with respect to the Sophists by aiming at the good in and for itself, whereas 'the Sophists stopped with the infinite refraction of the good in the multiplicity of the useful and the advantageous' (p. 232; in reality, for Kierkegaard, Socrates was much more negative – this is something Hegel does not say – than the Sophists, who, over and beyond their skepticism, always referred precisely to usefulness), in fact Socrates was not affirmative, for he did not proceed toward his own goal, the good in and for itself, but merely left the established order as it was. Socratic positivity is thus not the dialectical inverse of its infinite negativity, it is of a piece with the positivity that preceded it.

In Kierkegaard's view, then, Hegel recognized that Socrates was content to emphasize the negative side of the universal principle; he stopped at threatening the equilibrium of something that had been represented in a stable fashion. His universal principle was indefinite, and the gap attributable to its indefinite character was not yet filled – and could not be, because Socrates rejected the State without having arrived yet at the highest form of the State, where the infinity to which Socrates lay claim only negatively can be affirmed.

The result, then, for Kierkegaard (and this is the essential issue for him), is that the Hegelian view of Socrates as the founder of moral philosophy can be acknowledged. (Even while advancing Hegel's arguments in Hegel's own language, Kierkegaard manages to subordinate the Hegelian view to his own, by omitting the positive aspect that Hegel stresses just as strongly at a different point in his dialectics). 'Retranslated' and distorted in this way, Hegel's position becomes entirely compatible with Kierkegaard's own thesis: namely, that Socrates' point of view is that of irony.

For if irony takes nothing seriously, according to Hegel, the very same thing holds true for the moral subject whose freedom is strictly negative, assuming that true seriousness can be achieved only within a totality in which the subject no longer makes decisions at every point, no longer sees his mission as a task he has assigned himself but as one that has been imposed on him. Because they are not incorporated into the State, because they do not result from obedience to duty, the Socratic virtues lack seriousness: like words taken out of context, they are devoid of meaning; they *mean nothing*. And while Hegel does confer on Socrates the idea of the good, Socrates is unable to characterize this good in any positive way. If Socratic irony overpowers all reality, then it leaves room only for an ideality that is infinitely abstract in form, one that is barely hinted at in its almost imperceptible contours. What is essential in Socrates' life may well be that he is oriented toward the good, but also toward the beautiful and the true, and especially that he proceeds so as to enable others to head in the same direction. But his life never reaches its destination. Like Charon, Socrates strips souls of all that defines them as individuals, then ferries them across 'from the fullness of life to the shadowy land of the underworld' (p. 236). He conducts them from reality to ideality, but to an ideality so abstract that it is equivalent to nothingness. And after launching each soul in isolation, he himself comes back to earth, ironically, every time.

Because Hegel viewed Socratic irony as a simple human-relations device, a stage within a method, thus a controlled element of that method, he did not see that the founder of moral philosophy – though he suggests this in spite of himself, if one reads between the lines – is irony through and through, in the strong sense of the term. Socrates' 'divine mission' was in fact limited to carrying out a movement of generalized destruction, a movement of general embarkation toward a two-fold nothingness, that of perceptible reality and that of the Idea. By undertaking a closely-argued 'critique' of Hegel's reading of Socrates, Kierkegaard, like any thesis writer, has shown where Hegel was right and where he went wrong; and, in an entirely Hegelian fashion, Kierkegaard has adopted and highlighted only what supports his own conception, letting the rest fall by the wayside.

5. *The metaphoric front*

However, by viewing as 'positive' only those elements that point toward the negative aspect of Socratic irony and that turn out to be inscribed exclusively in the margins of the system to which he is paying special attention, Kierkegaard has simply overturned the Hegelian system in a straightforward way: without appearing to do so, he has also brought what was repressed in it to light. And in the process he has undermined the entire system in a way quite unlike that of an ordinary academic critique that overturns its object of study. He has revealed that the real stakes of the system, and of his 'critique', are not speculative in nature (and more than anything else, Hegel's peremptory, polemical, and envious tone every time he confronts the question of Romantic irony is indeed a symptom indicating that interests entirely different from those of reason govern dialectical rationality). Seen in this light, Kierkegaard's method of reading, which is more psychoanalytic or Nietzschean, by anticipation, than it is Hegelian, allows him to resist the system. For by paying attention primarily to what is marginal, Kierkegaard displaces the questions quite markedly. He makes it clear that Hegel's 'critic' is perhaps interested not only in discovering whether Hegel's conception of Socrates is true or false, whether it is right or wrong, but also whether it is viable or not, that is, whether it is a true 'conception' – a diagnosis that may derive not from critical or speculative philosophy, here, but from an entirely different philosophy, from a 'maieutics' that may also be somewhat different from Socrates' version.

The shift from the ground of Truth to the domain of instincts is often marked in Kierkegaard's writing by an abrupt leap to a register of extremely varied and violent metaphors that break with the seriousness of dialectics and its critique by situating the reading on different grounds.

Thus when he reproaches Hegel for not having been interested in certain questions – the question, for example, of Socrates' empirical reality, because he adopts a totalizing viewpoint that allows him to avoid getting bogged down in worthless 'details' – Kierkegaard compares Hegel's attitude toward phenomena to that of a 'commander-in-chief of world history' who 'is in too much of a hurry . . . to take time for more than the royal glimpse he allows to glide over [the troops]' (p. 222). He has assigned each of the soldiers a specific place in the ranks, and he makes them march in step, *ein, zwei, drei,* while looking up and to the right, toward him. This is an exercise for which German officers and non-commissioned officers, 'especially those who are subject to systematic recruitment', are exceptionally gifted. At least if we are to believe the 'Postscript to a Public Confession'[7] in which Kierkegaard compares Dr. Beck – who 'reviewed' his thesis and declared that he did not understand it fully but that he had very much enjoyed it – to a non-commissioned officer of limited ability who takes himself much too seriously and claims to be lining the author up with all the others, Strauss, Feuerbach, Bruno Bauer, and making him march in step; and he wonders how he could have made that serious army officer laugh, unless it was by suggesting that, furious at having bought a copy of the thesis, for 'nothing', he would have sent it back to the publisher, inflicting a real loss – of three marks – on the author; this obviously would have been a great joke at his expense! The tone of all this is exceedingly sarcastic – because the author for his part is not one of those systematic spirits who enjoys mobilizing the authors of the entire world and lining them up for review, and he does not like to rush forward when the master blows his whistle, does not tolerate staying in an assigned position or (a true *Janus bifrons*) looking only up and to the right.

By comparing Hegel to an officer, a more able one, to be sure, but still an officer, a commander, a commander-in-chief, Kierkegaard displaces the problem from the ground of 'truth' to the ground of the 'will to power', as one might call it anticipatorily. He reveals the will to power that governs the search for truth: Hegel's will to be the great master of world history, its great conqueror, Caesar's equal, or Alexander's, at the very least, triumphant over Athens and Socrates. But by adding that this commander, from his majestic height, simply allows his 'royal glimpse' to pass lightly over the troops, he overturns Hegel's pretensions to mastery and produces an unfavorable diagnosis as to the quality of his will. Despite its warlike manner, Hegel's will may well lack masculinity and may leave Truth unsatisfied: for woman – and Truth is a female figure – is not satisfied with caresses; she wants all of her features to be wholly embraced.

The comparison between Hegel and a commander-in-chief, which Kierkegaard makes in the Appendix to Part One, cannot be understood in all its ironic implications unless it is juxtaposed to a comparison he situates at the opening of the book, one with which the later one in its own way forms part of a coherent system.

In his Introduction, anticipating Nietzsche, Kierkegaard compares philosophy confronting its object to a conqueror who needs to know how to cope with his conquest if he is to hold onto it: he must understand that, while women like power, they also like to be treated with decent respect, which means that a man must wait for them to reveal themselves, wait until they take off their masks, until they are ready to show themselves of their own accord. The contemporary philosopher, by seeking vigorously to assert his masculine power as conquering knight, or commander-in-chief, has only frightened his prey by clicking his spurs. He has made much ado about nothing, and with poor timing, for by acting with the haste of a sovereign he has missed the essential features of his object. Under the circumstances, his haste has done violence to the silence, the reticence, the distance, the invisible murmur of the object of the conquest, irony. In the last analysis, many aspects of this object remain 'poorly illuminated' by the philosopher erotician who, having merely skimmed the surface of his conquest, managed to give birth only to an erroneous conception that merited abortion.

Hegel loftily disdained irony. Purporting to be teaching it a lesson, to be instructing it in morality, he addressed himself to irony in a most unsuitable tone. In so doing, he revealed his own weak point: his inability to grasp the woman/irony that caused him so much trouble and left him in a state of aporia. If Hegel missed the 'concept' of irony, it is because a good conception implies that one has grasped both the totality and the details, that one is able to win a woman erotically without being indifferent to any of her features, and that one is still capable of maintaining sufficient distance to avoid frightening her. Bemused by the contemporary Romantic irony that he sought, in vain, to dominate, Hegel minimized Socratic irony, the essential features of which he misunderstood. By relating his concept of irony constantly to Socrates, Kierkegaard seeks not only to grasp its truth more accurately than his rival had, but first of all – for the one is a condition of the other – to be a better erotician, a better lover than Hegel had been.

And if Socrates is the erotician par excellence, and if – such is the 'thesis', pure irony – he never grasps anything, what does it really mean to know how to cope with that woman/irony, to grasp her in her totality and in all her details? Does it not mean precisely that she is not to be grasped, not to be squeezed into concepts, but allowed to unveil herself, without alteration and without fuss, lightly and without appearing even to be touched? To grasp her, then, one must let her go; one must leave her in order to possess her. Not to master her the way commanders-in-chief or non-commissioned officers do, whatever their abilities, but to master without mastery, without violence or rape – by moving away from her.

6. *Irony or woman: how can either be possessed?*

While he is writing his thesis on irony, describing the detachment it necessarily entails and making clear that anyone who wants to possess it must detach himself from it, Kierkegaard has just detached himself from his fiancee Regina Olsen at the very same time and in just the same way. By writing the thesis in which he attempts to present himself as more 'masculine', as a better erotician than Hegel (than the father?), is he attempting to compensate for the lack of masculinity he has displayed by breaking with Regina, whose name suggests that, of the two of them, it was perhaps she who exercised mastery? Did he not break with her only so as to avoid being castrated by her? Or did he leave her only so as to be able, while keeping a respectful distance, to grasp her all the better, in all her features, without fear of being blinded by excessive proximity, without the risk of having to rape her? If, in order to possess a woman, in order to arouse or keep her love, one must be able to remain at a distance from her and give her nothing, Kierkegaard demonstrates more masculinity by breaking with Regina than by staying with her. He shows that he is more powerful than Hegel, that noisy, spur-wearing knight, by overcoming irony *incognito*, as it were, from a distance, and in silence, ironically: he does so, in other words, by identifying with irony (with the woman), by becoming a woman himself. If masculinity consists, then, not in warlike activity and power but in the feminine science of distance, respect, and silence, and if the conquering activity of philosophy makes up its mind to learn how to conceive correctly, it is obvious that the comparison that inaugurates the Thesis blurs the traditional distinction between the sexes to a considerable extent. The knight who goes off to conquer a woman and/or irony can only proceed in disguise, so far as his sex is concerned; he may not know himself which one of the two will impregnate the other. Kierkegaard's initial comparison reveals that behind the official subject of the thesis, *'the concept of irony'*, the unofficial subject may well be *'conception'*, or even, if conception is to be accomplished without physical contact, *'immaculate conception'*.

And the topic of conception has a necessary correlate: the question of *sexual difference,* another question skimmed over lightly, like the question of irony, by the commander-in-chief who let his glance fall briefly on Socrates when he was assigning him a place in world history inferior to that of Antigone, history's most magnificent figure. A passing remark made this clear. However, such questions cannot be relegated to asides; they are actually the 'true' subject of the Thesis. In this connection, another 'detail', located 'outside the text', is particularly revealing for anyone who – unlike the officer – pays sufficient attention. Kierkegaard's epigraph signals with the greatest appearance of seriousness (it is a passage from Plato given in Greek[8]), like a nod to the reader aimed over the jury's head, that – appearances notwithstanding – these are precisely the questions to be addressed.

The quote comes from Plato's *Republic,* a text that Kierkegaard will classify (with the exception of Book I) among the non-Socratic dialogues; more precisely, it is taken from Book V (403d), which deals with the question of women. Plato declares this question to be the most indecent and the most formidable of all, one that threatens to leave Socrates and his interlocutor in a state of aporia unless, to escape from their distress and get out of danger, they take the risk of swimming. They need to jump into the water to look for a *poros,* some unexpected dolphin that can carry them on its back and miraculously bring salvation. This well-known metaphor, used frequently by the Greeks to describe the aporetic situation,[9] is offered as an epigraph; it appears simply to announce that Kierkegaard too, obeying the Socrates of *The Republic,* is jumping into the water to get away from the daunting question (especially daunting if one has chosen it as a thesis topic) of irony, or women – for those who are capable of understanding know that the two questions are one and the same.

All this is still too simple, however. The remainder of the thesis shows that, for Kierkegaard, the Socrates-of-the-Plato-of-Book V-of-*The Republic* is not to be identified with the 'real' Socrates – whose viewpoint is indistinguishable from that of irony. Because he has nothing to assert, because his ignorance is real, far from inviting his interlocutors to leap into the vastness of the sea to find a *poros,* Socrates leaves them in *aporia,* in the most naked distress, that of shipwreck victims. When he does take them on board, he does not steer them toward salvation on the back of a dolphin; he puts them in Charon's boat, so that, like the ferryman of death, he can take them, through seduction, to nothingness.

Reread in retrospect, the epigraph thus proves to be doubly ironic. Through the context from which it is drawn, with seeming innocence, it reveals the real stakes of the thesis; through its content, in a duplicitous fashion, it attributes to 'Socrates' a discourse that is in contradiction with the one the author of the thesis will attribute to him by dedicating him to irony and to a purely negative 'mission'. It remains to be seen, then, whether Kierkegaard identifies with the 'real' Socrates – the one whose 'conception' he exposes – or with Plato's Socrates. A passage from the *Philosophical Fragments* may allow us to resolve this question.[10] In this later text, written in a different context, that of faith, Kierkegaard takes up the metaphor from *The Republic* on his own account, in a slightly modified form. Faith, by definition and in essence, takes the risk of jumping blindly into the water before it knows how to swim. If it were to put off 'believing' until it had all the proofs, it would never believe, and for want of uncertainty, it would no longer be faith but knowledge.

Kierkegaard does not reduce irony, as Hegel did, to a simple moment in the universal life of Mind. On the one hand, surpassing his predecessor, who thought he had attributed enough to the negative, Kierkegaard goes so far as to assign a role in every decisive turning point of world history to ironic subjectivity, as infinite and absolute negativity. On the other hand, taking the opposite tack from Hegel, he represents ironic subjectivity as a necessary stage in personal life, the initial stage; because in its essential aporia it is unable to bring salvation on its own, he is unable to give it the last word. The last word belongs to ethics and to religion, to which irony – if it is to avoid the risk of degenerating like its Romantic form into a diabolical nihilism – must be subordinated and by which it must be mastered: such would be the 'ultimate truth of irony' (which Goethe[11] had grasped after his fashion, since he put irony at the service only of something higher than itself, poetry). This truth is revealed finally in the very last words of the text, which reduce it, since it is not by itself a *poros*, to a simple *path* to salvation.

7. *Irony under control*

At the very moment when he is demonstrating that no authentic human life can do without irony, without detachment, Kierkegaard underlines the ultimate subordination of irony thanks to the ethico-religious metaphors and vocabulary he uses; thus he deprives irony on the one hand of what he is granting it on the other. Through this religious reappropriation he deprives it of mastery: if irony is to personal life what doubt is to science and philosophy (p. 326),[12] a necessary stage, this is so only provided that it keeps itself in its initial place and retains its pharmaceutical, corrective and purifying functions. From the infinite play of irony with reality, because it restricts truth, the ironic subject, and makes it finite (like Christ giving Judaism the coup de grâce by means of Judaism itself), using reality against reality (irony of ironies: Hegel had understood this, knowing that every historical reality bears within itself the seeds of its own destruction), Kierkegaard retains only the fact that irony is a strict disciplinarian: it corrects and chastises impatience, which 'wants to harvest before it sows' (p. 328); it prunes wild shoots and invests personal life with health and truth.

Kierkegaard asserts that those who remain deaf to irony's murmurs miss 'the absolute beginning of personal life' (ibid.), and he compares irony, because it saves the soul from finitude and opposes the idolatry of the finite, to the freshness and strength imparted by bathing in a fountain of youth, but he adds at once that the bath is a 'baptism of purification' (p. 326): anyone who takes off his coat in order to plunge into its waters does not intend to remain there, or even to start swimming – the pool is doubtless too small to allow anyone to behave like the Socrates of the epigraph and propose to seek a *poros* there, as one might in the open sea; no, one plunges in only 'in order to come out healthy, happy, and buoyant and to dress again' (p. 327). In the last analysis, one must protect oneself against irony as against a seducer, even while commending it as guide. Irony is not truth, but one of truth's paths.

Kierkegaard 'recuperates' irony as the possibility of a beginning. It brings enjoyment of freedom preserved; it offers the pleasure of soaring above the intoxicating infinity of possibilities, although only in the way the Church has authorized and illustrated: 'in the Middle Ages, [the Roman Catholic Church] tended to rise above its absolute reality at certain times and to view itself ironically – for example, at the Feast of the Ass, the Feast of Fools, the Easter Comedy, etc'. (p. 253). Ultimately, then, Kierkegaard recuperates irony in the service of faith. Irony as he understands it can serve faith because irony that is aware that life has no reality delivers just the same message as the piety to which it opens the way. It falls into the abyss of religious madness: the meditative spirit also maintains that all is vanity but (and here is what makes it superior) it uses this negation only to set disruptive elements aside and to support the appearance of eternal permanence; the meditative spirit effaces itself, the most miserable of all finite persons, in favor of the divine. By rendering all things vain, on the contrary (and this is where it goes astray, and needs to be brought under control), irony liberates subjectivity. While everything is becoming vanity, the ironic subject, inferior in this respect to the subject of religious humor, does not view itself as vain but preserves its own vanity. Thus Socrates' ironic point of view makes him choose death as a punishment, but this mere conveyor of souls nevertheless has not set off for Hades on his own initiative; he has in fact been *condemned* to die.

Later on, in the *Philosophical Fragments*, writing under the pseudonym 'Climacus', Kierkegaard reproaches himself for criticizing Socrates (in *The Concept of Irony*, in a way that is still entirely Hegelian), for privileging the individual at the expense of the collective, whereas it is precisely in this respect that he portrays Socrates as a great ethicist, in *The Sickness Unto Death* and *Practice in Christianity*. Under the name *Anticlimacus*, Kierkegaard shows that while subjectivity may be truth when it confronts the abstract objectivity of the system, it is error when it confronts the transcendence of God. Because God alone is the true master, irony can be acknowledged only as controlled; as for Hegel although not in exactly the same way, it can only be assigned a carefully circumscribed place: that of intermediary between aesthetics and ethics, just as humor will occupy the place of intermediary between ethics and religion. Notwithstanding all that separates him from Hegel, the whole subversive distance through which, by virtue of the subtle play of his writing, of his double language, Kierkegaard was able to detach himself from Hegel without opposing him; indeed, owing to his writing strategy and the displacements of problems it allowed, Kierkegaard seems finally to announce Nietzsche; the profound harmony between their critiques of Romantic irony might have hinted at this. In letting ethics and religion have the last word, Kierkegaard appears at least as akin to Nietzsche as to Hegel.

8. *Kierkegaard, Janus bifrons*

Although he recognized Socrates as a *Janus bifrons,* an embodiment of the bidirectionality immanent to irony, Kierkegaard was intent on stripping the philosopher of his positive aspect so he would be seen only from the perilous side of the void, so he would be swallowed up in the vast sea of aporia with no possible way out. Nevertheless, Kierkegaard's own sarcastic irony might not be the sign of the absolute negativity to which he sought to reduce Socrates. It might take the shape Hoffman gave irony[13]: it might be the reflection of a double 'soul', pulled painfully in opposite directions. This 'duality' in Kierkegaard, which is not susceptible to sublation by dialectics, would explain the fact that his thesis, in its presentation, exposition, and conclusions, is at once Hegelian and non-Hegelian, 'Nietzschean' and 'non-Nietzschean'; it would explain why his own bifrontality, which was prominently displayed at the outset, compelled him consistently to disobey all military figures who order their underlings to look up in one direction only.

Thus, beginning with the epigraph, Kierkegaard indicates that he sees things from both sides at once. On Socrates' side there is aporia and the emptiness of irony; on Plato's side there are audacity and risk, aiming for a secure refuge, a *poros,* a way out. In characterizing these two positions, Kierkegaard also describes the endlessly alternating structure of his own operation, as if he were watching himself watch himself in a mirror. He is taking the risk of presenting himself before a thesis jury studded with officers and non-commissioned officers of varying abilities; the risk is that he will be 'brought down' by them or even drowned. For this is the only way he can get himself out of the doubly aporetic situation in which he has landed. On the one hand, he has lost his father. Pastor Kierkegaard died in 1838, after hearing his son promise that he would take his final examination in theology. Jean Brun reminds us that, as a child herding sheep on harsh and solitary terrain, Kierkegaard's father was said to have cursed God for keeping him in a state of wretched poverty; presumably he despaired of God, or at least did not have enough faith to believe that God could always miraculously send some *poros,* a goat if not a dolphin, to bring men out of aporia, as he had done for Isaac. By having the courage to 'defend' his thesis in theology, the son at once obeys his father and shows himself to be more of a believer than his father was; it is as if he were attempting to pay for the latter's youthful error, or to wipe the slate clean. On the other hand (but perhaps this second point is not without relation to the first), Kierkegaard has just broken with his fiancee Regina. Unlike the commander-in-chief, he does not consider the institution of marriage important enough to keep him from wondering, before he commits himself fully, whether he will be happy or unhappy with the woman he has chosen, and especially whether he himself will be able to make her happy – and whether he would not do better to remain at the service of Christianity alone. Under the circumstances, then, he hesitates to jump into the water without answers to those questions. And since, facing such an interrogation, he may never be certain of anything, owing to his own lack of faith, he risks remaining in a permanent state of aporia – unless the thesis, by helping him to see more clearly into the question of women, his real subject, provides him with the unhoped-for *poros.*

The thesis cannot do so without plunging him into a new aporia, however. It is awkward for Kierkegaard, as a Christian, to accept being saved by writing. Later, identifying himself both with Socrates (who, as an authentic ironist, 'left nothing by which a later age can judge him' [p. 12], nothing in writing) and with Christ ('who did not get mixed up with writing' except for some traces in the sand), Kierkegaard refuses to 'conceive' – for conception would make him, a sinner, a rival of women and of God (who alone creates). He will write only under pseudonyms; only his religious work will appear under his own name (his father's name), because there he is speaking in the name of God.

No more than Socrates or Christ – who are quite similar in this respect – does Kierkegaard, at least in *The Point of View for My Work as an Author,* lay claim to the title of 'author'. He considers that for him as for his two 'models', his life as an individual has to bear witness rather than what he says or writes; language and writing are in any event no more than duplicitous masks.[14]

In other words, for Kierkegaard, too, *the concept of irony* turns out to be merely a stage in 'his' work, an aesthetic stage opening the way toward ethics and religion. The thesis supplies him simply with a provisional *poros.* Thanks to his incorporation of irony and the abandoned woman, he can give birth to a possible, actualized and necessary conception of Socrates. While his conception may not be more 'true' than Hegel's or that of his sources (since all human knowledge is necessarily finite), at least it may be more viable. He does not hesitate to 'expose' his conception, even though, in its irony, the Thesis on irony is perfectly aware that the offspring conceived, like any human child, is destined if not to be aborted then at least to pass away.

Did this official birth-giving allow Kierkegaard to reply as well to the questions underlying the unofficial subject of his thesis? By identifying himself with women and their irony, by showing that he was capable of writing and conceiving as they do, did he learn enough about them to know 'who' he was, man or woman, assuming that his gender identity was well-established and that his identification with women did not tend instead to destabilize him? To these unofficial questions, the responses, assuming they were possible, would have been in any case necessary if he was going to be able to commit himself to a marriage that might function according to a rhythm quite different from a military one, a marriage in which the two partners would not be compelled to line up one behind the other or to march in step, or to stay frozen for all eternity in the place assigned by the commander-in-chief; this holds true both for him and for her. But who is 'she', who is 'he'? Did Kierkegaard, even and perhaps especially after giving birth to his thesis, ever manage to find out?

1. An Impossible Painting

Leaving behind titles, epigraph and appendix, those hors-d'oeuvres to which we have thus far been paying special attention in feminine fashion, in Kierkegaard's own fashion, let us now address the work itself. In it, we shall once again discover a bifrontal approach.

In the Introduction, Kierkegaard justifies the fact that he has, in non-Hegelian fashion, attributed the most prominent position in his thesis on the 'concept of irony' to an individual, Socrates (although without reducing him to that position), and he stresses the methodological difficulties that he has to confront in order to try to circumscribe his object.

If his study of irony leads him to turn to Socrates, this is because, as the *tenth thesis* has already indicated, 'the concept of irony makes its entry into the world through Socrates' (p. 9). In other words, the concept is first of all a *conception* and, as Kierkegaard insists, in relation to Socrates the term 'takes on an entirely different meaning than it has for most other men' (and again: 'the question of a view in regard to Socrates is quite different from what it is in regard to most other people' [p. 12]). To conceive irony is to give birth not to an 'idea' that can be displayed 'in a discourse' that would presumably be 'the presence of the idea itself', but to give birth to a child the 'display' of whom threatens to reveal, at least in the eyes of the Greeks, its scandalous illegitimacy. For, contrary to expectations, this offspring's external appearance is not at all in harmony with its inner nature. The end result of its discomfiting inadequacy is that the atopic bastard will be put to death.

The child to which Socrates gives birth, the conception that makes its appearance in the world along with Socrates, is a self-conception. Irony is born with Socrates; it is one and the same as Socrates, at least in its inception; for, like every child, it will have its own history, and it will undergo many transformations before ending up in its modern form, Romantic irony. According to Kierkegaard's reading, Hegel believed that Romantic irony, coming as it does at the end of the developmental process, provides the 'truth' of the child and the concept; this belief led Hegel to neglect Socratic irony, treating it as if it were of secondary importance and reducing it to the status of a phase or 'moment'. In Kierkegaard's view, on the contrary, Socratic irony is of primary importance; for, despite all its vicissitudes, like all individuals irony harbors a certain nostalgia for its place of origin (even Hegel, in his own way, recognized the need to look to that country, the birthplace), a nostalgia for the mother's womb. In conformity with that infantile desire, Kierkegaard turns toward the mother, Socrates; however, he does not leave it at that, does not settle for a simple reversal. For no matter how satisfying childhood may be, it cannot supply the eternal truth of the concept on its own, because it is tied to the contingency of an individual history. Philosophy exploits its superior, sovereign status to look down on its little sister, history; it purports to be teaching history a lesson through its requirement of eternity. Under philosophy's orders, the historical moment, no matter how fertile, must be surpassed.

In this conflict between warring sisters, history and philosophy, Kierke-gaard does not take sides in a clearcut way, but he gives credit to each party while subverting both. He restores the exalted debate to an entirely different level, ironically, by comparing the 'speculative' relation between the two adversaries to the religious and psychological relation between a confessor and a penitent. The former's fine-tuned listening ability allows him to discover the penitent's secrets, enables him to grasp hidden connections that reveal the truth of the latter's history, above and beyond surface appearances.

Doing full justice to the phenomenon – to irony – implies that one must play the roles of confessor and penitent simultaneously. This is the only way the philosopher, operating in his elevated sphere, can avoid resembling the knight decked out in his spurs; it is the only way he can avoid worrying and frightening his feminine prey, and the only way he can escape from her magical seduction, from the distractions created by the profusion of detail. He has to position himself as close to her as possible; at the same time, he has to remain at a certain distance from her – the distance of a confessional, at least, a distance that allows him to 'restore' the seductive narratives heard in that dark chamber, by turning away from them and protecting himself against them in order to avoid being hypnotized by them.

While Socrates and irony make common cause, then, Kierkegaard is not about to let himself be fascinated by that particular aspect of Socrates' phenomenological existence at the expense of the truth of the concept. Still, that truth can be grasped only within and in relation to the phenomenological element. Kierkegaard makes it a rule not to neglect the penitent's confessions, although his attention to the details will fluctuate. Furthermore, without letting himself be hypnotized by the seductive profusion of those details, he does not fail to try to construct their meaning. Nevertheless, he ends up, subversively, paying closest attention to Socrates, to the phenomenological and historical aspect of the concept. Part One, by far the longer of the two sections of the thesis, continually refers the concept of irony back to the maternal womb, while Part Two, which addresses the *concept of irony* properly speaking, devotes yet another chapter to Socrates' irony, comparing it favorably to the modern forms.

Under these conditions, the thesis-writer's first priority is to present a solid, authentic conception of Socrates; such a conception is provided in great detail in Part One. In the process, the author exposes – so as to ensure their abortion – some conceptions that fail to present an authentic figure of Socrates (although these failures are quite different from Hegel's); rather, they offer some transfiguration, for example an excessively positive or negative image motivated by fervor or jealousy. For what the confessional of History secretly reveals to the philosopher is that History is not so much the site of the development of truth as the site of conflicts, polemics, settlings of accounts, and rivalrous or amorous relations among philosophers. There is a subterranean history of power relations that a 'perceptive ear' (p. 10) – Nietzsche will call it the 'third ear' – cannot fail to grasp, if it can avoid being hypnotized by all the all too human details. Thus it is with the greatest prudence and vigilance, while looking sharply in all directions, that one must lend one's ear to History, to the history of 'concepts', and in particular to the history of the concept of irony – or the concept of Socrates, who is even more difficult to grasp than anyone else. For, on the one hand, in keeping with the high value he attached to immobility, meditation, and silence, he wrote nothing; 'he has left nothing by which a later age can judge him' (p. 12). On the other hand, if one cannot trust the sources, as a last resort, it is because, even for his contemporaries, Socrates was already ungraspable. His outward appearance is a form of (his) irony; 'the outer was not at all in harmony with the inner but was rather its opposite' (ibid.), and his language was always at least double – it did not purely and simply reveal his thought.

Kierkegaard can only acknowledge this absence of harmony between the inner and outer Socrates by referring implicitly to Alcibiades' discourse in the *Symposium,* a discourse whose authenticity will not be challenged later on because it corroborates the thesis that Kierkegaard's point of view has dictated from the start. In his person and in his statements, Socrates is wholly double: 'only under this angle of refraction is he to be comprehended' (ibid.), Kierkegaard says, subordinating by that imperative the 'concept' of Socrates to 'his' own conception, to his perspective or his instincts. By emphasizing Socrates' dual nature, he announces a dissimilarity that he will introduce explicitly later on: the dissimilarity between Socrates and Christ, and between the available sources of information about Socrates and the narratives of the Evangelists.

Absent in his very presence, having left no written record, Socrates cannot be conceived and grasped except by a 'new combined reckoning' (p. 12), a reconstruction that may or may not correspond to the conception of his contemporaries (and after all, 'even his own age could not apprehend him in his immediacy' [ibid.]). Socrates' existence can only leave us in aporia, owing to the nature of his substantiality, which is ironic, paradoxically, but at the same time negative. It is impossible to produce *an image, a figure,* of Socrates, who never presents himself in person as such. In its positivity and unicity, an image would conceal more than it would reveal of his essence: through his duplicitous negativity, through his irony, the demoniacal Socrates in his malice defeats every attempt to capture his likeness. Kierkegaard offers a useful image for the endeavor: he says it is like trying to paint the invisible with visible means, a task 'as difficult as to picture a nisse [an elflike household creature] with the cap that makes him invisible' (ibid.).

2. Conception Becomes Possible

A. *Socrates' statements and those of his sources are not Gospel*

So how can one exit from aporia? How can one conceive the impossible? By jumping into the water. In Kierkegaard's case, this means presenting the conceptions of Socrates' contemporaries, Xenophon, Plato, Aristophanes as a point of departure. The first will be aborted because it caricatures Socrates; the second will be aborted because it idealizes him excessively. Between Xenophon and Plato, nevertheless, Kierkegaard leans toward the latter: like Aristophanes (who came closest to the truth of all three), Plato was able to penetrate the rough exterior of Socratic duplicity, while Xenophon apparently settled for surface appearances.

One must not equate the relation between Xenophon and Plato, however, as Baur does, with the relation between the synoptic gospels and John's gospel. According to Baur, the synoptic gospels, Jewish in conception, only grasped the external aspect of the Messiah, as Xenophon did with Socrates, whereas John's gospel grasped Christ's higher, divine nature, as Plato did with his master.

Despite the forceful character of the parallelism, Kierkegaard whose *first thesis* insists that the resemblance between Christ and Socrates lies in their dissimilarity, cannot adhere to it as such. To do so would presuppose a 'demonic' lack of congruence between outside and inside, an essential duplicity in both Christ and Socrates. If this were the case, the Evangelists would have been obliged to subject Christ's words to a more or less violent effort of interpretation, and it would have transformed the conception of the Apostles, who exhibited the truth of Christ's life in a tangible way, into a work of fiction, 'an ingenious work of art' (p. 14, note). Now, unlike the figure of Socrates, the figure of Christ, his essence and his words, cannot be transfigured, for Christ was tangible and visible. Socrates for his part is invisible, perceptible only to the ear (and at that, only to the alert and fine-tuned ear of a good confessor). Christ's existence was transparent, while that of Socrates was only apparent. Christ's words could be taken literally because they were life and spirit, while Socrates' words incited scorn and brought life only through negativity. Because Christ cannot be duplicitous, then, the synoptic gospels offer a direct image of Christ, a faithful image of his immediate existence, 'which did not signify anything else than what it was' (p. 14) and what it seemed to be (unlike the existence of Socrates, which Xenophon exploited for apologetic purposes). In the same way, John's gospel is based on a direct perception of the immediate divinity of Christ, whom it presents – while imposing silence upon itself – in its perfect objectivity. Plato, on the contrary, 'creates his Socrates by means of poetic productivity, since Socrates, precisely in his immediate existence, was only *negative*' (p. 15).

Kierkegaard's religious biases, which require him to get control of irony, to treat it as a simple stage subordinated to the stage of ethics and religion, compel him at this point to emphasize (as he is not always inclined to do[15]) the dissimilarity between Socrates and Christ. Thus, in the interest of his religious cause, he acknowledges the possibility of a perfectly transparent life, the possibility of a discourse that can be taken literally because it reveals the mind in full clarity in its own text, the possibility of a text without a reappropriating interpretation, the possibility of a truth that is not always already also a fiction. Kierkegaard, who is one of the first to establish (and before Nietzsche did) that Socrates oscillates between caricature and idealization because each of his two sources arrived at his conception by looking through his own stereoscope, nevertheless cannot be identified with Nietzsche in this respect. He remains attached to the whole metaphysical tradition that discredits duplicity and mystifying obscurity in all its forms, contrasting them with positively valued transparence, clarity, light, truth and/or Life. To reduce Socrates to an ironic or negative viewpoint is to claim that the philosopher is a malicious and invisible elf closer to infernal powers than to divine ones, that he is more like a demon than a God; and because he is Greek – neither Jewish nor Christian – Kierkegaard will ultimately identify him in his radical negativity, with Charon, the ferry-boat conductor of Hades; Kierkegaard reduces Socrates' 'divine mission' to the task of merely conveying souls to Nothingness.

Because Xenophon's and Plato's conceptions are not to be taken as Gospel, then, despite all the respect that scholars grant them as sources, it is fitting to cause them to abort by exposing their more or less fictional character – whether that fiction is sickeningly platitudinous, prosaic and boring, like Xenophon's, or divinely poetic, like Plato's.

B. *Xenophon's stereoscope*

Hegel prefers to turn to Xenophon when he seeks to illustrate the positive side of the Socrates figure. Nietzsche presents *Memorabilia* as the 'most compelling book in Greek literature',[16] one that he reads not out of curiosity but because he finds in it an 'unpretentious familiarity',[17] and he reads the same author's *Apology* ('The Defence of Socrates at His Trial') with 'deep personal feeling'.[18] Kierkegaard, for his part, uses his devastating irony to castigate Xenophon, because he does not find the least trace of irony in the latter's text (and he was looking for it; that aim directed his reading). 'The more Socrates tunneled under existence *[Existents]*, the more deeply and inevitably each single remark had to gravitate [in what sense? who or what, other than Kierkegaard's bias, is behind this requirement?] toward an ironic totality, a spiritual condition that was infinitely bottomless, invisible, and indivisible' (p. 19). Because the secret is invisible, Xenophon with his down-to-earth outlook completely misses Socrates' irony. Xenophon is like a crawling insect, hopelessly stuck to the ground and surely lacking in the refinement of hearing that allows one to perceive what is invisible. He offers his contemporaries a shopkeeper-Socrates in his own image, a good-natured, chatty, somewhat flighty bourgeois, a boring and harmless figure whose condemnation to death by the Athenians and subsequent immortalization by Plato is thus completely unbelievable in the end. Both the excessive honor and the infamy Socrates incurs would have to be explained by demonic bewitching, or perhaps by a state of shared dementia (a less-than-credible collective madness), or at least by some mistake or act of stupidity rather than by wrong-doing. The alternative is to acknowledge the ironic hypothesis that by trying too hard to defend Socrates (the apologetic intent already burdens Xenophon's text with a gap, leaves it lacking as a witness to truth), by depicting the philosopher as insipid and 'so fervently well-intentioned toward the world if only it will listen to his slipshod nonsense' (p. 16), Xenophon ends up justifying the death sentence, not so much because of the official charges against Socrates as because of the deadly tedium he radiates. This tedium is so pervasive that it might even seem more surprising to see Alcibiades remain so long in Socrates' company than to see him give in to debauchery; debauchery might be a reasonable compensation for spending so much time with such a mediocre character.

This hypothesis would lead us to acknowledge generalized insanity, would have us view the Platonic perspective as completely insane. Here is an authentic example of demonstration by way of the absurd, and it is also a way of begging the question (since it is a well-established 'objective' that is already a 'deficiency', to use Kierkegaard's own terms [p. 15], that guides and orients his own reading). No, Xenophon's conception is the one that must be condemned.

Playing off the 'wisdom of the world' against its 'irony', and Plato against Xenophon, in order to 'save' Socrates' irony, Kierkegaard goes after Xenophon's offspring with no holds barred; he wields ridicule more often than argument to rip Xenophon's conception to shreds, and he brings the author to his knees under the weight of his devastating metaphors. And Hegel is in for it along with Xenophon, even though on the surface Kierkegaard does not seem to be dealing with Hegel at all. For the

Xenophon to whom Hegel turns to illustrate Socrates' *positive* aspect is the very source whose deficiencies, gaps, omissions, lacks, and defects Kierkegaard puts on display. It is for not giving *enough* credit to his Socrates, for stripping him of too much, for leaving his offspring to languish, that Kierkegaard reproaches Xenophon, an unfit mother: in short, he reproaches the mother for inducing her own abortion, by leaving her offspring in an insubstantial and impoverished state. She reduces his bifrontal duplicity not in order to privilege the positive side but in favor of nothing at all. Unfolding Socrates' conversation in a linear, uniformly monotonous fashion, Xenophon *missed* the *two-faced* nature that makes him a 'torpedo fish', the *atopicity* that allows him to be everywhere and nowhere, never in the same place and always agitated – swimming in the empirical but able to fly off at the slightest contact and soar up toward reasoning and the Idea.

Unlike Hegel, however, Kierkegaard does not see the Idea as a positive reality. For him the Idea is a mere logico-dialectical abstraction of the same value as the phenomenon, because in his eyes both are pure images of the divine, and the divine is actually present nowhere. Being more or less deaf to Socratic sobriety, Xenophon could not perceive and thus could not render anything that contrasted with the braying of donkeys and the vain ruckus of the Sophists sputtering empty words, the deafening brouhaha of the marketplace; he could not detect the divine schema that Socrates *wove* (is that what dia-lectics means?) through the woof of existence – because everything was for him a sign, a welcome image of the Idea. Xenophon failed to perceive the underlying divine harmony; Plato, a better musician or confessor, was able to hear it and to make it heard, though in purely poetic form. Plato provided his offspring with excessive nourishment; this is another way, as we shall see, of being a bad mother. In any case, Xenophon kills his own offspring by not providing enough.

As further evidence of Xenophon's deficiencies, there is also his *lack* of the sense of repartee: questions and answers unfold in his text in a continuous one-directional *flow*. Socrates' interlocutors' rejoinders are deficient not because they are inappropriate but because they are too appropriate, too toughminded. And, because they follow on the heels of questions put too directly (something Hegel appreciated, for he did not think much of imper-tinent responses of the '*witzig*' type that sidestep the question; he sometimes attributes such responses to Socrates by relying on the same Xenophon – but is it really the 'same' one?), such rejoinders are exceedingly dull, for they are totally lacking in irony – the irony that (Kierkegaard asserts) is characteristic of Socrates. Xenophon was too short-sighted to see this, and he did not hear it either, because his ear lacked the finesse that would have enabled him to grasp what was said between the lines, beyond the plenitude of dialogue. For, in order to grasp the secret of irony, one needs an eye that Xenophon seems indeed to be lacking, an eye that Xenophon tore out himself in an access of anguish, an eye capable of grasping the void, nothingness. Such an eye would not have been superfluous, for that void, that nothingness conceal what is essential.

Xenophon listening to Socrates' discourse is like someone looking at a painting of Napoleon's tomb and seeing only two big trees shading the grave (p. 19). Xenophon hears only the immediate meaning of what the discourse implies, the way a superficial viewer sees nothing but trees and shadows. The viewer does not perceive the empty space between the two trees; if he were to follow its contours, the figure of Napoleon would suddenly leap out in hallucinatory fashion. Not a single line has been sketched in to indicate this figure, but once the viewer has seen it, he can never fail to perceive it again. Similarly, no one who has heard Socratic irony ring in his ears, even though nothing in the plenitude of discourse has hinted at it, can ever again fail to hear it: his ear has proven capable of confronting nothingness and the void without anguish, and it is positioned at the right distance to be able to hear accurately. One must not follow the example of Xenophon, Socrates' contemporary and favorite, and come too close. On the contrary, one must keep one's distance from irony, for, like a woman, irony only gives herself to someone who respects her, someone who withdraws without giving her anything in order to allow her to disclose herself: she then imposes herself abruptly, in her haunting nakedness, and will never leave again.

Because Xenophon stuck too closely to reality and to Socrates, he could not help but be mistaken; because he was too eager to be faithful to Socrates, he was inevitably unfaithful. Indeed, because the empty area was fully shaded in, he mistook the shadow (of the trees) for the only reality. He was fascinated by the plenitude of Socrates' discourse, without discerning in it the essential void that is self-evident only to someone who is afraid of nothing, someone undaunted by irony, or Socrates, or woman, or Napoleon – for Napoleon is a great man, who, like God, cannot be represented by himself; his presence is revealed in the void of a tomb. To anyone who knows how to deal with such figures, a 'nothing' suffices to make them self-evident.

By supplying this visual image of an auditory perception which for its part is offered and withheld simultaneously, does Kierkegaard mean to evoke once again the diabolical character of ironic discourse, as opposed to the Christic discourse which, in its plenitude and its presence, gives its meaning with full transparency? Or, since, after all, in the case of God's tomb, it is again the void that imposes a presence, without appearing to do so, is he hinting, without appearing to do so, at an entirely different conception of discourse from the one he presented when he emphasized the dissimilarity between Christ and Socrates, a dissimilarity that here on he will continually attempt to erase? In any case, the image of the painting suggests that it is the empty space, the nothingness, that conceals what is essential. This is perhaps because only that empty space allows each viewer's fantasy to take shape, as Freud indicates in his American anecdote.[19] Only that empty space allows the art critic to see the figure of Christ where there is merely the plenitude of a wall, a plenitude transformed into vacant lacunary space by the fantasy itself. Where Xenophon, looking at shadows (the plenitude of discourse), perceives only the emptiness that unfolds there between the lines, the same empty space allows Kierkegaard to make visible the irony that – because such is Kierkegaard's 'point of view' – has always already hollowed out the void that it can now fill, in a circular movement, with its own nothingness.

In the same way, the gaps in Xenophon's conceptions (owing to deficiency) and Plato's (owing to excess) provide space for Kierkegaard to expose and impose his own, as the only 'actualized' and necessary conception, provided that his own has already been able to show up the others' gaps as such. For Nietzsche and Hegel bring quite different fantasies to their readings, and they fail to perceive the gaps, or at least they do not see them in the same places in the texts. If Nietzsche delights in reading the *Memorabilia* while Kierkegaard experiences unforgivable boredom when he makes the attempt, this is ultimately because the similarities between 'their' Xenophons, and between themselves, lie especially in their dissimilarity – that of their fantasies. But this is precisely what Kierkegaard, unlike Freud or Nietzsche, does not say, at least not directly, not in so many words. His not saying so leaves room, however, for anyone capable of understanding to harbor an ironic sense of another interpretation, although his discourse can never – no discourse can – really authorize, on its own, a judgment as to the presence or absence of ironic duplicity. Taken in itself, then, Kierkegaard's discourse asserts that the two *defects* it has just unearthed in the plenitude of Xenophon's discourse – the failure to grasp the duplicity of Socrates' existence (his atopic bifrontality) and the lack of meaning in the responses given by Socrates' interlocutors – are fundamental deficiencies that prevented Xenophon from seeing, if not the character of Socrates in its totality, at least the 'ganglionic and cerebral system' of his personality (p. 17).

Xenophon comes up short on other grounds as well. As Kierkegaard examines a *collection of observations* attributed to Socrates,[20] he finds that Xenophon fails to rise to a poetic or philosophical level; he resembles a prospective elementary school teacher taking an oral examination, bleating ecstatically over the beauties of nature (p. 20) which Xenophon's own 'degenerate prose', in its wholesale banality, can only alter and stunt, retaining no trace of Socrates' 'heavenly' origin. At every turn, Xenophon misses the essential element, namely, irony.

By and large, as Kierkegaard's second thesis declared, Xenophon is a short-sighted, hard-of-hearing crawling insect who remains stuck at the empirical level. He operates at the level of the polygon, which he confuses – if he is translated into Hegelian language – with the circle, mistaking an angle of the polygon for true infinity. Thus he stresses usefulness in Socrates' teaching, and confuses it with the 'interior infinity of the good' (p. 21). Detached from its infinite dialectic, this spurious infinity becomes a 'kingdom of shadows' (p. 22) devoid of forms and contours, capable – this time Kierkegaard spells it out clearly – of adopting any form whatsoever (for if there is nothing absolutely useful, there is nothing absolutely useless) 'according to the observer's capricious and superficial glance' (ibid.). Taking the example of the dialogue with Aristippus,[21] Kierkegaard shows how, according to Xenophon's portrait (but not Plato's), Socrates demolishes his interlocutor's attempts to approach the Idea and is 'in dead earnest' (p. 23) in bringing the exalting infinity of his investigation into relation with the baseness of the spurious infinity. The *commensurable* is his proper field of operation. A 'positivist' before the fact, he sets up a cordon sanitaire around the all human sciences and actions, reducing them so as to make them available 'for use by everyone' (p. 23). In every realm, whether it be friendship,[22] Socratic erotics,[23] or life's various pleasures, Xenophon, unlike Plato, displays a narrow, prosaic outlook; he reduces Socrates to 'an aged coquette' who still thinks s/he is capable of pleasing – but with whom 'we are disgusted' (p. 24). With that phrase, Kierkegaard reveals less about Xenophon than about himself; he betrays a visceral bias that prevents him from acknowledging, without nausea, a version of Socrates' amorous practices that transforms the 'divine' philosopher (Plato's term) into a dubious go-between or a disgusting seducer.

Whereas, in the *Symposium,* Plato attributes to Socrates 'a kind of divine health' (ibid.) that does not deprive him of any pleasure and that never leads him into excess, Xenophon on the contrary interprets Socrates' ability to drink without ever getting drunk as the natural result of the moderation he was capable of practicing – not because he embodied the virtue of temperance but because he functioned like a more or less cynical shopkeeper capable of calculating what was in his own interest. This alone would suffice to make Socrates a detestable, 'disgusting' figure. However, his shallowness and lack of generosity are also revealed in Xenophon's version of his conception of death as a mere means of escaping the infirmities and burdens of old age.[24] Xenophon may grant him a few poetic features in the *Apology,* but in Socrates' refusal to defend himself Xenophon never perceives a supernatural dimension that would allow him to juxtapose his attitude of divine silence to that of Christ.

Judged by the standard of Plato and by Kierkegaard's own instincts, or instinctive repulsions (which can be read in his profound aversion for the portrayal by Xenophon that he has just translated, in terms that are sometimes Hegelian, sometimes Platonic, the better to discredit and ridicule it), Xenophon's conception displays only the parodic shadow of Socrates without retaining any trace of his irony. In place of irony, there is sophistics, whose noisy and endless tumult is substituted for Socrates' infinite silence. With a few exceptions, the sophisms cited in *Memorabilia*[25] lack 'the ironic infinite elasticity, the secret trap-door through which one suddenly plunges down' into an infinite void (p. 26).

Because Xenophon's conception, with its excessive positivism, its prosaic character, its excessive plenitude, has nothing to say about 'that infinite, absolute negativity' (ibid.), about the incommensurable void that no cordon sanitaire can circumscribe, about the irony of which it retains no traces at all, Kierkegaard in turn, unlike Hegel and Nietzsche, finds nothing at all worth preserving in Xenophon's conception of Socrates. The conception deserves to be aborted, and indeed it has always already been aborted by its own author, who condemned it to death himself by what he left out. Unless it was the child itself, at the moment of birth, who preferred to go straight back into its mother's womb, as if terrified at the prospect of boredom.[26]

Perhaps no one can do without a stereoscope, but Xenophon's served only to elicit a deadly tedium. His way of bringing Socrates into relief deprives the character of all depth, and that is not its least defect. The only benefit of his insipid portrayal is that its very gaps call up complementary colors to bridge them, and thus the text brings Plato into view at a distance, through gridwork, as it were; hence it is all the more successful in imposing, by contrast, the figure for whom Kierkegaard admittedly had a youthful predilection. By virtue of its sterile emptiness, Xenophon's stereoscope ultimately serves only to bring his rival into relief. Even though this rival is absent, even because he is absent, he has always been present, as if by anticipation, like a fetish called upon to fill Xenophon's gaps and to bring relief and comfort to Kierkegaard. As evidence of his gratitude, Kierkegaard takes his own good time to present the Platonic conception of Socrates; he is in no hurry to abort it or to burst it (the way he did with Xenophon) as quickly as a soap bubble.

C. *Plato's poetic fiction: Socrates' metamorphoses*

a) How to separate a child from its mother when she has fed it too well, or how Socrates becomes Samson

The question about Plato's conception of Socrates is not where it resides (quite clearly, for Kierkegaard, 'Plato saw in Socrates . . . an immediate conveyer of the divine' [p. 29]), but whether it corresponds to the real Socrates. Hegel did not raise this question, since, from his lofty position as commander-in-chief of world history, he only glanced casually at actual historical individuals: his interest lay in the necessary development of the Idea. For Kierkegaard (and later for Nietzsche), the question is inescapable. For if we confuse the real Socrates with Plato's Socrates, we run the risk once again, as we did earlier with Xenophon's Socrates but for the opposite reasons, of overlooking the essential element: his irony.

As Kierkegaard himself declares, 'every philosophy that begins with a presupposition naturally ends with the same presupposition' (p. 37). His own 'presupposition' thus leads him to seek traces of irony in Plato's dialogues: this is the only criterion, according to him (Nietzsche offers others, as we have seen) that makes it possible to distinguish, in Plato, between what belongs properly to the master and what to the disciple. The distinction is extremely difficult to make. For one thing, it seems very small-minded to try to dissociate individuals who are 'so inseparably fused' (p. 30); to do so would be to dismiss the gratitude that the devoted Plato shows toward his master by making him omnipresent in his work. In his youthful enthusiasm, Plato in fact attributes everything to Socrates, all the knowledge that he himself has already incorporated and that he shares with his master in return as if he were sharing secrets of love. By this dual operation of assimilation and depossession, the disciple is now one with the master. They are in perfect unison; neither now possesses anything of his own; each possesses all that belongs to the other, so that it is impossible to identify any portion that belongs to either one.

The deep need for 'unity of spirit' (p. 30), Plato's need to merge with Socrates, is such that he seeks to hear his own thoughts spoken in his master's voice. After the master's death, that need only increases; it leads Plato to confuse their respective originalities even more profoundly. He disinters the master in an effort to preserve him, and installs him within himself, in his work. He transfigures the master within this 'crypt', while at the same time, impelled by excessive humility or guilt, he treats the poetic figure he is creating as if it were historical reality and invites others do the same.

All this strikes Kierkegaard as perfectly self-evident. He knows that one cannot establish relationships among ideas without paying attention to relations among philosophers, whether amorous or rivalrous. To reach this understanding, he did not need to read *Mourning and Melancholia* or *Totem and Taboo;* however, the recent loss of his father may have enabled him to anticipate Freud. His father's death may have taught Kierkegaard that, once dead, the soul becomes more powerful than ever, that death is perhaps a gain for the soul, a 'good deal'.[27] He does not say as much in *The Concept of Irony* in connection with Socrates, for if he were to suggest that Socrates had everything to gain from dying he might be assenting to Xenophon's shopkeeper's spirit, which he finds repugnant. In *The Concept of Irony,* Kierkegaard is less concerned with the one who dies than with the survivor who keeps the loved one alive within himself as a way of surviving his loss. The survivor nourishes the loved one from his own substance. Renouncing his own 'narcissistic libido', he transfers it to the loved one at the price of shrinking his own ego and losing his own 'name' – for from that point on Socrates serves as Plato's only mouthpiece, and lends him his name. Kierkegaard, for his part, uses his father's voice in writing works that he would like to attribute to him; these he signs with his own name.

By recalling some general, elementary psychological truths that will also be immediately self-evident to Nietzsche, Kierkegaard pays homage to Diogenes Laertius, who had long ago raised the question of how to dissociate the two members of the couple. The question is inescapable, but it is very painful to contemplate – especially when one is passing through a period of mourning and rupture oneself. Diogenes brought about the intolerable break by distinguishing between *dramatic* and *narrative* dialogues in Plato's texts. For Diogenes, the narrative dialogues involve the real, historical Socrates; only the *Symposium* and the *Phaedo* belong in this category.

The formal criterion underlying the distinction does not appear any more clearcut to Kierkegaard than it did to Baur. Let us suppose Plato presented certain dialogues in the form of a narrative attributed to Socrates; might that not be precisely a device intended to make the text appear 'historical'? Nothing guarantees that the content of the dialogue, the discourse *attributed* to Socrates, was actually produced by him. Thus Baur suggests that, above and beyond the formal criterion, one should invoke the Socratic *method:* in this view, Socrates offered Plato his method as a gift. But things are not that simple. For if Baur was right, Kierkegaard ought to go along with Hegel in crediting Socrates with a positive side, precisely because Hegel cannot specify what was contributed to the 'Socratic' method by each member of the couple whose divorce he wanted to avoid in the interest of the dialectical cause.

By positioning himself in relation to the Hegelian dialectics and borrowing its language, Kierkegaard thus manages to extract 'his' Socrates from that of dialectics, and to separate him from Plato. The type of dialogue 'in which Socrates excels' is indeed an attempt to allow thought to present itself in its full objectivity, but the synthesis that alone makes the speculative trilogy possible is lacking. Socrates' method actually consists in 'simplifying life's multifarious complexities' (p. 32) by reducing them to an increasingly abstract summary. The particular skill required is the art of *asking questions* or *conversing*. This skill is different from the Sophists' technique, for, unlike Hegel, who 'lent' the Sophists' more negativity than he did to Socrates, Kierkegaard claims that they know how to *respond* and to speak, not how to converse; he finds them 'as uneasy as cows that have not been milked at the proper time' (p. 33, note), so impatient are they to show off their wisdom.

Conversation is authentic only if two conditions are met. On the one hand, the person speaking must keep in mind the topic under discussion; on the other hand – and Hegel had suppressed this – the person speaking must pay attention not only to the idea but also to the other interlocutor as an independent subject. Questioning cannot occur unless the person asking the questions has a relation both to the object at issue and to another individual.

That first point might allow us to juxtapose Socratic questioning to the Hegelian negative, except that the latter is a necessary phase in thought, whereas with Socrates, if one retains the term 'Hegelian' (although this is no longer very meaningful), the negative cannot be dissociated from the individual who is asking the questions. With Hegel, 'the thought does not need to be questioned from the outside, for it asks and answers itself within itself' (p. 35). 'With Plato', whom Kierkegaard is still coupling with his master so as to underline their shared difference from Hegel, 'thought answers only insofar as it is questioned' (ibid.), and it is questioned only in a contingent fashion, so it remains dependent on subjectivity. When the questioning is in a necessary relation with its object, questioning can no longer be distinguished from answering. When, as is the case with Plato/Socrates, 'the subject is an account to be settled between the one asking and the one answering' (ibid.), the exchange does not follow the straightforward and necessary linear pattern to which Hegel sought to reduce it; it is carried out in a rocking movement in which the interlocutors advance haltingly in alternation. Its progression remains dialectical (even if each response implies the possibility of a new question and even if the moment of synthesis is absent), but it no longer has anything in common with the Hegelian dialectics.

In this other dialectics common to Plato and Socrates, a dialectics that is distinct from the speculative version and that Kierkegaard has up to this point indifferently identified as 'Socratic' or 'Platonic', the strictly Socratic element can be discerned by distinguishing intentionality from interrogation. Either one can ask questions in order to get an answer, in keeping with the *speculative* method that presupposes a plenitude, or one can ask questions in order to exhaust the apparent content through the questions themselves and thus leave a void, in keeping with the *ironic* method. The latter, as we might expect, is the one Kierkegaard attributes to Socrates.

Questioning is the essential element for Socrates; questions are addressed to a knowledgeable subject in order to show him that he knows absolutely nothing; in this respect the type of interrogation practiced appears related to that of the Sophists. In fact, as the *Gorgias* (461d), the *Protagoras* (328e-329b), and the *Symposium* (198b)[28] suffice to prove, Socratic questioning differs as much from that of the Sophists as a 'slight draft' differs from hazy eloquence and from 'poetic vapors' (pp. 36-37), which it actually tends to dissipate quite readily.

The meteorological analogy reveals that, even as Kierkegaard is citing Plato for support, Aristophanes and his play *The Clouds* are what in fact unofficially 'inspire' Kierkegaard's point of view on Socrates and supply him from the 'outside' with the criterion for distinction between Plato and Socrates that the text of Plato alone, in its wilful amorous and melancholic confusion, could not have offered on its own. Officially, however, Kierkegaard turns to Plato and his *Apology* in order to illustrate Socrates' ironic activity, as if the text written by Plato could guarantee on its own the historical authenticity of the words attributed to Socrates, could be considered purely and simply as a 'document'. Actually, as Kierkegaard points out in a note, Xenophon's *Apology,* while it lays claim to the same authenticity, does not attribute the same words to Socrates and could not be a conclusive source for illustrating Socrates' ironic point of view; in Kierkegaard's eyes, this is sufficient reason to make Xenophon's *Apology* more suspect than Plato's. Plato's text, as Kierkegaard sees it, is an ironic statement from beginning to end, one in which the bulk of the accusations against Socrates are reduced to nothing, to the nothingness that Socrates offers as the content of his life.

Despite the title, the *Apology* contains no defense. Socrates finds a pretext for a pleasant chat; he mocks no one but his judges. His ironic attitude is confirmed by Diogenes Laertius, who recalls that Socrates saw no reason to read the discourse that Lysias had prepared for him and refused to do so, even though he himself acknowledged its excellence.[29] He tells how his life has been reduced to traversing the domain of intelligence only to find that everything is limited by an ocean of illusory knowledge. He explains that he has devoted himself to a 'divine mission' that has led him to neglect both private and public life; this mission consisted in showing, everywhere he went, that no human beings – not even poets, or artists, or politicians, or orators – possess wisdom. By the same token, he annihilates the futile claims of his three accusers and – this is the height of irony with respect to those who are condemning him to death – he manifests his joy at going to Hades so as to be able to question the dead themselves, in order to show them that they do not know anything either.

Socratic irony thus spares neither the living nor the dead. It reveals itself in the *Apology,* which 'in its totality is an ironic work, inasmuch as most of the accusations boil down to nothing' (p. 37). Socrates, of course, is not a Jew. His concept of dialogue symbolizes the Hellenic view of the relation between the gods and mankind: there is interaction without synthesis, dialogue without true dualism, since the relation consists entirely in simple reciprocity.[30] Still, Kierkegaard compares him to Samson, because of the negative power of his generalized irony that respects nothing, and because he causes the two pillars of the temple of knowledge to collapse into the nothingness of ignorance. Such a sacrilegious gesture could not be attributed to Plato, the divine Plato (who is more like a Christian than a Jew?); it is authentically Socratic. This seems so self-evident to Kierkegaard that there is no need to prove it: 'That this is genuinely Socratic everyone will certainly admit' (p. 40). In the confounding ambiguity and undecidability of the Platonic text, the only thing that makes it possible to draw distinctions is the reversing irony characteristic of Socrates. The traces of this irony need to be followed closely if one is to restore it to him, assuming one knows how to hear it, since in its duplicity it threatens to mask as well as to unmask that Socrates who, despite his blatant omnipresence, could just as well pass 'incognito' if we were to confine ourselves to this criterion alone.

That is why Kierkegaard adds a second, more obvious criterion: the difference between the *abstract,* which is linked to the method of confounding interrogation, and the *mythical,* which is linked more closely to the search for answers and which announces a richer speculation, one more characteristic of Plato than of Socrates.

Kierkegaard proposes, then, to examine certain dialogues more closely in order to show how abstraction is inflected into irony in one group (the *Symposium,* the *Protagoras,* the *Phaedo,* and the *Apology*) and that the mythical element in these texts points to a richer speculation. He provides a different reading of Book I of the *Republic,* the only one still marked with the stamp of irony.

b) The Symposium: how Socrates-Proteus becomes a telegrapher, a vampire, a counterfeiter, a diver, a seducer
The *Symposium* is a key dialogue for anyone seeking to develop a conception of Socrates' life, just as the *Phaedo* is crucial for forming a conception of his death. However, Kierkegaard is not taken in by the formulas in which Plato purports to be attesting to the authenticity of the narrative only so as to underscore its fictional character. Equipped with his twin criteria for selection – ironic dialectics belongs to Socrates, mythical exposition to Plato – Kierkegaard follows the traces of what 'properly' belongs to Socrates in the *Symposium.* Behind this overt aim, we may be able to detect another. Distinguishing between Socrates and Plato in the dialogue amounts to distinguishing between Greek love – the Socratic Eros – and Christian love. Once again, Plato's approach is closer to the Christian version, provided that Diotima's speech is attributed to him – which it is, by Kierkegaard, despite all the textual indications to the contrary. Were Kierkegaard to acknowledge the identification of Socrates with the priestess, it would annihilate his two criteria: myth and positivity would be on Socrates' side. In order to 'save' irony and 'lose' Socrates, he is thus constrained – begging

the question – to assert that the *Symposium* is the product of two different hands: one belongs to Plato, while the other is completely manipulated by Socrates.

Similarly, and with good reason, Kierkegaard is obliged to reject a dialectical reading of the *Symposium* (dialectical in the Hegelian sense) that would interpret the final discussion on the nature of Eros as a development that reappropriates and subsumes earlier arguments. Kierkegaard's own dialectics is, on the contrary, of the Socratic type; it reads the text as a continuous ascension, starting from the earth-bound stodginess of the presentations preceding that of Socrates. The heterogeneous discourses *on* love are inspired by heterogeneous viewpoints on life from which one needs to liberate oneself so as to rise higher and higher above the atmosphere until one reaches the essence of love. Such a view of dialectics might seem more Platonic than Socratic, if Kierkegaard were not transforming the topological image – ascension from the perceptible terrestrial element to an intelligible heaven – into a more Aristophanesque, more meteorological image: the final destination, in fact, is described as 'the pure ether of the abstract' (p. 41), which would take one's breath away if one were to get that far. However, one will not complete the ascent if one follows Socrates instead of Diotima/Plato; for Socrates, essence turns out to be invisible. It loses itself in the clouds; it is a pure abstract mathematical point from which the various earlier conceptions do not radiate.

Thus, after evoking and ironically deforming the Platonic metaphor, Kierkegaard attaches three other less familiar images to it, the better to displace it. The first, a military comparison, converges with the one proposed in the Introduction. Each speaker is the conqueror, ally or rival of the others; each aims to circumscribe the territory of love. This image is faithful to the agonal character of eulogies, in which everyone seeks not so much to find truth as to win first prize. A second simile, from the sphere of optics, suggests that each of the speeches is like a component of a sliding telescope; each segment is ingeniously adapted to the next. The third simile, which in its own way reutilizes the image of teaching that Socrates offers at the beginning of the *Symposium,* compares each of the speeches to cut crystal goblets that intoxicate as much through the infinitely multiple refraction of light as through the sparkling wine within. These three figures of speech illustrate not only the inebriating diversity of the lyrical qualities of the rival conceptions, but also the homogeneity of the search for a wholly positive and concrete object in relation to the existential experience of each individual; such an object has nothing in common with the 'abstraction' and invisibility of the Socratic ethos.

However, Kierkegaard deprives his reader of the intoxicating effects of these 'drunken' speeches, for he limits himself to a thoroughly insipid, disappointing, and unfaithful summary. His sole aim is to stress that even when the speakers grasp the ambiguity of Eros, they do not conceive of it the way Diotima does, in a negative synthesis (this viewpoint is highly contestable, if only because Kierkegaard is wrong to translate Plato into Hegelian language). Instead, they conceive of the duality of Eros as an external division; they neglect the moment of immediate unity, the unifying link that envelops ambiguity. Aristophanes himself fails to grasp this connection, even though he offers a deeper foundation for the opposition implicit in love by basing it on sexual difference. We may wonder whether it is not because Kierkegaard is blinded by the question of the difference between the sexes – the 'real' subject of his thesis – that, in dealing with Aristophanes' 'whimsicality' (p. 44), he neglects the two other human types, one wholly female and the other wholly male, that account for the origin of homosexuality: each had been split in two by Zeus. Does he have eyes only (like nearly everyone else)[31] for what he calls not bisexuality but the original sexual indifferentiation (that of androgyny) that gave rise, after the bisection by Zeus, to heterosexual love – a form of love that is perhaps less 'disgusting' to Kierkegaard than the other?

As if disgusted, Kierkegaard turns away from all these excessively concrete and detailed erotic scenes, in which no cut is spared, and looks toward Socrates and his more abstract love. He offers a summary account of Socrates' entrance onto the stage, his opposition to the rhetorical genre of eulogy and the use, in its place, of the interrogative method which does not remove the shell of Eros one question at a time in order to reach its kernel, but rather *removes the kernel*; that is, it liberates Eros from the contingent concrete content in which it had appeared earlier and brings it back to its most abstract characterization.

Kierkegaard neglects the 'poretic' side of Eros (in his view, the myth of the birth of Eros, son of Penia and of Poros, belongs exclusively to Diotima/Plato), the better to distinguish it from the Christian love of God that makes itself known in an infinite fashion and in all its plenitude. He emphasizes the strictly negative aspect of the Socratic Eros, which he reduces to nostalgia, to the search not for something that one has lost, as in Aristophanes' myth, but for something that one has never had and will never acquire. For this definition of love as nostalgia is the most abstract definition possible: shorn of all content, it is absolutely empty. And after rising up from concreteness to this abstract dimension, Socrates' investigation stops ironically right where it ought to begin. The halt is marked, as Kierkegaard sees it, by a break in the dialectical movement: Socrates passes the pen, as it were, to Diotima – that is, to Plato, who seeks for his part to supply the idea. In any event, Kierkegaard, who has been begging the question, cuts through the ambiguity of the text and settles it: he has decreed once and for all that what is negative and ironic belongs to Socrates, what is mythical and speculative to Plato. Still, he does not distribute roles to each character in quite such a simplistic way, for the profound communion between Socrates and Plato *is supposed to* leave room nevertheless (but here again, at whose demand?) for the supposition that their respective conceptions of love may converge at some point.

The convergence is to come in the person of Socrates himself, it seems: he 'exemplifies' in his person, as a supplement to the deficiency of dialectics, 'the idea', which would thus be rendered perceptible and which Alcibiades – unlike the other speakers, who are groping for it blindly – has grasped 'with immediate certainty' (p. 47). But to do this Alcibiades had to be in a drunken state, for when he is sober his love for Socrates leaves him instead (as it does everyone) in a state of uncertainty and anxiety, the gentle anguish of doubt.

Successful in being taken for a lover but never giving anything, Socrates becomes the loved one of all those he has duped and forever subjugated in this way. This unbearable position cannot fail to provoke ambivalence.[32] The love relation Socrates establishes with Alcibiades is not contingent, since it is repeated with everyone; the love relation is not only possible but necessarily bound up with Socrates' irony and the negativity of the Eros he embodies. Taking it for granted that the erotic relation between Socrates and Alcibiades is of a purely intellectual nature, Kierkegaard asserts that if Socrates had possessed the idea and had communicated it to Alcibiades, their love relation could never have given rise to 'such a passionate agitation' (p. 48). Agitation thus becomes the counterproof of the ungraspable Socratic irony that prompts a Protean changing of masks, and it can only produce the cruelest torments in the lover. Socratic irony tears the lover away from immediate existence, liberates him from it, seems to promise him something else, but leaves him finally in suspense – like the Socrates of *The Clouds* in his basket, one might say. However, Kierkegaard does not use this image here; instead, in a note, he uses the more sinister image of a coffin (which he will pick up again later in the body of the text). The coffin is not Napoleon's, this time, but Mohammed's, floating in suspension between two magnetic poles (p. 48). Irony buries immediate existence, which it both repels and attracts toward the idea, the true life that it cannot give any more than Mohammed (who is not Christ) can. But this 'suspension' in which all of irony's torment lies also constitutes its seductive charm, its enchantment. Irony holds captive in unbreakable bonds anyone who delights in its mystery, 'the telegraphic communication it prompts' (p. 48), like the woman who never gives herself when she gives in, unless it is through 'infinite sympathy' – and only from afar, fleetingly and without ever banishing the fear of scorn.

Such is the nature of the pleasure procured by the man whom Plato's Alcibiades calls a sorcerer, a charlatan, a magician more powerful than any other, and whom Kierkegaard calls a great seducer. It is a pleasure in negativity that one must be slightly perverse to appreciate, for the great seducer – and this is not the only metamorphosis of the one who always presents himself masked – also appears to the lover's eyes, if the lover is not completely blind, as an authentic vampire. The seducer merely alludes to the idea; he immediately takes back with one hand what he has just given with the other, as if he wanted to keep the idea all to himself (at least this is what the jealous lover supposes; in fact, the seducer does not possess the idea, but he gives the impression that he does through his strategy of seeking to dissimulate). In this way, the seducer leads his lover to perdition at the very moment when the lover thinks he is achieving his own objectives. In his infinite sympathy for the character, Kierkegaard offers an image of violence more evocative of Goya than Plato (who for his part chose the image of a poisonous snake): he transforms Socrates into a 'vampire who has sucked the blood of the lover and while doing so has fanned him cool, lulled him to sleep, and tormented him with troubled dreams' (p. 49).

The violence of this image is perhaps destined to conceal or mimic the violence to which Kierkegaard is in the process of subjecting Plato's text, so that he can more readily extract and separate from it not the divine Socrates, the divine *agalma* that is concealed behind the mask of the Silene according to Alcibiades, but a Socrates who is entirely demoniacal (in the Christian sense). This latter Socrates is a navel-gazer who focuses not on the idea but on himself; he inspires enthusiasm not through the divine, positive plenitude that he is thought to contain secretly within himself (and which he reveals furtively, at best, on rare occasions), but through irony alone: that is, through the negative element of love, which is the best stimulant of love because it never gives anything (Alcibiades acknowledges that Socrates has never granted them the slightest favor). In Plato's view, Alcibiades in particular has attempted to deceive Socrates, to exchange his own illusory beauty for the other's (presumed) knowledge in a real fool's bargain; however, Kierkegaard points out that Socrates would unquestionably have paid him back in kind. For another of this vampire's masks is that of counterfeiter: while the ironist may have something of solid value in his possession, the coin he produces has no nominal value. 'Like paper money, [it] is nothing' (p. 51). and yet it allows him to carry out all his transactions.[33] It is Socrates' positive plenitude – his solid value – that constitutes all the vital force and health of irony, that valueless, 'unhealthy' money. But this is a *poros* that Socrates keeps well hidden, dissimulated, when he takes up the diver's mask, with its tube connecting him to the life-sustaining atmospheric air.

Because he has made a gift of the divine *poros* of love to Diotima-Plato, Kierkegaard can only grant it surreptitiously to Socrates, offering it with one hand and withdrawing it just as quickly with the other. At the very moment when he has lent the ironist a certain solid value, and a definite plenitude, that of being not a mere destructive breeze but a life-giving air (this prefigures later images of irony as an air pump, a 'bath of regeneration and rejuvenation', a 'baptism of purification' (p. 326) and a necessary stage in a human existence worthy of the name), he brutally strips him of his breathing tube (or tubes).

Kierkegaard's reading in effect counters that of D. F. Strauss, who sees an analogy with the transfiguration of Christ in Socrates' sobriety at the end of the *Symposium,* when all the others are in a state of drunkenness. Baur characterizes the final tableau of the *Symposium* as a synthesis of the comic and the tragic; Kierkegaard accepts this reading only so long as the synthesis is located within irony itself. Socrates' meditative posture, his way of 'gazing into vacancy' (p. 52), may be a good plastic image for this synthesis, for Hegel is quite mistaken to make the philosopher's 'immobility' a figure of internal contemplation; once again he confuses Socrates with Plato. The fixity of his inward gaze signifies only that he is focused on nothing, to such an extent that he no longer sees anything but nothingness. The synthetic unity of the comic and the tragic is not their higher positive reconciliation, it is an '*abstract and negative*' reconciliation 'in nothingness' (ibid.).

Kierkegaard's reading of the *Symposium* thus turns out to have been a way of begging the question. To the Socrates of love he has granted nothing but nothingness: this is the only way to cut him off from Plato and Christ, to cut him off from himself, Kierkegaard, as well, to shake off the spell cast on him by the great seducer who promises much but delivers nothing, who leaves you finally deprived of your own vital substance, leaves you lifeless, with your air supply cut off. Through identification – 'infinite sympathy' – with the ironist, Kierkegaard has not resisted the diabolical temptation to offer Socrates the gift of these images, like so many masks, and to offer the reader, and his jury, the gift of his own highly seductive 'gentle anguish', a gift to be enjoyed with negative pleasure. Does he do this in order to charm them, or to turn them away from himself as well as from the demonic Socrates? Or is it so he can win their attachment by turning them away from the other? For Kierkegaard, a Christian author if we are to believe *The Point of View for My Work as an Author,* to proceed under the mask of a rogue and a seducer is a way of attracting large numbers of Christians: even for a saint such a task requires thoroughgoing self-denial. For a religious author, to seek to seduce is to offer oneself up for purifying persecution: the height of irony. If Kierkegaard is attempting to turn us away from Socrates, is this not after all the best way to bring us under his sway?

c) Protagoras: Socrates devours his own stomach, loses his hair, turns into a sleight-of-hand artist, a tyrant and an assassin
At the very outset, Kierkegaard announces that in his study of the *Protagoras,* he is going to 'show how the whole dialectical movement, which

is prominent here, ends in the totally negative' (p. 52). That this movement is therefore – he is begging the question again – essential if one is to conceive the real Socrates. That the *Protagoras* is the first dialogue governed, according to Schleiermacher's distinction, by the *dialogical* element, ironic controversy, as opposed to the *constructive* dialogues, which were written later and which are more objective and scientific. The latter are dialogues in name only, to such an extent that one can even wonder why Plato has preserved this mimetic form of utterance, which he condemns after all in *The Republic*. The ironic questioning has disappeared; 'Socrates' is no longer a real individual but simply a name, more like a common noun than a proper name, and the umbilical cord that connects the discourse to its author and makes him a true 'author' has been cut. In short, there is no point lingering over these pseudo-dialogues (although we should recall that for Hegel, these 'authorless' dialogues were on the contrary the only authentic ones): we shall find no trace of Socrates in them, according to Kierkegaard.

On the other hand, in the early dialogues, we have every chance of discovering Socrates. In fact, what characterizes them, or so Schleiermacher says, is that they end *without a conclusion*. Kierkegaard's use of the Hegelian expression rather than the Platonic term *aporetic* gives him more purchase on the Hegelian dialectic and facilitates the removal of Socrates from his defined place within the system, a place from which absolute negativity can only drive him away. For *without a conclusion* does not mean an aporetic, 'embarrassing' conclusion, a starting point for a new investigation, but precisely a *negative* conclusion, as Kierkegaard makes crystal clear. The *Protagoras* and Book I of *The Republic* supply the best examples. At the end of the *Protagoras,* a dialogue entirely infused with irony, Socrates and the Sophist find that their face-off leaves each of them facing nothing at all. Their disputes have produced no benefit whatever. They have split so many hairs it does them no good at all to find a comb: they have both grown completely bald.

In offering this image, Kierkegaard, who chose a passage from Book V of *The Republic* as his epigraph, had to be thinking of the paradigm for sexual difference proposed by 'Socrates' in that text. The difference between the sexes does not entail a difference in nature between man and woman, but simply the sort of difference that obtains, he says, between bald men and men with a full head of hair: this difference does not prevent them from exercising the same functions and trades. Suppose that bald men stand in for women (and this is not self-evident): does Kierkegaard, in returning to the image of baldness, not want to insinuate that Socrates, far from possessing the divine *agalma* that Lacan identified with the phallus and that Alcibiades supposedly tried to steal, could do nothing but use his irony to 'castrate' his interlocutor before castrating himself, leaving himself in a state of total impotence, 'vis-a-vis nothing'?

Kierkegaard complements the image of 'bald men' with another image that points toward the absolute negativity of irony: the image of Tantalus who first devours everything around him and then consumes himself, like the witch in the folktale who devours her own stomach. Because with its ravenous appetite it devours absolutely everything in its path, irony alone, much more than the Sophistic skepticism that always ends up 'positing' something, confers on the dialogue's absence of result a wholly negative character. Its negativity cannot be 'sublated', either by means of further study, as Platonic aporia suggests, or by being reduced to a simple phase or 'moment', as it is in speculative dialectics. For Socrates seems to enjoy the absolute 'negative' as if it were actually the avowed or unavowed object of his desire; the dialogue itself 'seems to take a certain pleasure in the fascinating game of demolition' (p. 56). (One might add, although Kierkegaard does not, that self-castration or self-devouring was the only way Socrates could protect himself against the castration that must have been inflicted on him by his wife Xanthippe – that 'high-spirited mare' whom he fled like the plague for the agora, where he 'invented' a no less lethal dialectics. In just the same way, Kierkegaard, who understood readily – as every man does, or so he declares in his *Journal* – what the word 'anthropophagic' means, was seeking, doubtless for the same reasons, and along the same routes, to escape from his fiancée, Regina, the Queen.

Socrates' strategy is to put himself in question in order to get his Sophist interlocutor to accept his critique (Sophists behave as thoughtlessly as Epimetheus in the Protagoras myth; if they want to be successful in their quest, they ought to be as vigilant as Prometheus[34]). Kierkegaard has nothing to say about this lesson; following his own all too Platonic criteria, he underscores only the ironic result reached by the two adversaries. After all sorts of disputes, they succeed only in exchanging roles, putting on each other's suit.[35] The one who was standing upright is now upside down, and vice versa. Protagoras espouses Socrates' position, while Socrates adopts that of the Sophist, just as (Kierkegaard says) a Protestant lets himself be convinced by his Catholic interlocutor and the Catholic by the Protestant. They have simply traded places and are ready to start arguing again. In the commotion, Plato may be the only real winner: he is the one who plays a game of toss-in-the-blanket with both Protagoras and Socrates; he is the one who puts into place the lever of irony. But Kierkegaard, who is eager to establish the *Protagoras* as a purely Socratic dialogue and to confer irony on Socrates alone, cannot accept this interesting hypothesis, which would complicate the scene of mastery: irony is Socrates's property, after all, since it is *he* who manifests surprise at seeing the game end in this curious reversal that annihilates all conclusions. (But this a very weak argument, since the question is precisely how to determine 'who' speaks through Socrates' mouth: is it Socrates or Plato?)

Like its structure, the dialogue's entire content derives from negative irony, Kierkegaard maintains. Each of the adversaries allows his method to be contaminated by the other's: Socrates does not hesitate to use sophisms and Protagoras resorts to an ironic dialectics. Concerning the first question of the dialogue, whether virtue is one or multiple, Protagoras looks at the qualititative unlikeness of the various virtues without being able to see the slightest unifying link among them. In order to preserve their oneness, above and beyond their relative disparity, Socrates sets out to rediscover the connection with the help of sophisms. However, in the name of essential unity he actually ends up with a pure abstraction of the weakest sort. Socrates, an authentic tyrant, begins in effect by assassinating his subjects, by draining virtues of all their blood, in order to reign more easily over this bleak shadow kingdom.[36] Putting Socrates ironically in the place of the prisoner in Plato's cave (or in Hades), Kierkegaard offers a proliferation of images destined to show the abstract inconsistency and negativity of the essential Socratic unity, a dangerous reef where 'real' virtues run aground like so many ships. Present in each of the virtues like a gentle murmur, their essential unity is audible nowhere. Like a watchword forgotten as soon as it is transmitted from one ear to another, the unity of virtue, in the last analysis – because it does not result from a genuine *sublation* that would preserve the various virtues while reconciling them – is completely volatilized, along with the concrete virtues, and its capital remains unexploited. Kierkegaard refuses to choose between his two equally inane hypotheses.

Concerning the second question addressed in the dialogue, whether virtue can be taught or not, irony can be discerned at various levels. Socrates starts with the idea that irony cannot be an object of teaching, while Protagoras begins with the opposite notion; each one ends up adopting the other's position. In the end, Socrates exhausts his adversary's presuppositions and takes up his defense ironically the better to ensure his defeat. But this is not the only locus of irony. Socrates announces that virtue cannot be taught, that it is natural (his error consists in denying history and life, while the Sophist, who denies the primordial nature of virtue, makes the opposite mistake). Then he goes on to present virtue as knowledge, but as self-annihilating knowledge; for what is in question, according to Kierkegaard, is recollection. Now, for Plato, recollection signifies something positive and comforting: 'that man is not driven empty-handed out into the world' and that he can '[call] to mind his abundant equipment through recollection' (p. 60). For Socrates, recollection – and this is why it is opposed to all teaching – is a regressive movement running completely counter to evolution: taken back through time immemorial, the recollection of virtue would constitute quite simply the forgetting of virtue. Kierkegaard presents this regressive conception of recollection even though he knows it is not supported in the text; simply begging the question, he asserts that it is 'Socratic' to deny the validity of reality without putting anything positive in its place, without offering something that at least might really be tested. Protagoras continually refers mankind to the school of experience, even though he knows (and here is where his irony lies) that, given its discontinuity and incoherence, such a school can never impart wisdom, for a mass of mute letters can express nothing by itself. Socrates, for his part, presents virtue in the guise of a woman, someone who is so cold and stiff[37], someone who holds herself at such an inaccessible distance, that none of her conquerors can see or touch her.

Here, then, is the locus of Socrates' irony: after denying that virtue can be taught, he reduces it to something that can be known, a form of self-suppressing knowledge, one whose pleasure, like woman's, is infinitely deferred. It may be the case that virtue cannot be taught by experience in the Sophists' sense, for the endless empiricism proclaimed by Protagoras can only leave one in a disastrously unsatisfied state. Socrates, however, in his ironic negativity, has no more to offer than Protagoras, whether he is opposing the latter's thesis or ostensibly espousing it the better to destroy it. And if Kierkegaard ultimately refuses to take sides, this is because when a Christian raises the question of virtue in terms of knowledge, whether the response is positive or negative, the problem has in any case been placed on a terrain other than its own. Socrates can no more be saved than Protagoras, because even if knowledge of virtue is inaccessible to him, he reduces sin to ignorance (Nietzsche calls this proposition devastating), to misunderstanding and blindness, 'and the element of will therein – pride and defiance – is disregarded' (p. 61).

d) Phaedo: invisible irony, or how the plebeian Socrates is infected with an aristocratic disease

Kierkegaard judges Socrates' position in the *Phaedo* in relation to the Christian position once again. Distinguishing between the Socratic and the Christian views on death, he uses the former as a supplementary example of his negative ironic viewpoint. According to Kierkegaard's criteria, the *Phaedo* is more Platonic than Socratic by virtue of the space allotted to myth; it has generally been judged tragic in tonality and deemed even more Oriental than Greek. Given this approach, it would seem that Kierkegaard ought to have a good deal of difficulty proving that irony actually constitutes the essential element of this dialogue, as it does in the case of the earlier ones. (And the irony in question is irreducible to the rhetorical flourishes and scattered ironic remarks that are compatible with text's presumed gravity and emotion.) Kierkegaard would be taking a real gamble here if this were something he wanted to prove; but in fact he begs the question yet again, in that he counters all objections with a repetitive, almost comical recourse to the necessary invisibility of irony. Only someone sufficiently in sympathy with irony to be able to 'hear' and acknowledge it without proof, despite the fact that it appears 'incognito', can be convinced of its ungraspable existence. Attempts at argumentation notwithstanding, Kierkegaard thus concludes that the text is inadequate to prove its own irony; he turns to Plato's *Apology* as a necessary supplement.

Nevertheless, he establishes what appears to him a justifiable distinction between what he calls subjective Oriental mysticism and Greek irony, and he contrasts these two conceptions with Christian mysticism. The first distinguishes itself from the second through its oppressive, heavy, murky, stifling atmosphere, which incites a soul languishing in the depths of melancholy to seek out some narcotic that will numb and stupefy it. The atmosphere of the Greek heavens is, for its part, light and diaphanous; it invites the soul to soar higher and higher. But the soul's aspirations are concentrated on a sublimated element so subtle that it ends up as a pure unmixed abstraction; its lack of consistency makes it indistinguishable from nothingness.

Thus in the *Phaedo,* progressive death to the self is conceived in a completely abstract way. The soul is conceived as abstractly as essence. Essence is a pure, phantomlike shadow that requires a correlative if it is to be grasped at all: a soul as shapeless as itself, reduced like the ideal – a pure abstraction in opposition to the concrete – to nothingness. Since both the object and the subject of knowledge are conceived so negatively, we can imagine what proofs of the immortality of a soul thus annihilated must be like; in any case, we may observe that they are not very compatible among themselves. Each of the arguments leads only to a corroboration of the completely abstract and negative character of the soul, whose future existence must be extremely abstract as well. If we limit ourselves to the dialectical portion of the dialogue, we find that it leads only to the conception of a lusterless, ethereal immortality, one still less substantial than Homer's, one that vanishes in a breath. In seeking to gain such immortality, one risks mistaking the shadow for the prey, grasping a cloud instead of Juno. That is why the living philosopher who has a nostalgic desire to die and leave reality behind is in a quite pitiful state of contradiction; he is not to be confused with the Christian who desires to die to himself. In the latter conception, a moral one, man desires to die to a positive reality, that of sin, in favor of something positive, namely, the growth of divinity within himself. In the intellectual, Greek conception, the thing to which one is to die is unimportant, and what is to develop in its place is purely abstract and negative.

Undertaking a typological reading of Greeks and Christians prior to

Nietzsche's, Kierkegaard ends up with an evaluation that is quite un-Nietzschean in character, for Christians turn out to be healthier, more life-affirming in the end than Greeks, who are assimilated in their nihilism to Buddhists (though it is true that with Plato the Greeks in question are 'post-Socratic'). Christians abstain from unhealthy elements and master their own appetites in order to attain good health; the more rigorist Greeks stop eating and drinking, which is actually unhealthy and which leads only to annihilation. For Christians, death is a new birth. They do not linger over negatives, such as doubt or pain; they rejoice in positives, such as victory, certainty and felicity. In Platonism (and here, given their common difference from Christianity, Kierkegaard no longer distinguishes the master from the disciple), death to the perceptible leads to the realm of ideas, the shadow realm where a deathly silence prevails. Socrates aspires only to die and to be dead, not out of enthusiasm for death but actually (and on this point, the final Nietzsche would not disagree with him), if not out of disgust with life – a feeling that might still imply some affirmative force, if only in repulsion – then at least out of lack of pleasure in living – a formula that better befits an ironist's conception of death.

The formula also allows Kierkegaard to remove Socrates' death from the calculation of interests to which Xenophon, with his shopkeeper mentality, wanted to reduce it, for someone who dies because he does not have the heart to live cannot desire another life, a new life: he is much too sick and tired for that. But the sickness in question, contrary to what Nietzsche thought – perhaps Nietzsche had read too much Xenophon – is not the contagious disease of some plebeian who infected the noble Plato. Perhaps the opposite is true, for the disease belongs to aristocrats: irony is a climacteric fever that is encountered only in lofty circles, a malady contracted by a select few and survived by even fewer. This illness turns out to be a bearer of health in that it saves the soul from the traps of relativity, so long as it remains a path and a guide toward something entirely different. Taken not as a simple stage but for its own sake, since it bears the absolute only in the form of nothingness, irony is a disease to the extent that one wishes to install oneself within it.

The irony of the *Phaedo* – provided that it is recognizable in the metamorphosis to which Kierkegaard has subjected it, a transformation in which the ancient form has been contaminated by the modern one – is located halfway between partial irony – a proof of health that breaks down only what is relative – and total irony – a malady that annihilates even the ironist himself. Leveling everything, dominating every exaggerated sentiment, towering over the fear or horror of death as over the pathos of the enthusiast, this form of irony gives Socrates a specific tone, impertinent and indifferent, that enables him to make death a subject for joking and to make annihilation, like any other object, a simple object of curiosity.

If you have not measured up to this tone, if you have not been up to enjoying it, you have only to open up the *Apology*, a decisive text that comes to the aid of the *Phaedo* and makes unmistakably clear that Socrates' viewpoint is indeed that of irony.

e) The Apology: 'either' . . . 'or'

Does Kierkegaard mean to imply that the *Apology*, more than other texts, may be conclusive on its own? Will this 'essential supplement' not need a supplement in turn, and so on, in a way that is ineluctable for a logic of supplementarity? How can that logic be interrupted if Socrates did not pronounce the address in the *Apology* as such (a hypothesis that Kierkegaard acknowledges)? And even if Plato had traced a faithful portrait of the real Socrates in his *Apology* (something that Kierkegaard did not do in his own), how can its authenticity be determined unless one invokes – but does this constitute proof? – the consensus of the commentators who view the text as a historical document (and it is indeed on this basis that Kierkegaard will turn to it in Chapter 2 to establish 'the actuality' of his conception)? Finally, since what is at issue is following the traces of irony, that is, detecting a certain tone, will the *Apology* not remain impregnable – whether or not it is authentic – for anyone who has a tin ear? Now, Kierkegaard was indeed sensitive to the tone of the text from early on; in his youthful naivete, where he expected a sublimely poetic heroico-tragic text he was disappointed to find only a prosaic narrative in which a most surprising tone of indifference prevails wherever death is in question. Yet this tone, because it is unusual and because it contrasts with Plato's idealizing and transfiguring portrait of Socrates, is precisely what attests to the dialogue's authenticity; this is the tone one must learn to hear in order to discern Socratic irony with accuracy.

All the passages about death show Socrates' complete lack of certainty on the subject. Far from being a source of anxiety, death gives him pleasure through the dizzying play that it authorizes, setting before him the alternative of his infinite importance or his nothingness. Socrates is neither a diversion-seeking man who clings with anguish to life in order to chase away the thought of death, nor a Christian who confronts death with enthusiasm while sacrificing his own life; he is a man who enjoys the alternation of light and shadow that is produced by the oscillation between day and night, between infinite reality and infinite nothingness. His pleasure is mixed, to say the least: pleasure in the control that his irony, a match for extremes, gives him over the onlookers, who, for their part, tremble in the face of death; pleasure in the vertigo produced by the speed with which the endless opposition appears and vanishes; pleasure, finally, in having his curiosity kept constantly on the alert by the intriguing enigma whose solution is necessarily pushed back ad infinitum. If ordinary mortals cannot

enjoy the thought of death, perhaps they can at least stop being afraid of it
– this is the gift Socrates offers, with his ironic generosity. If the thought
of death covers absolutely nothing, if ignorance of death is total, then fear
of death becomes ridiculous and absurd. The gift is both sophisticated and
poisonous, for in place of fear it substitutes the anguish of an ineluctable
nothingness in which no one, except perhaps the ironist, can find repose.
This nothingness leads the ironist, and the ironist alone, to prefer death to
any other punishment that he knows with certainty to be a bad thing.

At the end of the *Apology*, according to Kierkegaard, Socrates even shows
that dying is a good thing, that it offers benefits: the benefit of an eternal,
dreamless sleep, the benefit of escaping the judges of this world in order
to appear before a much more equitable tribunal, and finally, the benefit
of being able to question all the powerful figures of history in order to
show them their own ignorance. Presented as the result of a calculation of
interests that seems to allow one to win the absolute instead of and in place
of the relative, these benefits are actually reduced in each case to absolute
nothingness, since what is won is only negative: the absence of dreams,
the absence of injustice, the absence of knowledge. Moreover, the benefits
represent just one alternative, the one in which death is a simple change of
existence; the other, in which death is nothing at all, still remains possible.
Thus, in sum, the joy and the negative benefits won remain hypothetical in
any event. The entire scene Socrates plays out simply derives from irony in
its highest form. If, between the two alternatives, the *Phaedo* seems to come
down on the side of a benefit, the still negative benefit of ceasing to be a
burden to one's friends, Socrates' remarks on the subject must once again
be interpreted ironically. In Kierkegaard's reading, they derive from one of
life's clever ploys, in which life attempts the feat of tricking death itself. Thus
irony has the last word. The end of the *Phaedo* corroborates Kierkegaard's
reading of the *Apology*, just as the latter, whose end is no less ambiguous,
corroborates the plausibility of his ironic reading of the *Phaedo*.

Now, the passages on death are not the only ones that create an atmosphere
of ironic uncertainty. The entire text consists of irony, notwithstanding the
fact that Ast, against whom Kierkegaard unleashes his own most virulent
irony, was unable to hear it. For irony is exceedingly silent and cunning; it
snares the reader and holds him captive in its nets when he is least prepared.
To Socrates, at least if we are to believe Plato's *Gorgias* (but, unless we
are dealing with a vicious circle, how can that text lend its support to the
Apology, the only text whose presumably guaranteed authenticity would
allow Kierkegaard to distinguish between Socrates' part and Plato's?), the
obligation to defend himself before such a tribunal of children must have
appeared ridiculous in the highest degree. If we admit this, we have no
choice but to envisage the *design* of the *Apology* from the perspective of
irony: the text's irony would derive from the absence of any common

ground between the attack and the defense. Socrates does not refute the charges against him; he snatches them back from his accusers by showing that, in the face of his claim of ignorance, the accusations are so many blows struck for nothing, for there is nothing to annihilate. How can he be accused of introducing new doctrines, or anything new at all, when he knows absolutely nothing about new things or old? The death sentence in turn would have appeared supremely ridiculous, for several reasons. Since the 'crime' was identified as an aberration, only the most heterogeneous relation between crime and punishment obtains. It may be the tribunal's role to deliberate about Socrates' guilt, but it is not up to the judges to choose a punishment, to decide for or against a fine or the death penalty. Moreover, the decision is based on the number of votes, a procedure against which Socrates uses the frostiest irony.[38] Would a man's life or death thus depend on a single vote? And there are some who seek to declare him innocent by their votes, those whom, in a supplementary irony, he pretends to thank; would they be no less ridiculous than the others for believing that such a procedure could bring success? But the supreme irony in the *Apology* is the irony that turns against the ironist himself, as if in revenge, since in the last analysis the argument to which he succumbs is as ridiculous as the death penalty.

If we were to view the *Apology* as a work of fiction, if we were to suppose that Socrates never existed, every reader would savor the sting of this accusation, would appreciate the irony of the judgment. What makes readers deaf to irony, what makes them resist seeing it, is thus the idea that a real human being, putting his life on the line, can make 'indifferent' remarks, borrowed from the register of the utmost good fellowship and cordiality. In order to hear the gentle murmurs of irony in the *Apology*, it is thus not enough to be able to hear well; one must also be courageous. If one can summon up as much courage as Socrates did in the face of death, one may be able to capture the full irony of his defense, through 'infinite sympathy', and be captivated by it. Such courage is probably what Ast lacked. So there is no point in attempting to 'prove' the authenticity of the *Apology*, despite its irony; there is no point in piling up documents. The wrong way to go about attempting to capture irony would be to take away its edge by using scholarly procedures to strip it of its sharp, surprising, striking qualities. Kierkegaard lets Ast play the tedious role of professor; regarding other points in the *Apology*, he is content to reject Ast's arguments and his sublime pathos and then turn them maliciously against their author, and without seeming to do so, in a note or a passing remark.

Like Socrates, who manifests too much ironic indifference to commit himself seriously to the Athenians, Kierkegaard gives over the central portion of the text, its 'high point', to Ast and to the seriousness of sublime speech; he himself takes refuge, unarmed and unencumbered by baggage, in the text's margins, its 'low point'. From this vantage point, unburdened and infinitely free, like an elf or a child espying the primal scene, he can occasionally glance up above the line between the upper and lower 'regions' and sketch in features that are not angelic in the least. And Kierkegaard does not picture himself as a malicious elf; he reserves that comparison for the demonian Socrates. No, he imagines himself – here is the height of irony – with the features of an angel, like the one that can be seen in an etching of the ascension of the Madonna[39]: the Virgin, poised in all her sublimity at the highest point in the heavens, looks down on two angels who are situated at the very bottom of the painting and separated from her by a dark line over which they lift their eyes to the divine being on high.

Kierkegaard's profaning image overturns everything – the Madonna and the angels, Ast's sublime pathos and Kierkegaard's own irony, and also the university jury from which the timid candidate finds himself removed as well, as it were, by the vast distance that separates the seventh heaven from the lower ones, let alone from the earth. And, in a veritable ironic epiphany, it is by means of this image, found in a visible painting, that Kierkegaard attempts to bring something invisible to light: an invisible presence that, when it exists, neither displays nor introduces itself. It cannot be seen: it can only be watched for surreptitiously; it can only be heard in a gentle but none the less biting murmur. It is irony that reigns like a mistress, a Madonna (a *Regina?*) in the *Apology*.

f) Plato's dreams – how Plato fertilizes Socrates

Kierkegaard's study of dialectics in Plato concludes with the *Apology*. The search for something that would make it possible to follow the traces of the 'real' Socrates in Plato's writings is over. What remains to be examined is the mythical dimension. Kierkegaard began by establishing the dualism of myth and dialectics as a clue to the Socrates/Plato duality and discord, as trace evidence indicating that the tightly-bound pair had to be pried apart. Thus we might expect to find the mythical dimension attributed to Plato, since the ironic dialectic has been attributed to Socrates. And although Kierkegaard denies it – he says he is trying 'to forget the overall aim of the undertaking' (p. 96) – this is indeed what he will show, begging the question once more. Not without difficulty, for the 'mythical' is harder to circumscribe than the dialectical. There are 'myths' and 'myths' in Plato, a whole history of myth, and the mere mention or use of a myth does not make a dialogue mythical.

Despite his denegations, Kierkegaard's approach is actually a circular one, for the relation between the mythical and the dialectical in Plato can be understood only with reference to the Socrates/Plato relationship. As the final image he offers of this relationship reveals, after a detour through the examination of other concepts, Kierkegaard has already decided that the mythical belongs to Plato; it cannot belong, as everyone would readily agree (again, Kierkegaard appeals to consensus as sole proof) to Socrates' insatiable dialectics. (Nietzsche will call Socrates a pure theoretical type, although for the duration of a dream he will nevertheless lend him the possibility of falling back on myth as the ultimate explanatory principle; thus he allows for the possibility that Socrates too, like his disciple Plato, has an artistic nature.) According to Kierkegaard, the mythical belongs exclusively to Plato, a fair compensation for the disciple's presumed abandonment of his poetic productivity, at the age of twenty, under his master's influence, in favor of abstract knowledge of self; his mythical dimension contrasts with what more properly belongs to Socrates. So the union of the happy pair must not always have been idyllic. It is easier to understand, at this point, why Plato 'mythically' opposes Socrates in the early dialogues with great obstinacy, but then abandons the mythical dimension and re-places himself discreetly under the master's gentle authority. Viewed in this light, the so-called 'Socratic' dialogues are the most Platonic of all, and vice versa; especially after Socrates' death – when the painful need to unite with the master has made itself felt – the 'Platonic' dialogues compensate for the flaws of the Socratic dialogues. This means that only the vicissitudes of the relationship between Plato and Socrates can shed light on the specific nature of Platonic myth, the mythical dimension being identical with the poetic if the latter is understood, in Hegelian fashion,[40] as the enthusiasm of the imagination unleashed in dreams.

But what can Plato have dreamed? Did he dream of impregnating Socrates and succeeding where Socrates himself had failed?[41] In fact, his imagination toils in the service of speculation: that is, Plato claims to be filling the void left by the Socratic dialectics. The latter is drawn to the Idea, which it finds immensely attractive and desirable, whereas the mythical, in its fertility, stifles the Idea, at least in dreams. In other words, echoing Hegel's language, which in its own way echoes Aristotle's, the mythical delivers the speculative in figurative form; it permits the reader to take premature pleasure in the object to which the speculative leads only after lengthy detours. Only after he has awakened does the dreamer notice that the mythical is not the Idea but its reflection; it is an image, a simple mirage, the not-yet-ripe and never-to-be-ripe fruit of speculation. Plato will never succeed in 'really' impregnating his master. This is not, as Hegel thought, because the 'dialectical moment' to which Plato belonged required him to go further than Socrates, although without going as far in speculation as Aristotle went, or in any case without going as far as he himself, Hegel, was to go. Plato's failure is due rather to his sense of guilt, because he could not after all totally succeed where his master (father or mother or lover) had failed. He can produce only 'mythical' children with Socrates; if they deserve to live (for they are worth more than mere perceptible 'reflections'), they take the shape of children forever incapable of attaining adult maturity.

Thus in the mythical part of the *Symposium* (which cannot be equated purely and simply with Diotima's presentation of the myth of the birth of Eros, for other interlocutors offer other narratives that allude to mythology without having a mythical dimension themselves), 'Plato the poet daydreams and visualizes everything the dialectician Socrates was seeking; in the world of dreams, irony's unhappy love finds its object' (p. 108). Plato's imagination makes up for the deficiencies of the Socratic dialectics, which is insatiable because it is never satisfied and because it leaves all the interlocutors in suspense, hungry for more; thus imagination compensates for the loss of the speculative and of Socrates. Although Kierkegaard relies more on Hegel than on Plato for help in presenting his conception of the mythical, he still never reduces the mythical to a speculative function. The mythical does not engage knowledge, initially, but rather the imagination. It demands that one give oneself over entirely to the imagination; it requires Kierkegaard's presentation to oscillate between the production and the reproduction of imagination – which it can only do where dialectics leaves the way open to the broad visions of thought. What thought is incapable of grasping is excluded from thought and left to the imagination.

In this discussion, Kierkegaard is referring not so much to Hegel as to Kant, the Kant of *Religion within the Limits of Reason Alone*. Where thought is unable to conceive of radical evil, Kant leaves to the imagination the task of 'presenting' it in a myth. Kierkegaard's recourse to Kant allows him to introduce a certain distance between the dialectical and the mythical, a gap that the appeal to Hegel tended to fill in, since between the imagination and the speculative there was a linear dialectical continuity; the difference was only a matter a degree, namely, the degree of luminosity or maturity manifested by the speculative. The double recourse to Kant and Hegel to account for the relation between the dialectical and the mythical in Plato is intended to underline both their continuity and their discontinuity – the union, even the communion between Socrates and Plato, but also their divorce, their relation of mimetic rivalry and mastery. The history of the mythical in Plato, its evolution from the earliest dialogues to the later ones, where it disappears, can only be understood in the dual 'speculative' light provided by Kant and Hegel; it requires, too, the light shed by the history of the 'relations' between Plato and Socrates. While with one hand Kierkegaard is producing an academic critique of the various conceptions of the mythical in Plato, with the other hand he is manipulating an entirely different history, a much more subterranean one, the history of the loves of master and disciple, a history of which the *Symposium*, a dialogue on love, marks the apogee.

Thus, in the *Protagoras*, the mythical can be envisaged in relation to the dialectical as contributing simply a change in the *form of presentation*. The mythical element gives the presentation a form inferior to that of reasoned discourse, and makes it of direct pedagogical value for its youngest listeners. These two forms of exposition are conceptualized not in relation to the Idea but in relation to the listener; they can be compared to two languages, one of which is less articulated and more childlike than the other. When the mythical form is considered in relation to its listener, it is subject to no constraints beyond its psychopedagogical aims. Thus its content can be infinitely modified at the narrator's discretion; it is the presenter's free creation. In other words, Plato, in his youth, seeking revenge against Socrates, turns his imagination loose and invents myths that Socrates could have very well done without, myths that contribute nothing; at the same time, to punish himself for disobeying his master, he belittles his own 'production', his language. He judges his own language inferior to his master's, the latter being more vigorous, more solid, more articulate, more mature. Even when he is disobeying Socrates, then, Plato leaves him in a position of mastery, just as he does in the dialogues where myth is completely absent.

In other dialogues (for example, the *Gorgias,* the *Symposium,* or the *Phaedo*), myth is simultaneously linked to and independent of its contrary, abstraction. In such cases, the mythical dimension is not merely a free creation by Plato, one with pedagogical value, it also hints at a higher order of things that surpasses Plato's subjective authority. Whereas in the earlier dialogues the mythical is used to silence dialectics even as it purports to make dialectics easier to hear or to see, in the later dialogues mentioned above, the relationship between the mythical and dialectics takes a turn for the better. Plato is reconciled with Socrates, but this just allows the disciple to dominate the master more completely. The mythical element becomes what is presented in the form of images, and the images compensate for the deficiencies of the dialectics. Plato, a child who has grown up, now dominates his father and purports to be impregnating him (the father who has become sterile) in spite of himself, as if the child were repairing his progenitor. Whereas dialectics gives a wholly abstract and occasionally negative result, the mythical aims to supply much more, but it can only do so outside of dialectics. Myth is the exile of the Idea outside the field of dialectics; it always has a spatio-temporal form, the form of the imagination itself.

In a third type of dialogue that Kierkegaard labels *constructive,* myth takes on still another form, that of images. After waking from his dream of mastery and paternity, Plato observes that the child engendered in Socrates was a pure mirage. He then goes on to dream some more, but he knows that he is dreaming, that he is producing only images. The mythical is no longer positioned, like a sectarian, outside of dialectics, and the two are no longer in conflict. Instead, the mythical alternates with dialectics; the two interlocutors, Plato and Socrates, are on equal footing and each is raised to a higher order of things. Because Plato has never reached the movement of speculative thought, the image continues to play a role in the presentation of the Idea. Meanwhile, in another cycle of dialogues, the mythical dimension disappears: dialectics is wholly dominant, but no longer in the ironic sense. Socrates has triumphed, but he has been transfigured by Plato, poeticized by him. This is the only way left to Plato to make poetry; he triumphs at the very moment when he seems to have given up mastery.

Thus if his attention to the mythical in its relations with the dialectical is what allows Kierkegaard to credit Socrates and Plato respectively with what belonged to each, in circular fashion his attention to their relations of love and mastery is what allows him to attempt to categorize Plato's dialogues by taking as sole criterion the respective places attributed to the two figures – under the masks of myth and dialectics.

g) The scathing, devastating irony of Book I of the Republic

According to Kierkegaard, the first book of the *Republic* does not resemble those that follow; in Book I, the Socratic method appears for the last time. An examination of this book can thus serve to shore up the conclusions drawn from the other dialogues, just as those conclusions can help with the reading of the book in question; and there is no danger, or at least so Kierkegaard claims, that this reciprocal shoring-up will cause the whole carelessly-built structure to come tumbling down.

Kierkegaard's reading, which closely follows Schleiermacher's, consists in showing that Book I does not simply lack a conclusion but that it has a negative conclusion. He leaves it at that; and yet the nullity of the book's conclusion cannot be explained by its inaugural position in the *Republic,* for the other books are all different and do not 'follow' from the first. The final comment in Book I, marked with an ironic stamp, confirms the book's general tone, which is indeed ironic. The text's excessive, exuberant irony commands the entire dialogue like a master, like a military leader bent on destruction; partial and isolated manifestations of irony are drafted into its service like so many crafty spies. As soon as the skirmishes are over, when all the high spots have been leveled, the leader casts his eyes over the total annihilation and recognizes that nothing remains. Confronted with the nullity of the result, the Sophists, who argue with the utmost seriousness, are grotesque shadowy figures taking shape against a wall. This sort of irony escapes all dialectical 'sublation' in the Hegelian sense. It is not in relation with the Idea; the false and the partial are not suppressed so as to allow the true to appear; they are suppressed so that other equally false and partial paths may appear. The isolated manifestations of irony do not cluster together; instead, they disperse. No new beginning succeeds in constituting a new approach to the Idea: lacking any profound connection with the development of the Idea, each new beginning remains without relation to it. In short, the approach found in Book I does not belong to the dialectics of the Idea, whether the Idea in question is Hegelian or Platonic.

Book I of the *Republic* is closely related, then, to the preceding dialogues, the *Gorgias* and the *Protagoras* in particular, those that have been subjected to 'Socrates' influence and personal dominance' (p. 119). In other words, through their reciprocal shoring-up they open up the surest path toward a conception of a Socrates who deserves to live.

h) What haunted Plato

The sole aim of the investigation up to this point has been to make the Kierkegaardian conception of Socrates possible. Merely possible, however; for Kierkegaard knows perfectly well that a certain number of objections can be lodged against the reading he has just presented. And before abandoning Plato, he intends to respond.

First of all, concerning his choice of dialogues, he finds support in the general *consensus* of scholars according to which the ones he has chosen all open up a perspective on the *true* Socrates: even though not all scholars agree to call the dialogues 'Socratic dialogues', as Ast does, and even if they do not agree on the choice of dialogues, like Kierkegaard himself they grant special status to the *Protagoras*, the *Gorgias*, the *Phaedo*, the *Apology*, and even – Schleiermacher included – Book I of the *Republic*.

But Kierkegaard is not satisfied with this *consensus*. His own choices were confirmed, he declares, by an impartial examination of Plato's work, in which he recognized (as everyone else had, once again) two forms of irony and two forms of dialectics, along with the mythical and the imagistic (which compensate for the deficiencies of the first four forms). The mythical, which is not in a necessary relation with either irony or dialectics, opens up an anticipatory pathway toward something entirely different. The question is whether all those different viewpoints actually belong to Plato. If they do, one would expect to see his work pass through several stages; the final viewpoint would not incorporate the first one but would supplant it. The first viewpoint would be a sort of skeptical stage, an introduction supplying an impetus without leading to the goal. Such a conception does not do justice to the first viewpoint, which it obscures in favor of the second. Nor does it do justice to Socrates: flying in the face of all historical truth, it neglects Socrates' importance for Plato, who according to this view was content to make Socrates his front man.

An alternative hypothesis would be to acknowledge that one of the viewpoints, the first – that of total irony and dialectics in its liberating negativity – belonged initially to Socrates and that Plato merely 'reproduced' it. However, if you are having difficulty finding 'my' conception of Socratic irony in Plato's texts, this is because Plato is precisely the one who *reproduced* it: that is, he transfigured that conception to make it conform to his own image, the image of a poet who is incapable of understanding the influence that irony has had on his own nature and who has been unable to avoid contaminating it with his own positivity, with his own conception of irony as a negative power that is nevertheless at the service of a positive idea. Everything that is ambiguous in the early dialogues, everything that hesitates between the negative and the positive, is like an annunciatory sign of Platonism properly speaking, the mythical part of which is anticipatory. This Platonism comes into its own in the *Parmenides,* the *Theaetetus,* the *Sophist,* and the *Statesman.*

Because the Platonic 'reproduction' is thus not a faithful copy, if we are to grasp the 'first viewpoint' we shall require an interpretative 'critique' of the texts that will allow us to decide in favor of 'Socrates' or Plato – a task all the more difficult in that on many points their respective irony and their dialectics (would they have loved each other so much otherwise?) are uncannily alike. Both the ironic dialectics and the Platonic version (Kierkegaard calls the latter 'subjective' because, unlike Hegel's, it is not a dialectics of ideas developed in complete independence of the questioning subject and the responding subject) recognize that a personality in the process of exercising a liberating activity is a necessary point of departure: but the personality belonging to irony is purely negative, while the one belonging to subjective thought is positive. The former is content to cut the moorings, to dislodge speculation from the empirical sand banks that encumber it; if it helps the latter to venture forth, it still does not participate in the voyage. Plato, who does venture forth, makes the mistake of believing that he also owes to irony, to Socrates, what he 'brings back' from his speculative voyage to irony, and he rewards Socrates with his own 'gains', sowing confusion through an excess of gratitude. Although Plato no longer needs Socrates, later on, in order to free himself, he still never forgets his first emancipator. In the 'constructive' dialogues, he continues to make Socrates the main character, but the latter is no more than the shadow of 'himself' – the 'Socrates' of the early dialogues – and if he continues to haunt Plato and his dialogues, he does so less in the form of a faithful memory than in the obsessional form of a returning spirit, a phantom, a fantasy from which Plato succeeds in liberating himself only by mastering it in a free poetic creation that is entirely under his own control.

To acknowledge that Plato's Socrates is a poetic figure makes it possible to answer any objection that might accuse Kierkegaard of offering an erroneous interpretation of Socratic irony for his own part, since no trace of that irony, in the all-encompassing form he attributes to it, can be found in Plato's dialogues. Plato cannot serve as the ultimate reference: the delineation of his viewpoint, that of a limited irony and a dialectics that develops the interlocutor's responses and assimilates the world to itself, ends up as an abstraction with a positive form; it cannot include the viewpoint of an all-encompassing irony, of a dialectics that devours the world and the interlocutor's responses, a dialectics that leads to nothing and that in its self-sufficiency relies only on itself, that closes itself off to all solicitations and refuses to engage either with the world or with any other conception. Plato the poet might well have detected a certain irony in Socrates and been amused by it; he could not have grasped its infinite, monstrous and demoniacal quality. 'To conceive of irony in this way takes an altogether unique mental disposition' (p. 125). We are given to understand that Kierkegaard himself possessed such a mental disposition; it is what gave him such a good grasp of the irony in Socrates (by means of his 'infinite sympathy'), despite Plato's poetic transfiguration of the figure. Plato himself missed the irony, despite all the love he bore his master; as a result, he, Plato, a good poet but a bad painter, could not help but fail in his 'reproduction' of Socrates. He did not render him completely unrecognizable, however; he managed to leave some traces of Socratic irony that could support at least the possibility of Kierkegaard's conception.

i) Oscillation

Before Kierkegaard leaves Plato behind, he still has to compare Plato's conception with Xenophon's. Using a genealogical method ahead of its time, Kierkegaard seemingly refuses to come out in favor of either one. For neither conception delivers the 'real Socrates', but only the idiosyncracy of its author. Plato's Socrates wins *ideality*: like a good poet, Plato confers a supernatural dimension on Socrates. He depicts him as a philosopher who judges all things by the yardstick of the Idea, disdains profit, and remains indifferent to the established order. This Socrates is in every respect the opposite of Xenophon's. Xenophon makes his a Sophist; like a good grocer, by dint of bargaining, Xenophon consigns his Socrates to the service of finitude and an all too down-to-earth mediocrity.

Kierkegaard's 'genealogical' reading is not taken as far as it could be, however, since he does not apply it to his own conception. He can get out of the impasse, he believes, by going beyond the two earlier fictions and taking recourse to a 'real' Socrates. He believes he alone holds the key to the riddle of the real Socrates' existence, namely, irony. This is the right answer; it is at once the governing hypothesis of the entire 'Thesis' and the truth, for it alone explains, because it is ungraspable, why neither Xenophon nor Plato was able to perceive it plainly. Each was right up to a certain point: the former when he depicted Socrates strolling through the marketplace, because any external object at all is an occasion for the ironist to respond; the latter when he showed Socrates touching lightly on the Idea – so long as we recall that *touching lightly* does not mean opening oneself up to it. That is one thing the ironist never does: he simply steers speculation, guides it far enough out so it loses sight of the finite and can navigate in the open, but without ever reaching the infinite. The respective errors of the two authors arise from the fact that, as artists, each sought to perfect his creation: Xenophon by dragging it too far down (toward the profitable), Plato by tugging it too far up (toward the Idea). The truth occupies an intermediate position; invisible and ungraspable, it is an irony that oscillates between the empirical self and the ideal self. It traverses the earth with a light and airy step, ready to take off at any moment for a more heavenly realm where it has not yet chosen (and where it will never choose, for this 'not yet' is not that of speculative dialectics) to reside.

Socrates' ironic oscillation is made most obvious by Aristophanes in *The Clouds*. The playwright puts the philosopher in a basket suspended between heaven and earth. Here is a clue to the importance of this source: Aristophanes has been left for last, but he has nevertheless served as a guiding thread for the entire reading.

j) 'Suspense' in The Clouds

Indeed, Aristophanes' text is far from being a negligeable source. For one thing, in relation to the other two sources, each of which is deficient in its own way, it offers a helpful contrast. It brings in a third viewpoint, an additional nuance that cannot fail to be enriching, given the absence of direct evidence. Because the nuances in *The Clouds* are primarily comic, moreover, the portrait of Socrates that has been characterized up to now by Xenophon's prosaic quality and Plato's tragic ideality stands to benefit. Not only does the portrait become more amusing, but it also becomes a better and truer likeness, inasmuch as Greek comedy made a point of depicting real people on stage – even if it also presented them in idealized terms, as paradigms of an idea. Through the first, 'realist' aspect of Greek comedy, the public could not fail to recognize Socrates (by attending a performance of *The Clouds*, Socrates even gave the audience a chance to appreciate the likeness directly), while the distancing necessary to the work of art was established through the second, 'idealist' aspect. Unlike Hegel, Kierkegaard did not overlook the fact that *The Clouds* was a work of fiction, a theatrical fiction governed by specific rules, that requires us to distinguish between the discourse of the chorus and that of the characters, to distinguish between the two complementary aspects of every comedy, the realist and the idealist.

If Aristophanes' portrait of Socrates is thus a likeness, a precise assessment of the nature and degree of the resemblance is still required, and, since the portrait in question is a comic one, one has to try to see what can be looked at in a comic light in the model. While it is easy to exclude many features that put Socrates in the category of an 'original', a strange and bizarre being, more atopical than comic, it does seem – at least it is clear to Kierkegaard – that the comic, the infinitely comic aspect of Socrates consequently resides in irony. Because irony is a viewpoint that constantly cancels itself out, because in its omnivorous self-devouring negativity it is and is not everything at once, it conceals an infinite comic element. Kierkegaard attempts to make Socratic irony the constitutive element of his comic character; indeed, this is the view he seeks to impose, countering Hegel and the Hegelians, such as Rötscher (who has the sole merit, in Kierkegaard's eyes, of playing the role of a police force, poised to break up all sorts of scholarly gatherings and dubious historical conspiracies on the spot). For Hegel and his followers, the principle of interiority is constitutive of the comic as well as of the tragic: a thesis that Aristophanes would have been able to illustrate and anticipate marvelously in all seriousness and truth. It is only in a note – a very aggressive note – that Kierkegaard recalls Hegel's homage to Aristophanes, as if he could not forgive Hegel for recognizing the truth value of *The Clouds* before Kierkegaard himself did. In Kierkegaard's eyes, this is a pure contradiction on Hegel's part, since to the extent that Hegel confuses Socrates and Plato and grants the former an equally positive aspect, he should have found Aristophanes' portrait excessive, overstepping the bounds of truth. In any event, the seriousness of the principle of interiority and the seriousness of Aristophanes' comic thus reappropriated can only limit the comic, whereas the principle of irony on the contrary amplifies it ad infinitum. If Aristophanes depicted the real Socrates on stage, then his comic cannot be serious, true and rational, within the limits of reason alone, but it must actually reflect Socrates' irony with its much more profound laughter: here we have the 'realist' aspect of *The Clouds*.

Viewed in its idealist aspect, *The Clouds* reflects an idea that Kierkegaard seeks to refine. Following a suggestion found in Hegel's *Aesthetics*,[42] he attributes symbolic significance to the chorus, which represents the Clouds. Initially portrayed by women (an aspect Hegel neglects), the Clouds are beings that hold no value at all for Hegel, if we are to trust the lighthearted tone in which he speaks of them; they symbolize the hollow, meaningless activity that took place in the Thinkery. The Clouds are an inconsistent *reflection* of Socrates' own inner emptiness; they offer a perfect image for the sort of fluctuating thinking that loses contact with solid ground and lends itself – like the vaporous clouds – to all sorts of unstable configurations. Lacking content, such thinking can contain the whole world; like actors, whom Diderot called good-for-nothings, it offers the infinite possibility of becoming anything at all, without ever retaining anything 'properly'; and in the end, it drifts away like smoke. When Socrates calls the Clouds 'goddesses', his tone is derisive, for their only subjects are a community of idle folk, as empty as the clouds themselves. Their omnipotence appears to manifest itself through their power to become anything they like: a centaur in the presence of a hairy, hearty fellow, or a wolf in the presence of a thief. But in reality their omnipotence is a mark of their impotence, and that of Socrates, which they reflect: the irony lies in this reciprocal impotence,

which one might call a 'double Zelig effect'.[43] Socrates, a subject who tries
to grasp an object, simply gets hold of his own image; the Clouds, who seize
only the subject's image, reproduce it only in the presence of the objects to
which they themselves 'conform'. Thus Socrates' negative dialectics, which
may seem all-powerful owing to its very abstraction, is in fact like a king
without a country who enjoys only a negative pleasure – that of renouncing
everything precisely when he seems to have everything. This self-sufficient
dialectics, which lacks nothing and desires nothing, leaps over everything in
a single bound like a capricious, scatterbrained child.

Under the name 'goddesses' that is ironically attributed to the clouds,
one must thus read the hazy impotence of their feminine being, which is
hollow, empty, and *shapeless*. Aristophanes thus translated by Kierkegaard
anticipates the misogyny of Aristotle, for whom woman is shapeless matter,
pure power of contraries; she receives definite form and meaning only from
without, from men. When the men withdraw, when the various cloud
formations dissipate, nothing remains but a hazy mass: Socrates' Idea.
In other words, nothing, or virtually nothing: that is the 'reality' hidden
behind 'appearances'; it occurs only in this vaporous form. Between the
celestial Clouds, objective powers that are powerless to dwell permanently
on earth, and the subject, Socrates, suspended in a basket above the ground,
struggling to reach the heavens for fear that the earth might shatter his fragile
subjectivity, there is thus a profound and ironic harmony.

In their thoroughgoing vanity and impotence, the chorus and Socrates,
whom it reflects, represent the new order of things that is about to supplant
the ancient Greek culture. The new culture is that of the Sophists, ridiculed
through its representative Socrates: Kierkegaard at once subscribes and does
not subscribe to this Hegelian interpretation. On the one hand, he does not
want to give it up, for to identify Socrates with his hereditary enemies the
Sophists would be to make an odd conflation indeed, all the more ironic
in that in a certain sense Socrates himself really did identify with them, the
better to combat them, and he succeeded to such an extent that he surpassed
them, became master and 'high priest of this most subtle nonsense' (p. 139,
note). But on the other hand, Kierkegaard – who, unlike Hegel, grants more
positivity to the Sophists than to Socrates – cannot agree that Aristophanes
(who is the primary source for his own viewpoint) has purely and simply
identified Socrates with his enemies. Kierkegaard resolves the dilemma by
leaving the chorus with the responsibility of 'losing' Socrates among the
Sophists; the remainder of the play offers quite a different portrait of the
protagonist, as we shall see if we examine the argument of *The Clouds* more
closely in this light.

Kierkegaard proceeds, like Hegel, to 'summarize' the 'unsummarizable',
and in footnotes he cites long passages from the text, adding commentary
that points out the text's ironic and comic aspects. But at the same time he

lays special emphasis on the judiciously clever touch that consists in using the theft of Strepsiades' cloak to symbolize the Socratic method for ridding the disciples of their outmoded lines of reasoning. The situation is eminently comical. Strepsiades, who is heading for Socrates' Thinkery hoping to get some benefit from the new school, comes back without any booty, but he has acquired the privilege – a negative benefit – of being rid of his old cloak. He is happy enough that he did not lose his life and was not reduced to ruin by speculation; he is happy not to have been 'disposed of' himself the way his belongings and his ruddy complexion were disposed of. By way of food, Socrates has in effect offered him the same meal the stork offered the fox in the fable. Plunged into 'himself', like the fox in the neck of his vase, absorbed in the ecstatic contemplation of himself and his own emptiness, he displays the self-centeredness of a navel-gazer as he leaves his host – who has found someone cleverer than himself – disoriented, disappointed and unsatisfied. Goodhumored and modest, taking full responsibility for his failure, Strepsiades sends his promising son[44] off to the Thinkery. And the son actually keeps his promises: from Socrates' school, in exchange for the cloak, he brings back a double gift, a double poison. Thanks to dialectics, Pheidippides pays off his father's creditors with words (but the creditors turn to the reality of justice in order to win their cause). Not content to abolish the negative gift, the reality of the due dates, the cynical son brings his father back a positive gift, the irrefutable reality of a beating that is worth cash: dialectics has allowed him to send filial respect down the same path as the due dates. Somewhat belatedly noticing the pernicious character of the new wisdom, Strepsiades sets the Thinkery on fire.

In his 'summary' of the play – which is already an interpretation in itself – Kierkegaard's considerable debt to Hegel is apparent. And indeed, the father-son relationship is described essentially in terms of debt. Strepsiades is a ridiculous father who thought he could win on all fronts with that 'promising' son of his – in terms of reality, by requiring the son to help him get a finite debt repaid, and in symbolic terms, by requiring the son to pay him the infinite debt that a son, because he is a son, owes his father: obedience and infinite respect. Such is the 'promise' that Pheidippides, as a son, the promising son, is supposed to have to keep forever.

The lesson Strepsiades learns at Socrates' school – Hegel professed to be shocked by it – is that a son may disobey his father, may permanently settle his unpayable debt by settling a finite and partial debt, by *settling his account* with his father by means of a thrashing.

What Kierkegaard and Hegel both neglect to point out is, on the one hand, the fact that father's real debts are actually the son's, to the extent that Pheidippides' passion for horses has led to his father's ruin. Strepsiades sends his son to Socrates in order to turn him away from that ruinous passion; the decision will cost him much more dearly, in the end. On the other hand, there is the fact that, if an 'infinite debt' is indeed due to a father, Pheidippides no longer owes one to Strepsiades, for the latter has ceased to be a father. Aristophanes depicts him as a doddering old man in his second childhood who asks his son for help in meeting his most basic needs; thus he is quite as deserving of a thrashing in his own right as Pheidippides was when he was a child; this is fair compensation for the attentive care that Strepsiades, a 'good father', lavished on him. Neither Hegel nor Kierkegaard highlights this reversal of their situations (which Strepsiades acknowledges, moreover, recognizing the accuracy of his son's reasoning even while pointing out to him that he will be a father himself one day, even an old father, and that if he follows his current line of thinking he will end up being thrashed in his turn).

The reason for their oversight is that both Hegel and Kierkegaard neglect what they call the clownish elements of *The Clouds,* the 'low' comic side that retains trace of an idea' (p. 146). Thus they ignore Strepsiades' scatalogical language, which does seem to have regressed to the anal or urethral stage (his attachment to money, the passion of an infantile old man, attests to this as well); before he receives Socrates' scholarly interpretation of meteorological phenomena, Strepsiades views thunderclaps as explosive farts,[45] rain as Zeus urinating.[46] Pheidippides' lack of respect for Strepsiades thus echoes the latter's lack of respect for the gods, who are more thoroughly profaned by him than by Socrates. Reduced to an infantile state and lacking in respect for gods who deserve it even more than fathers, Strepsiades is no longer a 'father': thus he cannot appropriately require obedience. The teaching Socrates has lavished upon him is finally completed only through the supplementary lesson that his son administers to him freely and generously – this is his third poisoned gift – with a stick. Because he has let himself count too heavily on his son and his son's promises, he can do no more than display his infantile dependence with respect to Pheidippides, along with his lack of manliness: if Socrates was able to 'shear' him by depriving him of his cloak,[47] it is because Strepsiades had already shorn himself. Deprived by his son of his paternity, castrated and convinced of his castration, Strepsiades can react to this lesson only with an infantile gesture: he heads off to set Socrates' Thinkery on fire. If, like Freud interpreting the myth of Prometheus,[48] we acknowledge that fire can also represent its contrary, water, as it does in dreams, then we may say that Strepsiades is 'pissing' on Socrates' science (and his male organ can be of no other use to him from this point on[49]) in an attempt to put out the Promethean fire of dialectics. Strepsiades is the inverse of Prometheus, since he regresses to the stage preceding the conquest of fire: according to Freud, that is the stage in which fire was brought under control by men who learned to put it out in some way other than the homosexual practice of urinating on it.[50] Strepsiades also attempts to put an end to the impotent omnipotence of Zeus, or Socrates: the allusion in the text to Zeus's 'stream of urine' authorizes us, among other things, to interpret this gesture by Strepsiades as the regressive inverse of Prometheus's.

Seen in this light, the comic aspect of *The Clouds* might result from the general lowering of the sublime that is encountered in this play[51]: all fathers and all gods are profaned along with Socrates in the end. The spectator's laughter is due, in this case, to the economy of expenditure that he realizes by getting around the constraints that 'respect' for the powerful requires in 'real' life, for the duration of the spectacle, through identification with Pheidippides; Socrates' lessons are thus 'profitable', if not to Strepsiades, then at least to the audience watching *The Clouds*.

But Kierkegaard cannot conceive of laughter in this 'economic' light – not the Kierkegaard who makes fun of Xenophon the shopkeeper for depicting Socrates in terms of profit alone; nor can he do so, *a fortiori*, in the light of that 'other' economy, the economy of filial respect – not the Kierkegaard who knows that a son owes his father submission and knows that submission is a one-way street. The son, for Kierkegaard, is the very figure of renunciation and sacrifice on behalf of the Father's glory: a father who is made ridiculous, who is abased and castrated, must have shocked him, as it did Hegel, instead of making him laugh.

Thus Kierkegaard interprets the comic aspect of *The Clouds* more in a Kantian than a Freudian way. In his view, the comic results from a contrast between Strepsiades, who expects to get something from speculation, some material and finite advantage, and the dialectical movement, which is incapable of positing anything whatsoever. Exhausting itself in hollow experiments, the negative dialectic corresponds well, in a sense, to Strepsiades' expectations, but in a charlatanesque fashion. It is as if, through an act of authentic sleight-of-hand worthy of a Sophist, thanks to Strepsiades' artifices, his creative energy ends up producing the desired reality, but in such a form that, like the thrashing, the bargain struck with Socrates turns out in the last analysis to be a fool's bargain – indeed, it is actual theft. Kant's genuine 'one hundred dollars' are exchanged in the end for the representation of one hundred dollars. From these representations of coins, you will never be able to conclude, except by your sophistic speculation, that you actually have them in the form of hard cash clinking in your pocket. The only thing you have pocketed, and irrefutably, is that unexpected thrashing, more or less nothing at all, for the thrashing is neither the sort of spiritual benefit that Socrates purported to be producing, except ironically, nor the sort of material benefit anticipated by Strepsiades.

So Aristophanes was right to conceive of Socratic activity, if it is entirely ironic, from a comic standpoint: indeed, in relation to the *result*, irony cannot appear in anything but a comic light (even if in another sense it also liberates from the comic, since with irony the fact is that one should no longer expect anything at all except nothingness). That Aristophanes should have perceived Socrates in this comic light is thus a counter-proof of the accuracy of his conception – his and Kierkegaard's – and it invalidates Hegel's: if Socrates had not produced a negative, ironic dialectics but Plato's rich, subjective version, which Hegel also attributes mistakenly to Socrates, Aristophanes would not have been able to show Socrates in such a comic light, contrary to Hegel's belief.

Kierkegaard maintains the thesis that only Socratic irony could lend itself to the infinite comedy of *The Clouds*; this is why he cannot agree with Hegel that Aristophanes has identified Socrates with a Sophist in this play. Even if the chorus does so identify him – and let us recall that it does this only to a limited extent, since it also distinguishes Prodicus's competence and wisdom from the lofty gaze of Socrates swaggering down the street – the rest of the play portrays a character who has a fully-developed personality and the plastic aspect of a statue, a monolith engaged in monologue with itself. Aristophanes caught this aspect in a comic light, since he depicts a Socrates sliced up by billhooks, a Socrates whose huge feet were created on purpose to hold him upright, as if petrified. Such a personality has nothing in common with the Sophists. Not only are the latter much more positive than Socrates – they are always on the lookout for prey – but they certainly cannot have his 'outstanding personality' (p. 149), for they seem to exist only in the plural, as a family, always progressing by disorderly leaps in a noisy chorus proliferating on all sides. Socrates, on the contrary, exists in complete isolation. While he has disciples, he has no relationship with them[52] and indeed that is what they find intolerable: he soars above them, mysteriously attracting and repelling them, always focused enigmatically, for his part, on himself. Whereas the Sophists, the eighth plague of Egypt, can be identified with fantastic insects that drop like grasshoppers in huge clouds, Socrates advances in solemn silence, enjoying a solitude that befits a unique and innovative personality.

Kierkegaard credits Socrates with a 'plastic' personality (borrowing the term from Hegel) in order to distinguish him from the Sophists. But is Kierkegaard not forgetting that earlier, when he put Socrates in harmony with the Clouds, he credited him with a plastic nature in a completely different sense? That other version of Socrates had the fragile nature of a good-for-nothing; he was capable of 'hysterically' adopting any shape at all – except, precisely, the petrifying form of a statue. Does Kierkegaard not end up confusing 'his' Socrates with Hegel's, a Socrates whose subjective principle of focused unification is that of interiority? No: for according to Kierkegaard what endows Socrates with a personality is actually his irony. This personality, in its fragility, is stronger than the one Hegel might attribute to him, because with Hegel the empirical 'I' disappears in favor of ideal indeterminations and the individual evaporates, undone.

The ironist, on the contrary, is 'an abbreviation of a complete personality' (p. 149).

As for the Socratic version of dialectics, according to Aristophanes' representation it cannot be identified with the Sophists's version either. Ignoring the celebrated dialogue, a parody of sophistics, that takes place in Socrates' Thinkery between 'just reasoning' and 'unjust reasoning' (the latter comes out ahead), Kierkegaard easily demonstrates that Aristophanes' representation corresponds in every respect to the ironic and entirely negative dialectics that Kierkegaard has perceived in Socrates. Sometimes this dialectics gets bogged down in examining the worst ineptitudes, gets lost in trivialities, takes them with a morbid seriousness; sometimes it prepares to grapple with an important problem but pulls back at the very moment the problem is raised. It requires memory on the part of disciples (and here again, memory may be double-edged, like Strepsiades' version, or like the 'doublethink' Orwell speaks of in *1984*; Strepsiades remembers only what the old man is owed and not what he owes, a duplicity that is better suited to ironic dialectics). It also requires the gift of eloquence. It is inconsistent: it does not require a belief in the gods, only in 'the great empty space and the tongue' (p. 151). In short, Kierkegaard declares, borrowing the expression from Grimm, a good disciple owes it to himself to have 'an empty head and a tongue like the tongue in a church bell' (ibid.), that is, in perpetual oscillation.

In Kierkegaard's view, then, Aristophanes has got Socrates' viewpoint just right. It is the viewpoint of someone who is always in suspense: whether he is suspended in a basket or wrapped up in himself gazing at his navel, freed of earthly weight, he is always situated between heaven and earth; he is lighter than the world, even though he still belongs to the world. Like Mohammed's coffin, he is suspended between two poles. This oscillating position cannot be that of the interiority Hegel attributes to Socrates. For in that case, infinitely centered on itself, interiority would no longer even need the basket symbolizing the empirical reality that remains necessary to the ironist. Interiority would necessarily be eclipsed ad infinitum, for with Socrates – and Kierkegaard believes that Aristophanes saw this much more clearly than Hegel, who could not help misusing such a good source – subjectivity does not expand in an infinite plenitude, it is narcissistically inflected in irony. And thus irony on its own accounts for the comic element in its entirety.

Through its 'realist' aspect as well as through its 'idealist' one, Aristophanes' play thus at best 'reflects' the ironic conception of Socrates: Kierkegaard's conception, in any case. Compared to Hegel, Kierkegaard may have taken the fictional and theatrical character of *The Clouds* more fully into account; he may have distinguished more carefully between the chorus's discourse and that of the other characters, and he may have been more attentive to the play's textuality and to its metaphors. The fact remains that Kierkegaard, too, reads *The Clouds* as the illustration of a thesis. He reduces the play in its feminine inconstancy, if not Aristophanes himself, to a pure reflection of his theory.

Unless it is Kierkegaard who has always already reflected the play, as Socrates reflected the Clouds in the play. That would explain how the play can, in exchange, corroborate and confirm Kierkegaard's own point of view, countering Hegel's. Because Kierkegaard presents *The Clouds* as a 'thesis' play, he sees everything in it as symbolic, as a reflection of his thesis. While he does not neglect everything that fails to lend itself to serious and rational laughter, as Hegel did, he is led – as Hegel was – to exclude from consideration what he calls 'pure buffoonery', all the comic elements that retain no trace of the Idea: 'Since there is no trace of an idea in many scenes, I shall bypass them, because they contain nothing but foolish subtleties or slapstick jugglery and the swaggering that goes with such practical jokes – in short, a lot of what one could designate as leg-pulling' (p. 146). In support of his own thesis and in his own way, Kierkegaard, too, stifles outbursts of uncontrollable laughter, squelches any laughter that does not stem from irony. The hierarchy he sets up among forms of laughter has at a minimum the effect of repressing the 'low-level' laughter that stems from the lifting of taboos: sacrilegious and desublimating laughter, Strepsiades' 'anal' laughter – which might bring Aristophanes into communication with Bataille. Laughter that does not result from the contrast between expectation and outcome, from the fools' bargain of someone who pays his money and receives only wind and clouds in exchange: this is the laughter of irony, which may also be 'forced laughter', laughter that in any event never bursts forth frankly, laughter that remains in suspense, 'in the air', clinging to Socrates' basket like the smile of the Cheshire cat; and yet it is a laughter that overturns everything – gods, father and mothers (let us note that neither Kierkegaard nor Hegel breathes a word about mothers; Pheidippides evokes his mother, however, when, on the strength of 'unjust reasoning', he threatens, in imitation of his 'father' and the better to come to his aid, to join in pounding her – a proposition to be taken no doubt, in more than one sense). The outbursts of this laughter bring them all tumbling down from their lofty heights.

Too respectful of God, his father and his mother, Kierkegaard preferred not to hear this noisy, dazzling laughter at all, so he would not have to deal with it; he lent his subtle 'ears' only to the silent laughter of irony.

k) Baptism

After presenting the various conceptions offered by Xenophon, Plato and Aristophanes, Kierkegaard plays the role of conciliating mediator and subjects all three – as he has actually been doing all along – to the test of his own conception. Up to this point, Kierkegaard's conception has been held in suspension above the others, oscillating ironically among them; now, after his investigation of the others, his own turns out to be confirmed; it can come down from the heaven of possibility where it has been floating to the solid ground of reality. The test to which the three conceptions are subjected thus constitutes a rite of passage for Kierkegaard's own 'conception'.

Judged by the yardstick of the 'nothing' that is Socrates's life, in Kierkegaard's reading, Plato's conception seeks to fill the void, an eminently feminine void, by fertilizing it with the Idea. Xenophon's conception adds the prolixities of utility, while Aristophanes' lays particular stress on its inconstancy: Socrates plunges into himself, but he does not bring the eternal plenitude of the Idea back up from the depths. He always resurfaces empty-handed; even though (unlike Xenophon's Socrates, who refuses to accept any wages because he judges himself invaluable) Aristophanes' Socrates contrives – ironically – to be paid very well; he takes more from his disciples than he gives them, letting them all leave equally destitute. In comparison with Plato, Aristophanes takes things away; in comparison with Xenophon, he adds things, but what he adds is 'nothing', his addition is equivalent to a subtraction. The point of view that slips into the gaps left by the three others and fills them, reconciling their contradictions, is 'his', that of irony. Socrates maintains a negative relation with the Idea, which is the limit of dialectics. If he elevates phenomena to the level of the Idea, he also comes back down to reality. Reality prevails, however, only as an opportunity offered, without really being offered, to surpass that reality. In short, subjectivity brings everything back to itself and enjoys itself, self-satisfied.

None of these conceptions has 'restored' the Socrates figure: they all remain 'conceptions' to which one may turn only with prudence. But what can be said, then, of Kierkegaard's? Has the question not been begged, has the argument not been circular, has there not been, as he himself puts it, a certain 'Jesuitism' in the attempt to make his own conception float like a sword of Damocles capable of determining the truth of the others, even as it claims to prove through them its 'own truth', 'discovering' in those others, by which it is itself confirmed, what it has always already put in them?

To this accusation Kierkegaard has a reply. His own conception at once preceded his investigation and grew out of the investigation; it simultaneously exerted an attraction on the object of his research and was attracted by it. Like any birth, it results from a double attraction, in opposite directions. His 'conception,' because it existed prior to his investigation and did not simply 'become embodied' with it, is not born of the investigation but is reborn through it. The investigation is thus the equivalent of a baptism – it enables Kierkegaard's conception to pass from a first birth to a second, the only 'true' one. Through affinity with the 'object' that attracts him, irony, Kierkegaard takes its method as model in his first chapter: he plunges the various conceptions of Socrates into the waters of a fountain of youth, as it were, in order to rid them of their old unfashionable cloaks and to dress them in new clothes, his own. Thus baptized, purified and transformed, the 'old' conceptions allow his to 'pass' and to undergo a metamorphosis, from a conception that is simply 'possible' to an 'actualized' conception: they allow it to be reborn.

Through this second birth is also born a 'new' Socrates, a 'real' Socrates of whom Kierkegaard alone is the true 'father' or mother. For, like the one conferred by baptism, the second birth effaces the first and eradicates the role played by the first three maternal 'conceptions', which do not deserve to live. Through the image of 'baptism', Kierkegaard can thus break through the vicious circle of his method and respond ironically to the objections: purified by baptism, after the test, his conception is both the same and no longer the same. If, predating the investigation, it can also result from the investigation, this is because, in its repetition, it has changed form: once possible, it has been actualized; it has become real. The becoming-real of conception will take on definitive consistency, however, only when it is corroborated by the test of the historical 'givens'.

3. Conception Becomes Real: The Undeniable 'Facts'

In this chapter, Kierkegaard claims to be moving to a totally different sphere from that of the 'theses' or fictions inherent in the conceptions he has discussed; he intends to limit himself to historical data. But since these data appear only in texts, he is obliged to resort to texts once again. Thus the problem remains intact: what text to choose as testimony to the 'historical' reality of Socrates, to the extent that the textual evidence is divergent? Here again, Kierkegaard's conception is supposed to be corroborated by historical reality, and yet that conception is what determines the validity of one source over another – a vicious circle.

In Kierkegaard's view, Socrates' demon is one such historical 'datum', a 'fact' that Socrates acknowledges and that everyone mentions. But not everyone describes this 'fact' in the same way. It exudes a charm that seduces and captivates instead of leading philosophers to solve its mystery. It even induces some of them to see this divine, abstract thing – which is beyond specification, ineffable, refractory, like the name of God for the Jews – as a pure hallucination. How can one determine how that most abstract of things, that scarcely audible voice, operates, moreover, if one observes that Xenophon and Plato differ on the subject, the former characterizing it positively and the second negatively? For Xenophon, the demon gives orders, instructions to act; for Plato (and Plato's version is also Cicero's), it only produces warnings, instructions not to act. How can one decide between these two versions except simply in the name of one's own inclinations and preferences, which in Kierkegaard's case lead, unsurprisingly, toward Plato? He is thus inclined, as Nietzsche was but for different reasons, to opt for a negative demon, one in perfect harmony with his own conception of a completely ironic Socrates. In other words, a demon that is completely negative with respect to reality. Now, according to Plato, Socrates' demon intervened precisely to keep him from getting involved in public matters, in affairs of State, the highest form of reality for the Greeks. By obeying that silent and inhibitory voice, Socrates was putting himself in conflict with the religion of State, with the eloquence of the gods, as his accusers charged. For the demon's voice was not at all concerned with the substantive interests of public life, but only with the individual private interests of Socrates or his friends.

On the question of the demon, Kierkegaard seems to be going in entirely the same direction as Hegel; indeed, he goes beyond Hegel and takes his position one step further. He draws on Hegel's analyses for support, although he does not emphasize that Hegel for his part is referring to Xenophon rather than to Plato. That is, Hegel is referring to a positive definition that alone authorizes him to represent the demon *'that counseled [Socrates] what to do'* (p. 161) as an internal oracle replacing the external oracle of the Greeks. Kierkegaard notes that Hegel uses an analogy to solve the problems related to the demon's nature, an analogy with unhealthy phenomena that Kierkegaard has just found suspect in connection with others than Hegel; however, he goes on to assert that the study of Hegel is infinitely relevant and renders the mysterious phenomenon intelligible.

What does Kierkegaard seek to gain, then, by allying himself in this unexpected way with the commander-in-chief of history, whose 'true' name he reveals here – the name of Caesar, no less? By pretending to admit that the person on whom fortune smiles is right, not only does he stand to please his jury but he can also beat his adversary on his own ground – ground the adversary has so decisively conquered. Indeed, by describing the demon as an intermediary between the external aspect of the oracle and the pure interiority of the mind, Hegel acknowledges in spite of himself that Socrates' viewpoint cannot be that of the interiority of the mind. He continues, however, to assert that such is his principle; in order to get out of the trap, he is compelled to explain that this 'interiority' has not yet achieved full self-possession, so it can only show up in a pathological external form. Kierkegaard attempts to spare the unfortunate Socrates this pathology, by showing that if Socrates' subjectivity is not revealed in all his research as having a healthy, adult nature, it is not because it is still that of a sickly child, but because it is limited by the Idea that Socrates never attains and from which he returns into himself with ironic satisfaction. If Socrates is ill, his disease is irony. In his case, the influence of subjectivity is interrupted. It is inflected by personality: the demonic stems exclusively (and Hegel recognizes this in a sense, but for him it is only one aspect of the Socratic principle) from the individual personality and its egoistic satisfaction. Socrates may be preparing himself for a leap that will take him elsewhere, but he never lands on that other shore; he pulls back from it again and again to return into himself.

In short, as a tool for understanding all the conceptions of the Socratic demon, as Hegel describes them, the viewpoint of irony is much more heuristic than that of Hegel himself. Provided, of course, that one understands irony differently from someone who has not understood it at all, someone who has reduced it to an evanescent phase in a system.

If it is true – as Hegel acknowledges, moreover – that what is at stake in Socrates' case is not so much speculations as the life of an individual, his irony must be envisaged not in light of the system but in light of the life that can devote itself entirely to that irony, precisely because it is not a system. The struggles, victories and tribulations of that life, like any viewpoint, remove it from a rigid, systematic, linear, necessary development. Thus by starting with the Hegelian reading of the Socratic 'genius', by taking from that reading everything he can use, Kierkegaard has defeated Hegel on his own grounds. He grants Hegel with the one hand what he denies him with the other; like the Socrates of *The Clouds,* he leaves Hegel vanquished, empty-handed, the lucky Caesar transformed into a ridiculous Strepsiades, with no chance to understand anything at all, about Socrates, or life, or irony.

B. *Second fact: the condemnation of Socrates (and of Hegel?)*

After the 'demon', Kierkegaard summons up a second 'fact': Socrates' condemnation by the State. The State, in its *seriousness,* cannot be suspected of fabricating a transfiguring conception of Socrates through its accusations; nor, through the intermediary of the accusers, can it be suspected of holding a biased view of Socrates rooted in hatred and anger, since the accusers could not – this seems self-evident for Kierkegaard – have been too far from the truth, a certain truth. Does this mean that Kierkegaard admits from the outset that the Athenian State was right to condemn Socrates? Even while declaring that this question does not concern him, that his own position is not moral but historical, that he is examining the condemnation only as a document and in the very same historical terms that were transmitted by Diogenes Laertius when he retranscribed the Metroön temple archive, Kierkegaard nevertheless undertakes his reading with reference to the viewpoint of Hegel, who makes Socrates a tragic hero and presents him as both right and wrong. Kierkegaard, in his turn, presents the Hegelian conception – with which he appears preoccupied – as both right and wrong.

a) *First charge: Hegel is wrong and right*

Hegel is *right* on the first point of the accusation: Socrates does not accept the gods recognized by the State. But he is *wrong* on the second point: Socrates does not introduce new gods into the city-state. For Hegel, these two charges are connected as negative is to positive, shadow to sunshine. But they are dissociated by Kierkegaard, for whom the 'demon' that designates only Socrates' negative relation to the established order in the religious arena cannot be what it is for Hegel, a new oracle, a new god. There may be a form of negativity that is not the other side of a positivity:

this would be irony, which rejects the established order and then always falls back only on itself, in a self-centered fashion.

The core of Kierkegaard's demonstration consists in rendering Socrates' ignorance solely responsible for his religious negativism. The latter cannot be confused with atheism, which is still overly affirmative, since it implies knowledge of divine non-existence. Socrates' ignorance is also precisely what exonerates him from the second charge. For if the ignorance in question is not empirical (Socrates – and on this point Kierkegaard agrees with Hegel – was very well educated) but philosophical, Socrates must have been ignorant of the principle of all things: he was interested only in men, not in nature or in gods. For him, the Idea constituted a simple limit. If he did reach the Idea of dialectics, he did not possess the dialectic of the Idea: thus, knowing nothing about the gods, he could not introduce a new divinity. Against Hegel, Kierkegaard summons Plato's *Apology* once again to the witness stand. In this 'defense of Socrates', Socratic ignorance is affirmed and displayed under the name of *human wisdom* – the better to denigrate ironically the pseudo-knowledge of all powerful people. Socratic ignorance cannot be correctly understood as 'feigned'. If Socrates does not pass his time attempting to remedy ignorance, it is because that was not the mission entrusted to him by the gods: contrary to Christ, with whom Hegel seems to confuse him when he has him play the role of a Saviour, Socrates did not come to save the world but to judge it, that is, to rid each person of what he thought he possessed, sending him away empty-handed. Socrates does not introduce new gods; instead, he gets rid of the old ones. He succeeds in turning men away from their gods and inducing them to plunge deep within themselves; thus he is merely preparing the way for the appearance of a God different from the Greek gods. Socratic irony, which brings to light the negative character of all finite content, is a transitory path that is necessary for a deeper understanding of the real relation that divinity maintains with humankind.

Socrates points people in the right direction in the military sense of the term. He positions them to receive the good news simply by stripping them of their old acquisitions. His 'operation' consists in cutting off his besieged troops from their entire stock of opinions, leaving them famished; meanwhile, carried away by the flame of his own voracious zeal and his ravaging enthusiasm, momentarily satisfied after accomplishing his 'divine' mission, he savors the joy of irony. He can 'let go': he abandons himself to a sort of internal revery and remains immobile, his eyes proud; in this position, grasping not simply some kind of plenitude but an intoxicating nothingness, filled to the brim with nothingness, he is ready to take up his 'divine' or rather demonic negativizing activity once again. That activity allows him to free his interlocutors, although he cannot enable them to enjoy the total freedom of irony: after starving them, he induces in them a nostalgic desire for a different plenitude.

If Socrates' viewpoint ultimately turns him only toward himself, in a certain sense it turns the others toward a new viewpoint: we can thus understand how he could have been accused, however wrongly, of bringing in 'new gods'. In reality, he does not appease his negativity by speculation but by his eternal anxiety, an ironic correlative of the 'gentle repose' of his ignorance. Socrates knows nothing about the gods, either from a theoretical or a religious point of view, for, unlike the least of Christians – the *Second Alcibiades* is proof – he does not even know what prayer is[53]; he does not know what to ask of God, nor whether his prayer will be heard. But with his famous γνῶθι σέαυτον, did Socrates not at least invite men to know themselves? On this point, while Kierkegaard accepts the Hegelian reading to a certain extent, he also departs from it sufficiently to insist that, if Socrates did indeed invite all people to know themselves, to distinguish themselves from everything else, the exhortation had only a negative outcome. The dialectical air pump deprived his interlocutors of the air they were used to breathing, without supplying them with another way of getting air. The only thing they could do, to avoid dying of asphyxiation, was try to breathe the ethereal air of ideas.

Socrates' viewpoint is negative in theoretical and religious terms, and it is equally negative in practical terms. Disagreeing with Xenophon but in harmony with Plato's *Apology* and with Hegel, Kierkegaard affirms that Socrates, even though he carried out all his civic duties, could not enter into a real relation with the established order, with the State. His divine mission occupied him fully, and compelled him to live as a private individual. If we are to judge by the standards of the modern era – an era that nevertheless leaves a good deal more freedom to the individual – Socrates' confinement to the private sphere had to make him suspect in the eyes of the State. While he may not be the evanescent character lost in the clouds produced by Plato's poetic transfiguration, and while men did have infinite importance for him (so much so that he would even lose his irony in interminable palavers with Tom, Dick or Harry in dubious back alleys), his highly-developed human relations did not make either him or his interlocutors good citizens; that is why the State was right from its own point of view (and Hegel's) to condemn him. But Socrates was revolutionary, not because he brought a new, higher viewpoint to the State (or so Hegel thinks), not so much because of what he did as because of what he abstained from doing, for his irony could only preserve him from any positive commitments either *toward* or *against* the State.

The position of irony is that of an isolated entity (therefore situated outside any conspiracy), freely dominating its relationships from on high, relationships that for their part are inevitably ambivalent where irony is concerned. Irony occupies the position of the aristocrat who, in his purely negative and self-sufficient enjoyment of himself, is not far from evoking the figure of Diogenes the Cynic. This 'raving Socrates' is not a simple caricature. Socrates cannot be exonerated on the pretext that, in his remote negativity, he could not have 'done evil'; by pushing others to put themselves in the same situation as himself, he really was doing evil. Did he not corrupt youth in this way? And this was, as we know, his accusers' second charge against him.

Here is where Kierkegaard perhaps most clearly reveals himself to be a 'Hegelian fool', more 'Hegelian' than 'fool'. For the split between the private sphere and the public that condemns Socrates will lead Kierkegaard, elsewhere, to compare Socrates to Christ: 'The witness for the truth – who naturally has nothing to do with politics and must above everything else be most vigilantly on the watch not to be confounded with the politician – the God-fearing work of the witness to the truth is to engage himself if possible with all, but always individually, talking to every one severally on the streets and lanes'.[54] And again: 'The "crowd", when it is treated as an authority and its judgement regarded as the final judgement, is detested by the witness for the truth . . . that which in politics or in similar fields may be justifiable, wholly or in part, becomes untruth when it is transferred to the intellectual, the spiritual, the religious fields'.[55] Christ, like Socrates, was a victim of the anger of the State. The Christian religion is the domain of the individual, in his separateness, and in this respect it is necessarily in conflict with the State, which hinders its practice and condemns it to persecution. Socratic irony, with its practice of detachment and indifference, is a prelude to the Christian attitude of renunciation and sacrifice: 'Socrates was all his life and with his whole soul the declared lover of this impracticable attitude'.[56]

One may wonder, however, whether Kierkegaard is not already be imagining Socrates in the form of a Christ-figure in *The Concept of Irony,* where, always with a great deal of ironic force, he distinguishes between the Sophists – that vulgar plague from Egypt – and Socrates, isolated in his ironic loftiness. He does not say so openly; in his Thesis he is bent on stressing the differences between the two figures more than their resemblances. The one nevertheless serves as prelude to the other, and prepares a welcome for his good news.

b) Second charge: Socrates is a seducer
Hegel's analysis of the second point of the accusation seems to strike Kierkegaard as so brilliant that he has trouble producing an alternative reading. Hegel was right when he showed that the 'corruption' with which Socrates was charged lay essentially in his encouragement of young people to disobey their parents. He was right to argue that the moral interference of a third party, under the sophistic and wholly immoral pretext of greater

competence, is unacceptable in the sacrosanct parent-child relationship. Nevertheless, as always, like a good policeman Hegel did no more than clear the ground for others, for Kierkegaard's conception; for he failed to see that Socrates' lack of respect toward the State and the family was due not to the principle of interiority but to his own ironic point of view. Only such a point of view can invalidate both the substantive life of the State and family life; both State and family are reduced to some number of individuals with whom Socrates maintained the same relationships as with other individuals.

From the point of view of the State, Socrates' crime lay precisely in his neutralization of the value of family life. Was he seeking to limit the damage done by his interference when he refused to accept payment (unless one accepts the version given in *The Clouds*) for his teaching? Was he seeking to establish his superior competence, the absolute value of his teaching, as incommensurable with money? On this point, too, Kierkegaard rejects the Hegelian reading. For him, the Socratic gesture signifies, instead, a double irony. Irony toward the Sophists, who give 'so much' that they are properly speaking unpayable; and irony toward his own teaching: since he knows nothing, he can take no credit for dispensing free teaching to others. For it would not have been the least bit 'immoral' to accept good pay if he had 'truly' taught; that would not have been an 'abuse', even though, as Hegel points out, the use of compensation had begun only with the Sophists. ('Who' is Kierkegaard trying to defend in this defense of fair remuneration, since it is obviously not the Sophists? Nor is it himself, since he, as a good Christian, deems profit a sin, and, like Socrates, exploits his paternal heritage without working, except with his pen. Might he not then be seeking to exonerate his father, who became wealthy after having known severe poverty in his childhood? We may suppose that this is the case.)

But in fact Socrates did not teach 'seriously'. He did not adopt an edifying manner;[57] he did not take the place of fathers or take over their responsibilities out of concern for their sons' welfare. With his disciples, his relationship was strictly negative: he did not communicate anything at all, nor did he satisfy, nor did he enrich. The corruptor of youth was a *seducer*, not only in the etymological sense of turning young people away from their families (this is the meaning Hegel saw), but also in the modern sense which would make him first and foremost a *tease*. He gets young people excited when they are in contact with him, but he does not give them any strong, substantive nourishment. He 'abuses' them, fascinates them, awakens nostalgic desires in them without satisfying them. If this is not playing the role of a responsible father, it is – at least if we are to believe Freud – a way of playing a fully paternal role, by virtue of the fascination involved. Did not Alcibiades say as much in the *Symposium*? With Alcibiades, Socrates behaved like a father or an older brother, no more, no less. He abused Alcibiades by not abusing him. Socrates attracts and then withdraws just when his disciple thinks he has won the match and found satisfaction.

Like the psychoanalyst who provokes transference without ever giving the patient anything, Socrates enchants his victims, then breaks the spell, leaving his disciple painfully deceived and disappointed. And because he does not succeed in liquidating the transference before he disappears, he makes the disciple his slave forever. For Socrates, as for the God of the Old Testament according to Hegel, for the psychoanalyst, for all these 'abusive' fathers, there can be no reciprocity in the contract that binds a son to his father. The son has to be a slave; he is destined to make all the sacrifices. But, as Kierkegaard suggests more strongly than Hegel, this is a father fantasy constructed by a son. In fact, it is only because the disciple is unable to comprehend the infinite freedom of Socratic irony, which enjoys only itself, because he cannot grasp its negativity, that he imagines the master with a 'phallus' that he can desire and then nostalgically take away from him; or else the disciple desires to be fed with the master's knowledge. In keeping with the nature of fantasy, this one is not shared by all Socrates' disciples. Other disciples more distinguished than Alcibiades must have been grateful to the 'master' for having taught them to look within themselves and not to owe their wealth to anyone but themselves, even if like Plato, through an excess of gratitude, they believed they had an unpayable debt to him. And they too constructed, in their own way, a figure of Socrates as master; blinded by their love, they were incapable of seeing in Socrates the point of view of irony. Xenophon was too narrow-minded, for example, and Plato too well-endowed to notice it.

In reality, as Socrates himself proclaims in the *Apology,* he has been no one's master; he has only lent himself ironically to everyone's fantasy of mastery. Indifferent toward young people, he dominates them by his irony itself. As penetrating as a stiletto, it pierces their souls for an instant, forcing them to reveal their most intimate conversations and to comment on them out loud in his presence – as if they were in the presence of a psychoanalyst who looks only obliquely at his 'analysand'. 'He became their confidant without their quite knowing how it had happened, and while throughout all this they were completely changed, he remained unbudgingly the same' (p. 190). The culminating point of this relationship devoid of reciprocity is located at the decisive moment when, in the blink of an eye, Socrates turns everything upside down for them at once. After his patient efforts to undermine foundations, Socrates, an ironic observer, enjoys his interlocutor's surprise at seeing everything come tumbling down before his eyes, while the master offers nothing in place of what is lost; he enjoys the very moment of disappointment when the astonished disciple sees his lover transformed into the loved one. Unlike Hegel, Kierkegaard does not give any positive orientation to this Socratic art of maieutics: through his art, like a highly skilled midwife, Socrates simply speeds up the spiritual delivery of the individual, cuts the umbilical cord that attaches him to substantiality, without in any way engaging his own responsibility for the patient's future. The individual may well turn out badly, like Alcibiades; Socrates washes his hands of him.

While Socrates can thus be accused of having been a seducer of youth, he cannot be subject to the frequently invoked charge of pederasty. From that particular vice, once again his irony could only have preserved him. For if Socrates did engage in pederasty, on the one hand, it was purely intellectual – as Pausanias's valorization of the only intelligent love would prove (but here Kierkegaard forgets something he had demonstrated clearly in his analysis of the *Symposium,* namely, that the respective speeches of each protagonist are valid only for that protagonist). On the other hand, it was purely negative: Socrates' relationship with young people was only the beginning of a relationship. It remained at the same level of possibility as his enthusiasm, that is, without effect: the relationship gave way every time just when it might have taken on a deeper significance.

Socrates' relationship with men, like his relationship with his wife Xanthippe (whom Kierkegaard relegates, along with all her sex, to the lowly position of a footnote), can be explained only in the light of irony: if one accepts Xenophon's version, the only benefit Socrates gained from that shrewish woman is that he learned how to control her, and with her, *a fortiori,* everyone else. Scalded by Xanthippe, he could not abandon such a 'positive' conjugal love in favor of a pederastic love that would have been more positive: instead, he fled the 'reality' of all loves to take refuge in irony. As we have seen, he preferred to castrate himself and castrate others rather than be castrated by them and by her; he preferred to remain *indifferent,* to return to the sexual 'indifference' of Aristophanes' androgyne – to borrow the unusual term Kierkegaard uses to speak of the androgyne's bisexuality. Kierkegaard places particular stress on that aspect of Aristophanes' myth; he takes up the term again as well in his *Journal.* There, in the context of a curious allusion to Plato, he slips from *sexual indifference* to an originary *masculine unisexuality:* '[Plato] thinks that in the perfect life, the masculine, as originally, will be the only sex, that is, that sex-distinction is a matter of indifference'.[58] It is as if, like Plato (who gave thanks to the gods, Kierkegaard recalls in a note further on, for four things: 'that he was born a human being and not an animal, a male and not a female, a Greek and not a barbarian, but principally because he was born a citizen of Athens and a contemporary of Socrates' [p. 214]), he did not want to know anything about or see anything connected with female sexuality – like Pausanius favoring the celestial Aphrodite over the pandemien Aphrodite. This is perhaps because, if male sexuality were identical with sexual indifference, all sexuality properly speaking would be female; female sexuality would then be indomitable (like the high-spirited mare Xanthippe). It could not be tamed except in an oblique way by irony, by that other woman who, however silent and self-effacing she may be, has just as much bite. This 'female' is nevertheless compared by Kierkegaard, among other things, to a voracious witch, a bloodthirsty vampire, a murderous stiletto, and a tyrant assassinating his subjects. Given that irony accomplishes its devastating action under an innocent-looking exterior, one may wonder whether it would not be still better for a man to have to deal with a solid ill-tempered woman of the Xanthippe sort – whom there is every reason to mistrust, as he knows unequivocally – rather than to face irony, that haughty, enigmatic woman who is much more threatening in her silent indifference, and much too fascinating, but who never gives you anything, who leaves you dispossessed, deprived of air, blood, and life.

It is interesting that for Kierkegaard, it is still only a woman – or a man who has identified himself with women by castrating himself – who can win out over another woman and thus also over all men, just as only the disavowal of mastery can confer mastery. Thus Socrates' only crime, unpardonable because it is ungraspable as such, is his 'indifference' to women, to men, to the family and the State. This is his ironic self-satisfaction: he cares for no one and for nothing. He never holds onto anything, unless one of Strepsiades' rejoinders can be applied to him (and Strepsiades is his disciple, after all). Neither Hegel nor Kierkegaard makes use of the following passage, since both of them repress the 'low comic' elements of *The Clouds*:

> SOCRATES   Hey, he's asleep!
> STREPSIADES   No, no! no fear of that!
> SOCRATES   Caught anything?
> STREPSIADES   No, nothing.
> SOCRATES   Surely something.
> STREPSIADES Well, I had something in my hand, I'll own.[59]

He may have been guilty, but should he have been condemned to death for this 'private' activity? If we are to believe Hegel, it is not the State, it is Socrates himself who brings his punishment on himself through his attitude of sovereign scorn toward the popular sovereignty that would thus have quite justly condemned him.

Still, can we say that he dies a 'tragic hero' in defense of a principle – that of emancipatory interiority – as legitimate as the one in the name of which the people accused him? Not at all: for Socrates, at least, as for Kierkegaard, it seems, the judgment of the State does not stem from a legitimate objective conception opposing an individual subject who embodies for his part some principle that is just as universal. Socrates' irony leads him to underestimate all objective determinations. The quantitative order cannot be the equivalent of the qualitative order; numbers as such give judges, or the State, no superiority over the isolated individual; their sentence has only a numerical value. Far from being 'tragic', Socrates' death sentence actually underlines the comic aspect of a situation that is attempting to bring two unrelated things together – Socrates and the State are absolutely heterogeneous values; and yet his judges wish that Socrates had led his life in conformity with the paradigm of the State. And like an old arithmetic teacher, he amuses himself even when his life is at stake by trying to find some equality in that inequality, a dialectical operation that contrasts with the reality of his life; the life in its ironic isolation was completely marginal in relation to the judgments of the State.

As for the choice of punishment, Hegel was wrong. Socrates did not reject the freedom to choose; this freedom must have suited him perfectly, and it did not entail any acknowledgment of guilt. For Socrates, quite logically, chooses only a punishment – the imposition of a fine[60] – that cancels itself out and thereby cancels the wrongdoing; for, supposing that he does have some money, it has no value for him. In reality, he says, it would be just as fitting for him to receive all his meals at the State's expense; since his 'private' condition lacks common measure with the order of the State, it should be above any punishment and any recompense: from the ironic viewpoint, the two are equivalent. If one must choose, then, why not choose a recompense? The only acceptable punishment, in any case, is the one that is not one, namely, the death penalty. Death is preferable to a fine or exile, for the latter punishments might well cause him to suffer:[61] in the one case, because, being unable to pay the fine, he would risk going to prison, in the other case because he would be even less capable of living as a good citizen anywhere outside of Athens and would thus risk exile over and over, indefinitely; what is more, both forms of sufferings are unbearable because they are unjust. Death is obviously the punishment of choice: as suffering, it is null, because no one knows if death is a bad thing; any other punishment, any true punishment would be incongruous in Socrates' eyes.

If Socrates' attitude toward the State is thus completely negative, its negativity is not that of a personality sure of its absolute authority, opposing its 'principle' to another principle and resting in the plenitude of its subjectivity. It is that of the consummate ironic indifference against which the objective power of the State is mustered, along with the Hegelian system that validates that power and resists irony. Because irony is ungraspable, because it eludes all determinations, all definitions, it can no more be integrated into the system than Socrates can be integrated into the State. He is foreign to the world of the State and its determinations. He belongs to a different species, that of the bird of irony gliding contentedly, indifferent to life and death, above the strife-ridden crowd, borne by an infinite negativity from which no positivity – since Socrates is not Plato – has yet emerged. The height at which Socrates soars, however, is not that of modern Romantic irony, which mistakes itself for God. Socrates soars at an 'authentic' height, that of Ideas, which he attains as limits, as possibilities. This is why, even though it is totally negative, it is less disquieting than the modern form of irony, which in its abyss swallows up all reality, that of Mind as it does that of ideas, even insofar as they are limits, mere possibilities. You have perhaps often tended to confuse the one with the other: this is because, in my desire to distinguish myself from Hegel and from his 'reductive' conception of Socratic irony, I, Kierkegaard, have placed greater emphasis on his infinite negativity than on the positive *poros* that it signals at its limit, which is not however an endpoint. As I see it, this positive role has to be reserved for Plato.

4. Conception Becomes Necessary: Irony, Gift of the Gods

In the first chapter of his thesis, Kierkegaard exposes the various earlier conceptions of Socrates in order to make his own possible (his hypothesis having directed his reading even as it was being confirmed by that reading). In the second chapter, he lends 'reality' to his own conception by way of documents and historical 'facts'. In the third chapter, Kierkegaard goes on to show why his own conception is necessary: irony, Socrates' irony in particular, has a place in world history. Its place is not that of a phase within a method; it is the place of Socrates himself, in history, according to Hegel: the necessary place of the beginning, the place of a *Janus bifrons*. Kierkegaard's conclusion is thus once again simultaneously Hegelian and non-Hegelian, even though – perhaps because he is reaching the end of his trajectory (if we exclude the Appendix devoted to Hegel, and also Part Two, which goes beyond 'the case of Socrates'; each of these sections further displaces his results) – he seems to be trying harder than ever to be more Hegelian than Hegel, as if that would leave the jury with a favorable impression.

However, Kierkegaard's approach actually allows him to 'displace' his own viewpoint even more effectively than before. For when he puts irony in the place Hegel attributed to Socrates, he no longer means what Hegel meant by 'Socrates'. Socrates is no longer a figure of Mind, a stage in its development, but a real individual existence, and this is why irony cannot be reduced to a stage, or to a phase in a stage: irony is completely coextensive with Socrates, an individual who deserves to be taken into consideration on his own account, in his actual phenomenological totality. But precisely because his existence is conflated with that of irony and because it has all the characteristics of irony, it is strongly marked with a negative index. It is related less to being than to nothingness; it is ultimately much less 'positive' than the reality Hegel attributes to it as a 'moment' or stage.

Socrates' life is a sublime pause in the course of history, remarkable for its silence – a silence that is to be interrupted only by the numerous and exceedingly clamorous schools that come to claim him as their source. Socrates can be compared to a majestic underground river that bubbles over with renewed vigor where it resurfaces. He is a suspension point in world history. Since he cannot be directly observed, he can be turned into a symbol, as he was by Hegel. As the figure of a stage in the development of Mind, he can only be the ambivalent symbol of a beginning: for Socrates is and is not, or is not and yet is. But he is, in his infinite negativity, only in an abstract form. After maintaining an ironic distance from Hegel throughout his thesis, Kierkegaard ends up aligning himself with Hegel's position, appearances notwithstanding. For he inscribes Socrates within world history only so as abstract his actual existence from that history. Socrates' real existence, as such, cannot coincide perfectly with the ideal existence of a symbol. Socrates may be an authentic turning point in history, he may be inscribed in history, but he is nevertheless not in perfect, logical, rational, 'strict' continuity, as Hegel would say, with his own era. While he cannot be reduced to a divine being soaring above his era, he cannot be explained entirely by that era, either: Socrates contains more than what his premises promised. Against Hegel, Kierkegaard invokes Plato's *Apology,* in which Socrates describes himself as a *divine present* offered to the Athenians; by this he means that he is necessary to his era, but that the era does not suffice to give birth to him. Socrates brings a supplement that alone explains the role that Hegel attributes to him: the *great turning point* of history.

Kierkegaard borrows Hegel's description of the 'Socratic moment', that of the decadence of Athens, and pretends to go along with the commander-in-chief, whom he showers with praise – no one can speak better than he or his soldiers can about that decadent era, so propitious for the advent of a new principle. He characterizes the Athenian conflict between the ancient principle and the new one – in a way that Hegel, for whom both principles were just and legitimate and necessary, entirely failed to do – as a struggle between evil and good, a conflict between the arbitrariness of finite subjectivity and a more legitimate subjectivity, and finally as the combat between the Sophists, who are really false Messiahs, and Socrates, who is elevated for the occasion to the dignity of Christ.

In short, on the pretext of putting Socrates in his proper place in history, once again adopting an elaborately sarcastic tone, Kierkegaard settles his accounts with the Sophists, the extent of whose harmfulness in history Hegel failed to grasp – for Hegel found a way to put the Sophists (who through their multiple and varied forms of knowledge represent an uprooted culture and resist all systematic integration) in almost the same place as Socrates in the coherence of his system. Their knowledge is a result of the newly-arising reflection; far from being amenable to internalization in a fixed position, it might be described as nomadic: it *is detached* from immediate substantive morality and it lands anywhere and everywhere, like a fluttering leaf. As nomadic as their knowledge, the Sophists themselves circulate from city to city, slipping in everywhere like counterfeit coins. Loudly proclaiming their encyclopedic knowledge, they aim only to bring men a general culture, a universal key capable of opening any door, public or private.

Concerned above all with earning money and acquiring political power, they serve as scientific second-hand dealers, lowly vulgarizers, delivering instruction that is 'general' in every sense, lacking any particular content and taking into account no individual particularities; they force everyone into the same mold, using the same measures for all.[62] If, on the one hand, their instruction is negative compared to immediate consciousness, since it introduces a contradiction within the individual and leaves everything undecided, on the other hand, it is highly positive (a quality Hegel fails to see since he ascribes to the Sophists too much movement and treats that movement as excessively abhorrent).

The Sophists' instruction offers remedies for the defects it points out; it teaches its hearers to give reasons for everything, to base everything on solid grounds, to prove that everything is true. Sophistic is a monster that destabilizes everything but that can, when it is famished, get its fill of arguments and let them lull it to sleep. If, upon reflection, the statement 'everything is true' can always be quickly converted to 'nothing is true', this stage of negative conversion does not belong to the Sophists, who live in the moment and who are prepared to deal only with immediate danger: to protect against the disruption provoked by reflection, they fall back on the expedient of the finite subject's personal pleasure. They bind up the burgeoning autonomy of thought in the slavery of the instant; they cut its tendons to prevent it from escaping and paralyze it in the service of the useful. If sophistic nourishes within its bosom a highly disturbing secret, it refuses to become aware of this; it believes it is satisfying the requirements of the times by assigning itself the task of shoring up again what it has just disrupted. The Sophists are convinced that they are the healers of their era. They manifest their 'positivity' at its best in rhetoric, which they make their art par excellence. Indeed, because from the theoretical viewpoint this positivity is only an appearance (it conceals a repressed negative) and because from the practical viewpoint it is harmful, sophistic is less a remedy than an illness from which Greece had to be liberated after it ran its course.

The radical remedy resides in the person of the Sophists' hereditary enemy, Socrates: a necessary agent of dialectics and history, according to Hegel. Socrates' appearance on the scene is presented in a parodic and profanatory manner as the fruit of the confounding ingenuity of world history, of its cunning. History is a veritable *deus ex machina*: from its lofty heavens it has sent Socrates expressly equipped and armed to take up the battle against the Sophists. So if Socrates and the Sophists are inseparable, it is not in the way Hegel thinks: he fails to see the latter's positivity, while at the same time he attributes too much positivity to the former. When he credits Socrates with the Protagorean formula according to which man is the measure of all things, an ambiguous formula that circulates everywhere, for its part, too, like a counterfeit coin, he contradicts himself, since, anxious to make the Socratic principle a positive one, he gives a positive meaning to the sophistic formula. Neglecting the formula's negative and finite side, he reads it to mean that man is the goal toward which all things tend. As he had already done in connection with *The Clouds,* he seeks to exempt Socrates from identification with the Sophists – for if he had been as positive as they, why would they not have tolerated him? Why would they not have allowed him to set up shop alongside them?

In this context, Kierkegaard returns to his analysis of the *Protagoras.* This time he places less emphasis on the irony that sets the two adversaries on the same plane in an equal state of deafness. He stops distinguishing Socrates from Plato so he can distinguish them both from Protagoras; he pretends to give more credit to the Sophist than to Socrates, only to reverse the situation in the end. On the question of the teaching of virtue, Protagoras remains consistently positive, but only on the surface; Socrates for his part is consistently negative, but this too, to a certain extent, is merely a matter of appearances. 'He is positive to the extent that the infinite negativity contains within itself an infinity; he is negative because for him the infinity is not a disclosure but a boundary' (p. 209).

Because sophistic positivity is not true positivity (that is, not so much the positivity of the Hegelian Idea as that of Christianity), Socrates had to appear on the scene – with his 'apparent' negativity – to prepare the way for Christ, to purify the temple so that the truly sacred could take its place there and make its voice heard. If he arrives fully equipped, then, his weapons are silence and negativity: for even though for my own purposes I, Kierkegaard, have just told you that his negativity was only apparent, do not forget that the essence of my thesis is that Socrates was exclusively negative and that he acted as such. If he prepares the way for the coming of Christ (or Plato), he cannot be identified with either of them; this is attested by the anthropophagic ferocity that is just developed enough for the needs of his 'divine mission', that of annihilating all positivity by his irony. For such is the 'divine present', the wholly negative supplement awarded to the era by the *deus ex machina* of history: the gift of a subjectivity which, in the infinite exaltation of its freedom, was capable of putting an end to the Sophists' abuses by means of an indirect polemics directed ironically against them. For their responses, Socrates substituted his questions; for their encyclopedic knowledge, his universal ignorance; for their insatiable rhetoric and idle chatter, dialogue and silence; for their pretentiousness, his self-effacement and his modesty; for their wealth and drunkenness, sobriety and abstinence, for their interest in public affairs, his lack of interest in politics; for paid teaching, free teaching. In short, for the Sophists' ambition to be first in everything and for their claim to stand out, Socrates substituted a desire to be at the foot of the table; not to be everything but to be a nothing-at-all.

This conception of an 'ironist' Socrates does not diminish the individual in any way. Not only does it make a place for irony in world history – and a place considerably more important than the one Hegel allotted it – but, for whoever has ears to hear and eyes to see, and who thus knows that 'the last shall be first', this conception makes Socrates a true hero, much more than Hegel's does. Socrates is a great man who was able to help history give birth to a new principle that it contained within itself. He did not 'bring' that principle; he helped it to manifest itself; he himself possessed it only 'hidden' (in his womb?). He was and was not that principle: the formula only mimics that of speculative dialectics, the dialectics of each moment which always is no longer entirely this but is not yet entirely that, of which the 'this' always waits to be sublated by a 'that' that it is not yet. According to this movement of *Aufhebung*, Socrates is no longer entirely the Sophist that he is however still, because he is not yet entirely Plato whom he is however already. The meaning Kierkegaard gives his formula is more Aristotelian than Hegelian; Socrates is the new principle only potentially and not in act; he holds it hidden in his womb without giving birth to it himself. A less expert Heracles helping at his own birth, as a true *metaxu* or intermediary he only helps History give birth, however heroic he may be. Now, the position of intermediary, of obstetrician, is none other than that of irony. Hegel was wrong to separate maieutics and irony as two distinct stages in his method. Irony is the two-edged sword that Socrates, an exterminating angel, brandishes above Greece. A 'divine present' sent to Athens, as Socrates himself says, to prod that indolent mare like a horsefly, irony is a stimulant of subjectivity and, in Socrates, it is a passion worthy of world history.

From this point on, it is all very well for Kierkegaard to take up the Hegelian formulas more or less literally (and perhaps he allows himself to do this because while they circulate like Gospel, they are actually – as he would like to prove by his translation of them – counterfeit coins that serve for anything at all); the meaning he gives them is no longer speculative but ironic. Socrates is indeed a turning point in history; with him one cycle is completed and another begins. He is the ultimate classical figure. However, he spends all he is and has in the service of his 'divine mission': that of destroying classicism through the irony that classicism nevertheless allows him to bear. In other words, his completely classical irony is not the much more disturbing, morbid and self-centered Romantic irony. If Socrates' illness is a disease of the aristocracy (Kierkegaard does not ask how the plebeian philosopher might have 'caught' it), it remains, in his case, divine health. This does not mean serenity, however. Serenity belongs to the splendid individuality with which Hegel wrongly confused Socrates when he made him a plastic personality, comparable to a classical work of art. For his physical aspect attests much more to the disharmony of his entire being:

his ugliness dooms to failure any physiognomic reading that makes the body the expression of the soul. Socrates ought to have taken ironic pleasure in this: pleasure in the future mortification of Hegel, among others. For Hegel cannot get out of his bind by locating Socrates' beauty in his moral force. That force was considerable enough to have vanquished the 'naturally low and hateful qualities' (*Lectures,* p. 393) that were reflected in his ugliness, in favor of a second, 'divine' nature, his 'true' nature. For Socrates' plastic force was nevertheless not strong enough to regenerate his external aspect.[63] It thus left intact the initial disharmony between his 'soul' and his 'body', between inside and outside.

The point of view of irony, once again, can thus knowingly replace the speculative point of view; the former does a better job than the latter in making 'sense' of the Socratic disharmony. Is it not characteristic of irony, indeed, that it should disrupt harmony, even eradicate it? Does irony, for which divergence is in the order of things, not enjoy the disharmony between being and appearance? If one is determined, then, to grant Socrates historical necessity at all costs, one must follow Scripture more closely than Hegel did. Socrates and his irony are in fact to subjectivity what Jewish law and its skepticism are to Christian grace. Each had to appear, in its silent negativity, so that subjectivity and grace should not be taken 'in vain', should not fall into or remain in the hands of Sophists or Pharisees alone.

For, like the Law, irony has its requirements, real and infinite ones: it requires infinity and ideality at the expense of the reality it scorns. To the Sophists, who can be equated with the Pharisees, Socrates brings 'the next instant', the one that makes it possible to absorb the finite into the infinite by revealing the inanity of the preceding instant. Irony's requirement of ideality allows it to judge and definitively condemn all Hellenism along with the Sophists. However, having 'come not to save the world but to judge it' (p. 173), Socrates with his irony is not an instrument in the service of the Idea that he does not possess. As the viewpoint of irony, Socrates has nothing in view but destruction; as the one who announces the law, he does not dispense grace. However, between the Socratic requirement and its accomplishment (the comparison was merely analogical), there is not the unbridgeable gap that there is between the law and grace: there is only the Aristotelian relation between possibility and act. Irony is the beginning and, as such, it is and is not. The suppression of the preceding development constitutes its end, but it can only realize this end by virtue of the virtual presence of the new principle.

Thus Socrates indeed has the 'two-faced' aspect of beginnings that Hegel had rightly attributed to him; but his duplicitous bifrontality is that of irony, not that of a personality with two sides, negative and positive. For this beginning that is Socrates is, like irony, nothing but negativity:

but it is negativity with a destructive aspect and a fertilizing aspect. The latter accounts for the diversity of schools to which Socrates gave rise. This does not necessarily imply a high degree of positivity. Not only does irony suffice on its own, as we have seen, to charm and seduce minds, thus to attract numerous disciples to Socrates, but also, because it leaves them all hungering for more, it compels them to search for and to invent some sort of positivity, even if they have to attribute its invention to Socrates. Moreover, Hegel himself attributed Socrates' 'fertility' to his lack of a system, to the imprecision and formal abstraction of his principle, which wrongly authorized illegitimate filiations. But if Hegel does not highlight the positive side of Socrates in this connection, it is so he can better reproach him for the empty negativity that lends itself to any content whatsoever.

For Kierkegaard, on the contrary, negativity must not be the object of a reproach. It is not a fault, a limit that Socrates' positivity encountered and that regrettably prevented him from already being Plato. This negativity is Socrates through and through, and it is the infinite and infinitely fecund negativity of subjectivity, open to all possibilities, to all future novelties. It conceals within itself a prodigious resource; negativity and not its inverse is what entails and stimulates positivity. As a beginning, Socrates is an infinite beginning. This is his positivity, that of being, as a beginning, open to all possibilities. But being only this infinite openness, he is negative; he is and he is not. Kierkegaard, by making Socrates a beginning, thus only repeats Hegel in parodic form and displaces him considerably.

It would seem, too, that his language announces Nietzsche's in 'Die vorplatonischen Philosophen': indeed, for Nietzsche, the Socratic fecundity that gives birth to so many opposing schools cannot be explained either by 'negativity' or by 'positivity' – these dialectical concepts have no place in his terminology – but by the dawning abundance of impulses. Like all the early masters of philosophy, Socrates is a pure type, that is, complete: rival instincts still struggle within him, harnessed to the same yoke. The schools that 'issued forth' from him were born of cuttings, sectionings, divisions of that lovely complex and undivided completeness, each one taking what it needed where it could. For that 'Nietzsche' one can hardly qualify Socrates as poor, empty, abstract, or in any sense negative; rather, such terms apply precisely to those who, issuing forth from him, become his successors after making away with his original treasure and dividing it up among themselves.

For Kierkegaard, all the 'positivity' of Socrates' disciples comes from within themselves, even if Socrates was necessary for the pursuit of their research, even if world history owes him a debt for having set afloat the ship of speculation: he helps it set sail, but does not get on board himself. A *Janus bifrons*, he belongs to the old order but looks toward the new: a flying fish, he is prevented by his ambivalence from being pinned down by the categories of either old or new. He has the new world within himself, like a foreign continent, just as Christopher Columbus discovered America even before he set sail. Socrates' negativity prevents him from turning back, and it hastens the real discovery: the enthusiasm of an exterminating angel that he manifests resurfaces in his disciples' positivity in the form of energy.

The viewpoint of Socrates as a whole is inflected in an infinite negativity. With respect to the positivity that preceded it, that of the Sophists, as well as with respect to the positivity that followed it, that of Plato, his viewpoint takes on a negative aspect – even though one may also say, in a sense, that in both cases his negativity was positive: in the sense that Socrates made it possible to get rid of the Sophists, to 'surpass' them, and in the sense that he left to Plato the pleasure of 'fertilizing' him. If we accept this sense of the word 'positive', then we may say that his negativity is infinitely ambiguous; it is the ambiguity of irony itself. This irony manifests itself in him as sometimes partially controlled – as a stage – in the course of conversation (this is what Hegel wanted to reduce it to), and sometimes in its total and infinite aspect, as carrying everything in its wake, including Socrates himself.

In his final chapter, Kierkegaard thus outdid Hegel at his own game to a greater extent than before, since he even claimed to allot a determined and necessary place in world history to Socrates. But since the place was that of irony, in fact Kierkegaard was more than ever substituting his own viewpoint, that of irony, for the speculative viewpoint of view he was overturning. But he did this in the same way that Socrates substituted his own viewpoint for that of the Sophists: he used an 'indirect polemic' to put an end to the abuses of the commander-in-chief of world history. The latter, skimming over Socrates from his lofty height, did not hesitate to minimize, among other things, a mere detail, namely, irony: in other words, the essential thing.

And if Kierkegaard's jury is not convinced, if the jurors have been unable to hear and appreciate his irony any more than they could that of Socrates, if they refuse him his title of doctor or rank him 'last', he will not protest. For he knows perfectly well, he who has eyes to see and ears to hear, that the last will one day be first and that even if he is rejected he will nevertheless have been that 'divine present' sent from heaven above, equipped and armed to take up the battle against Hegel and to triumph, not so much by 'reasons' – on those grounds, like the Sophists, Hegel cannot be attacked – but wielding the icy stiletto of irony. If Kierkegaard ends up, where Socrates is concerning, having contributed nothing but the gift of the viewpoint of irony, a gift that is in no way positive, a gift that is a negative conception, at least he will have shown that it is possible to get around the Hegelian dialectics without appearing to touch it. If, unlike Socrates, he ends up not starting a school, at least through his perspective he announces that of

Nietzsche; he renders Nietzsche 'possible', even if the latter will never thank him for it. For Nietzsche's way of getting around Hegel is quite different from Kierkegaard's. He does not rely on a polemic that, however indirect, oblique and subtle it may be, leaves Kierkegaard ever so slightly dependent on speculative dialectics and keeps him both inside and outside the system. Nietzsche for his part will not profit from the solid ground conquered by that Caesar in order to vanquish him and reduce him to nothing. He places himself on entirely different grounds from Kierkegaard's at the outset, grounds that Kierkegaard ignored or repressed, grounds that he had indeed traversed but only on the sly, silently and 'unofficially': the grounds of instinct.

IV. NIETZSCHE'S SOCRATES(ES): 'WHO' IS SOCRATES?

> Simply to acknowledge the fact: *Socrates* is so close to me that I am almost continually fighting with him.[1]

1. Fascination with Doubles

Like many others, but for different reasons, Nietzsche is fascinated by Socrates. Seductiveness, magic, charm: these are all terms Nietzsche uses to describe the effect produced by that 'demon', that 'great erotician', on his contemporaries, the noble, handsome Greeks whom this excessively ugly man (a man whom Nietzsche – unlike Hegel and Kierkegaard who judged him highly cultivated – views as an uncultivated plebeian), this commoner endowed with the most violent passions, notably a serious penchant for anger,[2] managed to seduce. That is to say, at the same time, that he led them astray, corrupted them, poisoned them. For Nietzsche, then, as for Hegel and Kierkegaard, the Athenians' charge that Socrates had corrupted their youth was justified, and as punishment for having distilled his own poison he deserved to drink the hemlock: 'It meant standing truth on her head and denying *perspective,* the basic condition of all life, when one spoke of spirit and the good as Plato did. Indeed, as a physician one might ask: "How could the most beautiful growth of antiquity, Plato, contract such a disease? Did the wicked Socrates corrupt him after all? Could Socrates have been the corrupter of youth after all? And did he deserve his hemlock?"'[3]

Socrates practices a dangerous seduction. If you do not protect yourself against it, you risk the same misadventure that befell Plato. All at once, as if you were in a *camera obscura,* like prisoners in a cave (the prisoners whose illusions the same Plato believes he is denouncing), you may see everything upside down.[4] Because your fine poetic nature has been perverted by Socrates, you may suddenly believe in the permanence of goodness and good men; you may believe in Mind, in ideas in themselves.[5] And do not suppose that this generalized reversal is just a passing effect of the magic spells cast by a witch. Socrates managed to pervert and contaminate Plato's nature to such an extent that one must be armed with medical and genealogical flair if one is to succeed in restoring all its purity to 'the most beautiful growth of antiquity', in distinguishing what belongs to Plato in his own texts from what is overly redolent of the plebeian Socrates. It takes medical and genealogical insight, given the extent to which Plato was 'diverted', to succeed in characterizing Plato apart from Socrates,[6] to imagine what he could have become if he had escaped Socrates' spell, to picture what a fine model for philosophical humanity he could still have found, one that the demon Socrates – Nietzsche will not forgive him for this – caused to be lost forever.[7]

Now if Nietzsche more than anyone else has the gifts needed for such a discriminating task, the reason is, as he declares in *Ecce Homo,* that he himself is endowed with a double set of evaluative criteria: one inherited from his father, rooted in decadence, and one inherited from his mother, rooted in a rich and full life. His dual origin makes him at once a *decadent* and a *beginning,* gives him 'a subtler sense of smell for the signs of ascent and decline than any other human being' has ever had: 'I am the teacher *par excellence* for this: I know both, I am both'.[8] It is because he is his own double – because he is both Plato and Socrates – that he can so accurately detect the genealogical distance separating the two. If he is fascinated by Socrates, it is as if, like Alcibiades, he were drawn toward his own double, toward the polar opposite he carries within himself and by which he is both attracted and frightened. It is certainly no accident, that in order to show that he belongs to 'the lowest rung on the ladder of life, has reached the lowest point of [his] vitality,'[9] he underscores the fact that his approach to writing *Dawn* was characterized by an extreme form of dialectical clarity, and in this context he refers specifically to Socrates: 'My readers know perhaps in what way I consider dialectics as a symptom of decadence: for example in the most famous case, the case of Socrates'.[10]

When Nietzsche struggles against Socrates, then, he does so because he is as close to him as it is possible to get,[11] and because this is the way he can allow the other system of perspectives, the one he got from his mother, to triumph within himself over the paternal morality and moralism that have already killed him. The maternal system is the only one that allows him to keep on living and to grow old; insofar as Nietzsche is his own father, he is truly already dead.

The problem of Socrates that continually haunts Nietzsche is thus, for him, not a theoretical issue but a vital problem. With Socrates, the issue, above all, is which force will triumph in himself, life or death.

2. A Perplexing Case

Now, if we focus on Socrates' life, the case is perhaps not as simple as *Ecce Homo* and other Nietzschean texts contemporary with *The Twilight of the Idols* (1888) might suggest. As if to bring Nietzsche out of the aporia into which Socrates has never ceased to plunge him, these texts reduce Socrates to a caricature, a figure of decadence, a figure that is much more Jew than Greek. If Nietzsche carries 'Socrates' within himself, he does not seem to have a very clear idea of just 'whom' he is harboring. It is not a simple matter to evaluate the figure of Socrates genealogically, to offer a straightforward diagnosis of illness or health: for such is the typological question that perplexes Nietzsche and that he substitutes for the topological question Hegel raised. The issue, for Nietzsche, is not 'where' Socrates is, what position he occupies in world history, but 'who' he is; and only the answer to that question would allow him to confront the problem of the philosopher's historical position.

The topological question is dependent on the typological one because it is not a question about a stage in the dialectical development of Mind; instead, for Nietzsche it characterizes a specific state of growth or degenerescence of the vital forces. Because the history of philosophy is not the unobstructed history of ideas, one cannot attribute to it, as Hegel does, a continuous progression, a natural and regular course in which the appearance of Socrates would have a determined, necessary place in advance. While Socrates did not spring up 'like a mushroom', he is compared by Nietzsche to a stone[12] tossed into the machinery of the history of Greek philosophy; in a single night (for by bringing 'daylight' to the Athenians he actually plunged them into darkness), that stone was enough to blow up the whole works and to nullify its evolution, which had been 'wonderfully regular' up to that point. Socrates marked the contingent and accidental rupture of the history of Greek philosophy. Owing to the 'misfortune' of his arrival on the scene, the existence of the 'marvelous philosophers' who had preceded him was all for naught, and the 'combative and garrulous hordes of the Socratic schools' could take over.[13]

The fact that the Socratic stone, through bad luck, tipped Greek history in the direction of decadence is attributable to the contingency of the 'type' to which the individual belonged. But here is the problem: how can that type be determined with certainty? In Socrates' case, one cannot turn to his writings and decipher them as if they were symptoms. Since the absence of writing constitutes a symptom in itself, however, this would not be a cause for regret – except that that symptom, taken in itself, is not unambiguous. On some occasions, it allows Nietzsche to link Socrates with the earliest masters of philosophy who did not write either, according to him; at other points, he makes the absence of writing a ploy symptomatic of a weak person, a 'busybody'. The absence of writing can be a way of exercising one's mastery over others; one can limit oneself to questioning others without communicating anything to them. If Socrates does not write, his reasons are different from those of the thinkers whom the Aristotelian tradition, which does not have eyes to see, has labeled the 'pre-Socratics', using Socrates as the yardstick to judge them by. Socrates may not write, but he is an insolent magpie quite unlike the others. He belongs to a different type: 'These early Greeks did not *chatter* and *revile* so much; neither did they *write* so much'.[14]

'Socrates is the ideal "know-it-all". . . . Socrates as the "one who does not write": he does not wish to communicate anything, he only questions.'[15]

Is it possible, then, to produce a typological reading of Socrates by relying on the sources alone? Certainly not by relying on Plato as such: as we have seen, Plato depicted an entirely chimerical Socrates,[16] making him a supremely evanescent character by overloading him with qualities that never occur together in the same individual. Lacking dramatic genius, Plato was incapable of capturing the figure of Socrates, even within a single dialogue.[17] If he represented Socrates in such a dangerous, unstable position,[18] if he failed to 'pin him down', it is because his jealousy made him want to have Socrates all to himself. He wanted to impregnate him all by himself, to embellish him (does he not speak, in one of his Epistles, of a Socrates 'become fair and young'?), to steal him away from all the Socratics and to designate himself as Socrates' sole successor. In short, if Plato represented Socrates with no historical fidelity whatsoever, it is because he used him as a simple semiotic stand-in for himself.[19]

On the other hand, and contrary to Kierkegaard, Nietzsche is moved and gratified by his reading of the *Memorabilia*[20]; in his opinion, Xenophon offers a truly faithful image of Socrates, 'exactly as ingenious as the model'.[21] Nietzsche uses Xenophon as a yardstick to evaluate the 'truth' or lack thereof of Plato's portraits; and if he subjects Plato's idealizing and poeticizing reading to genealogical demasking, he spares Xenophon's texts a demystifying decoding, although he does declare that in order to judge the accuracy of the *Memorabilia* one must know how to read the text better than the philologists did – for they were bored by that poignant and admirable work.[22] But no matter how faithful this source may be, it still does not suffice on its own to resolve the typological enigma of Socrates: by itself it reveals only symptoms that one must then know how to interpret.

Now, as far as Socrates the individual is concerned, the certainty of the doctor's diagnosis seems to waver: as he himself acknowledges, if he repeatedly comes back to Socrates in order to grasp 'the meaning and purpose of this most questionable phenomenon of antiquity', it is like returning to a problem that leaves him, every time, 'in an extraordinary perplexity'.[23] Not only because Socrates wrote nothing, not only because the sources offer divergent information about him, but perhaps chiefly because he does not belong to a simple type, because in the end he resists the Nietzschean typological classification. He is neither a strong nor a weak type, neither a pure nor a hybrid type. In an attempt to break out of aporia, certain of Nietzsche's texts nevertheless attempt to pigeonhole Socrates, to combat his 'dangerous' atopia by assigning him to a specific category. But whenever this reductive operation is undertaken, Nietzsche always hints simultaneously at the character's extraordinary and irritating complexity. Socrates prevents anyone and everyone from grasping him, even in the subtlest fashion, and he leaves him, Nietzsche – as Nietzsche is forced to acknowledge every time – in aporia. As a result, on the subject of Socrates even more than on other topics, Nietzsche's texts are extremely heterogeneous in both content and tone (the tone ranges from highly admiring to highly pejorative), and they are almost always marked by an ambivalence with respect to the double from whom, like Alcibiades, he never quite manages to break free, and of whom he never quite succeeds in purging himself.

3. A Pure, Monolithic Type

In *La Philosophie à l'époque tragique des Grecs*, Socrates is classified in a thorough-going way among the pure, monolithic (*einseitig*) types, and thereby distinguished from Plato, the first of the great hybrids (*vielseitig*). Monolithic because a single principle orders and ranks all his instincts (and in this respect Nietzsche joins Hegel in attributing to Socrates a plastic personality unified by the single principle of interiority). Later, he calls this principle 'will' or 'perspective'; in his early texts, he calls it 'energy' or 'interest', specifying that this unique interest is moral interest: 'Socrates is an ethical autodidact . . . Monstrous energy directed toward moral reform. That is his only interest . . . What distinguishes him, however, is the *épistémè* as a means [of moral reform]'.[24]

As a pure type, Socrates is linked with those who are traditionally called 'pre-Socratics' whom Nietzsche prefers to call 'pre-Platonics'; in his early texts, Nietzsche identifies the beginning of the historical rupture with Plato. In general (to spite the metaphysicians who reduce them to the state of stammering infants[25] or as yet badly-trained soldiers) he calls the pre-Platonics the 'first masters of philosophy'. Modern philosophers have everything to learn from the pre-Platonics, and not vice versa; in their naivete – the absence of any internal divisions – and their dawning abundance, comparable to that of a fruitful pregnancy, the pre-Platonics are *complete*. It is they, not those who come after Socrates, who must serve as models and standard: the pre-Platonics represent the whole spectrum of possible types of philosophy. After them, there can be only repetition or degeneration: decadence owing to decomposition, isolation, some breach of solidarity among the instincts, between the individual and society, between life and thought. In Nietzsche's early texts, Socrates is situated on the same level as these old Greek masters who are carved out of a single block and whose thought and character are bound by strict necessity.

'It is only with Plato that something quite different begins, and that philosophers lack something essential if one compares them to the Republic of geniuses that stretches from Thales to Socrates. Socrates, a pure type. Plato, hybrid (Socratic elements, but also Pythagorean and Heraclitan)'.[26]

What *pure type* does Socrates embody, then? Just as Heraclitus is the prophet of truth and Pythagoras the philosopher of religion, Socrates embodies the sage who conquers the passions and whose knowledge is wholly at the service of life. 'He is the first to philosophize about life. A life directed by thought. Thought serves life, whereas with all the earlier philosophers life served thought and knowledge. The Socratic goal is a life of integrity, whereas the others sought a prominent amount of exact knowledge'.[27] (Here again, Nietzsche is in agreement with Hegel, and on this point both are inspired by the same source, Xenophon.) In the moral sphere, clear knowledge is the only merit: Socrates challenges the value of the moral instincts and holds that virtue can be taught. His belief is that morality lies in knowledge, a proposition whose corollary – an upsetting one in Nietzsche's eyes – maintains that wherever clear knowledge is lacking there is evil. This view has two consequences. Socrates becomes the censor of his epoch, which is subject to the instincts; and because knowledge is by rights universal, his philosophy is popular and democratic. In this text Nietzsche does not use the pejorative tone he adopts later on when he characterizes Socrates as plebeian, a corrupter of nobility. Here he simply underscores Socrates' suggestion that the humblest artisans are superior to statesmen, that what everyone 'knows' is presumption, based on words, that the human world is a world of ignorance.

Socrates embodies the accomplished sage, from whose person a moral radiance emanates. Like a prophet or a priest, he claims to be charged with a divine mission, and his death is the emblem of his radiant wisdom. If Socrates does not seek to defend himself before the tribunal, it is not out of pride, as Hegel maintains, nor through irony, as Kierkegaard argues; it is because he dies willingly and speaks for posterity, knowing that his death will be a powerful lesson: 'Socrates wanted to die. He had the magnificent opportunity to demonstrate his superiority over human fear and failing, as well as to demonstrate the nobility of his divine mission'.[28]

Later on, in *The Twilight of the Idols,* in a passage evoking Socrates' death, Nietzsche's tone changes remarkably. He now finds it quite suspect that a living person does not fear death and even seeks to die, and he sees in this death wish a symptom of decadence. In 'Die vorplatonischen Philosophen', the death wish is merely said to be in perfect harmony with the type of wise man Socrates embodies, in harmony with his life as a whole, which was characterized by the government of spiritual lucidity triumphing over the passions: 'Socrates is the last type of sage we meet: the sage as conqueror of the instincts through *sophía.* Thus is exhausted the line of original and typical *sophoi.* Now arrives a new age of *sophoi* – more complex characters, formed by the merging of streams flowing from the original and more one-dimensional *sophoi*'.[29]

In this text where Nietzsche nevertheless insists that virtue and merit lie in knowledge alone, how can he classify Socrates among the earliest sages, those in whom the knowledge instinct and the life instinct are still harnessed to the same yoke? He can do so because for Socrates, as for the 'pre-Platonics', in fact, life and thought are not separated. For the pre-Platonics, life is at the service of thought; for Socrates, thought is at the service of life, that is, it is *exclusively* at the service of life. Socrates' quest, as everyone has pointed out, is uniquely moral: the knowledge instinct is restrained, subordinated to the quest for happiness. In the same way, the goal of all the schools to which he gave rise is only a doctrine of moral good, a search for a human morality founded on the basis of a body of knowledge, as Nietzsche later notes in *Human, All Too Human*: '*The mischief-maker in science.* – Philosophy separated itself from science when it posed the question: what kind of knowledge of the world and life is it through which man can live happiest? This took place in the Socratic schools: by having in view the objective of happiness one applied a ligature to the arteries of scientific research – and does so still today'.[30]

Ethics is hostile to science because science attaches importance to something other than the autonomy of good and evil, whereas ethics seeks to command the obedience of all human energy. From the standpoint of ethics, it is wasteful to be concerned with stars and plants; that is why Socrates was hostile to science, even though he based ethics on the *épistémè*. In a later text,[31] Nietzsche adds that the imperative of having to avoid excessive expenditure applies especially to those who are not rich enough to be wasteful. In 'Die vorplatonischen Philosophen', the limitation on the search for knowledge is attributed to the 'artistic' mastery of the instinct that is content to seek what deserves to be sought, to search out what is beautiful and great; that instinct makes selections in a way that reveals the seeker's subtlety and nobility of taste. The indecent and disproportionate search for knowledge for its own sake – like the lack of interest in collective salvation and the formation of sects – is a post-Socratic phenomenon. Socrates is identified with pure and complete types: he is differentiated from Pythagoras and Heraclitus, while he is deemed comparable to Thales, Anaxagoras, Democritus and Parmenides, all of whom nevertheless seek to acquire knowledge. For this reason, his place is at the end of a cycle rather than at the beginning; and it is Plato, the first great hybrid (even though Empedocles, among the pre-Platonics, is already the very 'prototype' of a hybrid), who constitutes the break.

4. Monomania

At the other pole of Nietzsche's work, in *The Twilight of the Idols* and the contemporaneous posthumous fragments, Socrates is again presented in monolithic fashion. However, he is now merely a caricature of the pure monolithic type. What constitutes his *unity* is no longer characterized as the 'moral interest' of the sage; it is discredited by being labeled a 'monomania'. Socrates' mania is the madness of a *buffo*, not of a sage; it is an obsession with ethics, and as a correlative symptom it manifests a hypertrophy of his logical faculty. Both the obsession and the hypertrophy, in their excessive character, are indices of the decadence that Socrates inaugurates, in philosophy, ethics, art and culture. Socrates is no longer represented as completing a cycle; this time, he is placed at the origin of decadence, and he is held personally responsible for Plato's. The break comes with Socrates, a violent and revolting break owing to the upheavals that it provokes. For Nietzsche, as was the case for Hegel, Socrates now represents the great turning point in which consciousness turns toward itself – but this turning back is by no means a sign of progress. If, with Socrates, something changes, the change is actually a pernicious one in every respect.

In fact, starting with 'Die vorplatonischen Philosophen', alongside texts that classify Socrates among the first masters of philosophy, there are numerous others, more or less contemporaneous, in which Nietzsche declares that the Greeks who were particularly great and venerable, worthy to serve as models, were the ones who came *before* Socrates. Socrates is responsible for the Greeks' loss of their naivete[32]; his knowledge instinct is developed in monstrous fashion, without restraint or inhibition, and he declares that he is primarily concerned with the individual and his happiness rather than with the collectivity. In short, it was he, a true sculptor's son, who split the history of philosophy in two with hammer blows. Or, as Nietzsche asserts elsewhere, it was with the dagger strokes of his irony that he slashed the history of philosophy apart, in a violent, irremediable and unretractable split. Greece and philosophy have never recovered; they have never been 'sublated'.

'When the Hellenic genius had exhausted its highest types, Greece declined with the utmost rapidity. . . . One single powerful crank like Socrates, and the break was irreparable. The self-destruction of the Greeks is accomplished in Socrates. I consider it significant that he was the son of a sculptor. If for once the plastic arts could speak, they would seem to us superficial. In Socrates, the son of a sculptor, their superficiality emerged'.[33]

'With Socrates begins the optimism that is no longer artistic in the least, teleology and belief in a good god. Belief in man as good, because he knows. Disaggregation of the instincts'.[34]

'He breaks with science and with earlier civilization'.[35] 'Hostile to explanation drawn from the natural sciences. He denies civilization'.[36]

'Socrates *upset everything:* that is especially *ironic.*'[37]

'Every force (religion, myth, instinct for knowledge), if it is excessive, acts in the direction of barbarousness, immorality and stupidity because it exercises a rigid domination'.[38]

'The Pre-Socratics did not share the Post-Socratics' "detestable pretention to happiness". Everything does not revolve around the condition of their souls, for this is something that one does not think about without danger. Later Apollo's γνῶθι σεαύτον ["Know thyself!"] was misunderstood.'[39]

'Socrates . . .sought *to engender himself* and reject all tradition.'[40] 'Socrates: there remains nothing for me but myself; anxiety concerning oneself becomes the soul of philosophy.'[41]

'He struggles against the unconscious.'[42]

Thus Nietzsche very quickly makes Socrates responsible for decadence in philosophy and everywhere else. Because the destiny of art in particular is inseparable from that of philosophy, Nietzsche shows in *The Birth of Tragedy* how Socrates, the very prototype of the man of theory, the non-mystic par excellence, 'in whom, through a hypertrophy, the logical nature is developed as excessively as instinctive wisdom is in the mystic,'[43] and who is monstrously lacking in artistic talent, takes a vigorous stand against instinct, the unconscious, poetry, art, and tragedy. Hiding behind the mask of Euripides, Socrates uses his theoretical optimism to bring tragedy to its death agony. In short, Socrates is the very prototype of the Apollonian. His serenity is based on the illusion that through knowledge he can encompass all that is to come in his conceptual net, and can thereby gain mastery over it.

5. Socrates as Artist

The texts in which Nietzsche goes the furthest in 'typifying' Socrates, even to the point of caricature, still maintain a certain heterogeneity. Thus, in *The Birth of Tragedy*, Nietzsche depicts Socrates, with his great Cyclops eye 'in which the fair frenzy of artistic enthusiasm has never glowed',[44] as the anti-Dionysian par excellence. But he goes on to dream of an entirely different Socrates, one whom the despotic logician could only encounter in dreams – here is the only place Nietzsche hinted at any scruple, at 'any misgivings about the limits of logic',[45] at the possibility that there might be a region from which logicians would be banished, a region that would be a necessary supplement to science, that would fill its gaps. He dreams of an artistic, musical, Dionysian Socrates. As if in the grip of remorse, for the duration of a dream, Nietzsche seems to have perceived that Socrates' relation to art might not be exclusively antagonistic, negative and dissolving. The Apollonian, indeed, is only the shadow borne by the Dionysian. Anyone bold enough to look through to the other side (Socrates took that adventurous step only in dreams) will find behind Socratism and Apollonianism their true motor, Dionysianism. Behind logic and reason the most powerful instinctual forces will be found in all their horror: the best indication of their presence is the excessive character of the logical impulse itself, with its unrestrained unfurling.

This disproportion, this excess, monstrous because it is Dionysian, is what allows the wisdom of Socrates to communicate with the great figures of Greek tragedy,[46] Prometheus and Oedipus. With Prometheus, for Prometheus was torn apart by vultures because of his Titanic love of humanity;[47] with Oedipus, for Oedipus was thrown into the chaotic whirlwind of his crimes owing to his excess of wisdom.[48] Hegel was unable to turn Oedipus into a Socratic figure, a figure of light and clarity of consciousness who comes to terms with all riddles and all monsters, only because he did not grasp the excessive, Dionysian aspects of his 'wisdom' any better than he did in the case of Socrates. For one cannot separate the riddle-solver from the criminal, from the person who commits incest and parricide: whoever seeks to solve the enigmas posed by nature has no fear of violating natural laws. What the myth of Oedipus teaches is that monstrosity is at the origin of wisdom; it is a force that is necessary if one is to break the spell cast by nature and its laws, and that wisdom necessarily turns against the sage.[49] Socrates' Apollonianism, like Oedipus's, is thus only the other side and the shadow of his hidden Dionysianism, which reappears in his case just once, in the still-Apollonian form of a dream, an apparition ordering him to make music, and which he obeys in wholly Apollonian fashion once he wakes up, by composing a hymn in honor of Apollo and by putting Aesop's fables into verse.

In *The Birth of Tragedy*, Socrates' repressed Dionysian elements cannot yet be said to mark his belonging to decadence (although Nietzsche makes such a claim at a later stage, in *Ecce Homo*). For it does seem as though the same repressed Dionysianism may be found at work in Democritus, who is a pure type, the prototype of the scientific spirit and of rationalism. Behind the desire for serene knowledge, a desire directed and limited by the will to feel himself situated in the world as if in a well-lighted room, a desire that by that very token condemns all mythical intrusions, behind the lovely Apollonian Greek nature that is cold as a statue, Nietzsche in fact discovers a secret, Dionysian fire that is betrayed solely, in hard-to-discern traces, by Democritus's poetic enthusiasm and the faith he puts in his own system. Does Democritus, too, belong to decadence? Some clue allows Nietzsche to suspect, in any case, that the opposition between the man of theory and the artist is a pure 'theoretical' fantasy.

The desire to remove all the veils from the goddess Truth, to strip her to the point of total nudity, was a desire that Democritus did not have; it came into the world for the first time in the person of Socrates[50] along with the artist's desire to remain connected with what always remains of the veil after the unveiling; such desires finally refer to a single artistic desire for illusion. This is how desire on the part of the man of theory, taken to the extreme, suddenly turns into art: at its highest degree of perfection, in order to remain true to itself, theoretical serenity necessarily returns – as was the case with Socrates but not with Democritus – to the myth to which it appeals when 'reasons' are insufficient. In the process, over and beyond its explicit goals it proves the true aim of science, which is the same as that of art: the pharmaceutical aim of dissimulating the Dionysian, of attempting to make the intolerable tolerable – of curing, each in his own way, the 'eternal wound of existence'.[51]

If the 'pure' Apollonian is only an ideological fantasy – ideology itself – that wrongly separates the Apollonian from the Dionysian of which it is merely an illuminated apparition and a mirror image, Socrates cannot be 'Apollonian' for Nietzsche without being at bottom at least a little bit Dionysian as well. For the Nietzsche of *The Birth of Tragedy*, such would be the true meaning of the Socratic bifrontality (recognized also by Hegel and Kierkegaard), the same bifrontality as that of tragedy, and for the same reasons as tragedy.

6. Irony

Are we to conclude that the figure of Socrates resists being reduced to a pure and simple type – whether he typifies strength or weakness? If Nietzsche always finds himself in difficulty with this figure, is it not because he has sought to classify him in one category or the other – even though he suspected that there was something ridiculous about such classification? Ridiculous – although Nietzsche does not always seem to have been particularly aware of this – because the effort at classification presupposes that one takes the statements attributed to Socrates 'seriously' when he makes a radical distinction between reason and instinct, when he cuts off the theoretical, the 'Apollonian', from its instinctual, natural, 'Dionysian' roots and proposes knowledge, dialectics – and its syllogistic arguments – as the unique path to virtue, as the only way to conquer instinct and pleasure and to establish goals. If this is the case, then from the standpoint of truth, he is indeed an ideologue who, before Plato (whom he corrupted), presents a reversed world, a 'false' world, a world turned upside down; and, from the standpoint of life, he is a dubious, suspect, enigmatic human being, a singular phenomenon, a sick man, perhaps even a monster. But if the 'Apollonian' mask that Socrates displays is pure irony, and if on the contrary his avowal of ignorance is not feigned, if he knows nothing, as he claims, if he does not know what good and evil are, and thus cannot have taught Plato what is good and beautiful in itself,[52] if he knows perfectly well on the contrary that there is nothing divine but instinct and 'inspiration', what can the result be? Would Socrates, viewed from the standpoint of irony, be easier to classify and master in a typological category or, on the contrary, does this standpoint – and this would explain why Nietzsche was less sensitive to it than Kierkegaard – not resist the typological perspective? Or does it not at least require that the latter be ever so slightly complicated?

To pursue this question, let us take a close look at *Beyond Good and Evil*, §191, where Nietzsche formulates the hypothesis of an ironic point of view. From this point of view, Socrates would have known perfectly well that 'reason' cannot operate effectively in the realm of ethics; it is worth no more than 'faith', that is, instinct, for making ethical judgments; for reason, *ratio,* is simply able to appreciate and to act in accordance with motives and with 'a reason', that is, in conformity with a utilitarian goal and purpose. In the debate that opposes 'faith' to reason, Socrates' conduct reveals his 'taste': he behaves like a superior dialectician. At first, Socrates *allies himself with reason*. This initial gesture allows him to make sport of the noble Athenians, men of instincts like all aristocrats, who are incapable of giving 'reasons' for their behaviour. If we were to go no further, we might believe that Socrates is quite misguided in his mockery, that he who laughs last laughs best; what looks like notorious awkwardness and powerlessness to the eyes of reason could well turn out to be a symptom of the Athenians' power. After all, they affirm their instincts without any need for ratifications or demonstrations: anything that proceeds unmasked, reasons in hand, is plebeian and indecent. But in a second gesture, Socrates *also makes fun of himself:* he turns the formidable and merciless weapon of irony, which precludes all dissimulation or deception, against his own flesh. He knows that he is at the same point as the Athenians, that he is as diseased as they are, for his mockery is not directed so much against their rational awkwardness as against the pompous counterfeiting of the language used by those tired old conservatives. Their language no longer corresponds to the reality of their instincts – the worn-out instincts that he, as a good healer, can detect in himself as well as in them. His irony consists in reducing the aristocrats to the level of plebeians; it proclaims the equality of all with regard to the instincts and their weakness: '[His look] said clearly enough: "Don't dissemble in front of me! Here – we are equal."'[53]

Through this generalized leveling Socrates reveals his own plebeian instincts, but by the ironic distance that prevents him from taking himself more seriously than he does the Athenians he reveals his nobility and his greatness, the greatness no longer possessed by 'the aristocrats' who continue to use pompous old expressions to which they are no longer entitled in terms of the life they lead. For Socrates does not traffic in fine words: when he appeals to the Athenians, in response to the Apollonian imperative, 'Know thyself', he is not inviting them (as Hegel believes) to delve deep into their consciousness, that most superficial of organs, which they could explore thoroughly in short order. The Delphic imperative would have been quite useless if it had not called men not to know themselves as reason, but to know the limits of that reason, to find in themselves, underneath the Apollonian surface, the unconscious Dionysian impulses. If Socrates is also making fun of himself, it is because he knows the limits of the power of reason: he notes these limits every time his own reason vacillates and he falls back on what he calls the divine voice of his demon, on his instinctive wisdom. What makes this voice a 'strange phenomenon', completely abnormal, according to Nietzsche, is not so much that it stems from an auditory hallucination (although Nietzsche affirms this as well, but not here in *Beyond Good and Evil*[54]), a phenomenon Hegel thought was related to all the other bizarre illnesses that denote a state of psychic dissociation and passivity of consciousness. Rather, what is strange about the demon's voice is that, when it comes (Nietzsche, like Kierkegaard and unlike Hegel, offers the Platonic version of the demon), it always *dissuades;* it manifests itself only to '*hinder* conscious knowledge occasionally'.[55] What is unhealthy, even monstrous, is that instinct in Socrates does not take the form of an affirmative or creative force, as it does in all productive men, but that of a critical and dissuasive force, a task usually reserved to consciousness. This reversal of functions marks the 'weakness' of Socrates' instincts, his 'monstrosity *per defectum*,[56] but his strength lies in the fact that he ironically recognizes his own weakness when he mocks the power of reason as well as of that of 'instinct'.

But Socrates' irony does not stop here. In a third gesture that parodies in advance, by way of Nietzsche, the third moment of speculative dialectics, he attempts to reconcile the instincts and reason, by insinuating the impossible through 'reasoning'. He gives 'reasons' that authorize the abandonment of reason in favor of the only true guides to action, the instincts: this crafty compromise allows him to 'dupe' himself and others, ironically and deliberately. The ironist plebeian, in this respect, is being deceitful, is not 'playing fair': he proceeds with his 'reasons in hand', even more masked and mysterious than the aristocrat who, for his part, offers no reason that motivates his acts. For Socrates' 'reasons' are only superficial rationalizations that dissimulate his true, much more subterranean motives: the 'philosophy' he displays on the surface conceals in its 'underground' levels, its cavern, a totally different philosophy, a much vaster, richer, stranger, philosophy.[57] Under cover of reason, as Nietzsche sees it, Socrates actually penetrates the irrational realm of moral judgment.

In this respect the plebeian was much more cunning, much more the 'roué' than the noble Plato. Socrates treats reason as a tool of the instincts, worn-out instincts that have lost faith in themselves and thus need the illusory appeal of reason. Reason is the handmaiden of faith. Plato (perhaps because his own instincts were less unhealthy[58]), sees no conflict between reason and instinct. Both are masters; both are directed toward the same goal. But he was able to convince himself of this 'innocent' belief only by auto-suggestion, in order to avoid seeing the 'truth'. For, on the one hand, reason cannot be a 'faculty of ends'; on the other hand, the goal posited by instinct or 'faith' cannot be the one that Plato attributes equally – and wrongly – to reason: the pursuit of the good. The amalgamation of reason and faith has a doubly erroneous result: it elevates reason, which is a simple instrument, to the level of a faculty of ends, and it moralizes instinct, robbing it of its virulence, transforming its 'will' – which is not directed toward the good, the true and the beautiful but toward acquiring more and more power – into a 'good' will; thus it locates evil in an ignorance from which everyone can be cleansed by acquiring knowledge of good; that knowledge would suffice to make everyone good and happy. In the last analysis, by attributing to instinct (or 'faith') the finality of 'reason', the finality of the good, philosophy (or religion) lets instinctive spontaneity – and thus the 'herd' – have the last word: all human beings can authorize themselves, without reflection, to 'follow' their instincts, which would lead them all, on their own, to the common goal, namely, the good (or God). For 'instincts' cannot be deceptive: in recommending that they be followed, whatever 'good or bad reasons' may be invoked, neither Socrates nor Plato was mistaken, and both saw much further, with all their instinctive wisdom, than Descartes did.

Descartes alone is the true father of rationalism: he alone makes a genuine break in the history of philosophy.[59] He is the first ideologue, for he is the first to make a radical separation between soul and body, between instincts and reason. For him, reason is no longer the humble servant of 'faith', as it was for Socrates: it does not proceed, as it did for Plato, on equal footing alongside the instincts, directed toward a common goal. Reason is sovereign; it reigns alone. For Descartes is acting with the utmost seriousness when he brandishes reason and endows it with exclusive authority. That is why he is the father of rationalism and the grandfather of the French Revolution (Kierkegaard, too, had seen that Socrates' irony kept him from being truly revolutionary). Descartes alone is at the origin of a total upheaval of judgments; he alone turns 'truth' on its head and brings about the real triumph of the herd – for the full and entire authority of reason puts an end to all other principles of authority. Only the tyranny of reason can bring all tyranny to an end. But if 'pure' reason itself needs to become tyrannical in order to conquer, more tyrannical even than the instincts and the passions, it is because in reality, having cut itself off from the 'instincts', from its own depths, it is pure surface, empty of all substance and all strength. And Descartes, because he did not see that pure mind is a pure 'lie', because he mistook a means for an end, a servant for a sovereign, is a superficial mind whose authority is as illegitimate as that of reason.

7. Socrates as Jew

Might Nietzsche have confused Socrates with Descartes? Might he have 'forgotten' Socrates' irony (except in *Beyond Good and Evil*), when he represents Socrates as an incomprehensible, contradictory monster, not in relation to truth (for from this standpoint Socrates is never contradictory; he reasons almost too well; he always appears with his hands too visibly full of reasons not to be suspect[60]) but in relation to life? And he would be a monster on two grounds: because he privileges reason at the expense of instinct whereas reason is critical and dissolving, while instinct alone is creative; and because when he acknowledges that reason has a certain limit he grants a strictly negative, inhibitory, dissuasive role to instinct, which is his 'demon'; if Socrates is a paradox as far as his life is concerned, it is because, long before Descartes (if we disregard his irony) – in his person he truly presented 'the world inside out'.

'The unconscious is greater than Socrates' not-knowing. The demon is the unconscious, but one that only confronts consciousness here and there in the mode of inhibition. Its effect, however, is never productive, only critical. Most singular of upside-down worlds! Otherwise, the unconscious is always the productive element, and consciousness the critical element.'[61]

So Nietzsche must have recognized very early on a symptom of decadence in Socrates and his valorization of rationality at any price.[62] But how is such a 'living person' possible – supposing that he is living? How can such a monster have been born on Greek soil?

For such is the final Nietzschean hypothesis. His last word, still interrogative, is a reply to Socrates' last word, which was a word too many, 'ridiculous and terrible', a 'veiled, gruesome, pious and blasphemous saying' that betrays the fact that Socrates perceived the value of life as problematic, since he made an illness of it. Socrates' last word speaks against him; it attests to the ultimate nonwisdom of 'the wisest chatterer of all time'. For Nietzsche, it raises a question: 'Is it possible that a man like him, who had lived cheerfully and like a soldier in the sight of everyone, should have been a pessimist? He had merely kept a cheerful mien while concealing all his life long his ultimate judgment, his inmost feeling?'[63] Socrates' last word betrays the fact that he had suffered from life and that he had gotten his revenge – in short, that he was a decadent. Nietzsche's response – which allowed him to avoid reaching the point of despairing even of the Greeks[64] –

is that Socrates is no more a true Greek than he is a 'real' living person, that he is rather a Jew and a dead man. It goes without saying that, for Nietzsche as for Hegel[65], the terms 'Jew' and 'dead' cannot be dissociated.

The aspect of Socrates that best shows him as a Jewish 'type' is the one that seems to be his most 'characteristic' and most Greek aspect, the dialectics whose fanatic master he became. As is demonstrated by Jews, who are so good at argument and reasoning, dialectics is a sign of profound distress.[66] It is the ultimate weapon of those who have no other recourse (for it arouses mistrust and is not very convincing), of those who have to win their rights through fierce struggle. It is the defensive and reactive weapon of someone who has to be cunning because of ill health – Master Renard, the Jews, Socrates. It is the power of powerlessness itself. Owing to dialectics and to the optimism that it manifests the better to conceal its profound pessimism, Socrates can 'kill' tragedy, can substitute his own cure for that spectacular 'remedy' for pessimism. By taking on the role of questioner, he can persuade his interlocutors of their inferiority,[67] can bring them out of themselves and leave them dispossessed. For his part, after demonstrating to all the elegant noblemen that they do not know what they are doing or why they do what they do, he himself remains cold, reasonable, imperturbable, master of himself and others, thanks to the icy dagger of irony.

Nietzsche's analysis seems to match Kierkegaard's on this point. However, except in *Beyond Good and Evil*, §218, where irony confers a certain nobility on Socrates, it always receives a pejorative connotation, as it does for Hegel: 'Irony is in place only as a pedagogic tool'.[68] In other contexts, 'irony is ill-breeding, a vulgar affectation';[69] it aims to inflict shame and humiliation. The ironist belongs to 'the foolish species of men' who want to feel superior to others; in reality, in his malicious joy he only resembles 'a snapping dog which has learned how to laugh but forgotten how to bite.'[70] And the joy of the ironist, described in all its malice, seems quite distinct from the joy Nietzsche attributes to Socrates elsewhere, a smiling joy that differentiates him from Christ and reveals only a wisdom full of mischief[71] – for, in the hands of the dialectician, irony is a tool that spares nothing, it allows oppressed individuals to unleash their resentment in making sport of tyrants, to savor their own ferocity with each stab of a syllogism. 'The dialectician leaves it to his opponent to demonstrate that he is not an idiot; he is made furious and at the same time helpless. The dialectician *paralyzes* the intellect of his opponent. – What? Is dialectics only a form of *revenge* with Socrates?'[72]

However, the ironist dialectician is not really taken seriously, by and large, except by his seduced and charmed 'pupils' who believe for a moment in their own superiority over the 'master', while the master feigns ignorance the better to drive them into humiliation. He is a subject for amusement, like a clown. Socrates, for his part, brought off a tour de force: he was a clown who was taken seriously. Through what prodigious feat was he able to achieve such an illusion? By fascinating the Greeks, and doing so despite his clownish, grotesque nature, despite his revolting ugliness (which for the physiognomists would put him rather in the category of criminals). His ugliness was not so much a sign of the power of his instincts as it was a sign of their anarchy, their cross-bred variegation; this, more than the dawning fertility of a pure and complete type, explains in the last analysis why so many different schools sprang up in his wake.[73]

Despite his off-putting appearance as a monster hiding 'the worst vices and the worst appetites,' Socrates could seduce the handsome, noble Athenians owing to two subterfuges, two 'intuitions' that he was able to exploit to his own benefit. On the one hand, he knew how to charm the Athenians by addressing their 'agonal' instinct, introducing into the aristocratic milieux the new variety of *Agon* constituted by dialectics and its erotic games. On the other hand, a sick man, he managed to get himself taken ironically as healer and saviour by the Greeks of the decadent era (Nietzsche meets Hegel on this point) who were looking for a life preserver. The Athenians were diseased because their warring anarchic and bulimic instincts lacked a unique center of perspective capable of subjecting them by giving them *a style* and *a measure.* For them, Socrates represented a man capable of mastering his passions – and if no remedy is found, passions threaten either to transform men into wild beasts (that is what the moralists believed) or to destroy them.[74]

To the physiognomist who discovered in him not some divine *agalma* but a den of the worst appetites, Socrates, as we know, offered no disavowal; he merely responded, according to Xenophon, that he had managed to master them all. If Socrates fascinated people in that period of decadence and distress, it is because he represented in his person both evil and its remedy. Socrates' seductive cunning lay in his knowing how to offer, in the struggle against threatening tyrants,[75] an even more powerful counter-tyrant; against an 'excessive' evil he was able to propose a no less excessive remedy. For neither he nor the Athenians, for fear of wasting away, had a choice.[76] Becoming *reasonable to the point of absurdity:* that was the brilliant solution Socrates offered. At this 'moment' of Greek history, as Hegel believed, it was indeed necessary for Reason and its illuminating power to appear in broad daylight, but the necessity was not of the dialectic and speculative order, it was vital and instinctual. Against the nocturnal instincts, a perpetual light must be instituted at any price, for 'every yielding to the instincts, to the unconscious, leads *downwards* . . .'[77]

But the remedy Socrates offered the Athenians, rationality at any price, was in fact worse than the disease. It was really a poison; it allowed them not so much to live as to survive in ill health rather than die. Such was Socrates' malicious irony, his spitefulness. He passed himself off as a healer when he was actually a mere charlatan, so he could avenge himself, a diseased plebeian, against the noble Athenians, by poisoning them. For by proposing 'reason' to them, he knew perfectly well that he was proposing death in life, and that the only true remedy was the one he had chosen, that of drinking the hemlock. That is the medicine required in order finally to leave life behind, to cure the disease that has no remedy but death. And this is why, when Socrates was about to die, he asked – revealing his secret in an unfortunate, excessive word – that a cock be sacrificed to Asclepius. By entreating Crito to make a sacrifice – in the guise of an expression of gratitude – to the Greek god of sickness (venerated especially during the period of decadence), he revealed, at least to Nietzsche, the first to be able to understand him, that he was more Jew than Greek and that, far from having restored Greece to health, 'virtue' and 'happiness' by means of rationality, he had only served as a prelude to Christianity and to decadence.

Recalling that the text of the 'The Problem of Socrates', in *Twilight of the Idols,* along with the contemporaneous fragments published posthumously, constitutes Nietzsche's last word on Socrates, one can say that from beginning to end the representation of the character has not ceased to change; it has moved increasingly in the direction of caricature, while the author's tone has become more and more biting. It is as if Nietzsche could not forgive Socrates for disappointing him to such an extent. His disappointment is manifested in 'Socrates Dying', in *The Gay Science,* a text that is a turning point. Whereas he had first taken Socrates to be a Greek of the high period or its climax, seen him as a joyous and courageous soldier in love with life in all its forms, Nietzsche is disappointed to observe that Socrates was also a pessimist and a sick man, sick of life; he was a decadent moralist. While the disproportionate quality of Socrates' excessive instincts is attributed in *The Birth of Tragedy* to a Dionysian overabundance, and in *Human, All Too Human* to the richness of his temperament (his idiosyncracy is that he represents all possible temperaments), in 'The Problem of Socrates' his disproportion takes the grotesque form of diseased degenerescence; it is more Jewish than Greek.

Nietzsche will never forgive Socrates for tricking him so successfully that he has not always grasped Socrates' irony: it is because he had taken seriously the disturbing affirmation according to which virtue resides in knowledge and evil is ignorance that Nietzsche was able to see Socrates first of all as a pure and sublime type, as the Sage who conquers the passions by means of reason, and was able to see the philosopher's death not as the symptom of a sickness but as the emblem of that exemplary wisdom.

Disappointed and furious at having been duped, Nietzsche casts irony in the role of scapegoat. While Nietzsche maintains that irony invests Socrates with more nobility than can be attributed to the noble Athenians of the decadent period, owing to the distance irony institutes with respect to the philosopher himself, he reads irony also, and especially, as a symptom of the 'maliciousness' and the trickery of the weak; he declares that irony is the weapon par excellence of impotence and distress.

If, like Hegel, Nietzsche cannot ultimately 'feel' Socrates' irony, is it not because that irony resists genealogical flair as it does dialectical flair? Because it resists any simple and fixed position, and any overly simplistic typology? As Kierkegaard was well aware, irony is what makes Socrates an atopical being, a *Janus bifrons*, an enigmatic and uncategorizable monster, leaving those who attempt to deal with him, one way or another, in a state of aporia.

From this point on, if Socrates is Nietzsche's double, if the two are so close, perhaps it is not because Socrates represents the other pole that Nietzsche carries within himself, the set of evaluative criteria belonging to the weak and to decadence, but because, like Nietzsche, he is both at once, a beginning and an end, alive and dead: Nietzsche's true double through and through. Is Nietzsche's reduction of Socrates to just one of his aspects – the pejorative one – not an ultimate attempt on Nietzsche's part to project outside of himself the most unbearable part of himself, the morbid, paternal part, his 'Jewish' persona? A last attempt, before succumbing to madness, to expel and pin down outside of himself the most threatening and destructive element there may have been in himself, the caricatural and grotesque *buffo*? If, at the moment of madness, he can identify with Dionysus alone, it is because through his expulsion of Socrates to a position outside of himself he may have ceased to float in the most dangerous possible way without ever touching either the one or the other, as he did during the rest of his life, between father and mother, Jew and Greek, death and life. Is his madness the consequence of projecting that death-dealing aspect outside of himself, or does it mark the failure of his final attempt to avoid succumbing?

V. CONCLUSION: THREE SOCRATIC NOVELS

	HEGEL	KIERKEGAARD	NIETZSCHE
Method of reading	dialectical	indirectly or ironically polemical	genealogical, typological
Sources, in order of preference	Xenophon, Plato, Aristophanes	Aristophanes, Plato, Xenophon	Xenophon, Aristophanes, Plato
Position in the history of philosophy	threshold and turning point	beginning	– sometimes he ends a cycle – sometimes he begins a cycle and constitutes a break
Sophists judged in relation to Socrates	more negative	more positive	ancestors of the moral 'critique'
Ugliness	sign of the violence of his passions	sign of ironic disharmony	symptom of the variegated nature of his passions
The demon and its voice	positive – subjective and dawn-like aspect of Mind – 'not yet' the voice of consciousness	negative – the voice of irony	negative – the voice of degenerate instinct
Ecstatic immobility	youthful illness related to catalepsy	ecstasy of the ironist in the face of nothingness	symptom of ill health
Ignorance	sometimes called 'feigned,' sometimes called 'real'	real	feigned or real, depending on the text
Maieutics	positive moment of his method	inseparable from irony	means by which he aimed to produce geniuses
Irony	negative moment of his method – tragic irony	Socrates and his irony are one – comic irony	symptom of distress and impotence
Condemnation	just and unjust	just and unjust	just and unjust
Death	as a tragic hero	through irony	sometimes as a wise man, sometimes as a sick man and through irony
Socratic schools that sprang up after him, in their diversity	attributable to his absence of system	his negativity which gives nothing calls through nostalgia for positive creation of the most varied sorts	explained sometimes by the plenitude of the pure type, sometimes by the diversity of temperaments that he embodies, sometimes by the variegated nature of his instincts

By way of conclusion, the preceding chart sums up the diversity of viewpoints on the figure of Socrates. We have not been obliged to choose one among them that would present the true portrait. My entire reading has sought, on the contrary, to emphasize that each of these three perspectives constitutes a Socratic novel that is symptomatic only of its author. Kierkegaard, who shows that Xenophon and Plato 'fictionalized' Socrates (the one in an overly prosaic fashion, for he grasped him through a defective one-dimensional stereoscope, the other in an excessively idealizing poetic fashion), would not reject the title of novelist on his own behalf any more than would Nietzsche, who sniffs out in Plato's Socrates(es) a pure chimera. Hegel, who maintains that he is not interested in the 'literary aspect' of the sources but who proceeds to root around in them and to 'sublate' what, even without him, would have been preserved, the truth of the Socratic 'moment', is the only one of the three interpreters who might be shocked by the treatment I have inflicted on him and who might reject the proposed title of fiction-writer.

Does this mean that no one of these readings is 'worth' more than another? And in what sense? Kierkegaard, after demonstrating that all conceptions prior to his own deserve to be aborted, privileges his own, if not as the only 'true' one, at least as the only one that deserves to live, since it is the only possible, actualized and necessary one. Nietzsche, for his part, considers Xenophon a reliable source, and he relies largely on Xenophon as he develops his typological reading and attempts to immobilize the disconcerting and dangerous atopia of the 'most suspicious' character 'in Antiquity'. These variations in classification are not so much a sign of Nietzsche's failure to establish Socrates as one simple type or another as they are an avowal of the derision in which he would have liked to 'circumscribe' and capture 'typologically' what is uncategorizable.

If we may speak of a 'novel', in either case, it is not a purely imaginary construct. While Kierkegaard and Nietzsche would both recognize that, like all texts, their own are indeed confessions of their authors, each would claim that he had 'grasped' Socrates better than anyone else, not only because he used rigorous methods of reading – scrupulous textual criticism in the one case, honest philology in the other – but also because, more than anyone else, he has 'accounts to settle' with Socrates deep within himself; and that is what 'concerns' each of them in Socrates. Kierkegaard believes he is the only one who has been able to grasp the viewpoint of irony, precisely because irony (like Socrates, who is of a piece with his irony) does not allow itself to be grasped; it can only be perceived by someone capable of understanding it through 'sympathetic affinity'. Nietzsche was able to sniff out the decadent type in Socrates and his moralism, because, according to one of his systems of evaluation, Nietzsche himself – Nietzsche whose immoralism results from a moralism taken to its ultimate consequences – was as close to that authentic 'double' as anyone could get.

Both philosophers were able to identify with Socrates, at least in one of their aspects – an aspect powerful enough, nevertheless, to have made them both worry that the great seducer might turn them definitively away from their other system of evaluation: Kierkegaard, from the system of paternal judgments, and thus from Christ, whose similarities and dissimilarities with respect to Socrates he continually endeavors to foreground; Nietzsche, from the system of maternal judgments, and thus from Dionysus, whose triumph he was able to bring about only after expelling the accursed part of himself from within, in the form of a fascinating and repulsive, even persecuting double, 'Socrates', whom he seems to have conquered completely only in madness, and after having congealed him in the caricatural and grotesque figure of a buffoon who is more Jew than Greek.

In identifying with 'Socrates', but also in rejecting one of his aspects (and each rejected the opposite aspect), did Kierkegaard and Nietzsche not both 'grasp' and 'miss' what 'belongs' at best to Socrates? Both reveal, in any case, not only the 'embarrassing' aspects of that figure who resists – except through dialectical or typological reduction – all classification, all conventional categories and determinations, but especially the dangerous, life-threatening aspects of the character: not because he simply *wanted* death or nothingness, which is after all a masterable desire, but because, in the instability of his persona, he caused all 'narcissistic' stabilities and assurances to vacillate; he literally drove people crazy. Hegel managed to preserve himself and his system from madness by reducing the most symptomatic element of the Socratic atopia, his irony, to a simple stage within a method. Nietzsche, for his part, believed he could resist madness and save his typological reading by confining ironic oscillation to the category of weakness and impotence; thus he too ultimately hardened and congealed the figure of Socrates. If the monolithic character Nietzsche attributed to Socrates in his essay on the pre-Platonics[1] was attributable once again, in Nietzsche, to a whiff of Hegelianism, if in *The Birth of Tragedy*[2] he gave that lovely Greek statue a certain mobility by tolerating, for the duration of a dream, its oscillation between Apollonianism and the Dionysian, the final 'monomania' projected onto Socrates must be read rather as an ultimate defense against the internal collapse that Nietzsche felt coming.

By identifying Socrates with the point of view of irony and its oscillation, did Kierkegaard, although he may still have failed to grasp the 'truth' of Socrates, not manifest at least that he was more resistant than Hegel and Nietzsche to 'madness' and that his narcissism was less fragile than theirs? Is it because he had the system of paternal judgments as a rampart within himself that he was able to hear, without vacillating or trembling, the gentle but no less 'biting' murmur of irony? Is it not also because he had been able to accept the 'femininity' in himself (in a 'sublimated' and 'desexualized' form) that he could grasp the 'feminine' nature of irony by conforming to its requirements, by positioning himself, in order to be able to hear it from close up, as far away as possible – by putting between himself and irony at least the distance of a confessional? Is it not because Kierkegaard's 'position' is that of 'suspension' between father and mother (of his mother he breathes not a word, and he never touches either one) – a position of 'sexual indifference', of 'androgyny' – that he was so successful in maintaining the suspension between irony and/or Socrates?

Must we conclude from this that Hegel and Nietzsche were no more able to bear the 'femininity' in themselves and in Socrates than they were the oscillation? Hegel, as we have seen, skimmed lightly over the fact that Socrates inherited the art of midwifery from his mother. Even as he emphasizes the nobility of Socrates' attitude in the face of death – his manliness, he says parenthetically – he still judges Socrates' death less 'manly' than Antigone's. As for the relationship between Socrates and Xanthippe, he evokes it only to recall, with Plato, that Socrates made her leave the prison before he died so he could avoid hearing her all too feminine wailing and lamentations. Nietzsche does not forget Xanthippe, but this is so he can hold her partly responsible for Socrates' decadence, since by driving him out of the house with her yelling she compelled him to do his 'discussing' outside on the agora, and to invent dialectics. The couple she constitutes with Socrates interests him less, however, than the one, the only authentic one, that Socrates constitutes with Plato, a couple in which it is very difficult to discern what position each member holds, and whether that position is always the same. Only Kierkegaard was interested enough in this point to demonstrate the oscillating character of their two positions, showing that Socrates and Plato played the role of master by turns and that it was not always the same one who 'manipulated' the other.

As for Socrates' maieutic aspect, which Kierkegaard identifies completely with irony, Nietzsche alludes to it only in passing, in a remark in *The Birth of Tragedy* where Socrates is said to be teaching the youthful elite 'an altogether new form of "Greek cheerfulness" and blissful affirmation of existence that seeks to discharge itself in actions – most often maieutic and educational influences on noble youths, with a view to eventually producing a genius'.[3] In this text, is Nietzsche not acknowledging a maternal activity in Socrates, is he not identifying him with 'true' woman as he defines her – the one who produces children? But Nietzsche never returns elsewhere to this 'fertilizing' aspect of midwifery, increasingly determined as he is to establish Socrates' kinship with death rather than with life.

If the problem of Socrates has caused so much ink to flow, in the final analysis, is it not because behind the 'case' of this atopical and atypical monster, each interpreter is trying as best he can to 'settle' his own 'case', to carry out his reading in such a way that all of his own certitudes will not collapse with Socrates, that his own equilibrium and that of his 'system' – even if there is nothing obviously systematic about it – will not be too seriously threatened?

Notes

INTRODUCTION

1 Søren Kierkegaard, *The Concept of Irony with Continual Reference to Socrates. Kierkegaard's Writings, II,* ed. and trans. Howard V. Hong and Edna H. Hong (Princeton: Princeton University Press, 1989). Kierkegaard's first three chapter titles offer ironic echoes of Kant's categories of modality (or Hegel's categories of speculative dialectics): 'The View Made Possible', 'The Actualization of the View', 'The View Made Necessary'.

2 George Wilhelm Friedrich Hegel, *Lectures on the History of Philosophy: Greek Philosophy to Plato,* trans. E. S. Haldane (Lincoln, NE: University of Nebraska Press, 1995), vol. 1, pp. 389, 448.

3 Diogenes Laertius, *Lives of Eminent Philosophers,* vol. I, trans. R. D. Hicks (Cambridge, MA: Harvard University Press, 1972), p. 175.

4 *Lectures on the History of Philosophy,* vol. 1, p. 283.

5 Cf. Sarah Kofman, 'Aristotle and the "presocratics,"' in *Freud and Fiction,* trans. Sarah Wykes (Cambridge, UK: Polity Press, 1991), pp. 9-19; 'Le complot contre la philosophie', in *Nietzsche et la scène philosophique* (Paris: Union Générale d'Editions [10/18], 1979), pp. 13-19; 'Nietzsche et l'obscurité d'Héraclite', *Furor* 15 (October 1986): 3-33 (revised and extended republication in *Séductions: de Sartre à Héraclite* [Paris: Galilée, 1990], pp. 87-137).

6 'The greatest safeguard is to avoid writing and to learn by heart; for it is not possible that what is written should not get divulged. For this reason I myself have never yet written anything on these subjects, and no treatise by Plato exists or will exist, but those which now bear his name belong to a Socrates become fair and young' (Epistle II, in *Plato,* vol. VII, trans. R. E. Bury [London: William Heinemann Ltd., 1961], pp. 415-17).

7 *The Post Card. From Socrates to Freud and Beyond,* trans. Alan Bass (Chicago: University of Chicago Press, 1987); see pp. 47ff.

8 'There does not exist, nor will there ever exist, any treatise of mine dealing [with this subject]. For it does not at all admit of verbal expression like other studies. . . . Notwithstanding, of this much I am certain, that the best statement of these doctrines in writing or in speech would be my own statement . . . There is a certain true argument which confronts the man who ventures to write anything at all of these matters' (*Plato,* vol. VII, Epistle VI, pp. 521-33).

9 *Fragments Posthumes,* in *La Naissance de la tragédie* (Paris: Gallimard, 1977): 1 [24], fall 1869.

10 See *The Post Card,* p. 20.

11 These are Derrida's terms. They connect the first section of *The Post Card,* 'Envois', with the second section, 'To Speculate – on Freud' and Derrida's

'speculation' on Socrates/Plato with Freud's speculation on the death instinct in *Beyond the Pleasure Principle*.

12   *The Post Card*, p. 21.

13   Francis Wolff, in his *Socrate* (Paris: Presses Universitaires de France, 1985), notes that more than 16,000 academic works on the 'Socrates problem' were extant in the 1950s.

14   See Friedrich Nietzsche, 'Die vorplatonischen Philosophen', §17, 'Socrates', in *Nietzsche Werke, Kritische Gesamtausgabe*, ed. Giorgio Colli and Mazzino Montinari, II, 4, *Vorlesungsaufzeichnungen (WS 1871/72-WS 1874/75)*, (Berlin: Walter de Gruyter, 1995), pp. 351-62; see also the chapter on Nietzsche, below.
     Translator's note: an abridged version of the above text on Socrates appears in French in *La Naissance de la philosophie à l'époque de la tragédie grecque*, trans. Geneviève Bianquis (Paris: Gallimard, 1938). The English translation by Marianne Cowan, *Philosophy in the Tragic Age of the Greeks* (Chicago: Henry Regnery Company, 1962) and a later version of the Blanquis translation under the title *La Philosophie à l'époque tragique des Grecs* (Paris: Gallimard, 1969) omit the section on Socrates, among others. For Kofman's citations, I have used the Cowan translation where the French and English texts coincide; otherwise I have translated from the German, with the generous assistance of Geoffrey Waite.

15   See, among other texts, Kierkegaard's *The Concept of Irony*.

16   This is what Voltaire did in his *Socrates*. Let us recall that Socrates was more than a hero, according to Diogenes Laertius; he was also an author of tragedies who collaborated with Euripides. Thus, in Diogenes' account, Mnesimachus writes: "'This new play of Euripides is *The Phrygians;* and Socrates provides the wood for frying." And again he calls Euripides "'an engine riveted by Socrates".' Diogenes goes on to recall a passage from *The Clouds*: "'Tis he composes for Euripides / Those clever plays, much sound and little sense"' (*Lives*, p. 149). And Nietzsche, as we know, exploits this figure of Socrates-the-genius-behind-Euripides in *The Birth of Tragedy*.

17   In addition to Aristophanes, Diogenes Laertius cites Ameipsias, author of an old comedy, as someone who also depicted Socrates on stage. He quotes the following verses, among others:

   A.   You come to join us, Socrates, worthiest of a small band and emptiest by far! You are a robust fellow. Where can we get you a proper coat?
   B.   Your sorry plight is an insult to the cobblers.
   A.   And yet, hungry as he is, this man has never stooped to flatter.

(*Lives*, p. 159)

There is also a comic opera called *Le Socrate imaginaire* by Giovanni Paisielle (1740-1811) with a libretto by F. Gabiani and G. Lorenzi; it was performed in Naples in 1795. This information comes from an unpublished text by Françoise Metz, *Caractéristique de Socrate (à partir de Schlegel)*, Strasbourg.

Finally, let us note that Rousseau cast Socrates as a prophet of natural religion.

18 See Friedrich Nietzsche, *The Gay Science,* trans. Walter Kaufmann (New York: Vintage Books, 1974), §340: 'the dying Socrates', p. 272.

19 See especially Friedrich Nietzsche, *Beyond Good and Evil,* trans. Walter Kaufmann (New York: Vintage Books, 1966), preface and §190.

20 See Friedrich Nietzsche, *The Birth of Tragedy,* in *Basic Writings of Nietzsche,* trans. Walter Kaufmann (New York: Modern Library, 1968), §13.

21 See 'Die vorplatonischen Philosophen', and also 'The Struggle Between Science and Wisdom', in *Philosophy and Truth. Selections from Nietzsche's Notebooks of the Early 1870's,* trans. Daniel Breazale (Atlantic Highlands, NJ: Humanities Press, 1979), pp. 127-46.

22 Friedrich Nietzsche, *Nietzsche Werke,* III, 3, *Nachgelassene Fragmente. Herbst 1869 bis Herbst 1872* (Berlin: Walter de Gruyter, 1978), 8 [19], p. 328.

23 See the *Symposium,* in *Plato,* V, trans. W. R. M. Lamb (London: William Heinemann Ltd., 1961), pp. 73-245, and above.

24 *The Gay Science,* §340, p. 272.

25 Ibid., §340.

26 Socrates' ugliness is, for Hegel, a sign or a symbol; for Nietzsche, it is a symptom. For Kierkegaard, it is a way of deriving ironic enjoyment from the disharmony of his person.

27 See Xenophon, *Memorabilia,* trans. Amy L. Bonnette (Ithaca, NY: Cornell University Press, 1994), chapter XI, pp. 102-103, where Socrates is speaking to the courtisan Theodote:

> 'Then what source do you have for your provisions?' he said.
> 'If someone who has become my friend wants to treat me well', she said, 'he is my livelihood.' . . .
> 'Do you entrust it to chance whether some friend will light on you, like a fly, or do you yourself contrive something?'
> 'How could I find a contrivance for this?' she said.
> 'It belongs much more, by Zeus, to you to do this than to spiders', he said. 'You know how they hunt things for their livelihood: for, of course, they weave fine webs and use whatever falls into them for sustenance.' . . .
> 'And what sort of nets', she said, 'do I have?'
> 'To be sure, one that is indeed very entangling: your body', he said, 'and in it a soul, through which you learn both how you might gratify with a look and delight with what you say . . .'

28 Hegel, *Lectures,* p. 393.

29 Ibid., p. 384.

30 Ibid., p. 317.

31 'He . . . stands before us as one of those great plastic natures consistent through and through, such as we often see in those times' (*Lectures,* p. 393). See also G. W. F. Hegel, *Aesthetics: Lectures on Fine Art,* trans. T. M. Knox (Oxford: Clarendon Press, 1974), vol. II, section II, 'Sculpture', pp. 719-20:

In its poets and orators, historians and philosophers, Greece is not to be understood at its heart unless we bring with us as a key to our comprehension an insight into the ideals of sculpture . . . They are great and free, grown independently on the soil of their own inherently substantial personality, self-made, and developing into what they [essentially] were and wanted to be. . . . All of them are out-and-out artists by nature, ideal artists shaping themselves, individuals of a single cast, works of art standing there like immortal and deathless images of the gods, in which there is nothing temporal and doomed.

Socrates, Pericles, Phidias, Plato, Sophocles, Thucydides and Xenophon are cited as examples.

I. PLATO'S SOCRATES(ES)

1 *Symposium*, in *Plato*, vol. III, trans. W. R. M. Lamb (London: William Heinemann Ltd., 1961), 174e. Subsequent references will be supplied in the text.

2 See *Jokes and Their Relation to the Unconscious, The Standard Edition of the Complete Psychological Works of Sigmund Freud*, trans. James Strachey (London: The Hogarth Press, 1953-66), vol. 8, p. 74, and the third lecture in *Five Lectures on Psycho-Analysis, Standard Edition*, vol. 11, pp. 30-31. For a reading of this *Witz*, see Sarah Kofman, *Pourquoi rit-on?* (Paris: Galilée, 1986), pp. 82-92.

3 See Georg Wilhelm Friedrich Hegel, *Lectures on the History of Philosophy. I. Greek Philosophy to Plato*, trans. E. S. Haldane (Lincoln: University of Nebraska Press, 1995), p. 391.

4 *The Twilight of the Idols*, 'The Problem of Socrates', in *The Portable Nietzsche*, trans. Walter Kaufmann (New York: Viking Penguin, 1982 [1954]), §10, p. 478.

5 Ibid., §11, p. 479.

6 On this portrait of Eros, see Sarah Kofman, 'Beyond Aporia', trans. David Macey, in Andrew Benjamin, ed., *Post-Structuralist Classics* (London: Routledge, 1988), pp. 7-44.

7 Ibid. This text explores the way the figure of Socrates communicates with that of Prometheus, the first philosopher.

8 A legend holds that in the beginning gods and men lived and feasted together, until one day Prometheus was charged with dividing up what belonged to each group and tried to fool the gods to the benefit of men. Zeus then took over the distribution: mortal men were to have the cooked flesh of dead animals, while the gods would have nectar and ambrosia. Mortals like Penia were not to be invited to the banquet of the gods. Prometheus's crime was that he attempted to trick the gods into letting mortals participate in their feasts and into giving them immortality.

9 See Claude This, 'Au-delà du double: la bête', in Marie-José Baudinet and Christian Schatter, eds., *Du visage* (Lille: Presses Universitaires de Lille, 1982), pp. 91-101.

10 In 'Beyond Aporia', I argued that it is the indigent Penia who holds the *poros*

and that what she *does* contradicts what is attributed to her in *speech.* The myth projects the structure of the human soul and its desire onto three distinct characters: Penia (Poverty), Poros (Resource), and Eros (Love), all of whom make simultaneous demands. *Penia,* the soul's double, contains Poros within herself, and she is always already pregnant with Eros.

11 See Hegel, *Lectures,* I, pp. 394-95.

12 See Xenophon, *Memorabilia,* trans. Amy L. Bonnette (Ithaca, NY: Cornell University Press, 1996), Book III, Chapter 11, 4-18, and also, on this point, the introduction to the present volume.

13 See Hegel, *Lectures,* pp. 391, 422-25.

14 See *Phaedo,* in *Plato,* vol. I, trans. Harold North Fowler (London: William Heinemann Ltd., 1971), pp. 405-579.

15 See *The Twilight of the Idols,* 'The Problem of Socrates'.

16 'So now, for my part, I have no idea what virtue is, whilst you, though perhaps you may have known before you came in touch with me, are now as good as ignorant of it also' (*Meno,* in *Plato,* vol. II, trans. W. R. M. Lamb [London: William Heinemann Ltd., 1962], 80d).

17 See Eric Robertson Dodds, *The Greeks and the Irrational* (Berkeley: University of California Press, 1951). Shamans believe in a separable soul that can be withdrawn even from a living body if appropriate techniques are used. This soul is older than the body and will outlive it (pp. 146-47).

The shamanistic 'retreat' might provide the model for a deliberate *askesis,* a conscious training of the psychic powers through abstinence and through spiritual exercises; . . . tales of vanishing and reappearing shamans might encourage the belief in an indestructible magical or daemonic self. . . . The shaman's trance, his deliberate detachment of the occult self from the body, has become [in Plato] that practice of mental withdrawal and concentration which purifies the rational soul – a practice for which Plato in fact claims the authority of a traditional *logos.* The occult knowledge which the shaman acquires in trance has become a vision of metaphysical truth; his 'recollection' of past earthly lives has become a 'recollection' of bodiless Forms which is made the basis of a new epistemology; while on the mythical level his 'long sleep' and 'underworld journey' provides a direct model for the experiences of Er. (Pp. 149-50, 210)

It is thus clear that Dodds, like Socrates' disciples, thinks that Socrates was in the habit of looking within himself to find 'truth', 'bodiless Forms' (Dodds erroneously borrows this terminology from Aristotle to speak about Plato or Socrates).

18 See Jacques Lacan, 'Du "Trieb" de Freud et du désir du psychanalyste', in *Ecrits* (Paris: Seuil, 1966) pp. 851-54.

19 See *Protagoras,* in *Plato,* vol. II, trans. W. R. B. Lamb (London: William Heinemann Ltd., 1974), 309b-c, where Socrates neglects Alcibiades in favor of the handsomer Protagoras.

20 Phaedrus goes so far as to say that the gods themselves are more admiring and generous toward the beloved than toward the lover (*Symposium,* 180b).

21 Lacan, although we owe him the distinction between penis and phallus, wrote the following: 'It is because he has not seen Socrates' prick . . . that Alcibiades the seducer exalts in him the [*Agalma*], the marvel that he would like Socrates to cede to him in avowing his desire' ('Subversion of the Subject and Dialectic of Desire in the Freudian Unconscious', in *Ecrits: A Selection*, trans. Alan Sheridan [New York: Norton, 1977], p. 322).

22 'Thinking myself free at any time by gratifying his desires to hear all that our Socrates knew' (217a).

23 'For he brings home to me that I cannot disown the duty of doing what he bids me, but that as soon as I turn from his company I fall victim to the favours of the crowd. So I take a runaway's leave of him and flee away; when I see him again I think of those former admissions, and am ashamed' (216c).

24 In connection with this entire issue, see *Alcibiades* I and II in *Plato*, vol. XII, trans. W. R. M. Lamb (Cambridge, MA: William Heinemann Ltd., 1986).

25 See Plato, *Laws*, vol. I, trans. R. G. Bury (London: William Heinemann Ltd., 1952 [1926]), I, 637e-639a, pp. 45-49.

26 Freud also shows in *Jokes* how wine lifts inhibitions and, by putting people in a 'good mood', facilitates the return of the repressed.

27 Alcibiades' Dionysian drunkenness may recall the way the Greeks associated court trials with tragedy, thus with the emergence of Dionysus, that is, of drunken ecstasy or the persuasive power of living discourse. See Walter Benjamin, *The Origin of German Tragic Drama* (London: NLB, 1977), p. 116.

28 Although he refers to Xenophon when he speaks of Socrates' ugliness, Hegel remains dependent on Alcibiades' portrait and on the now-classic opposition between 'outside' and 'inside'. In Socrates' case, 'his appearance indicated naturally low and hateful qualities, which, as indeed he says, he himself subdued. He lived amongst his fellow-citizens, and stands before us as one of those great plastic natures consistent through and through . . . resembling a perfect classical work of art which has brought itself to this height of perfection' (*Lectures*, I, p. 393]. For Nietzsche, Socrates' external ugliness, on the contrary, is the expression of an internal 'ugliness', that is a symptom of the most violent impulses: 'Ugliness, in itself an objection, is among the Greeks almost a refutation. Was Socrates a Greek at all? Ugliness is often enough the expression of a development that has been crossed, *thwarted* by crossing. . . . The typical criminal is ugly: *monstrum in fronte, monstrum in animo*. But the criminal is a decadent. Was Socrates a typical criminal? . . . A foreigner who knew about faces once passed through Athens and told Socrates to his face that he was a *monstrum* – that he harbored in himself all the bad vices and appetites. And Socrates merely answered: "You know me, sir!"' (*The Twilight of the Idols*, 'The Problem of Socrates', section 3, pp. 474-75). We shall come back to the problems raised by these texts.

29 Marcel Détienne and Jean-Pierre Vernant, *Cunning Intelligence in Greek Culture and Society*, trans. Janet Lloyd (Atlantic Highlands, NJ: Humanities Press, 1978 [1974]), p. 46.

30 Let us recall that Socrates rejects this comparison, which depends on a

confusion between a blocking aporia, that of the Sophist, and a mobilizing aporia, that of the philosopher. Socrates compares himself rather to a gadfly or goad that provokes and arouses. See 'Beyond Aporia'.

31 According to Pierre Grimal's *Dictionary of Classical Mythology* (trans. A.R. Maxwell-Hyslop [Oxford: Blackwell, 1986]), Silenus, which is the generic name of satyrs who have grown old, is also the name of a character that was supposed to have reared Dionysus. One version of his story claims that he was born of drops of Uranos's blood when the latter was mutilated by Cronos. That Silenus possessed great wisdom, which he consented to reveal only under duress. This is how he was said to have been captured by King Midas, to whom he addressed wise words. Midas got the better of him one day when he found Silenus asleep after too many libations.

32 This is how Alcibiades might interpret the dream Socrates had in which Apollo exhorts him to make music (see *Phaedo*). See also Nietzsche, who dreams, in *The Birth of Tragedy*, of Socrates as an artist, a musician.

33 In the *Protagoras*, Socrates compares the voices of orators to those of flute-girls, extraneous voices: 'But when the party consists of thorough gentlemen who have had a proper education, you will see neither flute-girls nor dancing-girls nor harp-girls, but only the company contenting themselves with their own conversation, and none of these fooleries and frolics' (347d). See also the *Menexenus:*

> [Orators] praise in such splendid fashion, that . . . they bewitch our souls. . . . I myself, Menexenus, when thus praised by them feel mightily ennobled, and every time I listen fascinated I am exalted and imagine myself to have become all at once taller and nobler and more handsome. . . . Owing to the persuasive eloquence of the speaker . . . this majestic feeling remains with me for over three days: so persistently does the speech and voice of the orator ring in my ears that it is scarcely on the fourth or fifth day that I recover myself and remember that I really am here on earth, whereas till then I almost imagined myself to be living in the Islands of the Blessed, – so expert are our orators. (*Plato*, vol. VII, trans. R. G. Bury [William Heinemann Ltd., 1961], 234c-235c).

34 Love's bite is often represented by the sting of a serpent or scorpion. The image occurs in Xenophon's *Memorabilia,* where Socrates recommends that the love of young people be avoided, because of that sting: 'Don't you know that this creature called "fair and young" is more dangerous than the scorpion, seeing that it need not even come in contact, like the insect, but at any distance can inject a maddening poison into anyone who only looks at it?' (I, 3, [13]) The mix of styles is also what characterizes Plato for Nietzsche, the first of the great hybrids: 'The essence of the Platonic art, dialogue, is an absence of form and an absence of style produced by the mix of all possible forms and styles. . . . He hovers between all genres, between prose and poetry, narrative, lyricism, drama, since he has broken the strict ancient law of unity of form, style, and language' ('Socrate et la tragédie', in *Ecrits posthumes, 1870-1873* [Paris: Gallimard, 1977], p. 41).

35 Friedrich Nietzsche, *Beyond Good and Evil,* trans. Walter Kaufmann (New York: Vintage Books, 1966), §190, p. 103.

36 Ibid., preface, p. 3.

37 Ibid.; see also *The Twilight of the Idols,* 'The Problem of Socrates', §3: 'Was Socrates a typical criminal?'

38 On the genealogy of utilitarianism, see especially Friedrich Nietzsche, *On The Genealogy of Morals,* trans. Walter Kaufmann and R. J. Hollingdale, in *On the Genealogy of Morals and Ecce Homo* (New York: Vintage Books, 1989), 'First Essay,' §§1-3.

39 See *On The Genealogy of Morals,* 'Second Essay,' §7, and Friedrich Nietzsche, *The Gay Science,* trans. Walter Kaufman (New York: Vintage Books, 1974), §326, §338. This indissoluble union of pain and pleasure parodies in inverted form the relation established by Plato at the beginning of the *Phaedo.*

40 See *On The Genealogy of Morals,* 'Second Essay,' §7.

41 Ibid., 'First Essay,' §2.

42 See Friedrich Nietzsche, 'Die vorplatonischen Philosophen,' in *Nietzsche Werke, Kritische Gesamtausgabe,* ed. Giorgio Colli and Mazzino Montinari II, 4, *Vorlesungsaufzeichnungen (WS 1871/72-WS 1874/75),* (Berlin: Walter de Gruyter, 1995).

43 *Beyond Good and Evil,* §259.

44 Ibid., §191.

45 A variant of this text (in *Werke* I, 8, 207) speaks about the utilitarianism of this formula of 'Socratic foolishness par excellence' and the first draft says: '*Ancient foolishness of morality.* No one wants to harm himself *and therefore every evil is involuntary.* For the bad person harms himself, *but he believes the opposite.* Presupposition: good: what is *useful* to us' (*Werke* III, 4, 93).

46 There is no more an original text of Socrates than there is an original text of nature. In both cases, there are only interpretations. Cf. *Beyond Good and Evil,* §230, and Sarah Kofman, *Nietzsche and Metaphor,* trans. Duncan Large (Stanford, CA: Stanford University Press, 1993).

47 Cicero, *Tusculan Disputations,* trans. J. E. King (Cambridge, MA: Harvard University Press, 1966, V, 4, cited by Hegel, *Lectures,* p. 388: 'Cicero (Tusc. Quæs. V 4), whose manner of thought was, on the one hand, of the present, and who, on the other hand, had the belief that Philosophy should yield itself up, and hence succeeded in attaining to no content in it, boasted of Socrates (what has often enough been said since) that his most eminent characteristic was to have brought Philosophy from heaven to earth, to the homes and every-day life of men, or, as Diogenes Laertius expresses it (II. 21), "into the market place."' Cicero's text is also cited by Kierkegaard, who follows Socrates step by step down the unsavory alleyways of Athens where, according to Kierkegaard, Socrates loses his irony: he also reproaches Plato for excessively 'poeticizing' Socrates.

48 Homer, *The Iliad,* vol. 1, trans. A. T. Murray (Cambridge, MA: Harvard University Press, 1965), VI, 181, p. 275.

49 Friedrich Nietzsche, *Ecce Homo,* in *On the Genealogy of Morals and Ecce Homo,*

trans. Walter Kaufmann (New York: Vintage Books, 1989), §1, 'Why I Am So Wise,' p. 222.

HEGEL'S TWO-FACED SOCRATES

1 George Wilhelm Friedrich Hegel, *Lectures on the History of Philosophy: Greek Philosophy to Plato*, trans. E. S. Haldane (Lincoln: University of Nebraska Press, 1995), vol. 1, p. 283. Subsequent references to this work will be supplied in the text.

2 In this connection, and more generally speaking on the relation between Kierkegaard and Hegel, see Sylviane Agacinski, *Aparté, Conceptions and Deaths of Søren Kierkegaard,* trans. Kevin Newmark (Gainesville: University Presses of Florida, 1988).

3 See *Lectures*, p. 166: 'As we possess only traditions and fragments of this epoch, we may speak here of the sources of these.'

4 Contemporary legislation governing intellectual property rights remains Hegelian, since it declares that 'ideas' belong to no one and that there is plagiarism only if the 'form' remains unchanged.

5 The question of plagiarism seems to have been of special interest to Hegel. See *Hegel's Philosophy of Right*, trans. T. M. Knox (London: Oxford University Press, 1967), §69.

6 See Friedrich Nietzsche, *Beyond Good and Evil*, trans. Walter Kaufmann (New York: Vintage Books, 1966), §5.

7 This image, along with that of a flower (there is no 'reason' for a rose, either) seems to have become a favorite among philosophers especially to describe luck and fortune. It is found for example in La Mettrie: 'Who knows moreover whether the reason for man's existence does not lie in his existence itself? Perhaps he has been tossed up by chance on some point of the earth's surface, without our being able to know either how or why, but only that he is to live and to die, like those mushrooms that appear from one day to the next, or those flowers that grow along ditches and cover stone walls' ('L'homme-machine,' in *Oeuvres philosophiques*, vol. I [Paris: Fayard, 1987], p. 93).

8 Cf. Hegel, *Lectures*, p. 168:

> In the progress of Greek philosophy men were formerly accustomed to follow the order that showed, according to ordinary ideas, an external connection, and which is found in one philosopher having had another as his teacher – this connection is one which might show him to be partly derived from Thales and partly from Pythagoras. But such a connection is in part defective in itself, and in part it is merely external. The one set of philosophic sects, or of philosophers classed together, which is considered as belonging to a system – that which proceeds from Thales – pursues its course in time and mind far separate from the other. But, in truth, no such series ever does exist in this isolation, nor would it do so even though the individuals were consecutive and had been externally connected as teacher and taught, which never is the case; mind follows quite another order. These successive series are interwoven in spirit just as much as in their particular content.

9 Ibid, pp. 449-52:

The most varied schools and principles proceeded from this doctrine of Socrates, and this was made a reproach against him, but it was really due to the indefiniteness and abstraction of his principle. And in this way it is only particular forms of this principle which can at first be recognized in philosophic systems which we call Socratic. Under the name of Socratic, I understand . . . those schools and methods which remained closer to Socrates and in which we find nothing but the one-sided understanding of Socratic culture. . . . . There are . . . three schools worthy of consideration; first the Megaric School, . . . and then the Cyrenaic and Cynic Schools; and from the fact that they all three differ very much from one another, it is clearly shown that Socrates himself was devoid of any positive system.

In this text Hegel seems to accredit Kierkegaard's interpretation in advance: Kierkegaard explains the diversity of the Socratic schools by the 'void' of Socrates' thought. For Nietzsche, the text-of-Socrates has as many meanings as there are types of forces that make use of it, hence the necessary divergence of the schools that claim it as their origin. In Nietzsche's 'Die vorplatonischen Philosophen' (in *Nietzsche Werke, Kritische Gesamtausgabe,* ed. Giorgio Colli and Mazzino Montinari, II, 4, *Vorlesungsaufzeichnungen [WS 1871/72-WS 1874/75],* [Berlin: Walter de Gruyter, 1995]), the diversity of schools will be interpreted as the outcome, through schism and division, of Socrates' original complexity and plenitude, Socrates being a pure type like all the early masters of philosophy.

10   The distinction implies a very modern degree of attention to the staging of the text, which is something Hegel misses; as he himself declares with reference to the Socratic dialogues, 'they have ... only a literary interest, and hence I will pass them by' (*Lectures,* p. 450). From Kierkegaard's perspective, Hegel credits the Sophists with too much movement; according to Kierkegaard, the Sophists, unlike Socrates, never demolished opinions without putting something positive in their place.)

11   Leonardo da Vinci inevitably comes to mind here. In his Journal, he notes coolly and in full detail the expenses he incurred for his mother's burial; he adds them up, using this activity as an attempt to master and conceal the violent emotion produced in him by the death of the woman he calls 'Caterina'. See Freud, 'Leonardo da Vinci and a Memory of His Childhood', in *The Standard Edition of the Complete Psychological Works of Sigmund Freud,* ed. James Strachey (London: The Hogarth Press, 1953-66), vol. 11, chapter 3, pp. 93-106.

12   Cf. Diogenes Laertius, *Lives of Eminent Philosophers,* trans. R. D. Hicks (London: William Heineman, 1925), p. 175:

He was born, according to Apollodorus in his *Chronology,* in the archonship of Apsephion, in the fourth year of the 77th Olympiad, on the 6th day of the month of Thargelion, when the Athenians purify their city, which according to the Delians is the birthday of Artemis. He died in the first year of the 95th Olympiad at the age of seventy. With this Demetrius of Phalerum agrees; but some say he was sixty when he died.

Both were pupils of Anaxagoras, I mean Socrates and Euripides, who was born in the first year of the 75th Olympiad in the archonship of Calliades.

13 G. W. F. Hegel, *Lectures on the Philosophy of World History. Introduction: Reason in History*, trans. H. B. Nisbet (Cambridge, UK: Cambridge University Press, 1975), p. 45.

14 Ibid., pp. 45-46.

15 *Reason in History*, p. 89.

16 See Diogenes Laertius, *Lives*, p. 173, and Hegel, *Lectures*, p. 445.

17 One can see an 'illustration' of this gesture of immediate sublation after death in a small painting by Fra Angelico in the Louvre. In the foreground, we see four saints laid out on the ground, decapitated; their bloody heads lie in the background. Four palm trees, symbolizing the resurrection, stand in the middle distance, allowing the dead martyrs to hold their heads up, despite – and because of – their decapitation.

18 We should recall that Kierkegaard disagrees with Hegel on this point, reproaching him for giving the Sophists credit for too much movement and, on the contrary, not giving enough credit for negativity to Socrates. The Sophists are Hegel's real 'bête noire'.

19 Let us note that Heidegger does not attribute the same 'infinite importance' to Socrates, since for him the modern era, idealist and metaphysical, begins more or less with Descartes. Socrates, even more perhaps than the 'pre-Socratics', remains for Heidegger 'the purest thinker of the West', who would have known how to remain within the movement of withdrawal of what gives itself to thought. As evidence, there is the fact that he did not write. For Heidegger views writing as a sign of the decline of thought (and through this condemnation he reconnects with a decidedly metaphysical gesture). Cf. Jacques Derrida citing Heidegger, *Was heisst Denken*, in connection with the Heidegger-De Man relationship, in *Mémoires for Paul de Man*, trans. Cecile Lindsay, Jonathan Culler, and Eduardo Cadava (New York: Columbia University Press, 1986), p. 152:

> Socrates . . . is the purest thinker of the West. This is why he wrote nothing. For he who begins to write on coming out of thought *(aus dem Denken)* will inevitably resemble those people who run to seek refuge against a strong draft. This remains the secret of an as yet hidden history: that all Western thinkers after Socrates, notwithstanding their greatness, had to be such 'fugitives' [Heidegger does not, himself, place quotations around 'Flüchtlinge']. Thinking has entered into literature. And literature has decided the fate of Western science which, by way of the *doctrina* of the Middle Ages, became the *scientia* of modernity. In this form, all sciences have sprung, in a double manner, from out of philosophy. The sciences come here out of philosophy in that they must leave it.

20 'The Ionics founded natural philosophy, Socrates ethics, and Plato added to them dialectic' (*Lectures*, p. 387). At the end of his study of Socrates, however, Diogenes states: 'In my opinion Socrates discoursed on physics as well as on ethics, since he holds some conversations about providence, even according

to Xenophon, who, however, declares that he only discussed ethics. But Plato, after mentioning Anaxagoras and certain other physicists in the *Apology*, treats for his own part themes which Socrates disowned, although he puts everything into the mouth of Socrates' (*Lives*, p. 175). The citation to which Hegel is referring is found in Diogenes' chapter on Plato (*Lives*, p. 327).

21 In the *Phaedo*, in order to be able to converse in peace with his male disciples about the immortality of the soul, Socrates sends his wife away for fear that her cries and lamentations may prove disturbing.

22 G. W. F. Hegel, *Aesthetics: Lectures on Fine Art*, trans. T. M. Knox (Oxford: Clarendon Press, 1974), vol. II, section III, chapter III, 'Poetry', p. 1198.

23 *Philosophy of Right*, §140, note, p. 102.

24 *Aesthetics*, II, p. 1198.

25 *Philosophy of Right*, p. 102. This passage points directly at Sölger and Romantic irony: just before the text cited, Hegel writes: 'The arbitrary name "irony" would be of no importance, but there is an obscurity here when it is said that it is "the highest" which perishes with our nothingness and that it is in the disappearance of our actuality that the divine is first revealed' (ibid.).

26 *Aesthetics*, II, p. 1198.

27 '*Philosophy of Right*, p. 102.

28 Ibid., p. 101.

29 Ibid., note, p. 102.

30 For Hegel, the bequest was perfectly legitimate, for 'children have the right to maintenance and education at the expense of the family's common capital' (*Philosophy of Right*, §174, p. 117).

31 In *Aesthetics*, II, 'Poetry', Hegel rules out avarice as the object of an authentic comic action.

> Avarice . . . both in its aim and in the petty means it uses appears from beginning to end as inherently null. For the avaricious man takes the dead abstraction of wealth, money as such, as the ultimate reality beyond which he will not go; and he tries to attain this cold pleasure by depriving himself of every other concrete satisfaction, while nevertheless he cannot gain his chosen end because his aim and his means are helpless in face of cunning, betrayal, etc. But if an individual is *serious* in identifying himself with such an inherently false aim and making it the one real thing in his life, then, the more he still clings to it after he has been deprived of its realization, the more miserable he becomes. In such a picture there is none of the real essence of the comical . . . (P. 1200)

It is clear that Hegel felt obliged to pull out all the stops to exonerate Socrates of any suspicion of cupidity, Socrates being an authentic tragic hero but also a comic hero.

32 The ancient sources all stress this point. In *Memorabilia*, trans. Amy L. Bonnette (Ithaca, NY: Cornell University Press, 1994), Book I, chapter 5, p. 27, Xenophon writes: 'He overpowered not only the pleasures that come through the body but also the pleasure that comes through wealth, holding that the one who accepts wealth from one he meets by chance establishes a

master over himself and subjects himself to a slavery as shameful as any'. A little further on (chapter 6, pp. 29-30), Socrates compares the Sophists, who are paid for their science, to prostitutes. Alcibiades, in Plato's *Symposium,* gives up the idea of seducing Socrates by using profit as his bait, for he is well aware that 'as far as money was concerned [Socrates] was much more invulnerable through and through than was Ajax to iron' (219e).

Diogenes Laertius writes that, for Socrates, there existed 'only one good, that is, knowledge, and only one evil, that is, ignorance; wealth and good birth bring their possessor no dignity, but on the contrary evil' (*Lives,* p. 161).

Aristophanes alone represents Socrates on the contrary as charging a great deal and, worse, completely impoverishing his disciples; Kierkegaard dwells on this point.

33 *Hegel's Philosophy of Mind,* trans. William Wallace (Oxford: Clarendon Press, 1894).

34 In a youthful text, Hegel noted that Socrates' love of wisdom was what 'kept him from driving away his wicked wife so as not to have to look after her any more' (G. W. F. Hegel, *Werke in zwanzig Bänden, 1, Frühe Schriften* [Frankfurt: Suhrkamp, 1971), p. 00 [50-54]; in French in *Fragments de la période de Berne,* trans. Robert Legros and Fabienne Verstraeten [Paris: Vrin, 1987]), 4 [1793-94], p. 40). I owe Françoise Dastur thanks for bringing the *Fragments* to my attention.

35 Cf. Xenophon, *Banquet,* trans. O. J. Todd (London: William Heinemann, 1972). To Antisthenes, who asks him how he can put up with that exceptionally cantankerous creature, Socrates replies: 'I observe that men who wish to become expert horsemen do not get the most docile horses but rather those that are high-mettled, believing that if they can manage this kind, they will easily handle any other. My course is similar. Mankind at large is what I wish to deal and associate with; and so I have got her, well assured that if I can endure her, I shall have no difficulty in my relations with all the rest of human kind' (II, 10).

Cf. also Xenophon, *Memorabilia,* II, 2, where Socrates shows his son Lamprocles that his mother's difficult temperament must not keep him from revering and loving her in appreciation for all the good things he has received from her.

On Socrates and the courtesans, cf. *Memorabilia,* III, 1 in its entirety. Among other things, Socrates says to Theodote: 'Many affairs both private and public deprive me of leisure. And I also have female friends who will not allow me to leave them day or night, since they are learning love charms and incantations from me' (p. 104).

See also Diogenes Laertius, *Lives,* for example:

When his wife said, 'You suffer unjustly', he retorted, 'Why, would you have me suffer justly?' . . . When Xanthippe first scolded him and then drenched him with water, his rejoinder was: 'Did I not say that Xanthippe's thunder would end in rain?' When Alcibiades declared that the scolding of Xanthippe was intolerable, 'Nay, I have got used to it', said he, 'as to the continued rattle of a windlass. And you do not mind the cackle of geese'. 'No', replied

Alcibiades, 'but they furnish me with eggs and goslings'. 'And Xanthippe', said Socrates, 'is the mother of my children'. When she tore his coat off his back in the market-place and his acquaintances advised him to hit back, 'Yes, by Zeus', said he, 'in order that while we are sparring each of you may join in with "Go it, Socrates!" "Well done, Xanthippe!"' (*Lives*, pp. 165, 167)

Nietzsche, who had read and loved Xenophon (*Nietzsche Werke, Kritische Gesamtausgabe*, ed. Giorgio Colli and Mazzino Montinari, II, 3, *Menschliches, Allzumenschliches, II, Nachgelassene Fragmente, Frühling 1878 bis November 1879* [Berlin: Walter de Gruyter, 1967], 28 [11], p. 363; 41 [2], p. 442; 42 [48], p. 462) and Diogenes Laertius, does not fail to emphasize Xanthippe's decisive role in her husband's philosophical vocation. If, unlike the other great philosophers (Heraclitus, Plato, Descartes, Spinoza, Liebniz, Kant, Schopenhauer), the mischievous Socrates was married, confirming ironically the truth of the Nietzschean thesis according to which philosophers abhor marriage (*On the Genealogy of Morals*, 'Third Essay', 7), it is because he had found the woman who was just right for him: a woman who had managed to make his home so uninhabitable, his hearth so unwelcoming, that he wanted to spend all his time in the streets. 'She taught him to live in the street and everywhere where one could chatter and be idle, and thus fashioned him into the greatest Athenian street-dialectician: so that in the end he had to compare himself to an importunate gadfly which a god had placed on the neck of the beautiful steed Athens that it might never be allowed any rest' (Friedrich Nietzsche, *Human, All Too Human*, trans. R. J. Hollingdale [Cambridge: Cambridge University Press, 1986), I, §433, 'Xantippe', p. 159).

But 'if he had known her well enough', despite his heroism, he would not have sought her out, for 'in fact' it was she who poisoned the free thinker to the very end; the real hemlock, for Socrates, was Xanthippe. 'There are many kinds of hemlock, and fate usually finds an opportunity of setting a cup of this poison draught to the lips of the free spirit – to "punish" him, as all the world then says. What will the women around him then do? They will lament and cry out and perhaps disturb the repose of the thinker's sunset hours: as they did in the prison at Athens. "O Criton, do tell someone to take those women away!" Socrates finally said' (ibid., §437, 'Finally', p. 160).

All these texts obviously tell us more about Nietzsche's 'misogyny', or at least his ambivalence toward women, than they tell us about Socrates' attitudes. At a minimum Nietzsche can be credited with paying more than marginal attention to Socrates' 'women', whereas Hegel ignores them entirely, and Kierkegaard relegates Xanthippe to a footnote, tending to preserve Socrates from her fury in this way. As for Phaenarete, Socrates' mother, he says nothing at all. These two authors also maintain total silence regarding the mother of Pheidippides when they study *The Clouds*, whereas they both go on at length about the father-son relationship. These omissions and silences are highly symptomatic; we shall come back to them.

36   *Aesthetics*, I, 'The Symbolic Form of Art', p. 361.
37   *Aesthetics*, II, p. 1214.
38   Cf. *Philosophy of Right*, 'Ethical Life', §175, pp. 117-18:

Children are potentially free and their life directly embodies nothing save potential freedom. Consequently they are not things and cannot be the property either of their parents or others. In respect of his relation to the family, the child's education has the positive aim of instilling ethical principles into him in the form of an immediate feeling for which differences are not yet explicit, so that thus equipped with the foundation of an ethical life, his heart may live its early years in love, trust, and obedience. In respect of the same relation, this education has the negative aim of raising children out of the instinctive, physical, level on which they are originally, to self-subsistence and freedom of personality and so to the level on which they have the power to leave the natural unity of the family.

39 For a discussion of this gesture, see the reading of the *Symposium*, above.
40 When the dying Socrates asks Crito to sacrifice a cock to Asclepius, he is acknowledging that he has been a sick man. Nietzsche, as we have seen, does not forgive him for those last words, for going too far. Hegel could have interpreted Socrates' last words (but to my knowledge he did not do so) not as signifying that 'life is a disease', but as an allusion to the necessary illness through which Mind must pass in order to achieve full self-awareness. In *Fragments de la période de Berne*, Hegel writes only this: 'Socrates did not die like Maupertuis in a monk's robe while taking holy communion, but he died as a Greek, sacrificing a cock to Asclepius' (*Frühe Schriften*; in French in *Fragments*, 4, p. 41).
41 See the foregoing analysis.
42 We find the same approach in Auguste Comte, for whom the first two states through which the human mind necessarily passes, in its childhood and adolescence, before reaching the positive adult state – the only healthy and normal state – are states of illness. Cf., in this connection, Sarah Kofman, *Aberrations, le devenir-femme d'Auguste Comte* (Paris: Flammarion, 1978).
43 In §405, Hegel defines genius as the individuality of the subject's true self as distinct from the individuality that experiences feelings and that, inasmuch as it is immediate, is not a reflexive subject in itself and is thus passive. The genius may also be another individual.

Though the sensitive individuality is undoubtedly a monadic individual, it is because immediate, not yet as *its self*, not a true subject reflected into itself, and is therefore passive. Hence the individuality of its true self is a different subject from it – a subject which may even exist as another individual. By the self-hood of the latter it – a substance, which is only a non-independent predicate – is then set in vibration and controlled without the least resistance on its part. This other subject by which it is so controlled may be called its *genius* (pp. 27-28).

And Hegel continues:

In the ordinary course of nature this is the condition of the child in its mother's womb: – a condition neither merely bodily nor merely mental, but psychical – a correlation of soul to soul. Here are two individuals, yet in undivided psychic unity: the one as yet no *self*, as yet nothing impenetrable, incapable of resistance: the other is its actuating subject, the *single* self of the two. The mother is the *genius* of the child; for by genius we commonly mean the total mental self-hood, as it has existence of its own, and constitutes the subjective substantiality of some one else who is only externally treated as an individual and has only a nominal independence. ...

What ought to be noted as regards this psychical tie are not merely the striking effects communicated to and stamped upon the child by violent emotions, injuries, &c. of the mother, but the whole psychical *judgment* (partition) of the underlying nature, by which the female (like the monocotyledons among the vegetables) can suffer disruption in twain, so that the child has not merely got *communicated* to it, but has originally received morbid dispositions as well as other pre-dispositions of shape, temper, character, talent, idiosyncrasies, &c.

Sporadic examples and traces of this *magic* tie appear elsewhere in the range of self-possessed conscious life, say between friends, especially female friends, with delicate nerves (a tie which may go so far as to show 'magnetic' phenomena), between husband and wife and between members of the same family (pp. 28-29).

By granting such importance to 'genius', which he also calls 'heart' or 'profound sensibility', Hegel is opposed to Kant, whose categories of understanding divide up and parcel out what is profoundly and immediately united in an ongoing, anticipatory critique. It is not by chance that, in *Anthropology from a Pragmatic Point of View* (trans. Victor Lyle Dowdell [Carbondale: Southern Illinois University Press, 1978), precisely when he is arguing against the charge that the senses claim – illegitimately – to control the understanding, Kant shows that Socrates' demon or genius must not be identified with the inner sense. At the risk of being reduced to excitation and hallucination (a 'reduction' that Hegel will achieve to some extent when he depicts the demonic voice as a necessary manifestation of interiority through a form that remains external), the demonic inspiration has to be conceived as emanating from 'real, though obscure, deliberations of the understanding' (§10, p. 30). But further on, Kant refers to 'the gift of presentiment, inspirations similar to those of the genius of Socrates, and qualities purported to be grounded in experience but really based on such unaccountable influences as sympathy, antipathy, and idiosyncrasy (*qualitates occultae*)' as chimerical hobbyhorses of the soul (§75, pp. 98-99).

44 Ibid., §406, pp. 34-36.

45 Hegel uses this analogy to announce and dialectize positions that will be adopted later by Sigmund Freud and Sandor Ferenczi. For the latter thinkers, the relation between the hypnotist and the subject of hypnosis implies a regression of consciousness to a state in which the socius has its origin, a state anterior to the distinction of autonomous subjects as such: a 'panicking' state in which each one, separated from 'himself', identifies contagiously with another on whom he depends intimately and with whom alone he forms a complete whole. Freud (in *Group Psychology and the Analysis*

of the Ego [*Standard Edition,* vol. 18, pp. 67ff.]) and Ferenczi (in 'Introjection and Transference', in *First Contributions to Psycho-Analysis,* trans. Ernest Jones [London: Hogarth Press Ltd. and The Institute of Psychoanalysis, 1952], pp. 69-70) both identify paternal and maternal types of hypnosis. In the former, an all-powerful father, an absolute narcissist and leader of crowds, uses his gaze and his commands to operate a dangerous subjugation, reducing the hypnotized subject to helplessness, paralysis of the will, passive and masochistic behaviour (Thomas Mann's 'Mario and the Magician' offers a remarkable illustration of this type of hypnosis). In the latter, the hypnotist is a mother who lulls the subject to sleep with gentle caresses and cradles him with her soothing voice. Both types of hypnosis, by virtue of their regressive character and the type of symbiotic relation they establish between hypnotist and subject, ultimately take the intrauterine situation as their model. As Hegel had suspected, every hypnosis, in this sense, is of the maternal type. In *Thalassa: A Theory of Genitality* (trans. Henry Alden Bunker [New York: W. W. Norton, 1968], p. 32), Ferenczi declares that maternal hypnosis operates by way of seductive insinuation and that the hypnotised subject regresses to the stage of helpless infant in both types of hypnosis; he moves the regression back to the intrauterine stage. In *The Trauma of Birth* (London: K. Paul, Trench, Trubner, 1929), Otto Rank also posits that the nature of hypnosis can be accounted for by the primal relations linking infants and mothers.

46 On the awakening of consciousness, see Jean-Luc Nancy's decisive analysis in 'Identité et tremblement', in Michel Borch-Jacobsen, Eric Michaud and Jean-Luc Nancy, *Hypnoses* (Paris: Galilée, 1984), where Nancy draws principally on the same texts from the *Encyclopedia (Hegel's Philosophy of Mind)* that I have used. However, Nancy makes no mention of the passages in *Lectures on the History of Philosophy* that have to do with Socrates.

47 Cf. Kant's *Anthropology,* §12, pp. 34-35:

> Customary habit (*assuetudino*) . . . is a physical and inner compulsion to proceed farther in the very same way in which we have been traveling. Acquired habit deprives good actions of their moral value because it undermines mental freedom and, moreover, it leads to thoughtless repetitions of the same acts (monotony), and thus becomes ridiculous. Customary expletives (clichés used merely to stuff the emptiness of thoughts) make the listener apprehensive that he will have to hear these favorite expressions over and over, and they make the orator into a talking-machine. The reason for being disgusted with someone's acquired habits lies in the fact that the animal here predominates over the man, so that instinctively, according to the rule of acquired habit, that person is categorized as another nature, a nonhuman nature, so that he runs the risk of falling into the same class with the beast. Nevertheless, certain continued practices may be started intentionally and kept up when Nature refuses help to the free will; for example, to become accustomed in old age to the time of eating and sleeping, or to the quality and quantity of food, or sleep, thus making it gradually mechanical. But this is the exception to the rule, and it only occurs in a case of necessity. Generally, all acquired habits are objectionable.

48   See also Auguste Comte, for whom man cannot think continuously without risking madness, and who, at best, quickly tires of thinking.

49   *Hegel's Philosophy of Mind,* §410, pp. 41-44.

50   Ibid, §412, pp. 45-46.

51   Nietzsche also tells a story about a foreigner passing through Athens who was good at reading faces: he told Socrates outright that he was a monster who harbored the worst vices and the worst virtues. Socrates apparently was satisfied to answer: 'You know me, Sir' (*The Twilight of the Idols,* 'The Problem of Socrates' (in *The Portable Nietzsche,* trans. Walter Kaufmann [New York: Viking Penguin, 1982 (1954)], p. 107).

   Diogenes Laertius likes to tell stories that illustrate the strength of Socrates' instincts. For example, 'frequently, owing to his vehemence in argument, men set upon him with their fists or tore his hair out; and . . . for the most part he was despised and laughed at, yet bore all this ill-usage patiently' (*Lives,* p. 151). Diogenes also reports that Socrates had two wives and that he was married to them at the same time (p. 157).

52   He used to express his astonishment that the sculptors of marble statues should take pains to make the block of marble into a perfect likeness of a man, and should take no pains about themselves lest they should turn out mere blocks, not men. He recommended to the young the constant use of the mirror, to the end that handsome men might acquire a corresponding behaviour, and ugly men conceal their defects by education' (Diogenes Laertius, *Lives,* pp. 163-65).

53   Cf. Kant, *Anthropology,* p. 207. *On Physiognomy.*

   Physiognomy is the art of judging a person's disposition or way of thinking by his visible form; consequently, it judges the interior by the exterior. . . . It would be absurd to conclude that, by analogy to the human craftsman, the same holds true for the inscrutable creator of Nature; that he would have combined a beautiful body with a good soul . . . Taste, which merely expresses the subjective basis of satisfaction or dissatisfaction of one person with another (depending on their beauty or ugliness), cannot serve as a model for wisdom. Wisdom shares (with a purpose which we cannot absolutely comprehend) its existence objectively with certain natural qualities, but it is wrong to assume that these two heterogeneous things are united in a person for one and the same purpose. . . . It cannot be disputed that there is characterization by physiognomy. Yet it can never become a science . . . Thus there is now no longer any demand for physiognomy as an art of investigating the human interior through external, involuntary signs, and nothing is left of it but the art of cultivating taste, not taste in things, but rather in morals, manners, and customs, in order to add to the knowledge of man through a critique which would enhance human relations and the knowledge of man in general. . . . We should not charge any face with ugliness if in its characteristics it does not betray the expression of a mind degraded by vice or by a natural, though unfortunate, tendency to vice . . .

54   *Aesthetics,* I, 'The Idea of Artistic Beauty, or the Ideal', pp. 145-46.

55 *Philosophy of Mind,* pp. 44-45.
56 Ibid., p. 45.
57 Ibid., p. 151.
58 Ibid., p. 152.
59 Ibid., p. 154.
60 Nevertheless, Hegel writes that art, for its part, must strive to represent Socrates' spiritual beauty by physical beauty, as if his spiritual force had the power even to transform his bodily appearance. Art 'realizes' what 'nature' was unable to realize: 'A moral disposition and activity can dwell in the Silenus features of Socrates. Of course for the expression of spiritual beauty the artist will avoid what is absolutely ugly in external forms, or he can subdue and transfigure it through the power of the soul that breaks through it' (*Aesthetics,* II, 'Painting', p. 864).
61 Cf. *Lectures on the History of Philosophy,* pp. 150-53.

> The Greeks . . . made their world their home. . . . They certainly received the substantial beginnings of their religion, culture, their common bonds of fellowship, more or less from Asia, Syria and Egypt; but they have so greatly obliterated the foreign nature of this origin, and it is so much changed, worked upon, turned round, and altogether made so different, that what they, as we, prize, know, and love in it, is essentially their own. . . . Their spiritual development requires that which is received or foreign, as matter or stimulus only; in such they have known and borne themselves as men that were free. The form which they have given to the foreign principle is this characteristic breath of spirituality, the spirit of freedom and of beauty which can in the one aspect be regarded as form, but which in another and higher sense is simply substance. . . . They have also held in reverence this their spiritual rebirth, which is their real birth. . . . They have not only used and enjoyed all that they have brought forth and formed, but they have become aware of and thankfully and joyfully placed before themselves this at-homeness [Heimatlichkeit] in their whole existence . . . They represent their existence as an object apart from themselves, which manifests itself independently and which in its independence is of value to them . . . It is in this veritable homeliness, or, more accurately, in the spirit of homeliness, in this spirit of ideally being-at-home-with-themselves in their physical, corporate, legal, moral and political existence . . . that the kernel of thinking liberty rests; and hence it was requisite that Philosophy should arise amongst them. . . . To start from the self, to live in the self, is the other extreme of abstract subjectivity, when it is still empty . . . such is . . . the abstract principle of the modern world. . . . The stage reached by Greek consciousness is the stage of beauty.

See also Nietzsche, who shows how the Greeks were able to appropriate everything that was foreign to them in such as way as to assimilate and surpass it:

> It has been pointed out assiduously, to be sure, how much the Greeks were able to find and learn abroad in the Orient, and it is doubtless true that they

picked up much there. . . . As to specifics, very little has been discovered by such juxtaposition. As to the general idea, we should not mind it, if only its exponents did not burden us with their conclusion that philosophy was thus merely imported into Greece rather than having grown and developed there in a soil natural and native to it. Or worse, that philosophy being alien to the Greeks, it very likely contributed to their ruin more than to their well-being. Nothing would be sillier than to claim an autochthonous development for the Greeks. On the contrary, they invariably absorbed other living cultures. The very reason they got so far is that they knew how to pick up the spear and throw it onward from the point where others had left it. Their skill in the art of fruitful learning was admirable. We ought to be learning from our neighbors precisely as the Greeks learned from theirs, not for the sake of learned pedantry but rather using everything we learn as a foothold which will take us up as high, and higher than our neighbor. The quest for philosophy's beginnings is idle, for everywhere in all beginnings we find only the crude, the unformed, the empty and the ugly. What matters in all things is the higher levels. . . . Everywhere, the way to the beginnings leads to barbarism. . . . The Greeks . . . engaged in philosophy, as in everything else, as civilized human beings, and with highly civilized aims, wherefore, free of any kind of autochthonous conceit, they forbore trying to re-invent the elements of philosophy and science. Rather they instantly tackled the job of so fulfilling, enhancing, elevating and purifying the elements they took over from elsewhere that they became inventors after all, but in a higher sense and a purer sphere. (*Philosophy in the Tragic Age of the Greeks*, pp. 29-31)

62 Aesthetics, I, 'The Idea of Artistic Beauty', p. 154.
63 Ibid., p. 153 (the citation is from Diogenes Laertius, 'Plato', in *Lives*, 23, §29).
64 Trans. Hugh Fredennick (London: William Heinemann Ltd., vol. I, 1961 [1933], Book I vi, 2 (987 b 1-4).
65 'We can do no better in Greek philosophy than to study the first book of his *Metaphysics*' (*Lectures*, p. 167).
66 *Metaphysics*, vol. II, Book XIII, iv, 5 (1078 b 27-29): 'There are two innovations which may fairly be ascribed to Socrates: inductive reasoning and general definition. Both of these are associated with the starting-point of scientific knowledge.'
67 *Philosophy of Right*, §140, p. 101.
68 The passage cited was omitted from the Haldane translation. Cf. *Werke*, p. 459: 'dies ist das Wahrhafte der Sokratischen Ironie. . . . es ist um die Entwicklung dessen zu tun, was nur Vorstellung und deshalb etwas Abstraktes ist'.
69 See *Philosophy of Right*, §140, with the accompanying note, p. 101; the passage is in this connection quite characteristic:

The supreme form in which this subjectivism is completely comprised and expressed is the phenomenon which has been called by a name borrowed from Plato – 'Irony'. The name alone, however, is taken from Plato; he used it to describe a way of speaking which Socrates employed in conversation . . . Irony is only a manner of talking against *people*. Except as directed against persons, the essential movement of thought is dialectic, and Plato was so far from regarding the dialectical in itself, still less irony, as the last word in thought and a substitute for the Idea, that he terminated the flux and reflux of thinking, let alone of a subjective opinion, and submerged it in the substantiality of the Idea.

70 'Introduction', pp. 67-68.
71 Ibid., p. 67.
72 *Philosophy of Right*, §140, p. 101, note.
73 In *Philosophy of Right*, §140, Hegel also writes:

> It is not the thing that is excellent, but I who am so; as the master of law and thing alike, I simply play with them as with my caprice; my consciously ironical attitude lets the highest perish and I merely hug myself at the thought. This type of subjectivism not merely substitutes a void for the whole content of ethics, right, duties, and laws – and so is evil, in fact evil through and through and universally – but in addition its form is a subjective void, i.e., it knows itself as this contentless void and in this knowledge knows itself as absolute. (pp. 102-103)

And Hegel then recalls that, in his *Phenomenology of Mind*, he asked himself up to what point that sort of absolute complacency in the self is not an idolatry of the self – if it can also form something like a community of which the bond and substance would be reciprocal security in a clear conscience, good intentions, the joy of mutual purity, the splendid voluptuousness of the culture of the self – and he wonders whether what he described in that text as '"a beautiful soul" – that still nobler type of subjectivism which empties the objective of all content and so fades away until it loses all actuality' (p. 103), is kin to that sort of ironic consciousness. In *Aesthetics*, the identification seems to be made less hesitantly.

74 *Aesthetics*, I, p. 68.
75 Ibid.
76 In an early fragment on love, Hegel cites this play to show how true love is enriched by giving all it has to the loved one (*Early Theological Writings*, trans. T. M. Knox and Richard Kroner [Chicago: University of Chicago Press, 1948], p. 307).
77 *Aesthetics*, I, p. 69.
78 Søren Kierkegaard, *The Concept of Irony*, trans. Howard V. Hong and Edna H. Hong (Princeton: Princeton University Press, 1989) p. 309.
79 Cf. *Philosophy of Right*, §140.
80 See also Sarah Kofman, 'Nietzsche and the Obscurity of Heraclitus', trans. Françoise Lionnet-McCumber, *Diacritics* 17/3 (Fall 1987): 39-55.
81 This is why, in the *Theaetetus*, the images of the soul as wax – or dove – fail to account for the error, thus for science. Hegel does not refer to any specific text among Plato's writings, but he may be relying here on the *Theaetetus* or the *Meno*.

82 'Here we see land; there is no proposition of Heraclitus which I have not *adopted* in my Logic' (*Lectures*, p. 279; emphasis added).

83 See also *supra*.

84 See for example E. T. A. Hoffmann, *The Devil's Elixirs* (trans. Ronald Taylor [London: J. Calder, 1963] and *The Life and Opinions of Kater Murr* (in *Selected Writings of E. T. A. Hoffmann*, ed. and trans. Leonard J. Kent and Elizabeth C. Knight [Chicago: Chicago University Press, 1969]); the latter is a parody of apprenticeship novels. See also Sarah Kofman, 'Vautour rouge', in Sylviane Agacinski, Jacques Derrida, Sarah Kofman, Philippe Lacoue-Labarthe, Jean-Luc Nancy and Bernard Pautrat, *Mimesis des articulations* (Paris: Aubier-Flammarion, 1975), pp. 95-163, and *Autobiogriffures: Du chat Murr d'Hoffmann* (Paris: Galilée, 1984).

85 In the section on the Socratics in which he thematizes the question of sources, Hegel still favors Xenophon over Plato, but he seems to be a little less sure of their respective merits. 'And if we inquire whether he or Plato depicts Socrates to us most faithfully in his personality and doctrine, there is no question that in regard to the personality and method, the externals of his teaching, we may certainly receive from Plato a satisfactory, and perhaps a more complete representation of what Socrates was. But in regard to the content of his teaching and the point reached by him in the development of thought, we have in the main to look to Xenophon' (*Lectures*, p. 414; cf. *Werke* 18, p. 520). Hegel oscillates between Plato and Xenophon as he oscillates between a negative and a positive Socrates.

   Translator's note: In the Haldane translation, the passage cited above is included in the section on Socrates, immediately after an explicit reference to Xenophon that does not appear in the German text: 'If we consider the universal first, it has within it a positive and a negative side, *which we find both united in Xenophon's 'Memorabilia,' a work which aims at justifying Socrates'* (p. 414; emphasis added).

86 *Memorabilia*, p. 123.

87 'We ought not to object, he used to say, to be subjects for the Comic poets, for if they satirize our faults they will do us good, and if not they do not touch us' (*Lives*, p. 167) – and as we know, Socrates attended performances of *The Clouds* so that the Athenians could judge the resemblance for themselves.

88 On what is encompassed by German 'seriousness', see Nietzsche (*On the Genealogy of Morals*, trans. Walter Kaufmann and R. J. Hollingdale, in *On the Genealogy of Morals and Ecce Homo*, (New York: Vintage Books, 1989), 'Second Essay', section 3, pp. 60-62).

89 *The Birth of Tragedy*, §13. After recalling that Aristophanes' comedies always associated Socrates with Euripides, Nietzsche adds: '. . . to the dismay of the rising generation, who, while they were willing enough to sacrifice Euripides, could not forgive the picture of Socrates as the arch-Sophist. Their only recourse was to pillory Aristophanes in his turn as a dissolute, lying Alcibiades of poetry. I won't pause here to defend the profound instincts of Aristophanes against such attacks but shall proceed to demonstrate the close affinity between Socrates and Euripides as their contemporaries saw them' (pp. 82-83).

90 Hegel, *Aesthetics*, II, p. 1200; more generally, see *Aesthetics*, II, 'Poetry', 'The Different Genres of Poetry', pp. 1035ff.

91 These expressions are found in *Aesthetics*, I, 'Introduction', p. 67.

92 Immanuel Kant, *Critique of Judgment*, trans. J. H. Bernard (New York: Hafner Press, 1951), §54, 'Remark', p. 181.

93 *Aesthetics*, II, p. 1200.

94 *Aesthetics*, II, p. 1202.

95 Freud, in his *Jokes and Their Relation to the Unconscious* (*Standard Edition*, vol. 8), shows on the contrary that, in order to laugh, it is indispensable that one not know why or about what one is laughing. Cf. Sarah Kofman, *Pourquoi rit-on? Freud et le mot d'esprit* (Paris: Galilée, 1986).

96 An example of 'insane laughter' may be found in the laugh Milos Forman attributes to Salieri in his film *Amadeus:* a crazy person's laugh, which echoes the more anal laugh bestowed upon Salieri's rival Mozart.

97 On the practice of summarizing as a violent, 'reductive' approach to a text, see Sarah Kofman, 'Summarize, Interpret', in *Freud and Fiction*, trans. Sarah Wykes (Cambridge, UK: Polity Press, 1991), pp. 83-117.

98 In the chapter of the *Lectures* on the Socratics, Hegel declares in connection with the dialogues that he is setting aside everything that has 'only a literary interest' (p. 450).

99 Cf. §158: 'The family, as the immediate substantiality of mind, is specifically characterized by love, which is mind's feeling of its own unity. Hence in a family, one's frame of mind is to have self-consciousness of one's own individuality within this unity as the absolute essence of oneself, with the result that one is in it not as an independent person but as a member' (p. 110).

100 Translator's note: The French expression *au sein de,* literally 'at the breast of', lends itself well to the metaphor of mother's milk.

101 Cf. §175.

102 'In the case of maternal love it is generally true that a mother's love for her child is neither something accidental nor just a single feature in her life, but, on the contrary, it is her supreme vocation on earth' (*Aesthetics*, II, 'Painting', p. 824-25). The most singular form of this love is Mary's maternal love for Christ, a subject of painting par excellence (ibid., p. 824).

103 *Philosophy of Right*, pp. 117-18.

104 In *The Spirit of Christianity and Its Fate* (*Early Theological Writings*, pp. 182-301), Hegel had already described the unhappiness and injury that schisms and divisions inflict in life, and had prescribed the cure in a return to unity. If the Jews are unhappy, it is because they are cut off from God, with no possibility for reconciliation, whereas Christ forms an essential unity with his father. For speculative logic, this unity is nevertheless in other respects not incompatible with the 'separate' character of the son as an incarnate individual being, for from the standpoint of speculative logic, which is the same as that of life (and the best model for which is that of the child in the mother's womb), the part and the whole are one and the same being. 'Living things, however, are essences, even if they are separate, and their unity is still a unity of essence. What is a contradiction in the realm of the dead is not one in the realm of

life' (pp. 260-61). 'The Mosaic religion is a religion of unhappiness, for in unhappiness there is division. . . . In happiness this division has disappeared; happiness is the reign of love and unity. . . . Now there is a god who is not a master but a friendly being, beautiful, a living reality whose essence is total conciliation, whereas the Jewish God is the most profound schism; he excludes all free union, authorizes only domination or servitude' (*L'Esprit du christianisme et son destin* [Paris: Vrin, 1948], p. 135).

Translator's note: The French translation includes a selection of notes from a German edition of Hegel's early theological writings edited by H. Nohl: *Hegels theologische Jugendschriften* (Tübingen, 1907); this material is not included in *Early Theological Writings*.

105 On this logic, see Jacques Derrida, *Glas* (trans. John P. Leavey, Jr., and Richard Rand [Lincoln: University of Nebraska Press, 1986]). Derrida offers 'us', concerning 'Hegel's' family, some subtle and decisive revelations.

106 Cf. *The Spirit of Christianity and Its Fate:* 'As soon as intellectual concepts are opposed to imagery and taken as dominant, every image must be set aside as only play, as a by-product of the imagination and without truth; and, instead of the life of the image, nothing remains but objects' (p. 261).

107 Here Hegel's argument finds support in Books VIII and IX of Plato's *Republic*, which show that the passage from one political regime to another, paralleling that of the passage from one type of soul to another, is always driven by internal discord, by conflict between the paternal principles and those proposed by seducers who end up winning out over the parents. On this subject, see Sarah Kofman, 'Miroir et mirages oniriques, Platon précurseur de Freud', in *La Part de l'oeil* 4 (1988): 127-35 (revised version in *Séductions: De Sartre à Héraclite* [Paris: Galilée, 1990]).

108 In *Glas*, Derrida quotes a remark from *Philosophy of Right* that presents the concept of the morality of mores, even before the family is at issue, where Hegel writes: 'When a father inquired about the best method of educating his son in ethical conduct, a Pythagorean replied: "Make him a citizen of a state with good laws". (This phrase has also been attributed to others' (§153, p. 109). Derrida emphasizes that the German manuscript cited Socrates among the other philosophers; later, the name of Socrates was eliminated.

109 On the figure of Antigone, see also Hegel, *The Phenomenology of Mind*, trans. J. B. Baillie (London: Allen and Unwin, 1977, and Jacques Derrida, *Glas;* among other things, Derrida emphasizes that it is not by chance that the figure Hegel glorifies most highly is that of a sister.

110 'So he was taken from among men; and not long afterwards the Athenians felt such remorse that they shut up the training grounds and gymnasia. They banished the other accusers but put Meletus to death; they honoured Socrates with a bronze statue, the work of Lysippus, which they placed in the hall of processions . . . Not only in the case of Socrates but in very many others the Athenians repented in this way' (*Lives*, p. 173).

111 Cf. *The Spirit of Christianity and Its Fate:* 'Jesus died in the confidence that his plan would not miscarry' (p. 289, note). For a comparison of Christ with Socrates, see *Frühe Schriften*, pp. 50-54; in French in *Fragments* 4,

pp. 39-42).

112 Cf. *The Spirit of Christianity and Its Fate,* and Derrida's comment on this point in *Glas.*

III. KIERKEGAARD'S 'SOCRATES':
SOCRATES UNDER AN IRONIC LENSE

1 *Kierkegaard's Writings,* II, ed. and trans. Howard V. Hong and Edna H. Hong (Princeton: Princeton University Press, 1989). Subsequent references to this work will be supplied in the text.

2 Cf. *Concluding Unscientific Postscript to the Philosophical Fragments, A Mimic-Pathetic-Dialectic Composition, An Existential Contribution,* by 'Johannes Climacus' [S. Kierkegaard], trans. David S. Swanson (Princeton: Princeton University Press, 1944). Jacques Derrida cites this text in 'Outwork', in *Dissemination,* trans. Barbara Johnson (London: The Athlone Press, 1993), p. 28, n. 27.

3 The jury expressed particular reservations about Kierkegaard's writing style, finding it 'brilliant, sophisticated, and incorrigible', as Jean Brun points out in his introduction to the French translation (*Le Concept d'ironie constamment rapporté à Socrate* [Paris: Orante, 1976]). Brun does not offer much by way of objection to this verdict (is he thus endorsing it on his own account?).

4 *Søren Kierkegaard's Journals and Papers. Kierkegaard's Writings,* IV, ed. and trans. Howard V. Hong and Edna H. Hong (Bloomington: Indiana University Press, 1975), §4281, p. 214.

5 Translator's note: The cover page of the thesis, reproduced with an English translation in *The Concept of Irony,* p. 3, includes the date MDCCCLXI; the editors point out that this is a misprint for MDCCCXLI.

6 On this point, see Sylviane Agacinski, *Aparté, Conceptions and Deaths of Søren Kierkegaard,* trans. Kevin Newmark (Gainesville: University Presses of Florida, 1988): I shall refer to this text frequently.

7 From an article in *Faedrelandet* (1842).

8 Translator's note: Hong and Hong provide a facsimile of the original title page, which includes the epigraph, along with a translation (*Concept,* p. 419):

> but the fact is that whether one tumbles into a little diving pool or plump into the great sea he swims all the same. By all means. Then we, too, must swim and try to escape out of the sea of argument in the hope that either some dolphin will take us on its back or some other desperate rescue.
>
> *Republic,* I, 5 § 453 D

9 Cf. Sarah Kofman, *Comment s'en sortir?* (Paris: Galilée, 1983).

10 See *Philosophical Fragments / Johannes Climacus. Kierkegaard's Writings,* VII, ed. and trans. Howard V. Hong and Edna H. Hong (Princeton: Princeton University Press, 1985): 'When belief resolves to believe, it runs the risk that it was an error, but nevertheless it wills to believe. One never believes in any other way; if one wants to avoid risk, then one wants to know with certainty that one can swim before going into the water' (p. 83, note).

11 'In Goethe, irony was in the strictest sense a controlled element; it was a serving spirit to the poet' (*The Concept of Irony,* p. 325). Kierkegaard is referring

indirectly to *Wilhelm Meister's Apprenticeship* and to a study by Johan Ludvig Heiberg, who views Goethe as a speculative poet.

12 On this subject, see also *Johannes Climacus* or *De omnibus dubitandum est,* a tale written in 1842-43 right after *The Concept of Irony* (in *Philosophical Fragments / Johannes Climacus. Kierkegaard's Writings, VII.*

13 Cf. for example what is said about Kreisler's irony in E. T. A. Hoffman's 'The Life and Opinions of Kater Murr', in *Selected Writings of E. T. A. Hoffmann,* ed. and trans. Leonard J. Kent and Elizabeth C. Knight (Chicago: Chicago University Press, 1969). See also, on this subject, Sarah Kofman, *Autobiogriffures: Du chat Murr d'Hoffmann,* 2nd edition (Paris: Galilée, 1984).

14 Cf. *The Point of View for My Work as an Author,* trans. Walter Lowrie (New York: Harper Torchbooks, 1962). For the problem of Kierkegaard as a writer, his relation to language and to writing, the problem of pseudonymy, the identification to divine maternal activity, I refer to Sylviane Agacinski, *Aparté, Conceptions and Deaths of Soren Kierkegaard;* Agacinski makes this point with particular clarity.

15 Further on in his text, to counter the reading of Xenophon, who 'hears' Socrates' choice of death as a strictly self-interested move, Kierkegaard compares it with that of Christ, who refused to defend himself; for him, the two silences are comparable in this respect. On the death of Christ, who is the truth and who wills his death without however being guilty of it, see a poetic essay by Kierkegaard (signed H.H.), 'Has a Man the Right to Let Himself Be Put to Death for the Truth? A Poetic Experiment', in *The Present Age, and Two Minor Ethico-Religious Treatises,* trans. Alexander Dru and Walter Lowrie (London: Oxford University Press, 1940), pp. 77-135.

In *The Point of View for My Work as an Author,* Kierkegaard identifies with Christ and Socrates; like them, he gives up the idea of producing his own apology:

> What I write here is for orientation. It is a public attestation; not a defence or an apology. In this respect, truly, if in no other, I believe that I have something in common with Socrates. For when he was accused, and was about to be judged by 'the crowd,' his daemon forbade him to *defend* himself. Indeed, if he had done that, how unseemly it would have been, and how self-contradictory! Likewise there is something in me, and in the dialectical position I occupy, which makes it impossible for me, and impossible in itself, to conduct a defence for my work as an author. (pp. 6-7)

In the chapter of *The Concept of Irony* called 'Observations for Orientation' (pp. 246-58), Kierkegaard acknowledges nevertheless that the Church – the Roman Catholic Church, to be sure – agrees at certain periods of the year to 'view itself ironically'; however, he seems to concede only that 'the heavenly actuality' of the Greek gods was not 'spared the sharp blasts of irony' (p. 253).

16 *Nietzsche Werke,* IV, 3, *Menschliches, Allzumenschliches, II, Nachgelassene Fragmente, Frühling 1878 bis November 1879* (Berlin: Walter de Gruyeter, 1967), 41 [2], p. 442.

17 Ibid., 42 [48], p. 462.

18 Ibid., 28 [11], p. 363.

19 The lesson Kierkegaard draws from 'Napoleon's Tomb', a mere painting that is surrealist rather than realist, is comparable to the lesson Freud draws from the American anecdote to which I referred at the beginning of this study: only the empty space between the two portraits hanging on the wall allows someone who knows how to see it as such to discover the true meaning of the two portraits – they are portraits of the two thieves on either side of Christ. Christ's portrait then abruptly imposes itself between the two others, at least for anyone who knows how to see something other than surface appearances in the two paintings and on the wall between them.

20 See especially a long note, pp. 20-21, in which Kierkegaard refers to Xenophon's *Memorabilia* (trans. Amy L. Bonnette [Ithaca, NY: Cornell University Press, 1994], I, 1 [8], and I, 2).

21 *Memorabilia*, III, 8.

22 Ibid., II, 4, and I, 3 [14].

23 Ibid., III, 11.

24 Ibid., IV, 8 [8].

25 For example in IV, 2 and IV, 4.

26 Kierkegaard borrows this image from Abraham à Santa Clara (see *The Concept of Irony*, p. 28), without appearing to target Xenophon's 'conception', but rather modern ideas that do not take the time to flourish, that die of grief as soon as they are born.

27 Cf. *Journals and Papers*, vol. 3, §3200, in which Kierkegaard cites Christian Scriver with reference to a passage in Paul's Epistle to the Philippians.

28 See *Gorgias*, in *Plato*, vol. III, trans. W. R. M. Lamb (London: William Heinemann Ltd., 1961); *Protagoras*, in *Plato*, vol. II, trans. W. R. M. Lamb (London: William Heinemann Ltd., 1924); and *Symposium*, in *Plato*, vol. III.

29 Here is Diogenes' version: 'The philosopher, then, after Lysias had written a defence for him, read it through and said: "A fine speech, Lysias; it is not, however, suitable to me." For it was plainly more forensic than philosophical. Lysias said, "If it is a fine speech, how can it fail to suit you?" "Well," he replied, "would not fine raiment and fine shoes be just as unsuitable to me?"' (Diogenes Laertius, *Lives of Eminent Philosophers*, vol. I, trans. R. D. Hicks [Cambridge, MA: Harvard University Press, 1972 (1925)], p. 171). In this remark, Socrates' irony may not reside exactly where Kierkegaard situates it. Kierkegaard seems to take Socrates' reported praise of Lysias's speech seriously, substituting the term 'excellence' for the 'fineness' or beauty proclaimed by Socrates – and we know that for Socrates beauty is distinct from truth. Thus, in its invisibility, irony allows itself to be grasped only in places where everyone has an interest in hearing it.

30 Kierkegaard has emphasized this earlier, maintaining that true conversation is not 'identical with eccentric antiphonal singing in which everyone sings his part without regard to the other, and there is a resemblance to conversation only because they do not all talk at once' (*The Concept of Irony*, p. 34)

31 For example, Freud, in 'Beyond the Pleasure Principle', *The Standard Edition*

of the Complete Psychological Works of Sigmund Freud, trans. James Strachey (London: The Hogarth Press, 1953-66), vol. 18, pp. 7-64.

32 Cf. *supra,* the analysis of the *Symposium,* which is fairly close to Kierkegaard's on this point.

33 Jean-Joseph Goux, who highlights monetary metaphors in all his work, could find grist for his mill in this text. See Jean-Joseph Goux, *Symbolic Economies,* trans. Jennifer Curtiss Gage (Ithaca, NY: Cornell University Press 1990), and *The Coiners of Language,* trans. Jennifer Curtiss Gage (Norman: University of Oklahoma Press, 1994).

34 On the figure of Prometheus as the first philosopher, cf. *Philebus,* in *Plato,* vol. VIII, trans. W. R. M. Lamb (London: William Heinemann Ltd., 1962), pp. 197-399; see also Sarah Kofman, *Comment s'en sortir?*

35 Translator's note: in Kofman's text, the French word *habit,* 'suit,' reflects Kierkegaard's word play here. Referring to 'the well-known argument between a Catholic and a Protestant' in which each persuades the other to switch positions, Kierkegaard explains: 'There is only the relation of correspondence between them, so that the moment A is Catholic B becomes Protestant, and the moment B becomes Catholic A becomes Protestant, which means, of course, that neither of them changes his *habitus* [inner disposition] but each of them changes his suit [*Habit*]' (*The Concept of Irony,* pp. 56-57, note).

36 This image inevitably evokes the one Nietzsche later proposes for Parmenides: he is a vampire who has retreated to a cobweb castle, no longer possessing even the strength to drink his victims' blood. See *Philosophy in the Tragic Age of the Greeks,* trans. Marianne Cowan (Chicago: Henry Regnery, 1962), p. 80.

37 Here again, Kierkegaard can be compared with Nietzsche: see the foreword to *Beyond Good and Evil* (trans. Walter Kaufmann [New York: Vintage Books, 1966], pp. 2-4), and *The Twilight of the Gods,* 'How the "True World" Finally Became a Fable: The History of an Error' (in *The Portable Nietzsche,* trans. Walter Kaufmann [New York: Viking Penguin, 1968], pp. 485-86).

38 His Christian individualism will lead Kierkegaard himself to condemn democracy in favor of monarchy. The monarch at least keeps himself at a distance from men, like the Epicurean god.

39 'Presumably a copy of the *Sistine Madonna,* a painting by Raphael' (Hong and Hong, in *The Concept of Irony,* note 241, p. 503).

40 What Hegel calls the 'pantheism of the imagination', in *Lectures on the History of Philosophy: Greek Philosophy to Plato,* trans. E. S. Haldane (Lincoln, NE: University of Nebraska Press, 1995), vol. 1, part I, section II; Kierkegaard himself refers to this passage.

41 Long before Freud, Plato could describe dreams as a way of satisfying the most 'bestial' repressed desires: incest, parricide, cannibalism (cf. the beginning of Book IX of *The Republic* [in *Plato,* vol. 6, trans. Paul Shorey (London: William Heinemann, Ltd., 1935)] and Sarah Kofman [a reading of the same text], 'Miroir et mirages oniriques: Platon, précurseur de Freud', in *Séductions: De Sartre à Héraclite* [Paris: Galilée, 1990]). It seems that with Socrates he dreamed of simultaneously realizing all desires that are 'superfluous and prohibited by law', and that he was thus able to present death, putting the

words in Socrates' mouth, as a pleasure comparable to the one procured by dreamless sleep – since, to a person who is awake, as he says in *The Republic*, those delicious dreams seem like nightmares.

42 G. W. F. Hegel, *Aesthetics: Lectures on Fine Art,* trans. T. M. Knox (Oxford: Clarendon Press, 1974) vol. II, pp. 1210-11.

43 The reference is to Woody Allen's well-known film.

44 Kierkegaard stresses the term 'promising', which probably sums up the following passage from *The Clouds* (Strepsiades is speaking to Socrates):

> O never fear! he's very sharp, by nature,
> For when he was a little chap, *so* high,
> He used to build small baby-houses, boats,
> Go-carts of leather, darling little frogs,
> Carved from pomegranates, you can't think how nicely!

(Aristophanes, *The Clouds*, in *Aristophanes*, vol. I, trans. Benjamin Bickley Rogers [London: William Heinemann Ltd., 1960], 877-881, p. 345).

45 For example, see 386-90, p. 301 (but it would be easy to identify many other passages):

> SOCRATES Have you never then eat the broth-pudding you get
> when the Panathenea comes round,
> And felt with what might your bowels all night
> in turbulent tumult resound?
> STREPSIADES By Apollo, 'tis true, there's a mighty to-do,
> and my belly keeps rumbling about;
> And the puddings begin to clatter within
> and kick up a wonderful rout:
> Quite gently at first, papapax, papapax,
> but soon pappapapppax away,
> Till at last, I'll be bound, I can thunder as loud
> papapappappapapppax, as They.

(Ibid., 373)

46 Yet before, I had dreamed that the rain-water streamed
from Zeus and his chamber-pot sieve.

(Ibid., 373).

To this response, Kierkegaard attributes only a comic element resulting from the contrast between the scholarly and the naive.

47 The theft of the cloak can be interpreted as castration, not only because for a psychoanalyst a cloak symbolizes the masculine gender, but because Strepsiades himself identifies the two from the very beginning of the play, when he evokes his wedding day in front of his son (*The Clouds*, 48-55, p. 271):

> This wife I married, and we came together,
> I rank with wine-lees, fig-boards, greasy woolpacks;
> She all with scents, and saffron, and tongue-kissing
> Feasting, expense, and lordly modes of living.

> She was not idle, though she was too fast.
> I used to tell her, holding out my cloak,
> Threadbare and worn; *Wife, you're too fast by half.*

48   Cf. *The Acquisition and Control of Fire* (1932 [1931]), *The Standard Edition of the Complete Psychological Works of Sigmund Freud*, 24 vols. (London: Hogarth Press, 1953-74), vol. 22, pp. 185-93.

49   'The sexual organ of the male has two functions; and there are those to whom this association is an annoyance. . . . The child still believes that he can unite the two functions. . . . But the adult knows that in reality the acts are mutually incompatible – as incompatible as fire and water. . . . The antithesis between the two functions might lead us to say that man quenches his own fire with his own water' (ibid., pp. 192-93).

50   'I think my hypothesis – that, in order to gain control over fire, men had to renounce the homosexually-tinged desire to put it out with a stream of urine – can be confirmed by an interpretation of the Greek myth of Prometheus' (ibid., p. 187).

51   Cf. Freud, *Jokes and Their Relation to the Unconscious (1905)*, *Standard Edition*, vol. 8, p. 200: 'Caricature, parody and travesty (as well as their practical counterpart, unmasking) are directed against people and objects which lay claim to authority and respect, which are in some sense *"sublime"*. They are procedures for *Herabsetzung*, [degradation], as the apt German expression has it.'

52   In order to differentiate Socrates from Christ, Hegel also stresses (in *Frühe Schriften*, pp. 50-54) that Socrates was cut off from his disciples: 'Socrates did not live in them'. 'Each one remained for himself what he was'. (In French in *Fragments*, pp. 39-42.)

53   Hegel also writes: 'The essential thing [in prayer] is the assurance of simply being heard . . . [and] absolute confidence that God will give me what is best for me' (*Aesthetics*, II, 'Painting', p. 827).

54   *Point of View*, p. 115.

55   Ibid.

56   Preface to '"The Individual", the first of 'Two "Notes" Concerning My Work as an Author', in *Point of View*, p. 107.

57   Cf. Hegel, *Frühe Schriften*, p. 40: 'Socrates was never heard preaching from a pulpit or a mountaintop. . . . His goal was to teach people, to enlighten them and to encourage them in whatever awoke their major interest. He was not remunerated for his wisdom'. (In French in *Fragments*, 4, p. 40).

58   *Journals and Papers*, vol. 1, §45, p. 19.

59   *The Clouds*, 731-733 (pp. 333-335). Strepsiades has just put his head under his bedclothes and Socrates has peeked to seek what he is doing.

60   Translator's note: The French word for 'fine', *amende*, is also used in the expression *faire amende*, 'to make amends'; Kofman's play on this term is lost in English.

61   Translator's note: In French the term *peine* can mean both 'penalty', punishment and 'pain', suffering.

62   In 'Schopenhauer as Educator' [1874], in *Untimely Meditations* (trans. R.

J. Hollingdale [Cambridge, UK: Cambridge University Press, 1983], pp. 125-94), Nietzsche rails against general culture, using the same metaphors Kierkegaard used. But he is talking about the general culture of his own era, and not about that of the Sophists, whom he holds in higher regard than Kierkegaard does: he places them well above Socrates or Plato, whom he sees as 'Jews' compared to the authentic Greeks who are heirs to the pre-Socratics and whom any measure of theoretical or moral progress brings back to life. In other words, for him the Sophists are at the origin of the true 'critique' of morality, because they were the first to guess that every foundation for morality is necessarily sophistic. Cf. *Fragments posthumes,* III, VI, 1888 (XV, §428); XI, 1887-III, 1888 (XV, §427)-III, VI, 1888 (XV, §429). In the latter text, he praises them not for being paragons of virtue but for having the courage to recognize their own immorality, for not seeking to deceive the public at large with big words and lofty virtues.

63 For Hegel, as we have seen, this harmony between soul and body, which 'nature' was unable to achieve in Socrates, can only be established in paintings.

IV. NIETZSCHE'S SOCRATES(ES): 'WHO' IS SOCRATES?

1 'The Struggle Between Science and Wisdom', in *Philosophy and Truth: Selections from Nietzsche's Notebooks of the early 1870's,* trans. Daniel Breazale (Atlantic Highlands, NJ: Humanities Press, 1979), p. 127.

2 Cf. Friedrich Nietzsche, 'Die vorplatonischen Philosophen', §17, 'Socrates', in *Nietzsche Werke, Kritische Gesamtausgabe,* ed. Giorgio Colli and Mazzino Montinari, II, 4, *Vorlesungsaufzeichnungen (WS 1871/72-WS 1874/75),* (Berlin: Walter de Gruyter, 1995), pp. 354-61. Hegel too acknowledges these passions in Socrates, but he emphasizes that Socrates was able to master them and to create a second nature for himself, his 'true' nature. See *supra.*

3 *Beyond Good and Evil. Prelude to a Philosophy of the Future,* trans. Walter Kaufmann (New York: Vintage Books, 1966), preface, p. 3.

4 Cf. Sarah Kofman, *Camera obscura, of Ideology* (London: The Athlone Press, 1998), and 'Baubô, perversion théologique et fétichisme', in *Nietzsche et la scène philosophique* (Paris: Galilée, 1979).

5 Cf. Friedrich Nietzsche, *La Naissance de la philosophie à l'époque de la tragédie grecque,* trans. Geneviève Bianquis (Paris: Gallimard, 1938), p. 128.

6 Cf. 'The Struggle Between Science and Wisdom', pp. 134-35; see also *Beyond Good and Evil,* §190, and *supra.*

7 Cf. *Human, All Too Human: A Book for Free Spirits,* trans. R. J. Hollingdale (Cambridge: Cambridge University Press, 1986), I, §261, 'The tyrants of the spirit', pp. 122-25.

8 Friedrich Nietzsche, *Ecce Homo,* in *On the Genealogy of Morals and Ecce Homo,* trans. Walter Kaufmann (New York: Vintage Books, 1989), §1, 'Why I Am So Wise', p. 222.

9 Ibid.

10 Ibid., p. 223.

11 Cf., in addition to the text selected as epigraph, a passage from *Fragments*

8 (16) that is contemporaneous with *The Gay Science*: 'Why are the natures opposed to mine the ones that attract me most intensely? They make me feel the necessity of plenitude; they have a place within me'.

12   Cf. *Human, All Too Human*, I, 261.

13   Ibid., p. 160.

14   'The Struggle Between Science and Wisdom', p. 132.

15   *Nietzsche Werke*, ed. Giorgio Colli and Mazzino Montinari, III, 3, *Friedrich Nietzsche, Nachgelassene Fragmente, Herbst 1869 bis Herbst 1872* (Berlin: Walter de Gruyter, 1978), 1 [24] (fall 1869), p. 13.

16   Cf. *Beyond Good and Evil*, §190, and *supra*, chapter I, section B.

17   Cf. *Nietzsche Werke*, IV, 2, *Menschliches, Allzumenschliches, I, Nachgelassene Fragmente, 1876 bis Winter 1877-1878* (Berlin: Walter de Gruyter, 1967), 18 [47], p. 423.

18   In the same text, Nietzsche adds that Wagner did the same thing for Beethoven and Shakespeare.

19   Cf. *Ecce Homo*, 'Why I Write Such Good Books', p. 280. In discussing the third 'Untimely Meditation' ('Schopenhauer as Educator' [1874], in *Untimely Meditations*, trans. R. J. Hollingdale [Cambridge: Cambridge University Press, 1983], pp. 125-94), Nietzsche compares the way he uses Schopenhauer in that work – simply as a supplementary means of expression, a kind of sign language – with the way Plato used Socrates.

20   Cf. *Nietzsche Werke*, IV, 3, *Menschliches, Allzumenschliches, II, Nachgelassene Fragmente, Frühling 1878 bis November 1879* (Berlin: Walter de Gruyter, 1967), 28 [11], p. 363; 41 [2], p. 442; 42 [48], p. 462.

21   Ibid., 18 [47], p. 423.

22   Ibid.

23   *The Birth of Tragedy*, §13.

24   'Die vorplatonischen Philosophen', pp. 353-54.

25   Cf. Sarah Kofman, 'Aristotle and the "Presocratics"', in *Freud and Fiction*, trans. Sarah Wykes (Cambridge, UK: Polity Press, 1974), pp. 9-19; *Nietzsche et la scène philosophique* (Paris: Union Générale d'Editions [10/18], 1979), chapter I; and 'Nietzsche and the Obscurity of Heraclitus', trans. Françoise Lionnet-McCumber, *Diacritics* 17/3 (Fall 1987): 39-55.

26   *La Naissance de la philosophie*, p. 38.

27   'Die vorplatonischen Philosophen', p. 354.

28   Ibid., p. 360.

29   Ibid.

30   §7, p. 15.

31   Cf. *Le Gai Savoir*, 'Fragments inédits', 13 (32).

32   Cf. also *Nietzsche Werke*, V, 1, *Morgenröthe. Nachgelassene Fragmente. Anfang 1880 bis Frühjahr 1881* (Berlin: Walter de Gruyter, 1971), 8 [56], p. 724: 'Naivete of morality was lost because of Christianity (and earlier because of Socrates), just like French naivete under L[ouis] XV – for the same reasons'.

33   'The Struggle Between Science and Wisdom', §195, p. 136.

34   *La Naissance de la Philosophie*, p. 129.

35 Ibid.

36 Ibid., p. 131.

37 *Philosophy in the Tragic Age of the Greeks,* §189, p. 129.

38 *La Naissance de la philosophie,* p. 204.

39 *Philosophy in the Tragic Age of the Greeks,* §193, p. 132.

40 Ibid., §193, p. 134.

41 Ibid., §195, p. 135.

42 *Friedrich Nietzsche, Nachgelassene Fragmente, Herbst 1869 bis Herbst 1872,* 1 [27], p. 13.

43 *The Birth of Tragedy,* in *Basic Writings of Nietzsche,* trans. Walter Kaufmann (New York: Modern Library, 1968), §13, p. 88.

44 Ibid., p. 89.

45 Ibid., §14, p. 93.

46 Cf. *Nachgelassene Fragmente, Herbst 1869 bis Herbst 1872,* 8 [19], p. 238: 'The greatest figures of the Hellenic period remind us precisely of Socrates. He is at once Prometheus and Oedipus, but Prometheus before he stole the fire, and Oedipus before he solved the riddle of the Sphinx . . . But we have still said next to nothing about Socrates . . . whose influence, like an ever-lengthening shadow in the evening sun, has spread itself over posterity', a shadow that 'requires the transformation of art' and 'the infinity of that transformation'.

47 Cf. 'La Vision dionysiaque du Monde', in *Ecrits posthumes, 1870-1873,* pp. 47-70, and *The Birth of Tragedy,* §9.

48 *The Birth of Tragedy,* §4.

49 Ibid., §9. On the Socrates-Prometheus-Oedipus relationship, see Sarah Kofman, *Nietzsche et la scène philosophique,* chapter 2, 'Le masque de la sérénité' (Paris: Union Générale d'Editions [10/18], 1979), pp. 51-88.

50 Cf. *The Birth of Tragedy,* §15.

51 Ibid., §18.

52 In *La Naissance de la philosophie à l'époque de la tragédie grecque,* sometimes (p. 128) Nietzsche asserts that it was Socrates who taught Plato about the good and the beautiful in themselves, and corrupted him, and sometimes, on the contrary (p. 131), he writes: 'With Socrates everything is false. Concepts are neither fixed nor important. Knowledge is not the source of justice and is not fruitful. Socrates does not know what good is, what evil is, and he knows that only instinct, "inspiration", is divine'.

53 On this point, see *Beyond Good and Evil,* §218. This attitude on Socrates' part could be compared to Shylock's in *The Merchant of Venice,* when the latter treats both Jews and Christians as equals so far as the cruelty of their instincts is concerned. In this connection, see Sarah Kofman, 'Conversions: *The Merchant of Venice* under the Sign of Saturn', trans. Shaun Whiteside, in *Literary Theory Today,* ed. Peter Collier and Helga Geyer-Ryan (Cambridge, UK: Polity Press, 1990), pp. 142-66.

54 Cf. *Human, All Too Human,* I, §126, p. 68: 'Art and force of false interpretation': 'Thus the daemon of Socrates . . . was perhaps an ear-infection which, in accordance with the moralizing manner of thinking that dominated him, he only *interpreted* differently from how it would be interpreted now'. Cf. also 'The

Problem of Socrates', in *The Twilight of the Idols,* (in *The Portable Nietzsche,* trans. Walter Kaufmann [New York: Viking Penguin, 1976], §4, p. 475): 'Nor should we forget those auditory hallucinations which, as the *"daimonion* of Socrates"*,* have been interpreted religiously'.

55 *The Birth of Tragedy,* §13, p. 88.

56 Ibid.

57 Cf. *Beyond Good and Evil,* §289:

> No philosopher has ever expressed his true and definitive thought in books. Does one not write books precisely to hide what one has inside? [The solitary soul] will not believe that a philosopher *can* have 'ultimate and essential' opinions, that in his case, behind a cavern, there is not necessarily a deeper cavern, a vaster, stranger, richer world, below a surface, a lower level beneath every bottom, beneath every 'foundation.' All philosophy is a 'first-level philosophy.' . . . There is something arbitrary in the fact that [the philosopher] stopped *here,* that he looked behind and around him, that he did not dig deeper and that he tossed the spade aside; we have to see a dose of mistrust here. Every philosophy also *hides* philosophy, every opinion is also a retreat, every word a mask.

> Socrates does not 'write' books, to be sure, but his 'irony' is *writing [écriture]* and it dispenses him precisely from having to write in order to 'hide' his thoughts.

58 Cf. *The Gay Science,* §372: '*Why we are no idealists.* . . . All philosophical idealism to date was something like a disease, unless it was, as it was in Plato's case, the caution of an over-rich and dangerous health, the fear of *overpowerful* senses, the prudence of a prudent Socratic' (p. 333).

59 Heidegger agrees with Nietzsche on this point: the first true 'metaphysician' for him, too, is Descartes.

60 See 'The Problem of Socrates', §5: 'Honest things, like honest men, do not carry their reasons in their hands . . . It is indecent to put forth all the five fingers. That which requires to be proved is little worth' (p. 108).

61 *Nachgelassene Fragmente, Herbst 1869 bis Herbst 1872,* I [43], p. 17.

62 In writing the 'afterthoughts' presented in *Ecce Homo,* Nietzsche declares – leaving unmentioned the dream he had had then of at least making Socrates a musician, a Dionysian artist – that starting with *The Birth of Tragedy* he had recognized Socrates for the first time as an instrument of decomposition of Hellenism, as the prototype of the *decadent:* '"Rationality" *against* instinct. "Rationality" at any price as a dangerous force that undermines life. . . . My discovery that Socrates was a decadent proved unequivocally how little the sureness of my psychological grasp would be endangered by any moral idiosyncracy: seeing morality itself as a symptom of decadence is an innovation and a singularity of the first rank in the history of knowledge' (*Ecce Homo,* pp. 271–72).

63 See *The Gay Science,* §340, 'Socrates dying', p. 272.

64 The text cited just above ends with the following words: ' – Alas, my friends, we must overcome even the Greeks!' (ibid.)

65 Cf. for example *The Spirit of Christianity and Its Fate*, p. 259.
66 Here I am following 'The Problem of Socrates' very closely.
67 See 'Die vorplatonischen Philosophen', p. 355.
68 *Human, All Too Human*, §372, 'Irony', p. 146.
69 Ibid.
70 Ibid., p. 147.
71 'Socrates excels the founder of Christianity in being able to be serious cheerfully and in possessing that *wisdom full of roguishness* that constitutes the finest state of the human soul. And he also possessed the finer intellect' ('The Wanderer and His Shadow', in *Human, All Too Human: A Book for Free Spirits*, II, §86, p. 332).
72 'The Problem of Socrates,' §7, pp. 109-10.
73 Cf. 'The Wanderer and his Shadow'. In this text, the Socratic variegation is given a positive connotation, as allowing the affirmation of life in multiple forms:

> If all goes well, the time will come when one will take up the memorabilia of Socrates rather than the Bible as a guide to morals and reason, and when Montaigne and Horace will be employed as forerunners and signposts to an understanding of this simplest and most imperishable of intercessors. The pathways of the most various philosophical modes of life lead back to him; at bottom they are the modes of life of the various temperaments confirmed and established by reason and habit and all of them directed towards joy in living and in one's own self; from which one might conclude that Socrates' most personal characteristic was a participation in every temperament. (§86, p. 332)

74 Cf. *Le Gai Savoir*, 'Fragments inédits', 13 (33):

> The most strictly observant Greek philosophers had in themselves the choice of becoming either wild animals or severe, joyless animal-tamers: so already was Socrates. They were lucid enough to understand that someone who makes himself a human wild beast begins by *tearing* himself apart. Now, they believed that, like themselves, every person risked becoming such a wild beast – this is the *great belief* of all the great moralists, their power and their error – the belief that a frightful animality lurks near everyone. That is how far those men were from being beautiful.

75 In *Beyond Good and Evil*, §22, Nietzsche declares that the word 'tyranny' is an all too human metaphor for describing the forces that the will to power animates.
76 Similarly, in *Beyond Good and Evil*, §11, Nietzsche says that Kant was compelled to invent 'his' table of categories as the only remedy to German sensualism at the end of the eighteenth century. On this subject, see Sarah Kofman, 'Kant, médecin malgré lui', in *Nietzsche et la scène philosophique* (Paris: Union Générale d'Editions [10/18], 1979), pp. 271-288.
77 'The Problem of Socrates', §10, p. 112.

V. CONCLUSION: THREE SOCRATIC NOVELS

1 See Friedrich Nietzsche, 'Die vorplatonischen Philosophen', §17, 'Socrates', in *Nietzsche Werke, Kritische Gesamtausgabe,* ed. Giorgio Colli and Mazzino Montinari, II, 4, *Vorlesungsaufzeichnungen (WS 1871/72-WS 1874/75),* (Berlin: Walter de Gruyter, 1995), pp. 351-62; in English in part as *Philosophy in the Tragic Age of the Greeks,* trans. Marianne Cowan (Chicago: Henry Regnery, 1962).

2 *The Birth of Tragedy,* in *Basic Writings of Nietzsche,* trans. Walter Kaufmann (New York: Modern Library, 1968).

3 Ibid., §15, p. 97.

Bibliography

Agacinski, Sylviane. *Aparté, Conceptions and Deaths of Søren Kierkegaard.* Trans. Kevin Newmark. Gainesville: University Presses of Florida, 1988.

Aristophanes. *The Clouds.* In *Aristophanes,* vol. 1, trans. Benjamin Bickley Rogers. London: William Heinemann Ltd., 1960.

Aristotle. *Metaphysics.* Trans. Hugh Fredennick. Vol. 1. London: William Heinemann Ltd., 1961.

Benjamin, Walter. *The Origin of German Tragic Drama.* London: NLB, 1977.

Cicero. *Tusculan Disputations.* Trans. J. E. King. Cambridge, MA: Harvard University Press, 1966.

Derrida, Jacques. *Glas.* Trans. John P. Leavey, Jr., and Richard Rand. Lincoln: University of Nebraska Press, 1986.

—. *Mémoires for Paul de Man.* Trans. Cecile Lindsay, Jonathan Culler and Eduardo Cadava. New York: Columbia University Press, 1986.

—. 'Outwork'. In *Dissemination.* Trans. Barbara Johnson. London: The Athlone Press, 1993.

—. *The Post Card. From Socrates to Freud and Beyond.* Trans. Alan Bass. Chicago: University of Chicago Press, 1987.

Détienne, Marcel and Jean-Pierre Vernant. *Cunning Intelligence in Greek Culture and Society.* Trans. Janet Lloyd. Atlantic Highlands, NJ: Humanities Press, 1978.

Dodds, Eric Robertson. *The Greeks and the Irrational.* Berkeley: University of California Press, 1951.

Ferenczi, Sandor. 'Introjection and Transference'. In *First Contributions to Psycho-Analysis,* trans. Ernest Jones. London: Hogarth Press Ltd. and The Institute of Psychoanalysis, 1952.

—. *Thalassa: A Theory of Genitality.* Trans. Henry Alden Bunker. New York: W. W. Norton, 1968.

Goux, Jean-Joseph. *The Coiners of Language.* Trans. Jennifer Curtiss Gage. Norman: University of Oklahoma Press, 1994.

—. *Symbolic Economies.* Trans. Jennifer Curtiss Gage. Ithaca, NY: Cornell University Press, 1990.

Grimal, Pierre. *Dictionary of Classical Mythology.* Trans. A.R. Maxwell-Hyslop. Oxford: Blackwell, 1986.

Hegel, Georg Wilhelm Friedrich. *Aesthetics: Lectures on Fine Art.* Trans. T. M. Knox. 2 vols. Oxford: Clarendon Press, 1974.

—. *Early Theological Writings.* Trans. T. M. Knox and Richard Kroner. Chicago: University of Chicago Press, 1948.

—. *L'Esprit du christianisme et son destin.* Trans. Jacques Martin. Paris: Vrin, 1948.

—. *Fragments de la période de Berne.* Trans. Robert Legros and Fabienne Verstraeten. Paris: Vrin, 1987.

—. *Hegel's Philosophy of Mind.* Trans. William Wallace. Oxford: Clarendon Press, 1894.

—. *Hegel's Philosophy of Right.* Trans. T. M. Knox. London: Oxford University Press, 1967.

—. *Lectures on the History of Philosophy: Greek Philosophy to Plato.* Trans. E. S. Haldane. 2 vols. Lincoln, NE: University of Nebraska Press, 1995.

—. *Lectures on the Philosophy of World History. Introduction: Reason in History.* Trans. H. B. Nisbet. Cambridge, UK: Cambridge University Press, 1975.

—. *The Phenomenology of Mind.* Trans. J. B. Baillie. London: Allen and Unwin, 1977.

—. *Werke in zwanzig Bänden. 1. Frühe Schriften.* Frankfurt: Suhrkamp, 1971.

Hoffmann, E. T. A. *The Devil's Elixirs.* Trans. Ronald Taylor. London: J. Calder, 1963.

—. *Selected Writings of E. T. A. Hoffmann.* Ed. and trans. Leonard J. Kent and Elizabeth C. Knight. Chicago: Chicago University Press, 1969.

Homer. *The Iliad.* Trans. A. T. Murray. Vol. 1. Cambridge, MA: Harvard University Press, 1965.

Kant, Immanuel. *Anthropology from a Pragmatic Point of View.* Trans. Victor Lyle Dowdell. Carbondale: Southern Illinois University Press, 1978.

—. *Critique of Judgment.* Trans. J. H. Bernard. New York: Hafner Press, 1951.

Kierkegaard, Søren. *Le Concept d'ironie constamment rapporté à Socrate.* Trans. Jean Brun. Paris: Orante, 1976.

—. *The Concept of Irony with Continual Reference to Socrates. Kierkegaard's Writings, II.* Ed. and trans. Howard V. Hong and Edna H. Hong. Princeton: Princeton University Press, 1989.

— [Johannes Climacus, pseud.]. *Concluding Unscientific Postscript to the Philosophical Fragments, A Mimic-Pathetic-Dialectic Composition, An Existential Contribution.* Trans. David S. Swanson. Princeton: Princeton University Press, 1944.

— [H. H., pseud.]. 'Has a Man the Right to Let Himself Be Put to Death for the Truth? A Poetic Experiment.' In *The Present Age, and Two Minor Ethico-Religious Treatises,* trans. Alexander Dru and Walter Lowrie. London: Oxford University Press, 1940.

—. *The Point of View for My Work as an Author.* Trans. Walter Lowrie. New York: Harper Torchbooks, 1962.

Kofman, Sarah. *Aberrations, le devenir-femme d'Auguste Comte.* Paris: Flammarion, 1978.

—. *Autobiogriffures: Du chat Murr d'Hoffmann.* Paris: Galilée, 1984.

—. 'Aristotle and the "presocratics".' In *Freud and Fiction,* trans. Sarah Wykes. Cambridge, UK: Polity Press, 1991. Pp. 9-19.

—. 'Beyond Aporia'. Trans. David Macey. In Andrew Benjamin, ed., *Post-Structuralist Classics.* London: Routledge, 1988.

—. *Camera obscura, of Ideology*. London: The Athlone Press, 1998.

—. 'Conversions: *The Merchant of Venice* under the Sign of Saturn.' Trans. Shaun Whiteside. In Peter Collier and Helga Geyer-Ryan, eds., *Literary Theory Today*. Cambridge, UK: Polity Press, 1990. Pp. 142-66.

—. 'Miroir et mirages oniriques: Platon, précurseur de Freud.' In *Séductions: De Sartre à Héraclite*. Paris: Galilée, 1990.

—. *Nietzsche and Metaphor*. Trans. Duncan Large. London: The Athlone Press, 1993.

—. 'Nietzsche and the Obscurity of Heraclitus.' Trans. Françoise Lionnet-McCumber. *Diacritics* 17/3 (Fall 1987): 39-55.

—. *Nietzsche et la scène philosophique*. Paris: Union Générale d'Editions (10/18), 1979.

—. *Pourquoi rit-on? Freud et le mot d'esprit*. Paris: Galilée, 1986.

—. 'Summarize, Interpret.' In *Freud and Fiction*, trans. Sarah Wykes. Cambridge, UK: Polity Press, 1991. Pp. 83-117.

—. 'Vautour rouge.' In Sylviane Agacinski, Jacques Derrida, Sarah Kofman, Philippe Lacoue-Labarthe, Jean-Luc Nancy and Bernard Pautrat, *Mimesis des articulations*. Paris: Aubier-Flammarion, 1975. Pp. 95-163.

La Mettrie. 'L'homme-machine.' In *Oeuvres philosophiques*, vol. I. Paris: Fayard, 1987.

Lacan, Jacques. 'Du "Trieb" de Freud et du désir du psychanalyste.' In *Ecrits*. Paris: Seuil, 1966. Pp. 851-54.

—. 'Subversion of the Subject and Dialectic of Desire in the Freudian Unconscious.' In *Ecrits: A Selection*, trans. Alan Sheridan. New York: Norton, 1977. Pp. 292-325.

Laertius, Diogenes. *Lives of Eminent Philosophers*. Trans. R. D. Hicks. 2 vols. Cambridge, MA: Harvard University Press, 1972.

Metz, Françoise. *Caractéristique de Socrate (à partir de Schlegel)*. Strasbourg, unpublished.

Nancy, Jean-Luc. 'Identité et tremblement.' In Michel Borch-Jacobsen, Eric Michaud and Jean-Luc Nancy, *Hypnoses*. Paris: Galilée, 1984.

Nietzsche, Friedrich. *Aurore et Fragments Posthumes, 1879-1881*. Trans. Julien Hervier. Paris: Gallimard, 1970.

—. *Beyond Good and Evil*. Trans. Walter Kaufmann. New York: Vintage Books, 1966.

—. *The Birth of Tragedy*. In *Basic Writings of Nietzsche*, trans. Walter Kaufmann. New York: Modern Library, 1968.

—. *Daybreak*. Trans. R. J. Hollingdale. Cambridge, UK: Cambridge University Press, 1982.

—. *Ecce Homo*. In *On the Genealogy of Morals and Ecce Homo*. Trans. Walter Kaufmann. New York: Vintage Books, 1989.

—. *Ecrits posthumes, 1870-1873*. Trans. Jean-Louis Backes, Michel Haar, and Marc B. de Launay. Paris: Gallimard, 1976.

—. *Le Gai Savoir*. Trans. Pierre Klossowski. Paris: Gallimard, 1990.

—. *The Gay Science*. Trans. Walter Kaufmann. New York: Vintage Books (Random House), 1974.

—. *Humain, Trop Humain, Fragments posthumes*. Paris: Gallimard, 1981.

—. *Human, All Too Human: A Book for Free Spirits*. Trans. R. J. Hollingdale. Cambridge, UK: Cambridge University Press, 1986.

—. *La Naissance de la philosophie à l'époque de la tragédie grecque*. Trans. Geneviève Bianquis. Paris: Gallimard, 1938, 1969.

—. *La Naissance de la tragédie et Fragments Posthumes, automne 1869-printemps 1872*. Paris: Gallimard, 1977.

—. *Nietzsche Werke. Kritische Gesamtausgabe*. Ed. Giorgio Colli and Mazzino Montinari. Berlin: Walter de Gruyter, 1967-1995.

—. *On The Genealogy of Morals and Ecce Homo*. Trans. Walter Kaufmann. New York: Vintage Books, 1989.

—. *Philosophy in the Tragic Age of the Greeks*. Trans. Marianne Cowan. Chicago: Henry Regnery Company, 1962.

—. 'The Problem of Socrates.' *The Twilight of the Idols*. In *The Portable Nietzsche*. Trans. Walter Kaufmann. New York: Viking Penguin, 1982. Pp. 463-563.

—. 'Schopenhauer as Educator.' In *Untimely Meditations,* trans. R. J. Hollingdale. Cambridge, UK: Cambridge University Press, 1983.

—. 'The Struggle Between Science and Wisdom.' In *Philosophy and Truth. Selections from Nietzsche's Notebooks of the Early 1870's*. Trans. Daniel Breazale. Atlantic Highlands, NJ: Humanities Press, 1979.

Plato. *Plato*. Trans. R. E. Bury. London: William Heinemann Ltd., 1961.

Rank, Otto. *The Trauma of Birth*. London: K. Paul, Trench, Trubner, 1929.

Sigmund Freud. *The Standard Edition of the Complete Psychological Works of Sigmund Freud*. Trans. James Strachey. 24 vols. London: The Hogarth Press, 1953-66.

This, Claude. 'Au-delà du double: la bête.' In *Du visage*, ed. Marie-José Baudinet and Christian Schatter. Lille: Presses Universitaires de Lille, 1982.

Wolff, Francis. *Socrate*. Paris: Presses Universitaires de France, 1985.

Xenophon. *Banquet*. Trans. O. J. Todd. London: William Heinemann, 1972.

—. *Memorabilia*. Trans. Amy L. Bonnette. Ithaca, NY: Cornell University Press, 1994.

Index